IRELAND IN THE NEWSREELS

CIARA CHAMBERS
University of Ulster

IRISH ACADEMIC PRESS
DUBLIN • PORTLAND, OR

For my parents

First published in 2012 by Irish Academic Press

2 Brookside,
Dundrum Road,
Dublin 14, Ireland

920 NE 58th Avenue, Suite 300
Portland, Oregon,
97213-3786 USA

www.iap.ie

© 2012 Ciara Chambers

British Library Cataloguing in Publication Data
An entry can be found on request

ISBN 978 0 7165 3113 5 (cloth)
ISBN 978 0 7165 3114 2 (paper)

Library of Congress Cataloging-in-Publication Data
An entry can be found on request

Printed by Good News Digital Books, Stevenage, Hertfordshire

Contents

Acknowledgements

This book began life as a PhD thesis which was completed with the assistance of a studentship from the Higher Education Authority's North South Programme for Collaborative Research. My sincere thanks to Lisa Hyde for her time and patience throughout the process of editing this book.

Firstly I wish to express my heartfelt gratitude to Martin McLoone for his eternally constructive advice and encouragement as a supervisor, colleague and friend; he epitomizes all the best qualities of academic endeavour. I am also extremely grateful to John Hill for his comments on various drafts of this book. On many occasions, when completing this book seemed like an impossibility, I was fortunate to benefit from the support of my colleagues in the Centre for Media Research and the Faculty of Arts at the University of Ulster, Coleraine. I am particularly indebted to Robert Porter (or the 'legendary Bobby P' as he has been acknowledged in other publications) for helping me out on countless occasions in a variety of capacities and to Steve Baker and Alan Hook for providing spectacularly high levels of banter, even in the darkest days. Thanks also to Adrian Hickey for technical assistance with the illustrations. Special thanks are due to my postgraduate colleagues for ongoing friendship during the PhD experience we shared together and for leaving me with very happy memories of my time as a student of the University of Ulster. Conn Holohan and Niamh O'Sullivan in particular have continued to provide much welcomed distraction when it was most needed!

This book would not have been possible without access to the British Universities Film and Video Council's News on Screen database, a truly wonderful resource and I am grateful to Linda Kaye for consistently responding to repeated queries with patience and enthusiasm. Luke McKernan has also provided considerable help and advice. A big thank you to Jeff Hulbert and Richard Clarke, for sharing with me their work on the Newsfilm Online project and other aspects of their extensive expertise.

Thanks also to Sunniva O'Flynn at the IFI Irish Film Archive for initial guidance on their holdings and to Karen Wall and Kasandra O'Connell for repeated access to archival content and assistance with the provision of related images. My continued relationship with the staff of the Irish Film Archive is a constant source of inspiration!

Kevin Rockett and Eugene Finn provided invaluable guidance connected to material on the Irish Film & TV online database. Bob Monks offered helpful insights into the life of a newsreel cameraman and the complexities associated with shooting newsreel material. I am indebted to the staff at the British Film Institute, the Imperial War Museum, the Public Record Office of Northern Ireland, the National Archives of Ireland and the Military Archives of Ireland for consistently cheerful and practical help.

I have benefitted from some very important long-term (and more recent) friendships and am extremely grateful to my close friends for their ongoing patience and understanding. The utmost thanks are due to the wonderful extended family that I am lucky to be part of, for kindness and positivity, particularly during difficult times. A special thank you to one of my best friends, my brother Stephen, for intelligent and comic discussions about Irish history (amongst many other topics). A final thanks to my parents, for instilling in me a sense of the importance of the past and also for their unfaltering care and attention, irreverent humour, legendary cocktails and vinyl nights. This book is dedicated to them.

List of Illustrations

Introduction

The first newsreel to be produced in Britain appeared in 1910 and it did not take long for several core companies to grow and develop a genre which became a significant part of public viewing, at least until the advent of television in the 1950s. Often dismissed as a meaningless add-on to the cinema programme, the importance of what the newsreels tell us about how events were visually depicted for contemporary audiences is underestimated. Peter Baechlin and Maurice Muller-Strauss remind us that 'newsreels are not an extraneous branch of cinematographic work, grafted on to the essential business of film production. On the contrary, the cinema itself developed out of the presentation of topical events.'[1]

The formative years of the newsreels coincided with a period of political and cultural turbulence in Ireland as the nationalist revolt against Britain gathered momentum and the unionist resistance hardened. The newsreels offered contemporary audiences moving images of newsworthy events worldwide, but in Ireland this representation of news was to prove problematic. For a start, most available footage was produced by British companies and so for cinemagoers of a nationalist disposition, these newsreels were increasingly seen as partisan in favour of an occupying force. The newsreels were necessarily delayed, in any case, due to the nature of the production and editing process and their distribution through a hierarchy of cinema circuits. As a result, they often covered events already known to audiences through other media: the press, certainly, and, from the mid-1920s, radio. In Ireland, highly politicized audiences were already aware of the political events happening around them and often found themselves viewing representations that were contrary to an accumulated 'common knowledge' and the accepted norms of their

history and culture. Given that this would prove one of the most controversial periods in Irish history, the investigation into how the normally non-controversial newsreels would tackle such events for British and Irish audiences offers insight into both the nature of news-reel production and British attitudes towards the Irish (in the context of wider concerns about the empire) at a time of growing distance between 'north' and 'south'.

The main aim of this book is to examine an area which has been relatively neglected – the relationship between newsreels and Ireland. The body of academic work on newsreels is a comparatively small area of film studies, but within that work there is scant attention paid to Ireland. Even in the area of Irish film studies, a discipline greatly concerned with the representation of Ireland and Irishness, there has been surprisingly little consideration of the newsreels. There has been some coverage of newsreels which courted controversy, by historians such as Robert Fisk,[2] but there has been no sustained examination of the newsreels' ongoing and often problematic relationship with Ireland. Given the sheer amount of material produced in relation to Ireland (by my estimation, approximately 3,800 newsreels between 1910 and 1979, when the last remaining newsreel company ceased production) this has been a neglected area within Irish film studies, which has concentrated on a small amount of fiction and documen-tary material. The newsreels offer an exciting and rich opportunity for the exploration of images of Irishness – a central concern in the field of Irish film studies – and this becomes particularly significant when considering the wide ranges of audiences reached by newsreel coverage. This book begins the process of examination of newsreel material in relation to Ireland and opens up new avenues of research into how Irishness was constructed for cinemagoers in the only form of on-screen news available prior to the advent of television in the 1950s. It also explores the portrayal of Irishness for indigenous and British audiences at a time when there were significant changes in the relationship between Britain and Ireland, and indeed the relationship between Britain and the wider empire. Ireland's campaign for Home Rule and its eventual partition represented the potential fragmentation of the empire and it is against this backdrop that the newsreels constructed representations of Irishness which were often inconsistent and contradictory.

Given that a large amount of the material related to Ireland still exists, it was important to narrow the time frame that the book sought to investigate. The study covers three main periods. The first explores the movement towards partition and its immediate aftermath (1910–23). The next section covers the 1930s, which began as a time of relative outward calm within Ireland under the leadership of W.T. Cosgrave up until 1932. The relationship between Britain and Ireland became increasingly fraught as Cosgrave's successor, Éamon de Valera, set about dismantling the 1922 Treaty and entered into a period of economic war with Britain between 1932 and 1938.

This was a highly significant period as the Irish people slowly came to terms with partition, and the Irish government renegotiated its relationship with Britain, asserting its own strong-willed independence. These tensions were set against a backdrop of increasing international pressure, as the drift towards the Second World War continued. The final section of the book deals with the split in viewing in Ireland during the Second World War, and the newsreels' depiction of Irish neutrality and Northern Ireland's engagement with the war effort. The newsreels' depiction of 'the two Irelands' during this period presents the differing impacts of global events during a time when partition was truly cemented and the states of north and south reached a clear status of separation.

As none of the newsreel material related to Ireland has been previously examined as part of any study specifically related to the genre, this book sets out to offer an account of the representation of north and south through the only form of on-screen news available to the audiences of the time. This study begins with coverage from 1910 onwards which offers the chance to examine the newsreel genre from its establishment, through the height of its popularity and culminating in its significant and propaganda fuelled coverage of the Second World War. While there is a considerable amount of material produced on Ireland in the 1950s, this book will briefly consider two related instances of production, Universal Irish News (1952–56) and Amharc Éireann (1956–64). Given that, with the advent of television in the 1950s, daily on-screen news in the home was already beginning to replace the cinema newsreels, there will be no detailed exploration of this era.

I have also chosen these three periods to trace coverage of the

Home Rule movement, the partition of Ireland and the construction and representation of 'north' and 'south' as the two states grew further apart, concluding with the Second World War, an event which cemented the distance between north and south as a result of their differing roles in an international conflict. This study begins to reveal how support for partition emerges in the newsreels and how they initially prepared the way ideologically for the division of Ireland into two separate states by identifying 'Irish' and 'pro-British' communities. It also covers the portrayal of the events of partition, how both north and south came to terms with their new status and in turn positioned themselves in relation to the 'other' Ireland. What emerges from this is a reflection of an Ireland coming to terms with its division into two states and all the associated challenges to 'Irish' and 'British' identity that such a division created.

There have been no detailed audience studies of the reception of newsreels by British and Irish audiences during this period, but papers on cinema statistics and reports on the film industries in Ireland and Britain have been referred to alongside information published by the social research organization Mass Observation, in order to build up a context around audiences in the first half of the twentieth century. Given the lack of detailed information on audience reception, this book concentrates on a content analysis of the newsreels and the historical and political contexts in which they were produced. A filmography of all Irish newsreel stories produced between 1910 and 1949 has been included at the end of this book. This research has largely drawn on the British Universities Film and Video Council's database News on Screen (formerly the British Universities Newsreel Database or BUND). As I have frequently referred to News on Screen in the text and in the endnotes, it has usually been abbreviated to 'NoS' for ease of referencing. I have also indicated where there are items of Irish interest which are not included in the database and have attempted to highlight any discrepancies in titles or dating which have arisen.

The newsreels described in this book were, for the most part, filmed, edited and distributed by British companies. There is also exploration of two films completed by the American company March of Time which received assistance from the governments of both Northern Ireland and the Free State during the 1930s and therefore had a particularly local production focus. A small amount of material produced by indigenous companies in Ireland is also considered. Three broad cohorts of audiences viewed the material described in this book: audiences in the north of Ireland, audiences in the south of Ireland and audiences in Britain. While there is little data available on how audiences received newsreels, there is some evidence of items which were viewed on occasion by only one of these cohorts and where this evidence is available it is indicated in relation to the item in question and an explanation is given as to why particular stories were produced for particular audiences. The newsreels for the most part have been described in terms of their individual stories or 'items', as newsreels were edited differently for national and local audiences on the distribution circuit. Often, items of local interest were filmed for audiences in particular cities. In the case of Dublin, for example, issue sheets are sometimes stamped 'Local/Special: Dublin' to indicate that a story was spliced into the newsreel issue for Irish audiences. The item may have concerned a local sporting event and would most likely have been substituted for an item of general British interest, in some cases related to the monarchy. This information is not available for every item produced, but I have attempted to indicate where it is available.

By far the most significant cinematic account of this period in history is provided by the Pathé company. There are two reasons for this. Firstly, British Pathé is the longest-running newsreel operator (1910–70) to cover Ireland; secondly, it was the first to digitize its collection and make it available online. (Pathé offers 1,600 items in relation to Ireland, 42 per cent of the coverage mentioned above, and, as such, is highly representative of the material that audiences would have accessed, given that it was the main provider of newsreel content.)

One particular story sums up in its cataloguing discrepancies the difficulties in establishing the correct time, date and source of news-reel footage, even in the current climate of burgeoning digitization. *The Titanic Disaster* appears as part of both Pathé and Movietone's collections, yet its intertitles claim the production credits for Gaumont. News on Screen, the most comprehensive database of British newsreel content, offers no further clarification as it does not contain any records for this particular story. A further general feature of the newsreels is exemplified in the fact that although the newsreel is six minutes long and covers only one story, only the first minute presents actual footage of the *Titanic*. (It is most likely that this footage comes from a story listed on NoS as *The Titanic Leaving Belfast Lough Bound for Southampton April 2 1912*.) Furthermore, this is the only established authentic footage of the *Titanic* in existence. Mostly this was due to the fact that before its infamous collision with an iceberg the launching of the *Titanic* was not a signifi-cant news story. Although it was the largest liner of its kind in the world, it had two sister ships, the *Olympic* and *Britannic*, and it was the *Olympic* which took most credit (and media attention) as it was the first to be launched. *The Titanic Disaster* opens with the intertitle 'The "Titanic" leaving Belfast Lough for Southampton, April 2nd 1912' and is accompanied by a panning shot of the full length of the ship, along all four funnels (the last of which was added for purely aesthetic purposes). The next shots, according to the intertitle, show 'Captain Smith on the bridge'. In reality, the footage is of Captain Smith on the *Olympic*,[3] and the *Titanic* does not reappear for the rest of the newsreel, which consists of copious shots of icebergs, survivors, and crowds waiting for news outside the White Star offices in New York. In its artistry this particular item perfectly demonstrates the newsreel industry's skills in cobbling together library footage and whatever stock shots were available with powerful intertitles to create a film which is still compelling for audiences today. The newsreel even ends with shots of Marconi, inventor of the radio, accompanied by the intertitle 'whose marvellous discovery saved over 700 lives'. In fact, the rescue response was poor and in typical upbeat style the newsreel fails to emphasize the 1,500 victims, preferring to concentrate on shots of individual survivors, even at one point picturing some surviving crew in their lifejackets and the incredible 'Quarter Master Hitchins, who went down with the ship and was later picked up'. The survivors are shown relatively unscathed, happy to pose for pictures and chat to reporters.

This film of the *Titanic* illustrates the crucial problem with newsreel material – due to the nature of the genre, only the 'aftermath' of events could be covered. The scenes described above are not concerned with the sinking of the *Titanic*, but with the story that unfolds after the liner's tragic voyage. Unless the newsreels were covering staged events, it was difficult to get a camera crew to the scene on time to cover a story as it happened. Also, audiences in the cinemas would have already heard about most of the events screened in the newsreels through the printed press. (While Gaumont filmed the *Titanic* leaving Belfast on 2 April, the newsreel wasn't released until 18 April.) Crucially, due to the necessarily delayed nature of exhibition, constrained by editing and distribution, newsreels very seldom contained 'news'.

When Pathé digitized its entire British collection in 2002 and made it available for downloading, subsequent research determined *Titanic* as the most downloaded clip. This further testifies to an interest in how film presented historical events. Newsreel footage, like these shots of the *Titanic*, however sparse, can become iconic and can contribute, many years after the event, to the ongoing representation of history, communities and culture. How we interact with newsreel footage today can inform our understanding of past events and how they have shaped current identities. Newsreels can awaken and invigorate a sense of the past, and archive footage is increasingly being used in innovative ways in educational projects to enhance students' understanding of history and politics.[4]

Aldgate's *Cinema and History*: A Model for Research

Antony Aldgate's exploration of the newsreels in *Cinema and History: British Newsreels and the Spanish Civil War* (1979) offers a detailed history of the evolution of newsreel production and the financial, political and technological associations of the industry. Aldgate also explores content and censorship before offering a detailed case study of how the newsreels tackled and represented the Spanish Civil War. In a similar way, this book will explore the newsreel industry and its unique relationship with Ireland while providing a political and historical context to illustrate how the newsreels both covered Irish events and catered for Irish audiences.

Aldgate recognizes the importance of film as a source material but also highlights issues of source authenticity and ideological bias. While Aldgate reminds us that 'with the advent of motion pictures and the cinema, it became possible seemingly to traverse time and space, and to see at first hand the events and personalities which were shaping history',[5] he also reminds us that film is both a 'corporate' and 'technological'[6] art and subject to the economic and technical conditions of its production. Aldgate concludes that, as such, 'the limitations of its technology can sometimes impose a severe burden on the credibility of film as a record of what actually happened'.[7] Aldgate explores the development of the newsreel genre and its accompanying technology, the ownership of newsreel companies, audiences' relationship with cinema news and its content, and, most crucially, the relationship between the newsreels and the government, in particular in relation to censorship (concluding that the newsreels 'were committed to consensus not conflict'[8]). All of these issues set up a context within which Aldgate analyses the political ramifications of coverage of the Spanish Civil War. This book examines similar issues in order to construct a context in which to examine the newsreels' coverage of and distribution to Ireland throughout the first half of the twentieth century. It also interrogates the political connotations of the newsreels' representation of Ireland and their coverage of events as external news producers. In this context, Ireland and Irishness presented a difficult area for the newsreels both in their approach to Irish politics and in how they catered for different political opinions in Irish audiences.

Aldgate's examination of the Spanish Civil War is, of course, necessarily limited to newsreels of the 1930s, a time when the sound newsreel had become predominant and the genre was reaching the peak of its potential as a news medium. Aldgate recognizes that alongside the editor a new figure of power had been brought to the newsreels – the commentator: 'Next to the editor, the commentator and his scriptwriter had the greatest opportunity to influence the shape of an issue and to determine where its emphasis would lie. Where once the "picture told the story", eventually, after the advent of sound, it became a matter of the commentator "telling" and the picture "illustrating" the most photogenic incidents.'[9] This book, in spanning a larger time frame, has examined the messages conveyed by both silent and sound newsreels and has also investigated both the imagery and the language used to depict Ireland and its people. Aldgate concludes that in their coverage of events in Spain, it was 'impossible to ascertain whether the newsreels were successful in their purpose of engendering a consensus response'.[10] In coverage of

Ireland, gaining a 'consensus' was largely problematic for the news-reels, given the fragmented political leanings of their audiences throughout the country during the course of many instances of conflict, some local, some national, some international. Aldgate even suggests that the newsreels were deliberately selective in their coverage of Spanish events in order to prevent the politics of the situation from being fully understood by British audiences.[11] This book aims to establish whether the newsreels may have used a similar strategy in their coverage of Ireland, an ongoing story which was vastly more contentious, given its proximity and its potential to damage Britain politically and economically. It also examines how events in Ireland were covered for audiences within Ireland – and how these events were in some cases edited differently for (and differently received by) audiences in the north and in the south.

This book sets out to provide the first account of newsreel coverage of Ireland and argues that the newsreels reflected the development of a 'partitionist' mentality for audiences in the north and south of the country. Given the limitations on movement between the two states, the newsreels played an important part in showing audiences 'the other Ireland'. This contribution to the creation of the two states of north and south in the Irish public's psyche was a process which extended well beyond the signing of the Anglo-Irish Treaty in 1921. The ways in which north and south were conceptualized differently for cinema audiences will also be explored, with the creation of an industrially powerful, 'masculine' urban north in opposition to a rural, backward and 'feminine' south. This study will also consider the newsreels' relationship with the Irish, Northern Irish and British governments. A large part of this relationship involved the ongoing propaganda war to construct the 'Ireland' that matched each government's ideological leanings. To complicate this matter further, the audiences addressed were split by religion, political association and, sometimes, access to newsreel material.

NOTES

1. Baechlin and Muller-Strauss (1954–55), p.45.
2. Fisk explores Pathé's coverage of Irish neutrality during the Second World War and discusses British Paramount News's controversial *Ireland – The Plain Issue* (1942). See Fisk (1983), pp.390–6.

3. See notes on Northern Ireland Screen's Digital Film Archive (DFA) or on their database entry for 'Titanic' at www.digitalfilmarchive.net. The item is dated simply '1912' and is credited to Pathé.
4. One such project was Northern Ireland Screen's Creative Learning in the Digital Age which facilitated the use of newsreel footage in schools to assist students in learning history alongside filmic analysis and editing techniques. See http://www.digitalfilmarchive.net/clda/.
5. Aldgate (1979), p.ix.
6. Ibid., p.14.
7. Ibid., p.15.
8. Ibid., p.193.
9. Ibid., p.41.
10. Ibid., p.193.
11. Ibid., p.194.

2

The Newsreel Landscape: Industry and Genre

In 1925, an amusing animated spoof of the newsreel series Topical Budget, The Topical Bonzette, appeared featuring G.E. Studdy's popular canine character Bonzo. It is an interesting parody of the standard cinema newsreel of the time, containing such items as the unveiling of a new trough, the latest dog hats from Paris, labour-saving devices for watchdogs, and canine sporting events. It even alludes to the popular Topical company's perennial back-patting in suggesting how Topical Bonzette's slow-moving camera demonstrates the 'grace of movement and action' in depicting Bonzo boxing his own shadow! Topical Bonzette cleverly mimics many of the features which would come to be associated with the newsreel genre: the near-obsession with royal items,[1] the inclusion of trivial stories, the diversity of material covered, and the newsreel's swift gallop through its weekly issue with a typically self-congratulatory style that included upbeat music and authoritative tone. This chapter will explore the history of the newsreel and trace the development of this characteristic style. It will also explore the newsreel industry, considering some of the debates surrounding newsreel production, its content, its audience and, crucially, its relationship with propaganda.

The Formation of the Newsreel Genre: An Historical Perspective

Movietone's film cans generally carried the legend 'Useless if Delayed' as they hurried their way through the cinema distribution circuit. This statement could, however, have been applied to all of the main newsreel companies at the height of their popularity.[2] During the golden age of newsreel production, freshly shot footage, often obtained after ingenious 'scooping' of rivals, was hurried to the editing processing labs and swiftly dispatched to the cinema exhibitor.[3] The cinema newsreels, in other words, attempted from the beginning to aspire to the 'immediacy' of news. The first use of the word 'newsreel' seems to have been for the American International Newsreel in 1917 although it may have occurred in publicity prior to this date.[4] Before this, early news films borrowed from the press in a search to define themselves: they were often called 'topicals', 'budgets' or 'animated newspapers'. This reflected strong associations between early newsreels and the newspapers: in France, the birthplace of the newsreels, the first news film cameramen were also known as *chausseurs d'images* (picture hunters) – a name, according to Michelle Aubert, 'which indicates not only the work which these pioneers accomplished, but also the bond which united them to the illustrated press of the time – which paved the way for the development of cinematography'.[5] The newsreels did not, however, set the agenda in the way that news footage does today – the newspapers reported imme- diate news, and newsreels followed up with the images at a later date. An article from 1915 in *Cassell's Saturday Journal* – significantly called 'How Long After?' – described the newsfilm as 'a pictorial newspaper shorn of the greater part of its letterpress ... the picture paper of the moving picture world: an animated record of passing events'.[6] It also claimed that newsfilm editing was similar in practice to the editing of a newspaper. Raymond Fielding offers an interesting early example of the interrelationship between newsfilm and the press. In coverage of the Spanish–American war in 1898, one Vitagraph newsfilm entitled *Tearing Down the Spanish Flag* (which simply showed a Spanish flag being replaced with an American one) boosted newspaper sales among audiences eager to read more about the story.[7] Clearly, in the early days of onscreen news, the interdependence between newsfilm and the press was both substantial and mutually beneficial.

The Origins of News Filming

It could be said that the very first film news item originated on 10 June 1895 when the Lumière brothers filmed the arrival of the delegates to the French Photographic Societies' conference in Neuville-sur-Saône and screened the film for them the following day. A second film, showing a conversation between Jules Janssen, president of La Société Française de Photographie, and the mayor of the town was also shown, with a transcription of the conversation read in sync with the film.[8] The Lumières gave birth to the cinema largely by screening a series of *actualités* to paying audiences, while their contemporary, Georges Méliès, used to 'stage' news events as actuality footage for early audiences. Clearly, from the beginnings of the cinema, 'news-based' content inspired a great deal of interest.

Gradually and sporadically, more 'news' films were released and, in 1909, Charles Pathé, founder of the French Pathé company, issued the first specially edited newsfilm. In June 1910 Pathé's Animated Gazette became the first British newsreel. It was issued weekly to begin with and contained a selection of actuality items, each around a minute long. The items were taken from footage shot by two British-based cameramen and supplemented by material from Pathé's international organization. Gaumont quickly followed suit and by the end of 1910 it also was issuing newsreel editions for British audiences. Warwick Bioscope Chronicle was also established in 1910. Still leading the way by 1911, Pathé expanded to offer its news coverage to several more European countries and even American audiences: the Pathé crowing cockerel came to symbolize news coverage worldwide. Topical Budget first appeared in 1911 – it was destined to become War Office Topical Budget in less peaceful times – and, in 1913, the first edition of Éclair Journal was released. By the outbreak of war in 1914, the newsreel industry was a truly international one and was improving operations in order to cope more and more efficiently with world coverage. There was no shortage of stories: the British Pathé's Animated Gazette was even producing daily items which could be spliced into the weekly reel.

Newsreel stories were sourced from the ticker tape and shaped by an editor. Cameramen were often sent to cover stories in the same way that reporters were, but the emphasis was usually on speed rather than balanced reporting, although the practicalities of filming delayed newsreel correspondents – more so than newspaper reporters. John Turner sums up the qualities required of a cameraman in his memoirs: 'a cameraman has to be alert, imaginative, unemotional, able to cope with the unexpected. He must be able to approach the greatest and lowest in society equally. He is not concerned as to "who" a person is, only his or her newsworthiness.'[9]

The fact that the visual news industry had spread worldwide had a

2.1 H.S. 'Newsreel' Wong, Singapore c.1941 (Norman Fisher collection courtesy of BUFVC).

huge impact in terms of news coverage and distribution – no newspaper had managed to break the boundaries of language and accomplish this feat.[10] Newsreels covered four or five of the week's news items and, with each lasting around a minute, the standard issue duration was about five minutes. Like feature films, they were silent before 1927, with intertitles explaining the items on screen. The popularity garnered by early news films meant that by 1912 they were being issued bi-weekly to match programme changes in the cinema. (For instance, Pathé's issues appeared on Wednesdays and Saturdays, and Gaumont's on Mondays and Thursdays.) Ireland was on the British distribution circuit and, while the core newsreel items remained the same for British and Irish audiences, gradually the newsreels began to include items of regional interest, defined on the newsreel issue sheets as 'Local/Special', for various cities within the United Kingdom. Before and after partition there were often 'Local/Special' items produced with an associated 'Dublin' and less often a 'Belfast' classification.

Studies of the News Companies

Luke McKernan's *Topical Budget: The Great British News Film* offers an exhaustive history of the Topical Budget company (1911–31). (There are no similar accounts of any of the other newsreel companies.) Although not one of the longest-running newsreels, Topical is of special interest, given its role as the official War Office Topical Budget during the First World War. McKernan's book is split into three main sections: an introduction covering silent newsreels in Britain, focusing on Topical's news coverage; an examination of 'a view from the home front' during the First World War; and the aptly subtitled 'all pictures but no politics' for his exploration of Topical's coverage of the 1920s. McKernan also includes a useful appendix offering a detailed chronology of newsreel events from 1895 to 1986. He highlights the fact that the newsreels tended to cover events already familiar to audiences through the newspapers; accordingly, they 'did not make the news – they could only reflect it'.[11] McKernan also explains that newsreels prioritized stories with pictorial value, in particular prior to the advent of sound, as a reason why politics was sparsely covered – it was a difficult topic to visualize. Another interesting fact highlighted by the study is Topical's pride in advertising its British identity (in opposition to the French-owned Pathé and Gaumont newsreels). One example cited is from an item covering the 1922 British election, which contains an intertitle proclaiming ' "TOPICAL" IS BRITISH We Lead – Others Follow!'[12]

The Topical Film Company, unlike the other main newsreel players, did not have a parent company but did produce feature-length films which used newsreel material as well as the actual newsreels themselves. It also often produced regular regional stories using freelance cameramen.[13] In October 1915 an agreement was made between the War Office and the Cinematograph Trade Topical Committee to coordinate the filming, distribution and censorship of war films.[14] The government formed the War Office Cinematograph Committee (WOCC) which produced feature and medium-length films before making footage for regular newsreels. It took over the Topical Film Company in 1917 and renamed the newsreel the War Office Official Topical Budget. An advertisement in *The Bioscope* encouraged cinema owners to 'book the Topical Budget' and promised the inclusion of 'authentic and official pictures dealing with the war at home and abroad'.[15] This was the only newsreel to have access to film shot at the Front by official cameramen, and its proceeds went to military charities. Prior to this, the only cameramen permitted to film at the Front were those from Pathé, Éclair and Gaumont, with the sanction of the French War Office.[16]

Lord Beaverbrook, who became Minister for Information in 1918, claimed that screenings of Topical newsreels were crucial in maintaining public morale towards the end of the war, despite the fact that due to the practical difficulties of filming very little of the actual conflict was shown.[17] Proximity to the action was created by showing battle sites, military exercises and captured prisoners, satisfying a desire for those on the home front to see some form of representation of the conditions endured by friends and relatives involved in battle. Despite impediments to filming, Beaverbrook saw the newsreel as a perfect propaganda solution – 'guaranteed to be shown in the cinemas every week, not demanding too much footage, able to carry a simple message, and readily comprehensible by the audience'.[18] Given the *Bioscope*'s prediction on the outbreak of war that the cinema would be the last form of entertainment to suffer in wartime conditions, and that it was indeed 'the cheapest, the most easily carried on, and under current conditions, perhaps the most attractive to the public',[19] the significance of the medium for propaganda purposes was recognized and its use intensified.

From the outset, the usefulness of the newsreels in documenting events was recognized:

> The topicals, or news items, were of the greatest importance from the first in consolidating the popularity of the film. Once the people realized that the cinema could undertake the regular recording of events it became recognized as an indispensable part of the public service, although in a sense disguised always as entertainment. Only thousands could participate in the big national events: but by means of the living representations of the camera millions could now feel nearer to them.[20]

Feeling nearer to the unfolding events of the war was particularly important to audiences eagerly awaiting news from relatives, and the newsreels' visualization of the Front also offered a construction of the place of loss for those in mourning at home: they were a powerful source of wartime imagery. An added complexity was the fact that the newsreels had to be 'disguised as entertainment', causing much debate in the film industry over what it was appropriate to show during the war, especially when battle scenes had the potential to both remind audiences of loved ones at the forefront of the conflict and reinforce a sense of grief for those bereaved. Not surprisingly, *The Battle of the Somme* covering 'the big push' on the Western Front in 1916 was one film that caused some controversy, given the imagery of death it blatantly exhibited. Although it had 2,000 bookings and raised £30,000,[21] one Hammersmith exhibitor notified his audiences 'we are not showing *The Battle of the Somme*. This is a place of amusement, not a chamber of horrors.'[22] The Battle of the Somme has particular significance in an Irish context, given the involvement of Irish soldiers and, in particular, the 36th Ulster Division, which was made up largely of members of the Ulster Volunteers, formed before the war to oppose Home Rule. The political significance of the Somme, and the involvement of Irish soldiers from north and south, will be discussed in detail in the following chapter.

There were more than hints of disapproval of war films in other quarters, despite their popularity. The principle objection, as voiced by *The Bioscope*, seems to have been their exhibition in a venue of entertainment:

> The majority of us turn to the cinema for relaxation after the toil of the day. We go there to try and forget war and its horrors, but, instead of being able to do so, are continually reminded of the bloody struggle that is in progress, and have scene after scene flashed on the screen of happenings that may even at that very moment be occurring to those we hold most dear.[23]

The idea that war permeated every aspect of life – even entertainment – was often too much for cinemagoers, many of whom regarded the cinema as an instrument of escapism which took on added importance as a way of dealing with the difficult war years. Furthermore, images of war were highly emotive, and any depiction of loss or suffering could deeply affect public morale, which would, in turn, filter through to the troops through letters from home. With this potential to compromise military efficiency, the cinema was deemed a powerful force and given a significant function in the wartime propaganda arsenal. It was vital that newsreels, in particular, due to their visual reporting of wartime

information, were harnessed for the most efficient morale-boosting purposes possible. In this context, the newsreels' coverage of and for Ireland
would prove to be extremely political during the First World War. Ireland
had been on the brink of civil war over impending Home Rule before war
broke out in 1914. Home Rule and the potential conflict between
Unionists and Nationalists had been suspended on the outbreak of war.
The newsreels covered both Irish support for the war effort and also
ongoing dissent amongst Nationalists, manifest in the Easter Rising of
1916. The next chapter examines in detail Ireland's relationship with the
newsreels during the war and in the run-up to partition.

The Twenties: 'All Pictures but no Politics'[24]

The Pathé, Gaumont and Topical newsreels were to survive the war
and increase in popularity during the 1920s, joined by Empire News
Bulletin in 1926. Newsreel cameramen led an increasingly exciting
existence as they competed with rival companies for the latest scoop.
A 1921 Topical Budget Cup Final item[25] proudly proclaims that 'any
other films shown are without the consent of the FA authorities', alluding to the common practice of 'scooping' rivals with exclusive rights
to sporting events. In a 1933 piece looking back at developments in
the newsreel industry, *Picturegoer* compares the smuggling by female
accomplices of illicit cameras into sporting events with the 'gangster's
moll' in her quest to conceal a murder weapon. The article also
describes how 'high-speed cars, trained runners, expert track riders and
a feverish race against time' are involved in rushing exclusive footage
to the editing room.[26] Aldgate evokes the intense rivalry of the 1920s
newsreel industry in the nicknames which described competing newsreels: 'The Gruesome Graphic', 'Impure Screen News', 'The Comical
Budget'.[27]

The newsreels frequently congratulated themselves both on capturing
exclusives and on their use of technology. A 1922 Topical Budget item
showing new Prime Minister Andrew Bonar Law and his Cabinet claims
to be 'a film which marks an epoch in cinematography'.[28] Topical
claimed to be the only company granted permission to film inside
the 'historic and sacred walls of no 10 Downing Street'. In grateful
appreciation, the final intertitle describes the 'quiet and yet steadfast
dignity of the new Prime Minister' and this is followed by a flattering
shot of Bonar Law. When covering the discovery of Tutankhamen's

tomb in 1923, Topical apologizes in a series of intertitles for the poor quality of the pictures provided:

> no need to recount the extraordinary difficulties which have attended the taking of Cinematograph pictures of the tomb. They are also well known. The pictures therefore do not pretend to be other than they are. They are not of the high quality ordinarily associated with Topical Budget. But if they are crude they are vital. So vital that despite their imperfections we believe they will have irresistible appeal as the <u>first</u> to be shown to the public.[29]

And so Topical emphasizes the importance of getting the pictures into the cinemas before rival companies, as the first scenes will always be the most memorable.

A fascinating Topical Budget item of 1922 shows an outing of the Kine Cameramen's society, to which most contemporary newsreel men belonged. After showing close-ups of the men, an incorrectly punctuated intertitle states: 'Topicals' close-up of real film faces! Quite human aren't they?' – alluding to the still-elusive nature of film-making and the public's view of it as a rather mysterious art. This newsreel shows the cameramen as 'ordinary' people, suggesting that they are similar to the audience. This serves the function of making the newsreel appear more believable – if it is produced by 'humans' like the audience, they are likely to share similar interests and less likely to want to deceive their fellow men, or so it would seem.[30] This article attempts to demystify the newsreels and is symptomatic of this stage of the newsreel industry's relationship with its audiences. There was still an interest in technology and a certain amount of trust in the objectivity of newsreels. This would change as the audiences became more aware of the propagandistic potential of newsfilm. For the purposes of this particular item, the industry appears to be attempting to demonstrate the openness and objectivity of its productions.

The imagery forever associated with pre-sound 1920s newsreels is of the fashions, film stars and glamour of that era. To mirror the post-war shift in public interest to the more ephemeral, newsreel companies produced lighter cinemagazines in conjunction with their regular newsreels. Gaumont's 'colour supplement' was Around the Town (1919–23) and then Gaumont Mirror (1927–32) later in the decade, while Pathé Pictorial (1918–69) proved popular enough to merit Eve's Film Review

(1921–33), a sister cinemagazine produced for women, promising in its title 'fashion, fun and fancy'. In her book on the cinemagazine, Jenny Hammerton suggests that this review sought to tap into the new interest in 'what was seen to be a new visibility of female sexuality'[31] in traditionally male spheres. The newsreel was sometimes extended to male audiences as *Eve and Everybody's Film Review* and, given the frequent shots of scantily clad women, there is more than a suggestion of pandering to the male gaze. There are echoes here of P.D. Hugon's 1915 *Hints to Newsfilm Cameramen*: 'when it comes to girls, only the most strikingly beautiful specimens should appear'.[32] Men seldom appear in Eve's cinemagazine and although Hammerton claims that 'there is no male mediator of the look',[33] the reel is certainly not designed to appeal solely to a female audience, thus testifying to the 'all-embracing' nature of even 'specialist' newsreels. Once again the newsreel appears to be the obvious product of an entertainment package. The cinemagazines were even more eager than the mainstream newsreels to fit easily into the entertainment forum in which they were exhibited and though they took the form of longer factual films, they were quick to assert their differences from the documentary genre. The editor of Pathé Pictorial proudly proclaimed that 'the Pictorial does not attempt to enforce education upon an audience. Our primary business is to entertain, amuse and interest our audiences.' The remarks are concluded with the rather condescending caveat, 'though, if at any time anyone wishes to learn anything new from the pictures (and all of us are able to) he or she is very welcome'.[34] So the cinemagazine fitted neatly into the inoffensive, mildly-interesting-to-all category.

Distribution

Newsreels, like other elements of the cinema programme (feature films, cartoons, trailers) were rented to exhibitors and were distributed as part of a circuit. Given the expensive nature of prints, only a select few cinemas received the first newsreel prints. After screenings over three days, usually before feature films, the prints were then passed on to the next set of cinemas, and so on. The newsreel circuit took about three weeks to complete. Some trains, like the Leeds–London line, also had newsreel screenings and some large hotels provided newsreel screenings for their guests. Not surprisingly, cinema owners sought to thwart these practices, seeing them as unfair competition.[35]

2.2 Graham Thompson, Scotland 1928 (Norman Roper collection courtesy of BUFVC).

Another development for the newsreel industry was the opening of specialist newsreel theatres. Paris was the first city to establish news theatres in 1932 but London and other UK cities were soon to follow. The news theatre was most suited to the city, as it required a large floating public for feasible operation. By 1934 there were seven in London; this had risen to eighteen by 1936 and there were around fifty throughout the UK by 1938.[36] Some of these were found in railway stations (Victoria and Waterloo are two examples) and operated a fifty-minute programme for commuters. The programme would run from ten in the morning to midnight and a one-way traffic system ensured little congestion for outgoing and incoming patrons. Train times were clearly visible on a separate screen and these theatres boasted a staff of around twenty to ensure swift programme changes and continued screening throughout the day. The general programme of a news theatre consisted of alternating two or three newsreel services with cartoons, cinemagazines and travelogues. These were set to accommodate that percentage of the population interested solely in news rather than feature films (*The Cine-Technician* suggested this was as high as 10 per cent of the news theatre's clientele, with the other 90 per cent drawn from the passing public) and the patron wishing to see short films rather than a full programme. In fact, it was noted that the news theatres often boasted standing-room only and also accommodated those people who were in the practice of phoning the general cinemas to ask 'When does the news come on?'[37] The news theatre was perhaps the only arena where the discerning viewer could compare different newsreels' approach to covering events, but this worried the proprietor in terms of the repetition of material and the newsreels' use of pooled footage. In some circumstances unofficial editing occurred, a practice ignored by the news companies themselves, given the fact that their prime concern was maintaining contracts with exhibitors.[38] The news theatres occasionally put together their own newsreels, though they were careful 'to include only the sections that are likely to give no offence to any section of the audience'.[39] They also took the greatest care 'to do nothing to antagonise the Government in power in case it should bring a stringent censorship to bear on the newsreels'.[40]

The pattern here is worth pausing over. Newsreels were made for a large general audience and were distributed widely to all cinemas in strict rotation. The 'ideal' newsreel audience, in other words, was a large and undifferentiated mass audience. Yet local distributors and exhibitors retained the right to re-edit newsreels for a more differentiated local audience and to respond to particular local tastes and opinion as they saw it. The overarching desire was to avoid controversy, whether with the government or other authority figures or with the audience in the cinema. The result of all this was to ensure that newsreel content remained conservative and mostly unchallenging and that a degree of self-censorship operated at all levels of the newsreel circuit.

Introduction of Sound

By far the greatest development throughout the course of newsreel history was the advent of sound in the late 1920s. Fox Movietone News was the first to break the newsreel sound barrier in the US and the British newsreels were to follow within two years. The dominant tones of omniscient commentators were to change the way in which newsreels would be viewed and remembered. One of the most significant and perceptive observations about the use of sound in the visual news medium was made by Benito Mussolini in May 1927 when he addressed the camera directly, delivering a speech in English aimed at the US public. Having viewed the footage, he said: 'your talking newsreel has tremendous political possibilities, let me speak through it in twenty cities in Italy once a week and I need no other power'.[41] Although silent intertitles had begun to comment upon rather than simply to describe newsreel footage from the outbreak of the First World War,[42] the medium of sound brought newsreel commentary and interpretation to a new level. Sound had a huge impact on meaning as well as on atmosphere: 'the soundtrack gave a far greater sense of actuality to films ... It made you feel you were there – in the room, the store, the street, the ship, the plane ... it was the sound track that gave that added dimension, the feeling of actual contact with the places and people moving on the screen.'[43] Equally, this carried added responsibilities, particularly when considering the vital nature of newsreel propaganda during wartime, as suggested by Thorpe and Pronay: 'in a sound film an ill-judged phrase, or even an unfortunately chosen single word, can alter the effectiveness and the reception of the whole film'.[44] Ultimately, the soundtrack brought increased 'reality' for viewers, a heightened experience, a greater sense of a more accurate 'recreation'. John Grierson went as far as to argue that 'sound can obviously bring a rich contribution to the manifold of the film – so rich a contribution in fact that the double art becomes a new art altogether'[45] and that this 'new and distinct art' had a 'genius of its own' to be explored and used to fulfil the full potential of the combination of sound and image.[46] McKernan goes one step further, claiming that the dominant memory of newsreel coverage is of the 'rousing music' and authoritative commentary, rather than the accompanying images.[47]

After a strong rivalry between British Movietone News and Gaumont to rush out the first British sound issue, Movietone made it to the editing room first in June 1929. Gaumont's attempt to produce a sound edition on the same day was thwarted when their equipment failed but they were soon to follow in the race to get 'talking' newsreels to the theatres on time. But while the newsreel companies adopted the technology with the usual frenzied rush to outdo competitors, the cinemas adapted to sound at a slower pace, and Pathé, Gaumont and Empire continued to issue silent reels alongside sound issues for the following few years. Pathé Gazette yielded silent and sound issues; Gaumont Graphic continued in silent form alongside Gaumont Sound News, and Empire News Bulletin was the silent issue alongside the commentary-driven Universal Talking News. A major sound newsreel, British Paramount News, was born as the last issues of Topical Budget faded from cinema screens in 1931.

Towards the Height of Popularity – Newsreels in the 1930s

The upbeat music and authoritative commentary cemented the conventions of the newsreel genre, a genre which has been much parodied – most memorably perhaps in Orson Welles's *Citizen Kane*, with its 'News on the March' sequence cleverly parodying March of Time and its self-referential narrative is as much a record of news coverage as it is a study of the elusive news tycoon it portrays. In his book on March of Time, Raymond Fielding suggests that Welles 'meticulously imitates MOT style' in the opening ten minutes of *Citizen Kane*. The parody, 'complete with a booming Voice of Time narrator',[48] was the product of close study of the March of Time series by Welles, who sought to imitate it in every detail, even to the extent of coaching Bill Alland, who provided the voiceover, for weeks so that he could imitate the recognizable tones of Westbrook Van Voorhis, March of Time's most famous commentator.[49]

Before the advent of sound, newsreel stories had to be pictorial in nature to hold the audience's interest. By the 1930s, with more focus on sound and commentary, newsreels could quickly explain any subject appearing on screen. The fast-paced, somewhat monotonous tone gave the audience little time to assimilate information and increased the credibility of commentators – there was 'no place for the uncertain or informal'.[50] The commentator was always the unflinching voice of authority, entertaining, informing and *telling* the audience – perpetually didactic and unfaltering. Nichols argues that in a news-setting the reporter or commentator should always remain the apparently objective authority – there is no place in his role for obvious human response to the events covered. He is there simply to verify 'the omnipresence of the authoring agency, the news apparatus'.[51] It is only through his lack of response, his implicit impartiality, that room is left for audience reaction. Nichols always associates objectivity with the third-person 'omniscient perspective', a disinterested comment on the issue in question, 'letting the viewer decide on the basis of a fair presentation of facts'.[52] Newsreels sought to appear impartial in this manner, or at least to fool contemporary audiences into trusting their presumed objectivity.

The big newsreel players of the 1930s were Movietone (owned jointly by 20th Century Fox USA and Lord Rothermere, UK), Paramount (Paramount Pictures USA), Pathé (jointly owned by Associated British Picture Corporation UK and Warner Bros USA), Universal (owned by General Distributors UK) and Gaumont British News (owned by Gaumont British UK). Thus the majority of the newsreel market share was of American origin. The editors of these companies became more publicly prominent during the 1930s. Movietone was the only company with two editors – Gerald Sanger and Ivan Scott; the remaining four had only one – Tom Cummins at British Paramount, Louis Behr at Gaumont, Tom Scales at Pathé and Cecil Snape at Universal.

Four of the 'Big Five' joined the Newsreel Association of Great Britain and Ireland (NRA) in 1937 and the fifth, British Paramount News, followed in 1938. This was a body set up as the industry's trade association, offering the makers of screen news a forum in which to discuss pertinent issues, resolve disputes and protect collective interests. In his article on the NRA, Jeff Hulbert outlines the association's main aim: 'To promote the interests, financial welfare and success of the trade or business of manufacturing, producing and distribution of cinematic films of current events known as newsreels, and to devise means to promote co-operation amongst those in the said trade or business.'[53] It would continue to operate until 1960, during which time it helped the government to define legally the word 'newsreel', formed an agreement that the newsreels would avoid fakes and hoaxes, and decided to suspend normal sales competition during the Second World War, amongst other useful agreements. Whether or not the avoidance of 'fakes' was fully implemented is a questionable matter. In a Mass Observation report in 1940, it was suggested that clever use of sound could manipulate the images so that 'a completely false interpretation was conveyed'.[54] The report also alludes to 'prepared' or staged scenes set up by cameramen and voices the concern that the audience will continue to believe the images and sound, whether real or staged, fed to them through the cinema screen, given that 'nothing can be proved conclusively unless one of the newsreels makes a big mistake'.

Newsreels were at the height of their popularity during the 1930s, causing one newsreel editor to suggest that those who simply tolerated the news as part of the cinema programme were 'among the less intelligent section of the public'.[55] An article in the same issue of *Kinematograph Weekly* claimed that a cinema exhibitor cutting the newsreel from his cinema programme was 'cutting his own throat'.[56] However, the same article rather prophetically points to television newsreels as the news of the future, claiming that news is characterized by how quickly it is made accessible to the public. This testifies to a growing awareness of the increased immediacy of news coverage. The writer's 'extravagant peep into the future' visualizes the huge potential of news on screen as it actually occurs – 'red-hot news' – and alludes to the already archaic silent newsreel as a Victorian child to be 'seen and not heard'.

The newsreels' weekly diet consisted of royalty, sport and celebrities, and they grew to ten minutes or more on average by the 1930s. The prime requisite for a news item making it into the reel was its pictorial value. Generally, newsreel stories consisted of recent news stories, scheduled events and items of the 'magazine' variety. About sixty to ninety items were sent in by local cameramen and foreign agencies every week and eight or nine of these were chosen to be included in the final edition. Cameramen often faced difficulties in getting the best shots, and this pressure was well recognized: 'a newsreel cameraman never gets a second chance to retrieve his errors, and his mistakes are magnified on the screen many thousands of times for the whole world to view'.[57] Less newsworthy items were often included by editors simply because they presented more impressive footage. Staged events were particularly popular as they offered the chance of well-positioned cameras and preparation in advance. While royal weddings and sporting events were newsreel staples, newsreels approached politics with caution and avoided controversy in order to keep up a healthy relationship with the censor. The prime objective of the newsreel editor was to avoid alienating the audience by showing subject matter which would be off-putting or upsetting, particularly in relation to home issues. In contrast, the representation of conflict in other countries (in an appropriate manner) served to make life in Britain appear safer, calmer and more preferable.

There were many comparisons drawn between hard-drinking newspapermen and the equally ebullient newsreel cameramen. Peter Hopkinson's insightful comments on the March of Time series are included in an unpublished memoir, available on the British Universities Newsreel Database, entitled 'The Screen of Change: Film and Politics'.[58] Hopkinson seems to need to explain why, as a British cameraman, he chose to work for March of Time for several years after the war. He also defends the newsreel against criticisms about its staged sequences and highlights its unique position in the newsreel industry. However, there were also important differences between newspaper reporters and cameramen. F.A. Talbot suggested that the cameraman was more warmly received than the press photographer who 'often allows his zeal and enthusiasm to overstep his discretion'.[59] While newspaper reporters penned their own stories, cameramen recorded representations of locations and events but the overall commentary was not scripted by them and often included details from the press and radio. When authentic footage was not available, library or staged footage was used. The newsreels counteracted any doubt about the footage used for some items with the amount of staged events they covered (ship launches, sporting events), supplying well-shot, accurate footage, even actual sound effects in some cases, and maintaining public faith in the authenticity of newsreel pictures. Luke McKernan suggests that while sound newsreels benefited from sharper pictures, these images were 'often buried in music, commentary and the urgent need to cut to the next shot', as opposed to the 'special eloquence' of the longer shots of the silent newsreel.[60]

With the end of intertitles, newsreels became even more accessible to those without a formal education, whereas one had to be literate in order to read a newspaper. Newsreel viewing was also an experience shared with other audience members in a public place, as opposed to the individual act of reading a newspaper in a location of one's choice. Needless to say, the advent of sound had huge implications for internationally distributed newsreels. In the silent era, the order of a newsreel could remain intact for exhibition in a number of countries with a simple change of intertitles. With sound newsreels the timing of the commentary was crucial and foreign releases became more complicated.

Newsreel stories were designed to be covered as 'news flashes': there was little time to analyse and digest information before the next item appeared. This was an attempt to prevent boredom in the audience, but it gave little time to assimilate information. Similarly, commentaries were designed to be absorbed by 'speed, loudness and repetition'.[61]

Crucially, the public could reread a newspaper article to assess its objectivity; access to reviewing newsreels depended on how frequently one attended the cinema during a particular issue's three-day run. With a newspaper, the reader controls which stories will be read or ignored and in which order (although many readers will be guided by leading articles). With the newsreel, the editor controls which stories will be included and in which order – the modes of reception are fundamentally different for the end user.

Critiquing the Newsreels: A Review of Trade Paper Attitudes

Throughout the period of their greatest popularity the newsreels were often the subject of debate in the trade papers. The main points of discussion were about content, issues to do with censorship, the coverage of political material and controversies over exclusive rights. The most frequent critiques of newsreels were in relation to their form and content, often provoking interesting comments and responses from newsreel practitioners.

This ongoing criticism appeared as soon as the newsreels began to take shape in the 1910s. In 1914, for example, Lester Ruah criticized the newsreels for being trivial and predictable and for failing to cover real news.[62] This brought a swift and angry response from several newsreel editors in *Kinematograph Weekly*. Alec J. Braid, editor of Gaumont Graphic, reminded Ruah that great news stories were not always pictorial in their nature and also that newsreels were attempting to entertain the public through visual images. Val Steer of Éclair Animated Journal reminded Ruah that news film was still in its infancy, but stated: 'I feel certain that the news-film has not only come to stay, but to steadily improve in quality and importance until it becomes an essential adjunct to the ordinary newspaper press.' Steer suggests that improvements could be made if the 'authorities' granted 'the same privileges and courtesies extended to the press'.[63]

After the First World War there was a heightened awareness of the potential manipulation of audience opinion through the newsreels, highlighted in *Kinematograph Weekly*, which claimed in 1920 that 'ingenious attempts to utilise the public screens for partisan appeals have been several times attempted since the Armistice'.[64] The basic concern here seems to be the potential of a close relationship between screen news producer and newspaper magnate, suggesting that the political ties of the latter would sully the former. News tycoon Lord Beaverbrook is the principal figure of concern, with his preoccupation with 'the manipulation of public opinion' and his delight in 'pulling strings'. The article suggests that the power lies in the fact that the cinema reaches a higher number of the public than the press does, and that while one may avoid buying a newspaper one disagrees with, in attending the cinema to see a feature film it is impossible to avoid the newsreel. The article calls for continued 'entertainment undiluted by political flavouring'. In 1934, the then Managing Director of British News Theatres (an organization which managed a number of newsreel cinemas, particularly in railway stations) Norman Hulbert, made interesting comments in an article entitled 'What I Demand of the Newsreel Editor'. Hulbert believed the news film to be

> the greatest propaganda medium in the world, not even excluding broadcasting, for in the latter case it is easy to 'switch off' but when a news film is sandwiched between two feature pictures in a programme, I defy anyone to turn a deaf ear or a blind eye to its exhibition, and in this the newsreel editor has us at his mercy![65]

He warned that politics should be 'sparsely included', due to the near impossibility of representing the subject in an impartial manner. His attitude exemplifies the cautious nature of all of the newsreel editors. In their meetings through the Newsreel Association the five main editors generally agreed unanimously on how to deal with difficult subjects. In his keynote address to the 1996 International News Film Conference, Anthony Smith alludes to the problem of newsreels trying to present themselves as impartial against a backdrop of 'providing information inside a house of entertainment'.[66] Crucially, if a newsreel was seen to be propagandistic this could affect its purchase by exhibitors, and *Kinematograph Weekly* claimed that 'there is not an exhibitor in the country who will defend the policy of letting political views intrude upon the screen ... political propaganda in a kinema entertainment is an offence'.[67] It was a risk newsreel producers were keen to avoid.

By the 1930s, even though newsreels were at the height of their popularity, Charles Grinley was claiming that the public 'have become used to the newsreels being deleted or doctored'. The newsreels, he argues, play 'Safety first' and as a whole 'can't show us the world as it is'. He even suggests 'the newsreel isn't news, but a screen in front of it'. Equally, he recognizes that the public does not give its full attention to the newsreels and that people 'drop in, notice the items they want, doze through the rest'. Grinley was concerned that audiences were not questioning the content or production of the newsreels. He describes the resulting propaganda potential of the newsreels: 'slogans can be dinned into the audiences' ears till they become familiar with them, the first step towards accepting them. A viewpoint can be presented until it seems the natural one.' And 'certain reels are under the control of those from whom unbiased news is hardly to be expected'.[68] The potential existed for the government not only to use moving images for persuasion but also to divert audiences' attention away from serious issues or political crises and onto the trivial. J.B. Priestley referred to the newsreel editors as having the power to 'do much good or a great deal of mischief. They are among the most powerful educators of public opinion.' He also pointed out: 'Even the order "give us more light entertaining items" can have serious political-social consequences.'[69]

The whole censorship area in relation to the newsreels was a cloudy one. In discussing censorship issues, Rachel Low suggests that 'the assumption was that the majority of the audience was immature, and, in view of the great influence the cinema would have on them, in need of paternal guidance'.[70] This would prove particularly accurate during wartime, when the British (and, during the Second World War, Irish) governments were keen to police audience viewing. Outside wartime, all British films were subject to censorship by local councils who were guided by the British Board of Film Censors. The newsreels, however, escaped this censorship through a small loophole and were forever trying to ensure that they maintained this privileged position, particularly due to the necessity of swift editing and distribution procedures. Censorship would slow down the newsreels' race to the cinema screens, so it was important to avoid material which might further delay this process due to the mechanisms of censorship.

After partition, some cinemagazines (short films produced by the newsreel companies) in the Irish Free State were viewed alongside feature films by the Irish film censor and there were only occasional brushes with the censor, which, outside wartime, were not related to politics. Rockett cites some issues with the portrayal of beauty pageants, with the example of Pathé Pictorial: the company was asked to remove scenes of scantily clad women in 1936.[71] It is not clear if the newsreels were subject to consistent levels of stringent censorship during peacetime in the Irish Free State,[72] but they were intensely scrutinized during the Second World War, as will be explored in the penultimate chapter of this book. General film censorship in Northern Ireland after partition and up to the Second World War was 'less active and less centralized than its southern counterpart, there were fewer films censored and fewer records kept on the subject'.[73]

Politics was handled with acute sensitivity by the newsreel companies and there was a general reverence in the face of the huge propaganda potential of the film medium. British newsreels watched with caution the frequent brushes with the censor encountered by the American March of Time series and sought to avoid a similar fate. (March of Time produced twenty-minute issues usually confined to one event and often used impersonators or staged footage. It was produced once a month as opposed to the more common twice-weekly newsreel pattern and was much more controversial, sometimes even openly biased.[74]) There was a strong avoidance of the dramatization so rife in American newsreels, as this kind of re-enactment was considered 'rather repellent from a British point of view'.[75] The British newsreel was viewed by the public as more dignified and restrained in its commentary than the 'spurious verbosity' of American news, generating excitement in the audience 'by verbal and vocal artistry not always justified by the actual picture'. The British newsreel was comfortable with its apparently non-threatening, non-controversial stance – one that was also non-challenging to the censor. Raymond Fielding suggests that the March of Time series, more so than any other newsreel, tackled political content. One example given is that of newsreels produced in the Depression era which, even in a place of entertainment, reminded audiences of 'bread lines, unemployment and political demagoguery'.[76] This kind of provocative politicizing of newsreel content was far from common practice in British newsreel production. March of Time's coverage of Ireland, as will be seen in the three March of Time films discussed below, *Irish Republic* (1937), *Ulster vs Éire* (1938) and *The Irish Question* (1944), certainly courted the controversy for which March of Time quickly became famous. In fact, Fielding suggests the newsreel was 'the only film series, newsreel or not, regularly to exploit political issues on theatrical motion picture screens'.[77]

The Second World War: Propaganda and the Newsreels

Ireland would prove a contentious issue for newsreels during the Second World War. While Northern Ireland, as part of Britain, was fully involved in the war effort, the south of Ireland, despite increasing pressure from the British government, remained neutral for the duration of the war. Irish neutrality posed a particular problem for the newsreels. While audiences in Northern Ireland, like audiences throughout the rest of Britain, watched newsreels mostly containing war items, strict wartime censorship in the south of Ireland meant war stories had to be completely purged from the weekly cinema news. The newsreels responded to this by producing 'Irish editions' specifically packaged for Irish audiences which led to an interesting split in viewing in Ireland between north and south. While there was some variation between north and south in newsreel content before the war, during wartime the differences were extreme. This will be explored in more detail in the penultimate chapter of this book.

Ironically, in the lead-up to the Second World War the newsreels seemed even more obsessed with trivia than ever. In their attempt to avoid controversy they seemed to completely ignore the hotbed of European tension unfolding before them. The outbreak of the Second World War brought even more responsibilities for the newsreels to bear, with a newly defined 'rallying role'. The newsreels would be seen as vitally important in keeping up morale both abroad and at home, particularly when cities were under direct attack by aerial bombings. (Both Dublin and Belfast were bombed in 1941 but, despite the fact that Belfast suffered significant damage and fatalities, only the Dublin bombing made the newsreels.) Audiences at home also had to be kept from despair due to their links with troops fighting in distant locations, as any sense of despondency could filter through to the armed forces through letters from home. In the light of these responsibilities, the newsreels during the war were subject to censorship carried out by the Ministry of Information.

The main objective in planning the Ministry of Information, part of overall plans for war which were initiated in 1934, was to create a strategic propaganda campaign. It was firmly believed that the outcome of the war might depend heavily on the maintenance of civilian morale under sustained aerial bombardment. There was a general concern about the best way to appropriate recently established channels of mass communication, which meant that plans for the Ministry of Information were carried out intermittently. In the First World War, Britain had 'pioneered modern propaganda warfare', which also led to a certain degree of complacency about preparations for the Second World War.[78] Despite the protestations of Lord Beaverbrook, the Ministry of Information was one of the first ministries to be wound up at the end of the First World War, and there was no propaganda provision between the wars. Its function had been heavily praised by the press and was overall seen as a great success: any mistakes were glossed over, leading to the expectation of similar success during the Second World War. The British, it was claimed, had not only been productive in conducting a propaganda campaign at home during the Great War, but abroad as well, leading to accusations of a concerted and secret operation in the US which was instrumental in the ultimate American involvement in the Allied war effort. Thus British propaganda was seen as highly effective and 'could therefore be readily relied on as a pattern for future wars'; it was even praised by Hitler in *Mein Kampf*.[79] Public expectation was different by the Second World War, and the production of false stories of German atrocities during the First World War had led to a heightened scrutiny of war news.

While the Topical Budget company had conveyed the government's official message during the First World War , the RAF's The Gen (which ran from 1943 to 1945 and was intended for RAF personnel in bases throughout the world) and the home front Worker and Warfront bore this responsibility during the Second World War. Worker and Warfront was produced by Paul Rotha Productions for the Ministry of Information between 1942 and 1946. Warwork News was produced by Paramount in conjunction with the Ministry of Supply to show only war-related films with the aim of increasing wartime productivity.[80] The newsreels took to wartime reporting with the usual caution, and only one company, Paramount, was reprimanded for giving opponents to the Munich settlement the opportunity to voice their concerns in the run-up to war. When Paramount was asked to withdraw the item in question, which was critical of appeasement, it sparked much debate within the newsreel industry on the matter of censorship. This incident will be discussed in more detail in this book's exploration of Second World War newsreels.

In Britain, the newsreels were inevitably preoccupied with war news

– it was estimated that less than 15 per cent of newsreel coverage dealt with non-war items. It was also suggested by Mass Observation (a social research organization, founded in 1937 to document various aspects of British life) that the newsreels' interest in personalities shifted to events at this stage, with more coverage being given to wartime developments than to politicians.[81] This was perhaps due to perceived audience preference for scenes of soldiers supporting the Crown, and the comfort of 'uninterfering royalty' rather than 'troublesome members of parliament'. Mass Observation surveys designed to gauge public reaction to the wartime newsreels suggested that 'the only group that shows any strong objection to the newsreels are the men under 30 of the middle classes', seemingly on propaganda grounds, given the quotations cited by members of this group. The study attributed the general popularity of the newsreels to 'discovering public opinion and altering subject matter to taste'.[82] Again the newsreels were doing what they did best – showing audiences what they wanted to see and avoiding controversy at all costs.

The newsreel was an important propaganda weapon in Germany as well. Certainly Hitler and Goebbels were well aware of the importance of the newsreels in Nazi Germany and copies of each issue were sent to the Führer's headquarters and the Propaganda Ministry before distribution to the general public.[83] Goebbels supervised the newsreels during the early part of the war and nearly every entry in his diary during the Blitz contains some reference to a recent newsreel. He particularly voices his contempt for his adversaries' newsreels, claiming that English and Russian newsreels are 'absolutely no competition for us'. In contrast to Hitler's admiration of British propaganda in the First World War, Goebbels sees Second World War newsreels as amateur, ineffective and 'indescribably naïve'.[84] Convinced that Germany could certainly win the newsreel propaganda war, Goebbels even closed cinema box offices during the newsreel so that audiences could not skip the newsreel if they wanted to view a film.[85]

The British Ministry of Information had insisted on a heavy-handed propaganda campaign – all too transparent to audiences who still had fresh memories of the promises that a previous war would be over by Christmas. On top of the same scant supply of 'official' footage to each of the main companies, commentaries were heavily dictated by the official message. Also, when defeats had to be reported, and reported regularly (particularly between 1940 and 1942), the immediacy of audiovisual reporting made the losses seem all the more devastating.

On top of this was the entertainment framework within which the newsreel operated – even in the 'dream-house', the horrors of war could not be avoided. By the time victories began to appear, sceptical audiences were still regarding the newsreel with a cynical gaze and listening to the commentator with a cautious ear. Also, given the increase in middle-class cinema attendance during the Second World War, suddenly newsreel editors had to address a multi-tiered audience, making it more difficult to 'find the right level' and set the right tone. The broadsheets' readership was dipping into the tabloids, and expecting them to cater for their tastes. While in 1935 *Film Art* claimed 'the surest way of pleasing the largest number of people is to include the smallest amount of intelligent material in the reel',[86] ten years later this was no longer the case. It was also well recognized that the newsreels would be approached with more caution by the post-war public: 'the post war citizen, as the wartime citizen, will want realism because he is now and will continue to be a realist – in that way he is different from the average citizen of the complacent thirties'.[87] The damage witnessed during the bombings of British cities also meant that the British public experienced a greater engagement with the horrors of war than had been the case during the First World War.

Not even the jaunty commentary and upbeat style of cinema news could prevent the British public from seeing the newsreels as becoming the regular bearers of bad news. While the public appeal for the newsreels prior to the war had reached its height in terms of popularity and general respect, these had diminished by the end of the war. A series of Mass Observation reports charting audience reaction to the newsreels and the propaganda message they carried shows an early dip in popularity. Even by the end of 1940, Mass Observation was claiming that 'there is every evidence that the newsreels are still losing ground with the public'.[88] However, at least one of the trade journals seemed to rally against this trend by depicting the heroic duties of wartime newsreel cameramen, claiming that they 'belong to that fine band of people of the Fourth Service – propaganda and truthful news', recording 'the battle for freedom and civilisation'. One recollection in the article recalls how newsreel men in the First World War had been considered a nuisance, unlike current cameramen 'dressed like Colonels'. The article refers to them as 'front line warriors'[89] and its author seems happy to hand over responsibility for wartime reporting to the companies, and it was this attitude that gave rise to scepticism from many members of the public. In its tone the article itself appears overly propagandistic.

Post-War Decline

After the war, the growing dissatisfaction with cinema news is apparent in Granada's decision to cancel newsreels at their cinemas, claiming that 'they are of poor quality, lacking the sense of journalistic selectivity and showmanship'. This followed on from the Bernstein questionnaire (1946–47), reported in *The Daily Film Renter*. Bernstein's survey claimed that only 41 per cent of patrons thought the newsreels were good quality. Bernstein went on to condemn the newsreels as 'socially outmoded', incompetent in production and prone to political bias. He even went as far as to suggest they were damaging to the British film industry and far inferior to American and some European newsreels. There was some redemption for Pathé – 'it would be unfair to group their ethics and talents with those of the other companies' – but Bernstein delivers a clear and resounding message of discontent, appealing to the newsreel editors for improvement. Bernstein made an appeal for people to watch what would ultimately be the death knell for the newsreels – Television Newsreel.[90]

With the advent of television, the BBC initially transmitted cinema newsreels to those lucky enough to be able to afford television sets, but coverage of the 1953 Coronation increased public interest in more immediate news. The BBC's Television Newsreel began in 1954, and by 1955 there were daily news reports on TV, relayed by newsreaders. Gradually the newsreels faded from cinema screens. British Paramount News closed on 1 January 1957. Gaumont British News became the colour cinemagazine *Look at Life* after its subsidiary Universal News produced its last issue in 1956, and the cinemagazine was to follow suit on 28 January 1959. Pathé, the first and longest-running newsreel production company, valiantly battled television by producing colour issues of both *Pathé News* and *Pathé Pictorial* and continued to do so until 1970. British Movietone News adopted similar tactics, changing its name to Movietone News in 1969 and providing the Commonwealth newsreel British News overseas, and making it past its fiftieth anniversary before closing in 1979.

Retrospective Examination of Newsreels

Nicholas Pronay suggests that, in general, archival film has, from an historical point of view, been unable to offer comprehensive historical illustration, but recognizes that this is due to the fact that 'film (and radio) was a means of communicating, not a means of note-taking'.[91] Furthermore, due to the necessarily delayed nature of newsreel production, newsreels seldom offered audiences 'new facts', but provided the moving images pertaining to stories already familiar to audiences through press and radio. Film, like newspapers, demonstrates the information available in the public sphere, not that which is contained in government records. Its value, then, may lie in its revelation of what people were *shown* about contemporary events and figures rather than as a factual record of particular happenings. Pronay asserts: 'it is in the size, social composition and the attitudes of the *audience* of the newsreels that the strongest case for studying them is to be found'.[92] The historical significance of the newsreel as document is inextricably linked with its preoccupation with the audience. The newsreel editor set out not just to cover stories, but also to divert the public in an entertainment forum. Controversy was avoided, not simply to maintain the newsreels' cordial relationship with the censor,[93] but also to avoid upsetting cinemagoers on their evening out. The value in newsreels, then, lies with their record of *how* events were presented to contemporary audiences. Penelope Houston also reflects on the nature of the moving image as historical evidence, concluding that, on the one hand, it is 'untrustworthy, superficial, vulnerable to every kind of distortion', and on the other, 'irreplaceable, necessary, a source material that no twentieth century historian ought to disregard'.[94]

The technological advances of the cinema had a profound effect on public entertainment. From the first moving pictures to the application of sound, the foundations of mass communication were laid. Figures in Simon Rowson's 1934 statistical analysis of British cinemagoing suggest that up to 43 per cent of the population were attending the cinema weekly at this time. Rowson also suggests that the highest cinema density was in industrial areas rather than prosperous regions.[95] Rowson estimated that there were on average twenty-two visits per head per annum for Great Britain, while Thekla Beere's statistics for cinema attendance[96] in Ireland in 1936 suggested twenty-four visits per year for Irish Free State citizens, a significant increase from statistics quoted in the Dáil more than a decade earlier which suggested an attendance figure of six visits per year.[97]

Given that cinemagoing was a relatively inexpensive pastime, this would suggest that the technology was made available to all classes (but that the middle classes may have preferred the larger, more expensive and more comfortable cinemas). It became even more far-reaching by the growing frequency with which the medium was availed of and the atmosphere of 'communal participation' in which audiences accessed newsreel images.[98] Richard Dyer alludes to the idea of an experience not just shared with other local cinemagoers but also tapping into the even more universal nature of cinemagoing when he describes the 'vast assemblies of strangers gathered together in the dark to see flickering, rapidly changing fabulous images that they know are being seen in identical form across the world'.[99] In this context, Pronay suggests that the viewing of news in the cinema 'could evoke a greater degree of rapport and emotional involvement from the audience than printed words and pictures could, especially so in the case of the semi-literate majority of the ordinary people'.[100] Pronay also evokes the vocal audience responses to the newsreels and contrasts this idea of crowd responses with that of television: 'newsfilm could act upon the audience somewhat like a demagogue; it could reduce the individuality of the people in the audience and substitute a mass response for a critical and individual assessment'. If, as le Goff suggests, 'the mass media are the primary vehicles for the expression and ordering of mentalities',[101] then the newsreels' role in everyday life had the potential to influence, form and mould public opinion in a systematic way, given their homogeneity and regularity. Andrew Buchanan criticized the newsreels not only for their unfaltering sameness but also for perpetuating the norms of British life, for 'contributing consistently of the perpetuation of "things as they are" '.[102] Given their regularity, celebration of the monarchy and representation of traditional culture, the newsreels certainly did serve to reinforce hegemonic structures. Royalty and military were to be revered, politics avoided and certainly not interrogated. Despite their garrulous style the newsreels were cautious and diplomatic, reinforcing common ideas and attitudes in ways that made them seem invisible to contemporary audiences.

This 'diplomacy' also drew criticism. After noting the fact that newsreel companies never filmed Roosevelt being lifted to the speaker's chair (in order to shield the public from his disability), Penelope Houston recognizes that the newsreels 'speak with the authority not of impartiality but of national public relations'.[103] Cecil Day Lewis's anger about complacency towards international events lies not solely with the newsreels but also with the public for not taking seriously events depicted in contemporary news. In his 1938 poem *Newsreel* he objects to the newsreel juxtaposition that caused the American wit Oscar Levant to refer to the conventional newsreel as 'a series of catastrophes ended by a fashion show'.[104] Lewis describes a general public lack of recognition of responsibility for imminent warfare:[105]

> Enter the dream-house, brothers and sisters, leaving
> Your debts asleep, your history at the door:
> This is the home for heroes, and this loving
> Darkness a fur you can afford.[106]

As he begins his examination of the newsreel in these opening lines, Lewis alludes to the practice of leaving aside individual identity when audiences entered the cinema. While the cinema was seen as a place in which to be entertained and informed, Lewis would suggest in his poem that instead, audiences were dulled and almost hypnotized into apathy by the images presented. Later in the poem, he refers to the standards of the newsreel experience – 'the mayor', 'the oyster season', 'a society wedding'. He criticizes audiences for wishing to remain in a 'watery, womb-deep sleep' even when presented with images of war. He concludes the poem with the warning that 'out of the dream-house stumbling', audiences will eventually 'know you slept too long'.

The Advent of Sound

After the advent of sound, the significance of newsreel images was profoundly altered through the addition of spoken commentaries. Interestingly, when sound had been well established in the 1930s, *Kinematograph Weekly* described the commentator as 'a newspaper man, but gifted with the knack of boiling down a column story to a few pithy sentences'.[107] This was the task ahead for commentators. The same article called for commentaries that were 'essentially informative, clear in wording, bright yet interesting, decisive in style and typically English'.

The writer of the article clearly disapproves of the 'high speed, rapid fire, bombarding' nature of American newsreels. Given that the audience is composed of 'average people', a call is made for the commentator to 'speak to them in plain English with a plain English voice'. This was significant, given the newsreels' preference for Received Pronunciation rather than local dialect (even for local editions). The commentator was almost always male (even in cinemagazines produced for women, such as *Eve's Film Review*) with the exception of Louise Vance, who occasionally commented on fashion items. While regional accents intermittently crept in, Received Pronunciation was accepted as characterizing the 'voice of authority' (and for Irish audiences this 'authority' was distinctly British).

Paramount had two unidentified voices providing commentary, and Universal, Gaumont and Pathé each had one identifiable commentator – R.E. Jeffrey (Universal), E.V.H. Emmett (Gaumont), Roy de Groot (Pathé) – while Movietone opted for a number of well-known authorities as commentators for different subjects. However, even though they were deemed authorities in their subject area, they were not always permitted to script their own commentaries – with the exception of E.V.H. Emmett at Gaumont and R.E. Jeffrey at Universal (Emmett also controlled the editing of Gaumont stories, ensuring that picture and commentary always matched).[108] Movietone's producer, Gerald F. Sanger, proudly claimed that his newsreel commentary was 'no longer a voice – a background to the image – but an observation by an expert whose knowledge of that particular subject is recognised'. He then goes on to qualify this statement by adding: 'The commentary on Movietone is purely of an explanatory nature, and it should be hardly necessary to stress the fact that British Movietone News never has and never will abuse its influence as a news publishing medium to distort the significance of events or to give them propagandistic flavour.'[109]

The newsreels sought to reinforce the norms of British society, to perpetuate the traditional aspects of 'ordinary' life. Nothing illustrates this better than the lack of coverage of the abdication of King Edward VIII in 1936 in order to marry divorcée Wallis Simpson; any upset to the status quo was to be categorically avoided, leading one trade paper to condemn the newsreels as 'cowardly' and resembling 'frightened rabbits' in their commentaries.[110] In their usual spirit of self-censorship, the newsreels ignored the abdication completely while the film industry in general tackled it by producing a number of historical films about the monarchy, designed to 'restore confidence in the institution'.[111]

The tone of newsreels was always upbeat, completely ignoring the downbeat (very truly 'British'). Pronay claims the voice was dominant and the images were there simply to back it up.[112] Rachel Low suggests that the earliest moving images were made magical simply by the nature of their movement ('movement, without topical or dramatic interest, provided the necessary thrill to bring the first film audiences together. They were satisfied to see any simple scene from everyday life reproduced on the screen.'[113]). Low argues later that sound eclipsed the importance of onscreen images: 'in the end the greatest change brought by the sound film was the fact that what was said became almost more important than what was shown'.[114]

While scholars often prioritize sound over image when tracing the development of newsreels, the pleasure of looking has always been at the forefront of general cinema theory. What, then, makes the newsreel fall outside this paradigm? Michael Renov suggests that 'in psychoanalytic terms, one component of the spectator's cinematic pleasure involves the play of projection and identification with idealized others who inhabit the filmed world'.[115] Taking it at a superficial level, the newsreel supposedly provides an accurate picture of the real world, so where, in the absence of 'idealized' figures, would the viewer find pleasure in watching newsreel images? Partially, the newsreels compensated for this by providing multiple items about personalities, royalty and political leaders, depicted favourably by pleasant images and strong commentary. Equally, the villains – often in terms of dictators – were provided to fulfil the traditional role of the 'baddie'. The newsreels provided worldwide coverage (as demonstrated by the various cameramen's memoirs), therefore setting characters in exotic locations. What made the sound commentary all the more pervasive was that the characters (certainly in the early days of sound) spoke mostly through the commentator. The same all-knowing voice told all the stories, spoke for the characters and trundled through the items with little room for analysis, and thus the auditory resonance was more important than the visual, in conveying meaning.

D. Charles Ottley argued in 1935: 'the Cinematograph is free from bias; it neither condemns nor condones. It makes not statement, neither does it think; its function is to *record* ... The record is a record of truth,

since neither lens nor microphone can invent.'[116] However, even by
this time, increased understanding on the part of twentieth-century
audiences meant that the early faith in the accuracy of what appeared
on screen was already being interrogated and reconstituted with a more
discerning awareness of the creation of film. As Rachel Low points out,
'from the moment the film maker selected one subject rather than
another, one angle on it rather than another angle, bias or subjectivity
was present. And the film's capacity to invent and deceive was to prove
almost without parallel.'[117] Film, by its nature, will almost never reach
its audience in 'raw' form – it will always appear as the highly constructed
product of editor and cameraman. We can never pan or do a circular track
of 360 degrees to examine events surrounding the camera – we are offered
a story scripted by the news team cautiously seeking to please its viewer.
And it is within the confines of seeking to please that viewer that the
selection of news must take place, the prioritizing of one story over
another, the presentation of the facts from the angle best suited to the
viewer's disposition:

> Objectivity consists in reproducing the real world as faithfully as
> possible. But even within the boundaries of this rather simple
> conception, it is obvious that it is not technically possible to repro-
> duce all the events, to tell all the stories, to give every bit of infor-
> mation. So some selection must take place. Not all the events in
> the world, for instance, are of equal interest to the public; the
> newsman must therefore have a set of criteria, a 'news sense' with
> which to select his material.[118]

This caveat was consistent with the expectations of British audiences.
However, in Ireland, pleasing the audience was a highly complex
process, given the competing ideological dispositions of Irish viewers.
Often a newsreel distributed on the Irish circuit would be seen by
viewers with diverse political leanings. In this context, the content of
newsreels for Ireland and the construction of Ireland and its people
within cinema news offered unique challenges to newsreel producers.

Whatever the nationality or location, once established, the newsreel
genre tapped into the expectations of the spectator and was frequently
faked or distorted solely to offer that spectator what was desired and
expected. The single newsreel may lack explanation – simply offering
the audience a 'bird's-eye view' – or it may over-interpret, distorting the

visual image through heavy-handed commentary. Film images offer an impression of reality – a reproduction, an imprint rather than the genuine article. The camera captures a representation, as open to misunderstanding and interpretation as anything observed by the naked human eye. In fact, it could be argued that if it is not what the viewer expected, the images will be translated by the viewer into comfortable, predictable visuals:

> A person predicts that something will happen and this creates a mental matrix for easy reception and registration of the event if it finally does take place. Or he wants it to happen and the matrix is even more prepared, so much so that he may distort perceptions he receives and provide himself with images consonant with what he has wanted.[119]

When the event portrayed is rare, it continues to be 'good' news as long as it fits into an expected structure and sits neatly with society's ideological norms. Given the newsreels' preponderance of royal stories, it is easy to see how moving-image news was, from the beginning, 'elite-centred'.[120] Although elite, members of the royal family, as idealized figures, still served identification desires in the audience. Again, royalty constituted idealized figures for only a proportion of Irish audiences (whilst their news items served as general interest stories for other members of the population and a symbol of unwanted British links for further groups and individuals with strong nationalist and republican leanings). As such, the representation of monarchy on screen was more complex in Ireland than throughout the UK, particularly during the 1930s as De Valera's dismantling of the Treaty continued.

Film is defined as much by the audience as the camera – 'the presence of an audience is, in other words, an essential part of the very definition of the medium'.[121] The newsreels offer a guide to what film audiences were told about contemporary events; in their content and popularity they also offer an insight into what the public wanted to see and objected to in terms of news coverage and the inclusion of propaganda. They can potentially comment on not only the way in which news was released in the public sphere but also dominant attitudes towards government policy, use of propaganda and flow of information. This is particularly significant in relation to Irish audiences, who often watched a portrayal of their country which was distinctly at odds with their own lived experiences.

NOTES

1. While the British newsreels sometimes substituted items on the Royal family with local sporting news for Irish audiences, it appears this may have been short-sighted, given the popularity of royal publications recorded by Easons in the 1930s. See Russell in Augusteijn (1999), p.21.
2. McKernan (2001), p.86.
3. Gill (1963), p.71.
4. Fielding (1978), p.60.
5. Aubert, cited in Jeavons et al., p.11.
6. 'Running the Topical Films' (1915), cited by McKernan in Jeavons et al. (1998), p.19.
7. Fielding (1972), pp.30–1.
8. Pronay (1976), p.97.
9. J. Turner (2001), p.viii.
10. Pronay (1976), p.103.
11. McKernan (1992), p.68.
12. Ibid., p.137.
13. Ibid., p.14.
14. Ibid., p.10.
15. Advertisement, *Bioscope* (1917), pp.788–9.
16. Low (1950), p.152.
17. A.J.P. Taylor (1972), p.144.
18. McKernan (1996) in Jeavons et al. (1998), p.19.
19. *Bioscope* (1914) cited in Low (1950), p.13.
20. Low (1948), p.61.
21. *Bioscope* (1916) cited in Low (1950), p.29.
22. Ibid.
23. *Bioscope* (1918) cited in Low (1950), p.30.
24. McKernan (1992), pp.64–140.
25. *Cup Final 1921*. Topical Budget, Issue 504–2, 25 April 1921.
26. 'How your News is Rushed to You' (1933), p.22.
27. Aldgate (1979), p.21.
28. *The New Government*. Topical Budget, Issue 584–1, 2 November 1922.
29. *Tutankhamen's Tomb*. Topical Budget, Issue 600–1, 22 February 1923.
30. *Men Who Film the World for You*. Topical Budget, Issue 576–1, 7 September 1922.
31. Hammerton (2001), p.33.
32. Hugon (1916), available at http://www.bufvc.ac.uk/databases/newsreels/resources/texts/hints _to_newsfilm.pdf.
33. Hammerton (2001), p.67.
34. Watts (1928) cited in Hammerton (2001), p.117.
35. Pronay (1972), p.69.
36. Low (1979), p.15.
37. Neill-Brown (1939), p.199.
38. Sanger (1934), p.15.
39. Neill-Brown (1939), p.200.
40. Ibid.
41. Pronay in P. Smith (1976), p.109.
42. McKernan in Ballantyne (1993), p.37.
43. Manvell (1961), pp.44–5.
44. Thorpe and Pronay (1980), p.21.
45. Grierson (1946), p.92.
46. Ibid., p.118.
47. McKernan (1992), p.1.

48. Ibid, p.259.
49. Ibid, p.260.
50. Sorenssen in Smither and Klave (1996), p.53.
51. Nichols (1991), p.91.
52. Ibid., p.196.
53. J. Hulbert in McKernan (2002), pp.257–66.
54. Mass Observation File Report 16, *Faking of Newsreels*, 7 January 1940.
55. 'Editing and Presenting Film "Copy" ' (1934), p 20.
56. Simmonds (1934), p.4.
57. Bishop (1934), p.151.
58. The article can be viewed at http://www.bufvc.ac.uk/databases/newsreels/learnmore/docs/synopsis_hopkinson.pdf.
59. Talbot (1912), pp.277–86.
60. McKernan in Ballantyne (1993), p.37.
61. Pronay (1972), p.70.
62. Ruah (1914) cited in McKernan (2002), p.21.
63. Steer (1914) cited in McKernan (2002), p.28.
64. 'Newspaper "Boss" and the Kinema' (1920), p.79.
65. N. Hulbert (1934), p.5.
66. Anthony Smith cited in Jeavons et al. (1998), p.8.
67. 'Politics on the Screen' (1933), p.4.
68. Grinley (1937).
69. Priestley (1948).
70. Low (1950), p.141.
71. Rockett (2004), p.87.
72. Martin (2006) describes calls for stricter censorship on newsreel films after protests and vandalism at the Savoy cinema in 1934 during screenings of newsreel coverage of the Duke of Kent's wedding (p.175).
73. Ibid., p.172.
74. For more information on March of Time, see Fielding (1978).
75. 'Technique of the Commentator' (1935), p.17.
76. Fielding (1959), p.145.
77. Ibid.
78. Thorpe and Pronay (1980), p.2.
79. Ibid, p.4.
80. See Erhardt (1996).
81. Mass Observation File Report 22, *Content of Newsreels*, 28 January 1940.
82. Ibid.
83. Pronay in Short and Dolezel (1988), p.38.
84. Fred Taylor (1982), p.361.
85. Welch cited in Short and Dolezel (1988), p.85.
86. Buchanan (1935), pp.22–4.
87. Fennell (1945), p.5.
88. Mass Observation File Report 22, *Content of Newsreels*, 28 January 1950.
89. Sinkins (1943), p.41.
90. 'Bernstein Flays the Newsreels' (1946), p.1.
91. Pronay (1971), p.411. Pronay established the newsreel genre as a worthy subject of critical examination and recognized that up until the early 1970s newsreels had been virtually excluded from film histories.
92. Ibid.
93. The newsreels escaped normal censorship through a small loophole, a position the newsreel companies wished to maintain due to the necessary haste involved in production and distribution.
94. Houston (1967) cited in McKernan (2002), p.298.
95. Rowson (1936), pp.67–129.
96. Beere (1936), p.90

97. Rockett (2011), p.71.
98. Pronay (1971), p.414.
99. Dyer (1998) in Hill and Church Gibson (1998), p.8.
100. Pronay (1976), p.98.
101. le Goff cited in Sorenssen in Smither and Klaue (1996), p.44.
102. Buchanan (1935), pp.22–4.
103. Houston (1967) cited in McKernan, p.297.
104. Levant (1965) cited in Fielding (1972), p.228.
105. Sillars (2002), pp.91–2.
106. C. Day Lewis, 'Newsreel' (1938), quoted in McKernan (2002), pp.106–7.
107. 'Technique of the Commentator' (1935), p.15.
108. Aldgate (1979), p.40.
109. Pronay (1972), p.67.
110. 'Newsreel Rushes' (1937), p 29.
111. P.M. Taylor (1999), p.96.
112. Pronay (1971), p.417.
113. Low (1948), p.51.
114. Ibid, p.10.
115. Renov (1993), p.5.
116. Ottley (1935), p.23.
117. In Low, *Films of Comment* (1979), p.179.
118. Cohen and Young (1973), p.15.
119. Galtung and Ruge in Cohen and Young (1973), p.64.
120. Ibid., p.66.
121. Gripsrud (1998), p.202.

3

The Newsreels and Ireland: Home Rule and the First World War

While this book concentrates on the portrayal of Ireland in newsreels mostly produced by British companies, there are a few incidences of indigenous production which set up interesting contrasts and parallels with the representations constructed by the larger British companies operating in the industry pre-partition.

Local Newsreels – 'See Yourselves as Others See You'

In the early part of the twentieth century, as demand for newsreels increased, enterprising cinema owners began to produce their own. One such ill-fated attempt involved the exhibition of a newsreel in 1910 purporting to show the funeral of Edward VII. However, discerning viewers could spot Edward riding behind his own coffin looking in perfect health; the sequence was taken from coverage of Victoria's funeral.[1] This highlights a common newsreel practice – the use of library footage to compensate for lack of visual material to match a particular story, a custom which became increasingly difficult as viewers' experience and understanding of the new medium of cinema became more sophisticated.

The appearance of local newsreels served the regional cinema owner as a useful agent in the marketing of his premises. George Green, a pioneer of UK moving picture shows, proclaimed 'Come and See Yourselves as Others See You.'[2] It was believed that if people thought they had a chance of seeing themselves on the big screen they would attend the cinema showing local newsreels before any other. The idea of sharing the same screen as contemporary film idols was an attractive prospect to a public still fascinated by the technology of the cinema. Local newsreels were shown between the 'big' newsreel and the main feature, normally lasting three to five minutes. They often depicted local sporting or civil events, and the more local people caught on camera, the higher the numbers likely to turn up. Garrulous cinema audiences were often heard shouting out the names of friends or family as they appeared on screen. Normally only one print was made and exclusively shown at a particular cinema. The trend for these local (British) newsreels seems to have come to an end only slightly earlier than the demise of standard newsreels, given the cost of film stock and decreasing audiences.

The first instance of local production in Ireland was The Youghal Gazette, a series of actualities and topicals produced by the Horgan

3.1 *Leaving Sunday Mass* from The Horgan Collection, Courtesy of the IFI Irish Film Archive.

brothers in Co. Cork. Ruth Barton suggests that Thomas Horgan 'capitalized on the centrality of Church observance to Irish life, focusing in particular on its pageantry and communality'. This is exemplified in a 1917 item on the Corpus Christi procession, showing girls in communion dresses, women attired in white and wearing veils, and 'crowds spilling down the steps of the chapel after mass'.[3] Another item from the same year entitled *A Day by the Sea*[4] shows a seaside trip to the beach and children swimming, while *Leaving Sunday Mass*[5] echoes the Corpus Christi procession by showing men and women leaving church and descending en masse down a set of steps.

Sunniva O'Flynn suggests that The Youghal Gazette 'appears to transcend any political bias', citing the fact that the gazette included both footage of hunger strikers interned in Wormwood Scrubs after the 1916 Rising and coverage of the 'glorious return' of local soldiers from the First World War.[6] While the content of The Youghal Gazette might have been wide-ranging, the issues themselves were not without political comment. The opening footage of the hunger strikers identifies 'Mr Kelleher' in the first intertitle, telling the audience that he has been '17 days on hunger strike in the Scrubs'. The next intertitle describes 'Mr W.J. Bland who fought all through the war was arrested and deported without trial.'[7] The connotations of injustice are clear in the wording of the intertitle. Despite his service during the war, we are also told that he is the last to be released. Each of the men is shown in turn, smiling, lifting his hat and looking at the camera. All are dressed in suits. The footage of soldiers who served in the war is given no obvious political detail. The item is entitled 'Peace Celebrations'[8] and opens with footage of holidaymakers at the coast. The next intertitle, 'Comrades of the Great War', is accompanied with scenes of a band parade in the street before cutting back to scenes of the seaside.

A second instance of local production was the Irish Events series, which ran between 1917 and 1920, and will be explained in more detail below. After this, there were no further attempts at sustained indigenous production until the 1950s. Nevertheless, production of 'local' material for Irish audiences by British companies offers an interesting insight into the differing representations of Ireland and the newsreels' attempts to cater for Irish audiences amidst an atmosphere of conflicting ideologies and increasing political instability.

Irish Historians

While several Irish historians have proven invaluable in providing background details required to contextualize the events portrayed in the newsreels, the newsreels themselves have seldom been mentioned in these histories. The printed press has often been a starting point for debate, but the interpretation of the images associated with Irish news stories has not been undertaken in any significant form. That Irish historians have not fully interacted with the newsreels is symptomatic of the fact that historians have only recently begun to acknowledge the importance of mass media in society's perception of history. Accurate historical accounts can be drawn from histories, records and documents, but a further history can be discovered in what the public was told about events and their consequences. Communication is part of society – we understand society through information flow, and the media have a large part to play in this process. Ken Ward states that 'social interactions, acts of communication, define the society by reflecting and reaffirming particular forms of relationship between individuals and institutions'.[9] Clearly, in Ireland this takes on particular significance in examining newsreels, given that they were the only form of onscreen news throughout some of the most turbulent periods of Irish history and they marked the beginning and development of 'two Irelands'. Ward suggests that it was 'unlikely that the newsreels had an immediate political effect in any country, but in personalising issues and placing stories within a particular framework ... they were able to provide the cinema audience with a simplified picture of the issues affecting the national and international environment'.[10] It is clear that the newsreels found themselves in a particularly politicized environment in dealing with Ireland and faced huge challenges, not only in covering Irish stories, but also in dealing with the complexities associated with Irish audiences.

The issue of Irish audiences is a complex one due to the range of shifting sensibilities in terms of location and allegiances throughout the first half of the twentieth century. There are no audience studies of the reception of newsreel material by Irish audiences at this stage, and the information on newsreel issue sheets and cameramen's dope sheets is inconsistent and more readily available for some newsreels than others. Pre- and post-partition there are various splits in viewing in Ireland between north and south. The newsreels often produced items of local interest to be spliced into the main edition depending on location. On News on Screen's database, there will often (but not always) be information in the field entitled 'local/special' to denote an item's intended audience as Dublin, Manchester or other locations. These items will often have a particularly local interest and take on significant connotations when associated with Irish audiences. For the most part, items for inclusion in editions for Irish audiences are labelled 'Dublin' or, much less frequently, 'Belfast'. The label of 'Dublin' can connote a distribution to audiences throughout Ireland, which is significant, given the fluid range of allegiances and opinions spread throughout the country. Cinema exhibitors set up particular contracts with newsreel companies, but there is no information to suggest which of the newsreels was more popular and it is only possible to speculate on audience responses to the stories depicted. Where there is information available on items specifically targeted at Irish audiences, I have made this clear and have included references to the issue sheets where relevant. Equally, if a story about Ireland was intended solely for British audiences I have also outlined this fact, when the information is available. I have also attempted to speculate on the varying range of potential responses, given historical and political context and geographical location.

The 'partition era' was a time of uncertainty, turbulence and huge change in Ireland's history. This chapter will explore the way in which the newsreels covered these events and how they coped with the controversial nature of Irish politics, ultimately suggesting that the newsreels also contributed to the presentation of a partitionist perspective in the differing representations of north and south which appear in both content and coverage.

Early Newsreels in Ireland – the Problematic Construction of Identity On Screen

As has already been explored, the newsreels were conservative, even pro-Establishment in outlook. In order to avoid the delay which stricter censorship would incur, the newsreel companies sought to avoid controversy at all costs and were happy to market a cheerfully loyal and non-critical form of British identity in their films. Alvin Jackson recognizes that 'with the introduction of the cinema, a new vehicle for the propagation of British national imagery had been located'. Jackson emphasizes this point by stressing that among the first images projected for Belfast audiences were those of the Diamond Jubilee of Queen Victoria.[11] Equally, one of the first newsreels to be produced in Ireland was for the visit of Queen Victoria to Dublin in 1900. Sunniva O'Flynn, Curator of the Irish Film Archive in Dublin, describes it as 'a splendid affair with great pageantry'.[12] The item was filmed by pioneering English film-maker Cecil Hepworth, and opens with the intertitle 'Entering City Gates' accompanied with footage of the royal procession through the city, greeted by cheering crowds and men in bowler hats waving handkerchiefs.[13] Royal images like these became, as we know, a staple of the newsreels and, with limited indigenous newsreel production in Ireland at this time, Irish audiences mostly viewed footage produced by the British newsreel industry. In this footage they watched a general celebration of British pastimes and personalities. This constructed an essentially British imagery for Irish Nationalist viewers, often at odds with audiences' own political perspectives, and certainly the enthusiasm displayed in Hepworth's film depicts a degree of Irish loyalty to the Crown and at least a strong interest in the pageantry associated with the royal family. Unionists, on the other hand, could harness these images as a means of evoking a link with Britain. Philip Taylor suggests that newsreels often used the monarchy as means of evoking national stability and unity.[14] This ideology was likely to provoke dissension in Nationalist and Republican audiences. Kevin Rockett confirms that 'in addition to fiction film-making, foreign companies provided Irish audiences with most newsreel or actuality images during the first 25 years of film in Ireland ... The foreign source of actuality material was only one aspect of what was sometimes seen as overtly propagandist films shown in Irish cinemas.'[15] Rockett gives an example of a British Army recruitment film screened in Dublin's Grafton Cinema in late 1913 or early 1914, which led to the first organized protest against this type of film in Ireland. Fuelled by the Grafton's 'provocative external advertisements' depicting life in the British Army in 'glowing colour', two youth Nationalist movements (Daughters of Erin and the Fianna) met at Countess Markievicz's home to plan their protest. This was not approved in all quarters: one participant recalled that 'raiding a theatre' was not deemed appropriate by all.[16] Protesting at cinemas showing newsreels containing royal visits was not the only way to respond to such images, however. The Irish also sought to harness this new means of constructing identity to further Nationalist ideals, testifying to a growing awareness of the potential importance of moving images in the construction of identity. Another film produced in 1919 demonstrates acute awareness of the manipulation of images to further the Nationalist cause.[17] *The Republican Loan/Dáil Bonds* film ran for six minutes and promoted the sale of Republican loan bonds in order to finance the recently established Dáil Éireann. Produced by John MacDonagh, it featured Michael Collins, Arthur Griffith and relatives of the executed rebels of 1916.[18] The film's exhibition was somewhat unconventional: Irish Volunteers interrupted cinema programmes to force projectionists at gunpoint to screen the film. Nevertheless, it was a successful endeavour, publicizing a venture which ultimately raised £350,000. The production and exhibition of the film testified to a growing Nationalist awareness of the importance of film as a practical aid to furthering political ideals.

There are, however, only two instances of sustained indigenous

3.2 Irish Events: *The Agony of Belfast,* Courtesy of the IFI Irish Film Archive.

newsreel production in Ireland. One was General Film Supply's *Irish Events* which ran from 1917 to 1920 amid the tumultuous years of political and military upheaval, while the other, *Amharc Éireann* (1956–64), was produced in a very different era by Gael Linn, the Irish language and culture pressure group. *Irish Events* was produced by English-born cameraman Norman Whitten and filmed by Gordon Lewis, also a cameraman for Pathé Gazette. Whitten's company, General Film Supply, had made two recruiting films in 1914, *Britannia's Message* and *Sons of John Bull*.[19] There are only a few surviving *Irish Events* editions in the Irish Film Archive. These contain footage of the funerals of Republican hunger strikers Thomas Ashe and Terence MacSwiney; Peadar Clancy and Dick McKee, prominent Republicans interrogated in Dublin Castle and later shot; and the funerals of Thomas MacCurtain, Seamus Quirke, R. McKee, Lieutenant Col. Beattie, Captain White and Major Smith.

Only some of this footage is still extant and the funeral footage in particular is only available in a series of compilation shots. However, two significant items – coverage of the funeral of Terence MacSwiney and *The Agony of Belfast* – are discussed in more detail below. Other topics included an Irish pilgrimage to Lourdes and the return of Sinn Féin prisoners. Ruth Barton describes the general content of *Irish Events* as consisting of 'a mixture of sporting news, religious pageantry and political events'.[20] Sunniva O'Flynn describes some material shot prior to 1917, 'incidents surrounding the Rebellion in Dublin in 1916, the subsequent execution of its leaders, and activities leading up to the war of independence', and also credits Whitten with filming the Bachelor's Walk funerals (of Irish Volunteers involved in gunrunning, shot by British soldiers) and the funeral of O'Donovan Rossa,[21] at whose graveside Patrick Pearse gave his famous oration.

According to Rockett, *Irish Events* quickly established itself as part of most cinema programmes, and according to *Irish Limelight* it produced films that not only contributed to the Irish film industry but 'were made with an Irish audience in mind'.[22] The events filmed were not of an exclusively Nationalist flavour – the Twelfth of July celebrations in Belfast also featured in *Irish Events*' content. O'Flynn cites an advertisement in *Irish Limelight* listing the following as part of an Irish Events issue:[23]

The Galway Races
Puck Fair
The Lucan Horse-Jumping Competition
A Red Cross Pageant
Ford Works at Cork
Jockeys' Football Match
A British Military Tournament
Films Taken by Aeroplanes
The First All-Irish Cartoons Drawn by Frank Leah and Filmed
by Gordon Lewis.

The fact that British military activity is included testifies again to a broader political perspective than might be expected from indigenous news production. The diversity of the above list highlights the fact that these newsreels sought to both inform and entertain audiences (with a diverse range of interests and allegiances) with a blend of politics and pageantry.

Whitten proved a competent and efficient producer: after filming the Sinn Féin convention in 1917, he had the film edited and in the cinemas by that evening. On filming the release of Sinn Féin prisoners in July 1917, Whitten was able to beat Gaumont in the race to exhibition by delivering the footage to Dublin cinemas within hours, while Gaumont's cameraman had to send his film to England for editing.[24]

While most Irish Events material was far from controversial, one particular film was challenged by the military authorities. *The Sinn Féin Review* (1919),[25] a thirty-minute compilation film covering the Sinn Féin Movement for the previous three years, was investigated prior to exhibition on the basis of provocative advertising posters. The film was referred to the press censor and ultimately submitted for police inspection. The subsequent report described the film as 'a glorification of Sinn Féin', suggesting that 'wherever exhibited [it] would, no doubt, be good Sinn Féin propaganda and might in that way be objectionable to members of an audience holding different views'.[26] The film was seized by police to prevent any further exhibition. This raises interesting questions in relation to the coverage of contentious Irish subjects in the newsreels. One of Whitten's arguments against censorship was that the film contained a great deal of footage from Pathé and the War Office Gazette. Irish politics was most certainly being covered by the newsreels, but their representation only became problematic when approached from an Irish perspective. Unfortunately, *The Sinn Féin Review* is no longer in existence, but the fact that the film was made demonstrates the Irish opposition to the predominant newsreel imagery of British imperialism by appropriating the genre to explore Irish political matters. It was the furore surrounding the *Sinn Féin Review* that ultimately brought Irish Events to an end, although Whitten did continue to shoot occasional newsreel footage and also turned his hand to fiction film-making.[27]

Beyond Irish Events there was a smattering of sporadic local newsreel production. An early instance was the filming of the 1913 Wolfe Tone commemoration ceremony in Bodenstown, Co. Kildare, by J.T. Jameson, a newsreel cameraman and exhibitor who owned the Irish Animated Picture Company. The footage was shown at the Rotunda and in Rathmines to 'tremendous applause', according to Thomas J. Clarke, later to be executed as one of the 1916 Easter Rising leaders.[28] Such was the success of the film that there were plans to show it throughout the country, and Clarke also believed that there might be some benefit in screening the film in America, in particular to raise money for the Wolfe Tone Fund and to 'further the Irish Nationalist cause in the United States'.[29]

From the beginning of the newsreel era there were various attempts by indigenous film-makers to establish Irish newsreel production, but these attempts were never sustained. Rather, Irish audiences continued to be catered for by the major British newsreels, with their peculiar brand of onscreen Britishness. These images would become even more significant as Ireland's campaign for independence intensified.

The Impact of the Home Rule Debate

Through countless images of monarchy and unionism, the newsreels projected for Irish audiences a set of imagery that was essentially British. Nationalists strongly perceived this as British imperialist propaganda and recognized that images of Irishmen (particularly during this turbulent period when identities – north and south – were being redefined) were seen as 'other' to the mainstream images of British unionism which proliferated in cinema news. While Nationalists resented these images of Britishness, Unionists actively embraced them. Newsreels became major players in the Unionist propaganda campaign as they offered a means through which impressive Unionist demonstrations of solidarity (like the signing of the Ulster Covenant) could be screened both locally and throughout Britain as a display of the strength of Unionist resolve.

Throughout the Home Rule debate, Unionists pursued all means necessary to further their plea to the British government to maintain the Union. Acutely aware of the power of propaganda, the Unionist leadership consistently and cleverly marketed Unionist ideals to harness support from both the local community and the Westminster government. The leading personalities in Unionism became important figureheads for the cause, and their appearance as strong, impressive and unyielding leaders was carefully constructed. Carson's image was very meticulously marketed, and Alvin Jackson attributes Unionist success in the years 1912–14 to successful 'salesmanship'[30] in the area of image building, suggesting that James Craig in particular was responsible for clever promotion: 'Carson's grimly ironic features appear everywhere: in dozens of poses on tens of thousands of cards, on mass-produced lapel badges, on charity stamps. German porcelain manufacturers supplied parian busts of Carson and the Tory leader, Andrew Bonar Law, to the china cabinets of suburban Belfast.'[31]

This was also, of course, a time when Unionist identity was under pressure, particularly through its complex relationship with Britain and the monarchy. Loughlin asserts:

> The longest sense of betrayal on the enacting of the Home Rule Bill found expression, briefly, in demonstrations of antagonism towards the King. His picture was booed when it appeared in Belfast cinemas and walk-outs occurred in Protestant churches during the playing of the national anthem, the King being focussed on, apparently because his signature was necessary for the Bill's enactment and was deeply offensive to a community with an especially deep affection for the monarch and prone to interpret his approach to the Home Rule question, as being very close to their own.[32]

The complex nature of Unionist desire to maintain links with Britain is outlined here. The monarchy inspired feelings of rejection, given that the King's signature could grant Home Rule, and Unionist agitation operated like the force of an unruly child seeking attention from a distant parent. Jackson further stresses that by 1912, 'Unionist leaders like James Craig had been made fully aware of the importance of the cinema as a means of manipulating public opinion both within Ireland and beyond. Unionist festivals such as Ulster Covenant Day, 28th September, 1912, were filmed for the benefit of the Irish public outside Belfast and for the benefit of British voters.'[33] The signing of the Ulster Covenant remains a monumental event in Unionist history. A huge demonstration of Unionist solidarity had been organized for that day. A brief statement of policy was drawn up and copies were distributed throughout the north of Ireland. It was signed by 200,000 people on the day, and nearly half a million signatures were collected in all. Edward Carson was the first to sign, at a ceremony in Belfast City Hall. By signing the Solemn League and Covenant, these signatories pledged themselves to use 'all means which may be found necessary to defeat the present conspiracy to set up a home rule parliament in Ireland'.[34] It was important that such a huge demonstration against Home Rule should be captured by the cameras. Craig was aware of the importance that footage from the event should be screened throughout Britain to inform viewers throughout the United Kingdom of the intention and resolve of Ulster Unionists.

Warwick Bioscope Chronicle's[35] *Ulster Day* announces in its first intertitle: 'Impressive scenes in the capital. Sir Edward Carson signs the Covenant. March of the Orange Battalions'.[36] (Describing Belfast as the 'capital' was prophetic rather than accurate at this stage.) There are scenes of Orangemen in bowler hats, wearing sashes, marching uniformly through the crowd (some of them holding sticks). The streets are crowded with people watching. Carson walks behind one group holding a walking stick. He has no hat and is walking alone. Another group of marchers follows him, carrying a large flag with a white background and a cross in the top right-hand corner. Next there is a cut to a static shot of a photograph of Carson signing the Covenant, James Craig to his left, at a table draped in a Union Jack; a large group of men is standing in the background. The camera movement begins again with a cut to crowds outside, pushing and filing through to sign the covenant, many still holding hats. Only men are depicted; the 234,046 women who signed a separate covenant are not shown or alluded to. Alvin Jackson suggests that 'The Covenant of 1912, again partly Craig's inspiration, and on which the first signature was Carson's, carried echoes of the Scots' covenants of 1638 and 1643. Indeed the evocation of God in the Ulster Covenant, and its pious language, suggested even more ancient, Judaic precedents for Loyalist strategy.'[37] Tradition and history were to be used repeatedly in Unionist propaganda, a pattern which still exists today.

The episode summed up the Unionist awareness of the potential of manipulating public opinion through film, as John Hill explains: 'As early as 1912, James Craig had recognized the propaganda value of film newsreels by arranging for the recording – "under the fierce glare of electric light and to the click of a dozen cinematograph machines" – of the signing of the Ulster Covenant by Edward Carson and others on "Ulster Day."'[38] It was to characterize the beginning of a Unionist relationship with newsreels which would seek to maximize the publicity potential of the medium throughout their subsequent struggle to maintain the Union with Britain and to carve out an identity which was both British and unique to Ulster. Alvin Jackson describes the years 1912–14 as a time of 'Orange genesis' providing 'a creation myth for Unionism in the twentieth century'.[39] Jackson further asserts: 'what is most impressive about the marketing of Unionism in 1912 is, perhaps, the comprehensive application of Edwardian technology to the task'. The fact that film was exploited to promote and consolidate images of Unionism is characterized by the shrewd adaptation of this new technology to promote Unionist ideals to audiences in Ulster and throughout Britain. This furthered the cause of northern Protestants at a time when their identity was being challenged from internal national forces and the British leadership.

Unionism was at this stage, particularly through its leaders, firmly associated with the Westminster government. Dublin-born Carson was educated at Trinity College before becoming a highly successful barrister, remembered in legal circles for his involvement in two famous cases: the Winslow Boy case, and Oscar Wilde's first libel case against the Marquess of Queensberry. He was elected MP for Trinity College from 1892 to 1918 and was leader of the Irish Unionist Parliamentary Party from 1911 until 1921. He also served in the British government as Attorney General, First Lord of the Admiralty and in the War Cabinet and was given a peerage in 1921. Through his statue at the gates of Stormont, the seat of the Northern Ireland parliament, he is constructed as an iconic figure in the politics of the north of Ireland. In the early part of the twentieth century he was closely associated with the British government, thus, for many, legitimizing Unionist opposition to Home Rule. His links with the British government are exemplified in a 1913 Pathé item featuring a suffragette march calling for the arrest of Bonar Law and Carson. Bonar Law, leader of the Conservative opposition, and Carson, leader of the Unionists, had actively opposed votes for women. This sparked a protest march by the suffragettes, who are shown in the newsreel item wearing hoods and carrying protest boards calling for the arrest of both leaders. The women are also shown distributing leaflets about the protest which was filmed in London. The newsreel demonstrates the extent of Carson's profile throughout the UK and, more specifically, his association with the British Establishment and his staunchly conservative political inclinations.[40]

An early Topical Budget item entitled *Derry Election Day* (1 February 1913) tells us through its intertitle that 'Colonel Pakenham, backed by a host of loyal supporters, is not downhearted. Result of polling: Mr David C Hogg (Nat.) 2,699, Colonel Pakenham (Unionist) 2,642).' Colonel Pakenham and his supporters are shown outside Derry Town Hall. There are shots of a group of men; some are wearing bowler hats, some wear flat caps. A close-up on a heavily moustached Colonel Pakenham shows him jovially chatting with some working-class men. He takes off his hat and acknowledges the camera. Although the item is essentially covering a Nationalist victory, the perspective is that of the defeated Colonel Pakenham, a supporter of the ongoing union with Britain. This reflects the fact that at this time newsreels tended to follow the Establishment, and in 1913 Unionism represented and appealed to the mainstream British Establishment. However, the item also demonstrates the fact that Unionists did struggle to gain a majority in some areas, making the possibility of Home Rule loom as an even larger threat.

In January 1913 the Ulster Unionist Council announced the formation of the Ulster Volunteer Force. Some military drilling had already begun and, before long, 90,000 men had been recruited under the command of Sir George Richardson, an experienced soldier. The force appears to be featured on a Pathé item entitled *Ulster's Guardians of the Peace.*[41] The newsreel shows the men being reviewed by Lord Derby. There are also scenes of speeches from a podium lined with lambeg drums, followed by shots of the men singing a hymn. Alvin Jackson records that 'Mr Copeland Trimble, commander of the Enniskillen Horse (an outpost of the Ulster Volunteer Movement) demanded a full turn-out of his men, in May 1913, "because of the presence of cinematographic operators" ',[42] clearly demonstrating an awareness of the potential publicity generated by the newsreels. It is worth noting that Nationalists responded to the formation and drilling of the Ulster Volunteer Force by forming the Irish Volunteers to support Home Rule in November 1913 but there is no coverage of early drilling on the part of the Irish Volunteers – they are not featured in the newsreels until the 1916 Rising.

In general, the Ulster Volunteer Force was poorly equipped until the Council commissioned a Belfast businessman, Fred Crawford, to purchase arms secretly in Germany. In April 1914, 35,000 rifles and a large amount of ammunition were smuggled into Larne harbour. This amounted to sedition and treason on behalf of the Unionist establishment but just months later many of these 'Guardians of the Peace' would be fighting against Germany in the First World War, pledging their full allegiance to the British Crown. Unsurprisingly, the newsreels did not cover the gunrunning, partly due to the practicalities of providing suitable pictures to illustrate the story, or to make the story visually interesting retroactively. Also, such a subversive reaction on the part of those Unionists claiming to be loyal to the British government did not fit easily with the standard representation of devout Orangeism.

There are three Topical Budget items related to Ireland in 1914, all with a strong Unionist flavour, which effectively illustrate the generally positive coverage that the newsreels of the time gave to Unionist opposition to Home Rule. The first, Topical Budget's 15 July edition, introduces an item on the 12 July celebrations with the intertitle: 'Orange day. The 224th Anniversary of the Battle of the Boyne celebrated throughout Ulster with stirring enthusiasm.'[43] Large crowds are shown in Belfast city centre, with Carson travelling through the streets in horse and carriage while people wave and raise their hats. The camera then cuts to a procession at Drumbeg where a large canopy, carried by four men, is blown in a strong wind. There are Union Jacks flying from a constructed arch in the background while Carson speaks from a platform covered in flags. Craig sits to Carson's right. Two days earlier, Carson had consulted the Ulster Unionist Council and warned during the secret meeting that he expected civil war. The tone of the coverage here, however, is celebratory and the general atmosphere more that of patriotic enthusiasm than preparation for communal conflict.[44] It was characteristic of the newsreels to cover superficial celebration and ignore conflict growing under the surface, but there is also here a sense of sympathy with Unionist opposition to any plans the British government may have had to enact Home Rule.

The next item covering Carson in Belfast is the first of a five-item newsreel. The intertitle reads: 'The Ulster leader hurriedly inspects the Lady Signallers and Ambulance Corps and departs for London.'[45] Carson, clearly identified at this stage with 'Ulster' Unionists rather than those in the south, is shown inspecting troops wearing what appear to be suits with flat caps, knee boots and shoulder bags. Carson looks stern as he walks along the line accompanied by a moustached man in suit and flat cap carrying a stick. The camera cuts to an inspection of Lady Signallers in a field. They are wearing long skirts, jackets, ties and wide-brimmed hats and holding some form of weapon. Carson shakes hands with a woman accompanying him, probably the Signallers' leader. There are then sun-filled shots of Carson on a lawn with Lord and Lady Londonderry and Sir Reginald Pole-Carew. Carson is talking to a little girl while two smiling women look on. These scenes are followed by a cut to Carson with uniformed officers beside a UVF ambulance. He checks the back of the vehicle before climbing in and is then shown jumping out again and speaking to two officers. The item finishes with a medium close-up of Carson. This five-story newsreel begins and ends with Irish items – the first covering Carson's visit, while the final item is entitled 'Dublin Civic Exhibition'[46] and covers the Lord Lieutenant's opening of a Dublin civic exhibition, including shots of Lord and Lady Aberdeen receiving guests. The newsreel is framed by Irish items of a Unionist and pro-Establishment flavour.

These images of Craig and Carson during a period when Unionism felt most under threat are significant. Jackson suggests that 'the images propagated in 1912–14, the personality cult of Carson, and the imagery associated with the idea of a besieged and self-reliant northern Loyalism have, by and large, survived as the distinguishing features of contemporary Unionism'.[47] The iconic features of Craig and Carson and in particular the images of masses of people queuing to sign the Covenant remain potent symbols of Unionist identity, even a century later.

The First World War would call on the newsreels to consolidate their promotion of British ideals and to deal sensitively with any opposition to government policies from either the Nationalist or Unionist movements. No crack in the empire could be exposed, as will be demonstrated in the paucity of Easter Rising footage which made it into the cinemas in 1916. The newsreels were called on more than ever before to promote British loyalty in Ireland and to normalize British presence in times of crisis. There was to be no debate on Home Rule until after the war. Ireland was expected to unify, put differences aside and help the Allies win the war before local problems were aired again. The newsreels were part of the propaganda machine intended to fulfil this aim. Ruth Barton suggests that indigenous Irish production also had an agenda in the turbulent years leading up to independence. There was, Barton suggests, amongst local producers like the Horgan brothers,

> [an] awareness of the importance of controlling news and other images in a climate of war. Their success with cinema audiences similarly indicates a popular desire to imagine the nation in a particular fashion ... The variety of Irish Events subject matter, from the activities of Sinn Féin to sporting occasions to British military displays, suggests that the demographic group of the time admitted to a wide range of allegiances and interests. Indeed, this willingness to subscribe to such an eclectic view of Irish contemporary life hints at the existence within the popular audience of a much more plural outlook than Nationalist histories have allowed for.[48]

Whether or not this 'plural outlook' was as widespread as Barton suggests, both Unionists and Nationalists were eager to utilize newsreel material to present and construct various facets of both southern and northern Irish identity. Newsreel coverage of the war years is particularly interesting in this regard.

The War Years

The outbreak of the First World War meant the postponement of Home Rule. All resources and energies were to be focussed on the war and the British government hoped for the support of the whole of Ireland in this time of international crisis. Both Carson and Redmond pledged their support for the war effort. Each had hoped for a reward for loyalty when the war was over, with Home Rule for the Nationalists on the one hand and a continuing link with Britain for Unionists on the other. As Beckett suggests, 'each side felt that it was establishing a claim on the gratitude of Great Britain, and that its services during the war would entitle it to full satisfaction when victory had been won'.[49]

The Ulster Volunteer Force formed most of the 36th Ulster Division, and recruits from the Irish National Volunteers entered the 10th and 16th Irish Divisions. The two forces would supply a combined number of 50,000 recruits to the British Army over the course of the war and approximately 210,000 men living in Ireland joined the British forces altogether.[50] More militant Nationalists, however, saw the war as an opportunity to advance the struggle for complete independence from Britain. In opposition to Redmond's support for the war effort, this group did everything possible to hinder recruitment. The Unionists, on the other hand, were delighted at this new opportunity to demonstrate their loyalty to the Crown in an international arena. Loughlin quotes from A.D. Smith in suggesting that 'of all the factors that shape national identity warfare is recognized as having a central role, especially as a mobiliser of ethnic sentiments and national consciousness ... [and] a provider of myths and memories for future generations'.[51] Loughlin asserts that this is the role Carson believed the war would perform for Ulster Unionists, 'consolidating beyond question their membership of the British nation'.[52] Given the ongoing relationship between Unionism and the symbolism of the First World War, it is clear that the 'myths and memories' of warfare have provided ample sustenance for Unionist consciousness for nearly a century.

1916 – a Crucial Year

1916 presented two significant events in Irish history: the Easter Rising and the Battle of the Somme. Both events have played a crucial role in symbolizing each community's commitment to a chosen political belief and both continue to consolidate Nationalist and Unionist identities respectively today. Given the historic nature of each event, there is little contemporary newsreel footage covering, explaining or predicting the significance of Easter 1916 or the Somme for Irish politics at the time, probably due to the difficulties in obtaining footage in times of conflict at this stage of the newsreels' development. It is possible, however, that this lack of availability of moving images played some part in the construction of the 'myths and memories' that emerged around both events.

The Easter Rising

The events of Easter 1916 have been revised, mythologized and used by both Unionist and Nationalist politicians to define, condone and condemn the subsequent struggle within Irish politics. What was also unique about the events of 1916 was the huge shift in opinion following the collapse of the Rising. The media had a large part to play in reporting and commenting on the Rising, the executions and their legacy. The newsreels' relationship with Ireland during this turbulent era would prove problematic, given the controversial nature of many of the unfolding events and the practical difficulties for British companies attempting to film in conflict-ridden zones. In times of war in particular, the newsreels sought to portray cheerfully even the worst of events in order to bolster morale and promote participation in the war effort. Their motivation was always to support the Establishment and, in coverage of Irish events, violent attacks or disturbances were often simply ignored by the newsreels in preference for their usual staple of personalities, sporting events and royal visits.

The date set for the Rising was Easter Sunday, 23 April 1916, a symbolic occasion in line with Patrick Pearse's belief in a 'blood sacrifice'. However, confusion about dates meant that the *Aud*, a German ship carrying arms for the volunteers, arrived in Kerry with no one to meet her. As a result, she was captured by the British and scuttled by her captain, delaying the insurrection until Easter Monday. On the following Saturday, Pearse surrendered and the insurrection came to an end. Around 1,600 rebels had participated in the Rising, which lasted for a week, but the rebellion (initially at least) failed to ignite the popular imagination of the country and thus there was general resentment towards the British military occupation and curfews imposed in the immediate aftermath.[53] What was ultimately to change popular opinion was the subsequent action of the British government. Over the two weeks following the Rising, fifteen of the insurgents were executed (all of the leaders with the exception of Eamon de Valera, who had escaped execution due to his American birth[54]). Probably the most abhorrent execution from the public's viewpoint was that of James Connolly. Badly wounded, he was strapped to a chair before being shot by a firing squad.

There were only two films produced covering the Rising – one news-reel featuring 'exclusive' pictures for Topical Budget, and another item, *Aftermath of the Easter Rising*,[55] currently stored in the archives of the Imperial War Museum. Both films feature smoky shots of burnt-out buildings and hazy scenes of the devastation of the Rising's aftermath. This footage would become characteristic of the depiction of Irish warfare with Britain during the War of Independence and the internal conflict of the Civil War. Both films juxtapose scenes of the everyday bustle of Dublin life with shots of streets littered with the remnants of conflict. The connotations arising from this type of footage, whether accurate or not, are of a country accepting of violence and willing to self-destruct in order to further political ideals.

Topical Budget, which would later become War Office Topical Budget, offering official reports, covered the events of the Rising in an item entitled *The Dublin Rebellion*.[56] In its introductory intertitle it boasts 'exclusive pictures of the scene of the fighting in Dublin', accompanied by panning shots of ruined buildings in Sackville Street (later renamed O'Connell street) and along the Quays. Pedestrians walk through the shots in comparative normality and from the ground up this looks like a depiction of Dublin before the Rising: it is only as the eye rises to the battered skyline that the evidence of destruction becomes clear. Soldiers are shown marching through the streets while civilians stand beside piles of burning debris. We are also shown scenes of the interior of the post office, described in an intertitle as 'completely gutted' after the battle, the footage amply evidencing this claim by showing a ransacked shell of a building. Members of the fire brigade are shown inside as the camera pans up slowly to the open air – the entire roof gone. Again civilians are shown, this time clearing rubble and debris. A third and final intertitle describes 'a street barricade, batches of rebels being marched off to the Quay, one of the looted shops, soldiers on guard having their meals in the street'. A close-up on broken windows is followed by shots of a soldier on guard. Again armed troops march while civilians stand outside a shop with all its windows shattered. A final shot of soldiers eating concludes the item before the newsreel moves on to its second and final item: Allies' Bands in Paris. This story featured 'Mlle Paule Andral singing the National Anthem of the Allies'. Andral is shown singing and posing as Britannia.

This juxtaposition offers an interesting insight into the divided opinion that was to follow the events of the Rising. The fact that the rebels had chosen wartime to strike was particularly abhorrent to the families of the thousands of soldiers from throughout Ireland who had enlisted in the war effort. Writer and broadcaster Tim Pat Coogan reports a comment by prisoner Frank Thornton: 'if it weren't for the fact that we were so strongly guarded by British troops, we would have been torn asunder by the soldiers' wives in the area'.[57] Coogan goes on to explain that these 'separation women' (described as such because of the separation allowance paid to them while their husbands were off fighting for the Allies) were angry that the rebels' actions put at risk the financial assistance afforded to soldiers' wives by the British government. The fact that the newsreel moves from Irish insurgents to 'Britannia' is also characteristic of the newsreels' tendency to jump from stories of conflict to lighter fare, often in what appears to be an insensitive manner. The juxtaposition here, however, does not seem to be coincidental. Ireland is shown as a small and violent nation pitted against the connotations set up by everything that 'Britannia' epitomizes and perhaps, by association, Irish audiences are being persuaded that loyalty, rather than insurrection, is preferable in a time of global war.

Details are obscure for the other film featuring the Rising. Currently held in the Imperial War Museum and entitled *Aftermath of the Easter Rising*,[58] it was most likely an official film, but there are no further details available on its production. The film opens with a shot in the shape of a shamrock (the rest of the screen is blacked out) of Sackville Street before the Rising. The scenes are similar to those in the Topical Budget film except for the fact that all the buildings are intact. There is a sharp cut to shots of Irish Volunteers, in civilian clothes and carrying rifles, drilling before the Rising, followed by shots of uniformed volunteers. In both cases the volunteers are openly marching, in some shots in crowded Dublin streets. This was a standard sight in Dublin at the time and it was for this reason that the rebels were able to take control of the General Post Office without difficulty: no particular attention had been paid by civilians to the marching volunteers. The next set of scenes shows the damage done to Liberty Hall, the head office of the Irish Transport and General Workers Union. The camera lingers over the damaged building showing the devastation in minute detail and from every angle. Buildings on O'Connell Bridge are also shown to have been damaged. British soldiers are depicted outside the Customs

House while shots of the interior of a hospital show three wounded British soldiers in beds. One is alert and chatty, another has a bandaged head and a third is propped up and sleeping. The nurses converse in a relaxed manner with two of the soldiers. All except the sleeping third soldier are aware of the camera's presence. Subsequent shots show barricades, improvised armoured cars and more damaged buildings. The film concludes with a posed shot of Thomas Clarke with Miss O'Donovan Rossa.[59] Clarke was one of the rebel leaders to be executed in the aftermath of the Rising: in these shots he looks thin and frail. This film is appropriately entitled *Aftermath of the Easter Rising*, since the footage consists of scenes of the volunteers drilling before the Rising and shots of the damage done to buildings after the events, rather than any footage taken during the events of the rebellion.

In a newsreel dated 17 May, opening with the trial of Roger Casement, two items featuring the inspection of Irish troops are included, probably to stress the restoration of order in Dublin after the Rising. These are immediately followed by an item entitled *German Rifles* showing rifles and equipment used by the rebels.[60] Topical Budget deals with the Rising again just a few days later in an item entitled *Sinn Féin Rebels*, introduced by the intertitle 'disarmed rebels marching from the military barracks in Dublin to Kingstown for deportation' and accompanied by shots of rebels under military guard walking past the camera, and then posed shots of six rebels with close-ups.[61] Topical Budget was showing its audiences what the rebels looked like at a time when many of their leaders were being executed day by day. It is interesting here that a British newsreel will include shots that might potentially humanize the insurgents for audiences. A year later, Gaumont Graphic would show the release of many of these same prisoners (nearly 1,500, including Constance Markievicz, had been interned) and their return to a rapturous response in Dublin.[62] The vast crowds shown welcoming prisoners back into their community demonstrated the post-Rising change in Irish attitudes, which was often attributed to the British government's execution of the rebel leaders.

The complexity of the politics behind the Easter Rising does not manifest itself in newsreel coverage. The reporting of the events of 1916 in the two main films to cover the insurrection summarizes many of the characteristics of early newsreel portrayals of Ireland. Sometimes these were produced by government-sponsored companies (like War

Office Topical Budget, as explored in the previous chapter) and naturally these official agencies policed newsreel output very carefully. A British, pro-Establishment agenda is clear in the coverage of all three main companies operating at this stage (Topical, Gaumont and Pathé) (although, ironically, Topical's coverage, as Luke McKernan has suggested, is perhaps more sympathetic in its treatment of Ireland). Scenes of Ireland are often smoky, conflict ridden, full of the 'aftermath' of destruction – hardly surprising, given the time lag and the practicalities associated with capturing footage at this stage. However, Irish politics are seldom contextualized or explained. In contrast, the more frequent representations of Unionist demonstrations are more easily covered due to the 'staged-managed' nature of the events. These show well-organized displays of British loyalty that tapped into and reflected the general tenor of newsreel coverage with its predilection for the political, military and cultural establishment. These representations largely germinated due to a lack of indigenous newsreels and the practicalities associated with newsreel production at the time.

The Battle of the Somme

Due to the heavy losses incurred by the Ulster Division, a regiment made up largely by members of the Ulster Volunteer Force, the Battle of the Somme has become an evocative symbol of Unionist sacrifice for Britain. It presents Unionists with a 'blood sacrifice' of their own, situated in the same historic context as the Easter Rising. Ulster Protestants had proven that they too were prepared to die for their country to maintain their British identity.

The Battle of the Somme took place in the French region of Picardy. There were huge casualties, particularly from the Ulster Division, and the events of the Somme are still commemorated by the Orange Order as a contemporary equivalent to the Battle of the Boyne in 1690. Although the Battle of the Boyne is celebrated on 12 July, according to the calendar in use in 1690, it fell on the first day of the month, also the first day of the Battle of the Somme. The Ulster Division's main objective was to take the Schwaben Redoubt, one of the most closely guarded German strongholds along the Somme. Newsreel cameraman Geoffrey Malins (believed to be of Irish origin)[63] was part of Topical Budget's crew during the First World War, shooting battle scenes at the beginning of the 'big push'.

Malins provided audiences with a unique vantage point in terms of footage of the battle – up to this point it had been unheard of for cameramen to be permitted so close to the action. Previously the newsreels would only have covered training and drilling exercises and military parades, given the dangers and the unpredictability of real warfare. The resulting film, *The Battle of the Somme*,[64] was over an hour long and featured scenes shot in the trenches; wounded soldiers being carried to safety on stretchers and on the shoulders of their fellow soldiers; shots of barbed wire, sandbags and barricades; explosions in no-man's-land; and a dramatic 'over the top' scene. This particular scene shows soldiers moving up a small hill to make their dangerous move 'over the top' into no-man's-land. Firing starts as soon as the soldiers begin their charge – one man immediately slumps down and lies motionless (it is generally accepted that this part of the film is staged).[65] Soldiers are then depicted stepping gingerly over barbed wire in no-man's-land. Another falls to the ground. One soldier left standing seems to dissolve into the background, leaving only a ghostly silhouette.

The film was dramatic and completely new to audiences. There was orchestral accompaniment for all of the film except the 'over the top' sequence. Even in hindsight, Malins remembers the events he filmed at the Battle of the Somme with a disconcerting cheerfulness, true to the genre in which he worked. He describes the men on several occasions as 'keen as mustard'.[66] Nowhere does he mention any sense of fear or foreboding which must have been present in the minutes before the battle began at 7.20 a.m. on the morning of 1 July. Malins also describes his own actions as 'cold, cool and calculating'[67] despite his proximity to dangerous shelling. He looks on the action 'from the purely pictorial point of view, and even felt annoyed if a shell burst outside the range of my camera'.[68] The lack of emotional involvement on behalf of the cameraman perhaps goes some distance to explain the nature of the newsreels themselves. Often the finished product seems unfeeling, irreverently cheerful, and in some cases the tone seems inappropriate to the gravity of the story portrayed. Malins goes on with enthusiasm to describe the troops going 'over the top': 'What a picture it was! They went over as one man. I could see while I was exposing, that numbers were shot down before they reached the top of the parapet; others just the other side. They went across the ground in swarms and marvel upon marvels, still smoking cigarettes.' Malins, in true news-reel style, skips cheerfully over the men shot down in no-man's-land, preferring to comment on inane details like cigarette smoking which bolster bravado while ignoring the reality of battle.

Even though the famous 'over the top' scene in the finalized film was staged, *The Battle of the Somme* had widespread release in cinemas, demonstrating audience desire to see what real conditions of battle were actually like. Malins's own comment on the reception of the film is characteristically bumptious, but does emphasize the important role film played in the war effort:

> The Somme film has proved a mighty instrument in the service of recruiting; the newspapers still talk of its astounding realism, and it is generally admitted that the great kinematograph picture has done much to help the people of the British Empire to realize the wonderful spirit of our men in almost insuperable difficulties; the splendid way in which our great citizen army has been organized; the vastness of the military machine we have created during the last two and a half years; and the immensity of the task which still faces us.[69]

Further comments by Malins on the process of editing also back up a belief ingrained in the newsreel industry that war film should always be packaged in a positive way:

> But after seeing a battle film, though full of suffering and agony, as it unavoidably must be to be genuine, you must not leave the public with a bitter taste in their mouth at the end. The film takes you to the grave, but it must not leave you there; it shows you death in all its grim nakedness; but after that it is essential that you should be restored to a sense of cheerfulness and joy. That joy comes of the knowledge that in all this whirlpool of horrors our lads continue to smile the smile of victory. Therefore the film must finish with a touch of happiness to send you home from the picture theatre with a light heart – or at least as light a heart as circumstances permit.[70]

The general tenor of these remarks could stand as the defining manifesto of the newsreel throughout its years as a significant cultural and informational medium.

Malins goes on to discuss military censorship in the same glib terms. He comments on how the War Office 'corrected [intertitles] from a military point of view' and how they are 'printed for insertion in their appropriate position'. Appropriate positioning of intertitles was vital as, prior to the development of sound newsreels, these gave the overall commentary for the newsreel and could contextualize and propagandize footage according to the motivation of the producer. Once an official film was completed it was shown to War Office officials who had approval on whether or not it was forwarded to the Chief Censor to be viewed at a specially constructed theatre at General Headquarters in France. At this point 'it may happen that certain incidents or sections are deleted in view of their possible value to the enemy. These excisions are carefully marked and upon the return of the film to London those sections are taken out and kept for future reference. The film is now ready for public consumption.'[71] Malins's story of his filming of the First World War contextualizes the process of production of propaganda footage and highlights the importance attributed to this material.

Despite the involvement of the 10th and 17th Irish Divisions (regiments present on the first day included the 1st Battalion of the Royal Dublin Fusiliers, which was part of the 29th Division, situated next to the 36th) and the particular losses suffered by the 36th Ulster Division, the film does not feature the contribution of any of these regiments.[72] At the opening of the 'big push', 120,000 were involved; nearly half of these were killed or wounded. Within the Ulster Division there were 5,500 killed, wounded or taken prisoner during the first two days of battle. The lack of coverage of the Ulster Division's contribution in *The Battle of the Somme* may simply have been due to practicalities involved in organizing the film. Also, Malins was present for the first day of the attack – it could not have been predicted that the regiment's losses would have been so great, despite claims afterwards that the men were deliberately selected as 'cannon fodder'. Another possibility was that the authorities believed that any undue attention given to Irish soldiers' involvement in the war might have been problematic, given the hotbed of tensions in Ireland before the outbreak of war. As long as there was a straightforward contribution to the war effort, perhaps Ireland and the Home Rule debate was best left ignored while war was raging. The Somme, however, was to prove more significant in Irish history than could ever have been anticipated.

On the first day of the Battle of the Somme, the 1st Battalion of the

Royal Dublin Fusiliers was part of the 29th Division situated beside the 36th Ulster Division. This was a stage where soldiers from north and south did indeed fight side by side. The opportunity to exploit this was missed by the film-makers of *The Battle of the Somme*, but was taken up in a later film entitled *With the North and South Irish at the Front* which offers a useful insight into how wartime propaganda capitalized on international events in order to address domestic tensions.

North and South at the Front

Due to a lack of official involvement in newsreel production during the early stages of the war there is little authentic footage of the First World War prior to 1915. Stephen Badsey explains that this was due to the British official attitude of 'indifference and concern about security'. To counteract this gap a number of compilation films were made towards the end of (and immediately after) the war.[73] One such film is *With the North and South Irish at the Front*, produced by the British Topical Committee for War Films with the assistance of the Ministry of Information. However, on closer examination it is clear that the motivation behind this film transcends the need to address a gap in coverage of the war. The film's ultimate goal was clearly to produce propaganda demonstrating camaraderie between soldiers from the north and south of Ireland, thus stressing a unity of support in the war effort despite any prior tensions caused by debates on Home Rule.

With the North and South Irish at the Front[74] was made from footage taken between 1915 and 1917, and ultimately released in 1918. Its original release details shed further light on its use as a propaganda piece to demonstrate Irish unity. Parts of it were initially released as a one-reel film entitled *With the Irish at the Front*. Significantly, it was released by the War Office on 1 May 1916, just days after the Easter Rising, as part of a series of official films. This would have appeared to counteract the display of insurgence by the Irish rebels during the Rising. This first film dealt only with the 16th Division, a division made up largely of Nationalist volunteers, and appeared days before Topical Budget's film covering the Dublin Rebellion (which had the standard newsreel delay due to the necessities of editing). This original footage was later re-edited to include material of the 36th Division, comprising mostly members of the UVF, the division which was to suffer heavy losses during the Battle of the Somme the following July. The final two-reel version of the film was released in 1918 as *With the North and*

South Irish at the Front. The footage of Irish regiments appearing in the 1916 version was repackaged and juxtaposed with footage of northern soldiers to produce a propaganda film displaying unity amongst Irish soldiers in their support for Britain in the war effort. In the Imperial War Museum catalogue, notes on the second, longer film state: 'British propaganda towards Ireland during the war was understated and covert, at least in films. This episode makes no effort to enlist sympathy for the British cause or the Irish soldiers. It merely provides evidence for the fact that the British Army on the Western Front contained a number of organized formations made up exclusively of Irishmen.'[75] The film's priority may not have been to engage audiences' sympathies for soldiers at the Front (this had been done in previous films) but its propagandistic comment on Irish politics was clear, particularly at a time when war was coming to an end and the resumption of the Home Rule debate was in sight.

The first intertitle informs the audience the subsequent scenes depict the 'issue of dinners in billets to a Company of the Connaught Rangers'.[76] Footage of this southern regiment near Hulloch in March 1916 is immediately juxtaposed with 'the Royal Inniskilling Fusiliers on their way back to a rest camp'. This footage is taken over a year later, in June 1917 at Messines, as dated on Northern Ireland Screen's Digital Film Archive. While this can be established by looking at catalogue notes for the item, contemporary audiences watching the film in 1918 would not have been aware of any major jumps in time or place unless informed by the intertitles.[77] There are shots of the soldiers parading back into camp, looking relaxed, some waving their helmets and smiling at the camera. Some are drumming on large and medium-sized drums. The Royal Munster Fusiliers are featured next, shown – as the intertitle tells us – 'going to Mass'. With this footage the film has moved back in time again to March 1916, near Hulloch, as in the opening shots of the Connaught Rangers. There are scenes of the Munster Fusiliers marching to Mass but no shots of an actual church. The march-through appears like any other military parade: there is no religious imagery – the association with churchgoing is set up only through the intertitle. The next intertitle announces: 'the flag of the Irish Guards. The regiment carried this flag thro' the Battle of Loos.' This footage goes back even further, to December 1915, near Aubers Ridge and shows the 2nd Battalion of the Irish Guards clearing water from their trenches. A flag is shown flying in what looks like no-man's-land: it has a dark background with a shape (possibly of a harp) in the middle. Men carefully traverse the rough ground around the flag. The next intertitle states: 'Irish Regiments, which specially distinguished themselves coming from the trenches to a rest camp.' This features the 16th Division at Messines, possibly prior to the Battle of Messines, which began in June 1917. Again the soldiers are shown looking relaxed. There are shots inside the camp of the soldiers washing. After what an intertitle describes as 'a good wash', the following intertitle introduces 'an issue of stout to men of the Royal Irish Regiment'. The soldiers are shown happily lining up for mugs of stout while an officer keeps an eye on proceedings (presumably to check that each soldier receives his fair share).

The following shots are of 'the Late Major Redmond, MP, leading his company'. Willie Redmond, brother of Irish Parliamentary Party leader John Redmond, died from wounds received during the Battle of Messines on 7 June 1917. This is footage from 1915 and it is likely that these scenes of Redmond were included in the first film, released in May 1916 to further stress Irish constitutional support for the British Army, given that Major Redmond and his brother were well-known figures in Irish Nationalist circles. We see Redmond marching in front of his soldiers while the next intertitle states: 'Royal Irish on their way to the trenches'. The marching troops are interspersed with military bands. The expression on soldiers' faces is more serious than in previous scenes.

The action then moves to the front line, depicting soldiers clearing drains between the trenches. There are shots of 'Connaught Rangers ready to attack' and 'bombing enemy's sap'. Overhead shots of soldiers firing from the trenches are followed by panning shots of what appear to be explosions in no-man's-land. After the intertitle 'the Irish occupy a position' there are overhead shots of men climbing out of the trenches, like insects appearing from crevices in the ground, and rushing towards no-man's-land. The next shots are of 'well constructed German dugouts'; the intertitle urges the audience to 'note the evidence of comfort'. Particularly poignant scenes appear when 'German prisoners help to carry the wounded'; men on stretchers are carried towards the camera. The depiction of the Irish as jovially enjoying a drink in what appears to be a relatively convivial atmosphere is starkly contrasted with scenes of shelling and the wounded. A sense of destruction deepens as motionless German soldiers are shown lying on the battlefield in particularly graphic and shocking scenes of death and mutilation. This is where part one of the compilation ends – a still shot of two dead bodies, with the feet of three soldiers standing beside them. We cannot identify the faces of either the living or the dead in these shots. The inclusion of these violent and disturbing scenes is significant, given the debate raging in the trade journals as to what was suitable viewing in a place of entertainment.

The second part of the compilation begins with the 'ruins of Wytschaete Village, captured by north and south Irishmen fighting side by side'. Wytschaete was taken on 7 June 1917, the same day Redmond died, by the 16th Irish and 36th Ulster Divisions. Northern soldiers are clearly positioned here 'side by side' with their southern counterparts for propaganda purposes; they actually fought on either side of the bridge in Wystchaete, some distance apart. The shots immediately following the intertitle show only barren battleground. There is no evidence of any human contact with the desolate place depicted. Another intertitle states that 'men of the Ulster Division who fought side by side with their compatriots from other parts of Ireland'. There is a close-up on three rows of seated men, wearing what appear to be officers' uniforms, arranged as if for a photo. The camera then cuts to casually dressed soldiers seated on the ground outside tents, eating and drinking. A cut back to soldiers and officers shows a larger group of men, again arranged in rows and seated on the ground.

The next intertitle announces 'the Royal Dublin Fusiliers with their trophies'. The camera pans a large group of soldiers waving German helmets and weapons at the camera. One soldier, wearing a German helmet and dancing with a bayonet, stands out from the rest of the crowd. Other soldiers look on laughing. The next intertitle introduces 'some of the men who were led "over the top" by the late Major W. Redmond, MP'. We see these soldiers in camp, milling around outside their tents, many smoking and some looking towards the camera with interest and amusement. The next shots are of 'the graves behind the Irish lines' and 'a memorial service for the dead'. An addition to the intertitle at the bottom states 'With the Irish at the front', suggesting that this section is from the earlier version of the film. It is juxtaposed, however, with scenes of Redmond's grave, which would definitely have been added later. Tribute is paid to 'a great and noble Irishman, Major

W. Redmond, MP'. We see nuns praying beside Redmond's grave in the grounds of the hospice at Locre before the film moves on to 'Irish and Australian wounded landing in Blighty'. There are panning shots of wounded soldiers, before the next intertitle announces 'Canadian Irish visit the old Homeland'. A following intertitle reads: 'The citizens of Cork fete the Irish Canadians as they march through the streets.' This was the 55th Canadian Battalion (the Duchess of Connaught's Own Irish Canadian Rangers), on tour in Ireland between 25 January 1917 and 2 February 1917.[78]

The tone shifts drastically with scenes of soldiers marching along the streets of Cork with enthusiastic crowds watching and waving from the street and the windows of buildings. The film then moves north to Belfast with scenes of an inspection at Belfast City Hall where large groups of soldiers are depicted in orderly lines while inspected by the Lord Mayor. Footage of enthusiastic crowds cheering troops in Cork is juxtaposed with an impressive inspection of soldiers at Belfast City Hall, demonstrating in a very propagandistic way that soldiers were being welcomed throughout Ireland, a portrayal which was not entirely accurate, given the range of both positive and negative responses to soldiers who had served in the British military. The movement back and forth, north and south, which continued throughout this 'lighter' section of footage backs up the film's attempt to create a sense of unity amongst northern and southern soldiers and, connected to this, an Ireland unified, north and south, in its support for the war effort.

The film continues with a move south again for shots of 'Blarney Castle: famous for the Kissing Stone which is on the outer walls. The Irish legend says that he who kisses the stone, a difficult operation, will be blessed with a fluent tongue.' There are shots of one man being lowered to kiss the stone with the help and amusement of fellow soldiers and civilians. These shots are followed by 'fair souvenir hunters at Limerick'. White cross nurses are shown chatting and bantering with officers, pinning and removing badges. 'At Armagh. Cardinal Logue entertains the Officers' is accompanied with shots of Cardinal Logue in the centre of a group of smiling officers, and then of the regiment attending Mass. We see soldiers walking up a long set of steps to the cathedral and then shots of the interior, while Cardinal Logue preaches, according to the intertitle: 'we are all longing for peace, but it must be a just peace, it must be a stable peace, it must be a permanent peace, and not a halting one'. A large band is shown leading soldiers out of the cathedral in an orderly and jaunty stream as the intertitle announces 'The End'. The final message of the film, Cardinal Logue's plea for peace, transcends international conflict to refer to political instabilities closer to home. The message calls for a measured and permanent solution to the Home Rule conflict – a propaganda plea cleverly set up just as war was ending and focus would return to events in Ireland.

The contribution of Irish soldiers in the British Army remains problematic even today, as can be seen in ongoing debates surrounding Nationalist participation at the Somme and throughout the war. By concluding a film which began by demonstrating conviviality between troops from throughout Ireland with the message of peace from Cardinal Logue, the newsreel creates a utopian ideal of what Ireland can achieve through unity and as a valued member of the United Kingdom. Through references to Canada, this also extends to allude to Ireland's connection to the wider empire. The grisly shots of bodies testify to the horrors of war, evoking the nature of loss not just for Germany but for any future army defeated in battle. These shots also testify to the military prowess of the British Army, poised to defeat any enemy of the Allies.

The scenes at Belfast City Hall juxtaposed with scenes from the south extend the camaraderie of the battlefield to the home front, projecting onto audiences the suggestion of continued good relations between both communities. With the inclusion of footage of Canadian battalions there is a hint at both national and international unity through the process of unified action in time of war. The fact that there are scenes of soldiers eating and washing as well as drilling, and, crucially, at times in civilian clothes or relaxed uniform, humanizes the military and stresses the importance of individuals' contributions. Frequent close-ups on the faces of men further stress that individuals from each community are contented and happy to interact with one another and unite against the common enemy. This is a British propaganda message to the truculent Irish – that if times are difficult enough, communities can work successfully together for common gain. As often occurred in the newsreels, the British representation of Irish affairs was overly simplistic.

While the full version of *With the North and South Irish at the Front* was not released before 1917, other newsreel items ensured that the idea that Ireland was unified in its support was evident through cinema news. *Irish soldiers at Mass*[79] or *Nationalists in Khaki* served this purpose. While the footage for *Nationalists in Khaki*,[80] a 1915 item, no longer exists, the intertitle 'the Kaiser pinned his faith on the disloyalty of the Irish and they are eager to fight him' makes clear the newsreel's aim: to demonstrate Nationalist support for the war effort and to refute claims that Irish support lay with Germany. Similarly, Irish Victoria Cross winner Mike O'Leary is acclaimed by the newsreels as 'our famous hero'.[81] Gaumont Graphic shows O'Leary at an enthusiastic reception in Dublin, where, the intertitle tells us, he also addresses a recruitment meeting. Not only is O'Leary's success celebrated by the newsreel, but there is also the message that other Irishmen could gain such honours by enlisting in the British Army.[82] The emphasis on Irish support for the war effort was more problematic after 1916. To claim united Irish support after the Rising was, even for the ever-upbeat newsreels, no longer completely plausible propaganda. There were still items showing inspections of Irish troops, but the aftermath of the Rising and protests against conscription were also reported. When Cork man Frederick Edwards was awarded the Victoria Cross for valour during the Battle of the Somme, it was not reported in the newsreels, unlike the interest shown in O'Leary in 1915. Instead, the newsreels sought to normalize British presence in Ireland and balance reports of subversive activity (like the Rising) with inspections of Irish troops, demonstrating a continuing support for the British war effort, at least amongst some of the Irish people.

The Home Front

Beyond the specific case studies examined above, the newsreels operated on the home front to normalize British presence through the promotion of repeated images of Britishness in Irish places of entertainment. While propaganda films were essentially about keeping up morale throughout the UK, in Ireland it was also important that they consolidated Irish unity to garner as much support for the war effort as possible in what were subversive times, particularly after the events of Easter 1916. Due to the Rising, however, it was not possible to be overtly propagandistic, so images of British presence in Ireland, or Irish participation in the war, sought to construct 'British Ireland' as the status quo, the correct order of being, and to instil in the Irish psyche a sense of normality in relation to a continued link with Britain.

These images were also shown to audiences in Britain, of course, so the process of consolidating and normalizing the Britishness of Ireland was as important there as it was in Ireland itself.

In 1915, a new viceroy, Lord Wimborne, was appointed, and the story was amply covered by the newsreels. The steady flow of stories on the viceroy reminded cinemagoers of a British presence in Ireland and therefore the link with the Union, after Home Rule proceedings had been placed on hold during the war. Topical Budget's coverage was very typical in its mixing of the human, the celebratory and the ritualistic, showing the viceroy's arrival with his wife in Cork, scenes at Dublin Castle and the inspection of the Guard of Honour.[83]

Gaumont Graphic also covered the event, with the following description appearing on the database entry: 'Lord and Lady Wimborne leaving ship in Dublin. Guard of Honour Cavalry ride through Dublin and into courtyard with Wimborne's carriage.'[84] The following month, Gaumont covered Wimborne's inspection of the Boys' Brigade in Dublin.[85] However, Topical Budget claims in August that Lord and Lady Wimborne's visit to Limerick is 'their first official visit to the south of Ireland' where they 'receive a most hearty reception from the town council', according to the intertitle accompanying scenes of Lord and Lady Wimborne's procession through Limerick and subsequent inspection of soldiers.[86] A second item shows the Lord Lieutenant inspecting the Leinster Regiment at Ballincurra.[87]

Coverage of Ireland during the war, as already discussed, is sporadic. Interestingly, for most years throughout newsreel history, the Twelfth of July celebrations are reported in cinema news, probably due to the staged nature of the event which provided a convenient and altogether typical filming opportunity for the newsreels at this point of their development. In 1917, an early July item for Gaumont Graphic features 'Lady Carson's Ulster Fund'[80] which provides 'gifts' for the sick and wounded of the Ulster Division. Even in this reference to the Ulster Division, its losses at the Battle of the Somme the previous year are still omitted. The following Twelfth of July celebrations are also reported in 'Orange Day Demonstrations in Belfast' showing the usual Union Jack decorated parades and speeches.[89] The images of Carson on screen would most likely have had a profound effect on his Unionist supporters. Bardon suggests that 'in public Carson's tall frame commanded respect and the grim set of his lower jaw seemed to show

a great deal of concern for the Irish Parliamentary Party. The execution of the leaders of the Easter Rising had created a wave of sympathy for Sinn Féin, and in the December 1918 election Sinn Féin replaced the Irish Parliamentary Party, winning nearly three-quarters of Irish seats.[103] Sinn Féin refused to take up its seats at Westminster, establishing its own Irish parliament in Dublin (Dáil Éireann) in January 1919 and formally declaring that a state of war existed between Britain and Ireland. A Volunteer raid in Tipperary on 21 January ended with the death of two RIC (Royal Irish Constabulary) policemen and confirmed Republican intentions. The ensuing War of Independence (coverage of which will be explored in the next chapter) lasted until a truce was signed on 11 July 1921. From 1918, Ulster Protestants increasingly promoted the idea of ensuring that at least the northern counties would ultimately be excluded from any Home Rule arrangements. John Redmond, leader of the Irish Parliamentary Party from 1900, died in March 1918. His son campaigned in his British Army uniform and defeated Sinn Féin in the subsequent Waterford by-election. His victory was covered by Pathé, proclaiming 'Captain W.A. Redmond defeats the Sinn Féin candidate by 474 votes.'[104] Redmond is pictured in his uniform with crowds cheering and congratulating him enthusiastically. This item, celebrating the success of a nationalism sympathetic to Britishness over the more extreme Sinn Féin, summed up the dominant British thinking at the time but underestimated the nature of the conflict that would ensue after the war was over. The turning point had been the conscription debates of April and May 1918.

The Conscription Debate

Germany's last great offensive towards Paris was launched in the spring of 1918, and in April conscription was imposed on Ireland to provide more men for the Allied war effort.[105] The opposition to this move on the part of Nationalists of all persuasions was featured by Pathé, Gaumont and Topical Budget. In an item in Gaumont's 1 April 1918 edition, entitled *Ireland Refuses Conscription*,[106] crowds are shown protesting. They are not identified and there is a suggestion in the title that the whole of Ireland is in opposition to conscription. Pathé's *Conscription in Ireland. To Be – or Not to Be?*[107] conjures up more of a sense of debate on the issue and depicts a more organized form of protest. This item deals with a one-day anti-conscription strike which took place throughout Ireland on 23 April (with the exception of Ulster which did not participate).[108] There are shots of an unidentified man facing a large crowd, with his right hand raised, apparently reading an oath. Most members of the crowd also have their right hands raised. There are also shots of men signing a petition. Topical Budget's 8 May item features John Dillon and de Valera's anti-conscription speeches at Balla-gradereen. An intertitle reports a crowd of 15,000 to hear the protest speeches.[109] There were a series of speeches made throughout the country during April and May in 1918. Under the combined opposition of the Church and all the Nationalist political parties the attempt to impose conscription was abandoned.

Once again the newsreels demonstrated their ability to propagandize any situation. To counteract the spring images of protest, and to help with the drive for voluntary recruitment, summer images of war effort support were provided for audiences. Two consecutive Gaumont Graphic issues in August 1918 deal with military support from Ireland. The first, *Recruiting in Ireland*,[110] features a speaker from the RAF, while the next issue includes *Off to France, Irish Contingent QM WAAC Leave Dublin for Front*, showing the women's corps on a railway platform preparing to leave for France.[111] The next Gaumont issue features an item showing Lord French at an Inter-Allied Exhibition in Dublin[112] – another item stressing the normality of British presence in Ireland. Viscount French's appointment as Lord Lieutenant was covered with the newsreels' usual enthusiasm for personalities and ritual. Subsequent to his appointment, French is shown by Pathé, Gaumont and Topical Budget visiting exhibitions, inspecting men at Dublin Castle, and 'among the fashionable people'[113] at the Dublin Horse Show. These items showing French in Ireland during the last months of the war reminded viewers of a strong British presence and associated this presence both with the war effort and with various activities – often leisure activities separate from the war, suggesting a time beyond the war when British association with Ireland would continue in everyday political life. (In May, just after he had been appointed Lord Lieutenant, Viscount French announced his suspicions of a 'German Plot'[114] and arrested over seventy Sinn Féin activists, as reported in Topical Budget's *Firm Hand in Ireland*.[115] The item shows de Valera and Countess Markievicz addressing crowds, and reports that they were among those arrested. The 'German plot' was bogus, the arrests unpopular, and Sinn Féin's deep involvement in the anti-conscription protests would work to its advantage in the post-war election.)

There are no items featuring Ireland in September of 1918; the next Gaumont issue containing an item of Irish interest appears at the end of October when the Red Cross pageant in Dublin is featured.[116] The last newsreel item featuring Ireland in 1918 appears in Gaumont's item *Dublin School Cadets Inspected* which shows an inspection by General Scallon.[117] Again a British presence is demonstrated along with connotations of Irish involvement in the war effort, stressing southern involvement by depicting scenes in Dublin. Thus within a few months we are shown the conflicting efforts of Ireland and Britain to gain support on either side of the Home Rule debate, each with the realization that Irish politics would come to the fore once again on the cessation of war. For Ireland, the end of a world war would soon give way to more localized conflict, firstly through the War of Independence and then through the Civil War. Ongoing conflict in Ireland offered the newsreels a challenging but frequently featured topic which was covered with a wide-ranging variation in tone, echoing the complexities of Irish politics in the 1920s.

NOTES

1. Norman cited in McKernan(1971).
2. McBain (1996) cited in Jeavons et al. (1998), p.75.
3. R. Barton (2004), p.15.
4. *A Day by the Sea.* Youghal Gazette, 1917, Irish Film Archive.
5. *Leaving Sunday Mass.* Youghal Gazette, 1917, Irish Film Archive.
6. O'Flynn in Smither and Klaue (1996), p.58.
7. *Sinn Féin.* Youghal Gazette, 1916, Irish Film Archive.
8. *Peace Celebrations.* Youghal Gazette, 1918, Irish Film Archive.
9. Ward (1989), p.5.
10. Ibid., p.104.
11. Jackson in Patten (1995), p.347.
12. O'Flynn in Smither and Klaue (1996), p.58.
13. *Late Queen's Visit to Dublin*, 1900, filmed by Cecil Hepworth, in Irish Film Archive.
14. P.M. Taylor (1999), p.103.
15. Rockett et al. (1987), p.32.
16. Ibid., pp.32–3.
17. *Republican Loan Film/Dáil Bonds Film*, Ireland, April 1920, directed by John MacDonagh.
18. For more information on this film, see O'Flynn in Smither and Klaue (1996), p.60.
19. Rockett (2004), p.72.
20. R. Barton (2004), p.15.
21. O'Flynn in Smither and Klaue (1996), pp.58–9.
22. Rockett et al. (1987), p.34.
23. O'Flynn in Smither and Klaue (1996), p.59.
24. R. Barton (2004), p.15.
25. *Sinn Féin Review.* Irish Events, 1919.
26. Kevin Rockett discusses this incident in detail in *Cinema and Ireland* (1987), pp.34–6.

27. R. Barton (2004), p.16.
28. Rockett et al. (1987), p.33.
29. O'Flynn in Smither and Klaue (1996), p.58.
30. Jackson in Patten (1995), p.354.
31. Ibid., p.356.
32. Loughlin (1995), p.78.
33. Jackson in Patten (1995), p.347
34. See http://www.proni.gov.uk/index/search_the_archives/ulster_covenant.htm for a searchable database of Covenant signatories.
35. Warwick Bioscope Chronicle appeared as a competitor with Pathé in 1910 but never became a major newsreel player.
36. *Ulster Day*. Warwick Bioscope Chronicle Issue 58, 28 September 1912.
37. Jackson in Patten (1995), p.335.
38. Hill (2006), pp.27–8.
39. Jackson (1992), pp.164–85.
40. *Suffragettes calling for arrest of Bonar Law and Carson*. Pathé circa 1913. This item appears on the Digital Film Archive. There is no corresponding entry on NoS.
41. *Ulster's Guardians of the Peace*, Pathé, date unknown. *Ulster's Guardians of the Peace* appears on the Digital Film Archive dated as 1913, it appears on the British Pathé website twice – once dated as 1914–18 and as a second clip (with the same footage) dated as 16 April 1923. Furthermore, NoS dates this item as 16 April 1923.
42. Jackson in Patten (1995), p.347.
43. *Orange Day*. Topical Budget, Issue 151–1, 15 July 1914.
44. Item's accompanying notes on Northern Ireland Screen's Digital Film Archive database: www.digitalfilmarchive.net.
45. *Sir Edward Carson in Belfast*. Topical Budget, Issue 151–2, 18 July 1914.
46. *Dublin Civic Exhibition*. Topical Budget, Issue 151–2, 18 July 1914.
47. Jackson in Patten (1995), p.357.
48. R. Barton (2004), p.16.
49. Beckett (1966), p.434.
50. Fitzpatrick, David, *Militarism in Ireland, 1900–1922*, p.388.
51. A.D. Smith, cited in Loughlin (1995), p.74.
52. Loughlin (1995), p.74.
53. McGarry (2010), p.279.
54. Beckett (1966), p.443.
55. *Aftermath of the Easter Rising*. Imperial War Museum, 1916.
56. *The Dublin Rebellion*. Topical Budget, Issue 245–2, 6 May 1916.
57. Coogan (2003), p.60.
58. *Aftermath of the Easter Rising*. Imperial War Museum, 1916.
59. Identified in Roger Smither (ed.), *Imperial War Museum Film Catalogue, Vol. 1: The First World War Archive* (Trowbridge: Flicks Books, 1993), p.69.
60. *German Rifles*. Topical Budget, Issue 247–1, 17 May 1916.
61. *Sinn Féin Rebels*. Topical Budget, Issue 247–2, 20 May 1916.
62. *Sinn Féin Released and Return to Dublin*. Gaumont Graphic, Issue 652, 21 June 1917, and *Countess Markievicz returns to Dublin*. Gaumont Grapic, 2 July 1917. There is no entry for the second item on NoS.
63. See comments by Nicholas Hiley in the introduction to Malins (1993), p.xv, which suggest that Malins had Irish roots but also that he would only admit to being born 'somewhere in the British isles' around 1883. Elsewhere in the book (p.152) Malins comments on observing the action on the first day of the Somme; he 'felt like going down on my knees and thanking God I was an Englishman'.
64. *The Battle of the Somme*. British Topical Committee for War Films, 11 August 1916.
65. Clips of *The Battle of the Somme*, including the staged 'over the top' sequence, are available for viewing at the Imperial War Museum's website at www.iwm.org.uk.
66. Malins (1993), p.160.

67. Ibid., p.163.
68. Ibid., p.163.
69. Ibid., p.177.
70. Ibid., p.181.
71. Ibid., p.182.
72. A full listing of the regiments filmed is available on the Imperial War Museum's online catalogue at www.iwmcollections.org.uk.
73. Stephen Badsey in Roger Smither (ed.), *Imperial War Museum Film Catalogue*, vol. 1 (Trowbridge: Flicks Books, 1994), p.vii.
74. *With the North and South Irish at the Front*. British Topical Committee for War Films, 1915–17.
75. See the Imperial War Museum's catalogue entry on *With the North and South Irish at the Front* at www.iwm.org.uk.
76. The Connaught Rangers was the county regiment of Galway, Leitrim, Mayo and Roscommon.
77. See www.digitalfilmarchive.net for contextual notes and shot list.
78. This information, as with many of the above details on dates and regiments, comes from notes for the Imperial War Museum's catalogue entry on *With the North and South Irish at the Front* at www.iwm.org.uk.
79. *Irish Soldiers at Mass*. Topical Budget, Issue 239–1, 22 March 1916.
80. *Nationalists in Khaki*. Topical Budget, Issue 215–1, 6 October 1915.
81. *Sergeant Mike O'Leary, VC. Dublin's Welcome to Our Famous Hero*. Gaumont Graphic, Issue 448, 8 July 1915.
82. *Ireland Welcomes O'Leary VC*. Topical Budget, Issue 202–2, 10 July 1915.
83. *Ireland's New Viceroy*. Topical Budget, Issue 190–2, 17 April 1915.
84. *Ireland's New Lord Lieutenant Arrives*. Gaumont Graphic, Issue 425, 19 April 1915.
85. *The Lord Lieutenant of Ireland Inspects a Good Muster of Boys Brigade at Dublin*. Gaumont Graphic, Issue 434, 20 May 1915.
86. *Viceroy at Limerick*. Topical Budget, Issue 208–2, 21 August 1915.
87. *Vice-Regal Procession*. Topical Budget, Issue 208–2, 21 August 1915.
88. *Ulster Division Fund*. Gaumont Graphic, 2 July 1917. This item does not appear on NoS.
89. *Orange Day Demonstrations in Belfast*. Gaumont Graphic, 14 July 1917. This item does not appear on NoS.
90. Bardon (1992), p.433.
91. *At Fortwilliam Park*. Gaumont Graphic, Issue 719, 11 February 1918.
92. *Dear Little Shamrock*. Pathé, 1914–18. This item cannot be dated more precisely.
93. *St Patrick's Day*. Topical Budget, Issue 238–2, 18 March 1916.
94. *Irish Soldiers at Mass*. Topical Budget, Issue 239–1, 22 March 1916.
95. *St Patrick's Day*. Topical Budget, Issue 291–1, 21 March 1916.
96. *Shamrock Day*. War Office Topical Budget, Issue 343–1, 20 March 1918.
97. *Recruiting in Ireland*. War Office Topical Budget, Issue 358–2, 8 July 1918.
98. *War Time Orange Festival*. War Office Topical Budget, Issue 360–1, 18 July 1918.
99. Smither (ed.), *Imperial War Museum Film Catalogue, Vol. 1: The First World War Archive* (1993), p.315.
100. *Ruthless Sea Hun Victims*. War Office Topical Budget, Issue 362–1, 1 August 1918.
101. *Irish Mail Boat Leinster Torpedoed by the Huns*. War Office Topical Budget, Issue 373–1, 17 October 1918.
102. *Sinn Féin to Be Suppressed*. War Office Topical Budget, Issue 359–1, 11 July 1918.
103. Kee (1981), p.179.
104. *Waterford Election*. Pathé Gazette, Issue 472B, 23 March 1918.
105. Bardon (1992), p.459.
106. *Ireland Refuses Conscription*. Gaumont Graphic, Issue 733, 1 April 1918.
107. *Conscription in Ireland. To Be – or Not to Be?* Pathé Gazette, Issue 476B, 25 April 1918.
108. Bardon (1992), p.459.
109. *Ireland and the War*. War Office Topical Budget, Issue 350–1, 8 May 1918.

110. *Recruiting in Ireland.* Gaumont Graphic, Issue 772, 15 August 1918.
111. *Off to France.* Gaumont Graphic, Issue 773, 19 August 1918.
112. *Visit to Inter-Allied Exhibition, Dublin.* Gaumont Graphic, Issue 774, 22 August 1918.
113. *Lord French at Dublin Horse Show.* Pathé, 1918. This item does not appear on NoS.
114. Bardon (1992), p.459.
115. *Firm Hand in Ireland.* War Office Topical Budget, Issue 352–1, 23 May 1918.
116. *Red Cross Pageant, Dublin.* Gaumont Graphic, Issue 794, 31 October 1918.
117. *Dublin School Cadets Inspected.* Gaumont Graphic, Issue 800, 21 November 1918.

4

Ireland at War:
Revolution and Reprisals

On 21 January 1919, Dáil Éireann, the assembly of elected Sinn Féin representatives in Ireland, met in Dublin's Mansion House. The event was reported in Topical Budget's 27 January issue as *Sinn Féin Parliament*.[1] The Dáil, consisting in the majority of Sinn Féin representatives after widespread success in the December election, proclaimed Irish independence. This was the first newsreel to report the establishment of the Dáil. On the same day as the Dáil's first meeting, masked volunteers shot two RIC constables.[2] This was the beginning of a spate of violent incidents. Initially the newsreels avoided reporting violent incidents in Ireland, but later images of Ireland would see a return to the 'aftermath' shots of smoky scenes of violent conflict.

1919 – the 'Peace' Agenda

In their reporting of Ireland during 1919, the newsreels were pulled between the news agenda of reporting the growing conflict and the 'peace' agenda of marking and celebrating the end of the First World War. Throughout the year, there were many items that drew attention to the role Ireland had played in the Great War and commemorating the war effort in general. Of particular significance are the items marking the first anniversary of the death of John Redmond.[3] An intertitle describes 'impressive scenes in Wexford in memory of the great loyal Irishman'. There was also acknowledgment of overseas troops. *Canadians in Ireland* features Cardinal Logue bidding farewell to overseas battalions, with some of the soldiers kissing the Blarney Stone before departing.[4]

The newsreels were also quick to focus on the return and commemoration of soldiers. A light-hearted item *Nurse vs Tommy* features recuperating soldiers in a hospital in Lucan, Co. Dublin.[5] The soldiers, many dressed in suits, are shown playing a game of golf with nurses dressed in white uniforms. There are long shots of the golf course and panning shots of a cheering crowd. The winning nurse is shown holding her prize – a piglet. Such items focussed on the contribution offered by everyday Irishmen to the war effort – a semi-comical item like this one also humanized such men at a time when violence and sectarian attacks in Ireland were growing. Stories such as *Dublin's Peace Day Procession*,[6] *Man of Ulster*[7] (featuring another 'peace' procession in which troops are inspected by Lord French), *Irish Guards Visit to Belfast*[8] (the same story covered by another newsreel) and *Ulster Celebrates Peace*[9] all celebrated the contribution by Irish servicemen to the war. A Gaumont item from April focuses on *Comrades of the Great War*[10] showing a procession of horse-drawn carriages filled with soldiers. Such scenes of impressive and orderly parades contrasted with the growing tension and turbulence in many areas throughout Ireland.

The newsreels had to cover this growing turbulence as well, and in many issues celebratory post-war items jostled with stories about increasing social and political unrest. In January 1919, Michael Collins, who had been elected MP for Cork South in the general election held at the end of 1918, was unable to attend the first meeting of Dáil Éireann as he was in England planning de Valera's escape from Lincoln jail. De Valera had been held in connection with the so-called 'German plot' to stage a second insurrection.[11] Topical Budget covered de Valera's escape in February 1919 in an item entitled *The Mystery of De Valera*, describing the 'Sinn Féin leader, who escaped from Lincoln Gaol, addressing a meeting in Ireland', according to the intertitle listed on News on Screen.[12] Collins would have been satisfied with this publicity – de Valera had wanted to go straight to America on his escape, but Collins advised him to return to Ireland first to maximize the publicity surrounding his escape.[13]

April begins with a Topical Budget item entitled *Re-Enter de Valera*, and the intertitle explains that 'Sinn Féin Leader's first appearance in public since his escape from Lincoln. He is accompanied by the Lord Mayor ... ' (rest of description unavailable).[14] Some of the tension came from industrial unrest as well. Just a few days later, Gaumont dealt with the Limerick strikes (in which the Limerick Soviet was established) in an item called *Under Martial Law*. The first intertitle proclaims: 'Under Martial Law, Military holding the bridges of Limerick against the strikers'.[15] There are shots of a checkpoint at a bridge and several well-attired people cycling through. A boy carrying a package walks away from camera, turns to look back at camera and then walks without much difficulty through the checkpoint. He is clearly more interested in the camera than the checkpoint. The checkpoint is an ordinary part of daily life while the camera is an unusual sight for locals. The cut to the next shot is more threatening – a panning shot of a soldier on a bridge, standing to attention in front of large tank which almost fills the whole frame. We do not, however, see any sign of conflict between the strikers and the soldiers manning the checkpoint.

There were also strikes in Belfast, covered in the newsreels of February 1919. As the war ended, Lord Pirrie, Chairman of Harland and Wolff, issued an announcement at the end of Armistice Week which would lead to strikes in the early part of 1919. Pirrie stated that the war was 'over in the fields, but not in the shipyards' and urged that there should be 'no slackening of effort in shipbuilding as ships are as vitally necessary today as at any period in the history of this country'.[16] Shipyard engineers downed tools early in the new year and demanded a forty-four-hour week. Other shipyard workers and gas and electricity workers soon joined them. Gaumont Graphic covered these demonstrations, reporting 'Unrest. Scenes in Belfast where over 100,000 men are "out" '.[17] The accompanying footage shows demonstrators marching with a banner proclaiming that 'pattern makers want 44 hours'. This newsreel followed just a week after disturbances on 25 January when strikers vandalized shops still using gas and electricity. The trams shut down, cinemas were closed, the newspapers could not produce their daily editions and even food was growing short. None of these consequences are dealt with in the newsreel, although an item immediately following *Strikers' Demonstrations in Belfast*, dealing with a fire in Donegal Street, probably relates to disturbances caused as a result of the strikes.[18] Characteristically, the newsreels do not comment on the conflict caused by the strikers.

In the summer of 1919, whilst Topical Budget depicted 'a great Irish pageant' in Belfast (where Marshall French and Edward Carson reviewed 'loyal victory men'),[19] Eamon de Valera was on a trip to America. Pathé

Gazette, describing him as 'President of the Irish Republic' (albeit with accompanying quotation marks), reports that he is touring the USA in search of funds.[20] (Harry Boland had introduced de Valera to a group of reporters in the Waldorf Astoria as President of the Irish Republic and he even received mail addressed to the hotel with this title.) De Valera is shown smiling surrounded by a group of suited men. Many of them are cheering and waving their hats in the air. There are panning shots of a large crowd gathered in the grounds of Fenway park stadium, showing people waving American flags, Tricolours and banners, one of which reads: 'let us carry the cross of Ireland'. Dave Hannigan describes the crowd's enthusiastic reception as it surged forward towards de Valera: 'Women fainted in the crush, several appeals were made to try to calm the masses, yet still they pressed forward. Even when de Valera finally reached the stage, reporters stationed at tables directly in front of him found themselves immediately under siege as men clambered over them in a quest to get ever closer to the action.'[21] The trip was generally seen as highly successful for publicity purposes, as analysed by Irish-American historian Francis M. Carrol: 'De Valera spoke before State legislatures, conferred with Governors, was given the freedom of several cities, and received two honorary doctorates ... always, he addressed large public audiences ... perhaps de Valera's travels throughout America, more than any other event since the 1916 Rising, dramatised for the American people the dimensions of the Irish struggle.'[22] Pathé was the only newsreel to cover the story, which appeared as part of the main edition for British and Irish audiences. Gaumont's item on De Valera's visit was not released.[23] For Irish audiences, America's enthusiasm for De Valera cemented the potential for Ireland's construction as an independent nation on a global stage; for British audiences De Valera's American campaign signified the fragmentation of the empire.

1920 – 'The Year of Terror'

Jonathan Bardon describes Ireland in 1920: 'Full-scale guerrilla warfare had developed over much of the south and as the year advanced it spread northwards, inflaming ancient hatreds, plunging Ulster into the most terrible period of violence the province had experienced since the eighteenth century. The civil war, postponed by a general European war in 1914, had begun.'[24] Newsreels from this period onwards would be characterized by reports of violent incidents and the return to the kind of smoky shots typical of the 'aftermath' scenes from the Rising. One such incident was the murder of the Lord Mayor of Cork, Thomas MacCurtain, in March 1920, whose killing by the Black and Tans caused widespread outrage. The only newsreel to cover the event is Pathé, in an item entitled *Funeral of Lord Mayor of Cork*. There is one intertitle at the beginning of the item, stating: 'Irish Mayor Shot. Alderman Thomas MacCurtain, Lord Mayor of Cork, buried with full Sinn Féin honours.' There are various shots of the funeral cortège processing slowly through crowded streets. No further explanation of the cause of the shooting or its perpetrators is given – such controversial fare had no place in standard newsreel coverage. Equally, the newsreels carried an inherent sense of 'orderly' Britishness – to evoke the unruly and anarchic nature of the Black and Tans would have been unheard of by newsreel companies, who avoided provocative material at all times. On one occasion only was this deemed acceptable – when the newsreels reported government condemnation of the actions of the Black and Tans.

Smoky footage of burnt-out shop-fronts and houses is shown in *The War of Reprisals* in Pathé's 27 September 1920 issue. The intertitle reads: 'Police and Auxiliaries raid and sack another Irish town.'[25] On 20 September the infamous Black and Tans had attacked and sacked the north Co. Dublin town of Balbriggan as a reprisal for the shooting of a head constable earlier that day, and it was this kind of swift reaction that gave the 'Tans' their fearsome reputation. On the surface, the British authorities condemned such excessive use of force by Crown officers. Thus a newsreel the following week, under the title *Reprisals in Ireland condemned by Sir Hamar Greenwood*,[26] reports the Irish Secretary saying that 'government condemn excesses at big review of RIC and the Black and Tans'. There are shots of the secretary and his wife, with rows of soldiers in the background. These scenes are followed by shots of military display, with the secretary to right of screen; he raises his bowler hat to the marching soldiers. The newsreel follows the conventional pattern of showing formality and ceremony (and a practical preference for staged events). The end result is a piece that seemingly endorses a positive reading of Hamar Greenwood and his security policy. 'Reprisals', however, was a word that would recur in the newsreels throughout this period, and 1920 became known as 'The Year of Terror'. The Black and Tans were composed of ex-servicemen and were an ill-disciplined and largely uncontrolled force – Coogan claims that this resulted in the death of 200 civilians as part of the government's campaign of 'frightfulness' – a policy designed to wreak terror and torture throughout Ireland during the War of Independence. Hamar Greenwood repeatedly denied any misbehaviour on behalf of the Crown forces to the extent that 'telling a Hamar' became a new description for lying.[27] Whether these reprisals, like the murder of MacCurtain, were actual policy or the result of poor discipline and lack of leadership is a debating point. However, the policy of reprisals alienated the general population even more, and in their reporting of the reprisals the newsreels – unsurprisingly, given the context of their production – do not acknowledge this declining support for the British presence in Ireland.

Pathé covered the appointment of General Sir Neville Macready in April 1920 'to command police and troops in Ireland'.[28] The first shots are medium close-ups of an austere-looking man wearing a suit and reading through some notes. He does not acknowledge the camera. The subsequent shots are of a side profile of Macready lighting and smoking a pipe. Further shots show him checking through his notes. Next there is an intertitle stating: 'Irish Loyalist demonstration outside the House during debate on Home Rule Bill'. At this time the 'Better Government of Ireland Bill', which would become the Government of Ireland Act in 1920, was being considered. Protestors are shown walking along a busy road carrying placards reading 'People of England do not hand Ireland over.' A close-up of two demonstrators shows two placards, reading 'Englishmen will you abandon Irish Loyalists to men who fought for Germany' and 'Sinn Féin helped Germany. Irish Loyalists fought for Britain. Which will you stand by?' respectively. Traffic and pedestrians move past the protestors nonchalantly; some pedestrians even cross the protestors' path, weaving in and out between them. The protestors' placards look cumbersome and heavy and impede their movement. These two separate stories are treated as one item, the juxtaposition associating Macready with the Loyalist demonstrators, suggesting that his sympathies lie with them.

A contentious and divisive incident was the death in Brixton prison on October 25 of hunger striker Terence MacSwiney. MacSwiney was

at the time the Lord Mayor of Cork, having succeeded Thomas
MacCurtain when the latter was murdered in March. After being found
with illegal documents, MacSwiney refused to recognize a military
court and went on 'a prodigious hunger strike'.[29] Pathé introduces its
item on his death with the intertitle: 'Lord Mayor of Cork Dead. Cork
was outwardly calm on receipt of the news – but military patrolled the
city unceasingly', giving a typically upbeat, positive spin to the sombre
mood in Cork at the funeral.[30] Pallbearers bring the casket through the
centre of the shot. To the right are clergymen – priests and altar boys.
To the left are policemen in uniform with helmets. The bishop, flanked
by priests, anoints the coffin with incense. The coffin, completely
covered by a Tricolour, is loaded into the funeral carriage. The funeral
cortège is shown processing through the street. It is preceded by a
lengthy religious procession. After the procession there are shots of a
police presence surrounding a large crowd of mourners at the graveside.

4.1 Irish Events: *The Funeral of Terence MacSwiney*, Courtesy of the IFI Irish Film Archive.

Some of the newsreel's concluding shots show a human chain of police holding onlookers back from the road. The newsreel's next item re-establishes a sense of normality with stories on the Mayor of Arras visiting Newcastle, a golf tournament and 'honours to firemen'. The Irish Events footage of MacSwiney's funeral is markedly different, particularly in its lack of police presence. (The indigenous material shot for Irish Events had a different production agenda to the main British newsreels and was viewed only by Irish audiences.) The Irish Events cameraman also gets much closer than Pathé's production crew. This is particularly evident in overhead shots of an open casket. Other shots show the procession following the coffin, again clearly draped in a Tricolour while crowds look on, and, as in the Pathé film, shots of Arthur Griffith closely following the coffin.[31]

A group of British officers dubbed 'the Cairo gang' arrived in Ireland in October 1920 as part of an attempt to unify intelligence-gathering operations. Collins obtained detailed information on these 'hush-hush men', and a dozen of the alleged[32] British agents were killed in a pre-dawn raid on 21 November 1920 as part of a broader attempt to 'meet British reprisals in Ireland with a massive counter-reprisal'.[33] (The campaign also involved activity in Dublin, Liverpool, Manchester and London.)

The funeral of the officers was held in London and covered by Gaumont Graphic.[34] An intertitle states: 'Murdered Officers Dublin's Tribute. Impressive procession thro' Ireland's Capital' – which presumably refers to the military procession through Dublin before the bodies were returned to England. There are scenes of a processing military brass band followed by coffins covered with Union Jacks and pulled by horses through the streets, with soldiers parading behind. The event is also covered by Pathé in an item showing the military ship carrying the officers' bodies, and the military procession through the streets of Dublin, with the intertitle 'Dublin. The Murdered Officers. With full Naval and Military honours the bodies were borne through the Irish Capital and embarked on the Destroyer "Sea Wolf".'[35] The newsreel coverage is typically reverential but, as usual, characteristically reactive to the aftermath of monumental events. It is not clear from the items' records whether this coverage was shown only in Britain or if it was also exhibited for Irish audiences. The attacks on the Cairo gang spawned a reprisal in the form of an attack on players and spectators at a Gaelic football match in Croke Park in Dublin. Indiscriminate firing towards players and spectators left a dozen or more people dead (numbers are disputed) and hundreds injured in a stampede.[36] The incident became known as 'Bloody Sunday' and was not reported by any of the newsreel companies.

As the violence escalated, newsreel coverage appeared increasingly hostile to Sinn Féin and Republicans. The Pathé Issue of November 25 illustrates this well.[37] It opens with the intertitle 'No-one can insult our flag. Sinn Féiners – who had on Armistice day, of all days – torn down the Union Jack – were made to parade the village and rehoist it.' There is footage of two Black and Tans carrying a large Union Jack down a street flanked by several RIC officers. The camera then cuts to a panning shot of two civilians, flanked by RIC officers, holding the flag and looking at the camera while a crowd behind looks on. The flag is nearly completely draped over one of the men, eclipsing most of his body apart from his head and feet; the other stands to the left of the shot, unmoving, almost like a flagpole. He glances for a second at his fellow flag-bearer. There is a cut to a country lane where a large number of officers accompany the two men, still carrying the Union Jack, into a field. One Black and Tan towards the rear of the ungainly procession slaps an RIC officer on the back. It is clear that tensions were running high at this stage, further demonstrated by an item released on the same date as part of a separate Pathé issue. *Side Lights on Sinn Féin*[38] showed footage of 'May Connelly – who was kicked and had her hair shorn for the "crime" of speaking to Black and Tans'. The victim is shown in a doorway, turning to reveal her shorn hair to the camera. The fact that the intertitle uses inverted commas on the word 'crime' suggests an implied judgement on the perpetrators of the attack.

A Topical Budget item from December 1920 describes 'Ireland's Agony – desolation follows mystery fire in Cork.' The film shows people sifting through wreckage, shots of the fire brigade arriving and smoky pictures of burnt-out buildings.[39] The newsreel does not report that Cork had been sacked and set on fire by the Black and Tans and the Auxiliaries during 11–12 December as a reprisal for the IRA ambush at Kilmichael which killed seventeen Auxiliaries. Some soldiers also prevented firefighters from tackling the blaze. At a time when Sir Hamar Greenwood was denying such riotousness on the part of the British forces it could not have been openly shown by the newsreels,

even if they had been in the habit of courting controversy. This particular item gives an interesting insight into what the public in Ireland and
in Britain were told (or not told) about the increasing violence. While
the audience is asked to sympathize with 'Ireland's agony' and with the
people shown picking their way through devastated buildings, there is
no search for the perpetrators of the attack. The newsreel's focus is to
invoke sympathy, not to condemn the attack or to offer contextual
information. It is not clear if this item was exhibited to Irish audiences,
but there are two other items listed as part of this edition. The first
covers a London murder trial and the second, entitled *Our Wonderful
Weather*, features contrasting weather conditions in London and
Torquay, and it is likely that this 'general interest' edition was shown in
the same format for British and Irish audiences.

The final Pathé newsreel of 1920 of Irish interest relocates Sinn Féin
activity to London. The intertitle announces: 'Sinn Féin Outrages in
England. Many cotton warehouses and timber yards set on fire by Sinn
Féin agents.' This is accompanied by footage of burning buildings being
hosed down, the smoky imagery of Ireland for once associated with
England. The perpetrators of this fire are firmly identified as Irish and
blame is allocated, unlike the 'mystery' fire in Cork. The fact that the
threat of IRA violence had spread to England was seized upon by the
newsreels and would certainly have evoked anti-Irish sentiment in
British audiences.

1921 – Violence and Reprisal

By January 1921, Ireland was still embroiled in a circuit of violence
and reprisal, as Pathé's first Irish item of the year demonstrated.
Reprisals by Order reports on seven houses destroyed by the British
Army because of the occupants' failure to inform on the participants of
an ambush in which three policemen were killed.[40] Shots of damaged
houses reveal that several of them were also shops with residences
upstairs – a stern warning to both residents and businessmen who failed
to inform on crimes perpetrated against the British Army. Civilians are
shown picking through the wreckage of buildings which look as if they
have suffered aerial bombings. The camera cuts to pedestrians walking
up and down a reasonably quiet street which is patrolled by RIC
officers, one of whom stops to converse with a woman. Two others are

shown stopping an elderly man, obviously much less reluctant to talk. They are half slouched against a wall, holding rifles and look bored. He looks back hesitantly before one soldier nods permission for him to continue on his way. These are images of an Ireland at war.

The next Pathé items of Irish interest follow a couple of weeks later and reinforce the pro-Establishment, pro-British leanings of the newsreels. The first begins with footage of Sir Hamar Greenwood reviewing the RIC Auxiliaries in Phoenix Park. In an item clearly convenient for the newsreels to cover as a 'scheduled' event, Greenwood is shown inspecting the men and then addressing them. They stand in formation, listening intently as he waves his walking stick in anger. The men respond by lifting their caps in the air in four successive cheers led by an officer.[41] The message behind these images being projected from Phoenix Park is one of strength and defiance. Greenwood is clearly motivating the men towards victory in the fight against the rebels. Another item listed for the same newsreel was the funeral of District Inspector Tobias O'Sullivan, shot in an ambush in Co. Kerry on 20 January 1921. The fact that the item was not assigned a running order number suggests that it may only have been viewed in Ireland and not as part of the general release British issue.[42] This is interesting, given the nature of the item, which depicts a full military funeral in Dublin with a coffin clearly draped in a Union Jack. On the NoS database it is identified as 'Dublin' in the 'local/special' category, further suggesting that this item would have been screened only as part of an Irish edition.

Another February issue for Pathé deals with political events in an item entitled *All's Fair in ...* with an intertitle explaining that 'hostages are now being taken in military patrol lorries' and showing military vehicles.[43] Another item in this issue shows attempts by the some prominent Irish figures to 'relieve suffering in Ireland' through the first meeting of the White Cross at the Mansion House in Dublin. Amongst those attending are: 'Mrs McBride, Mrs Sheehy Skeffington, Mrs Kettle, Lord Monteagle, Mr Erskine Childers, Mr George Russell, Ald. O'Neil Mayor of Dublin'.[44] A third item of Irish interest is introduced by the intertitle 'Lady Sykes – of "Peace with Ireland Movement" – visits scene of reprisals at Sixmilebridge Co. Clare.' There are scenes of completely burnt-out cottages with residents clearing rubble from inside the ruins of their homes. Lady Sykes, attired in furs, is featured watching from a distance with a clergyman.[45] Another February item features further aid for war-torn Irish villages. The intertitle 'American Mission to relieve distress in Ireland visit devastated villages' is accompanied by scenes of well-dressed men promenading along a street of ruined houses, pointing out features of the damage in a casual way. They go into houses for a closer look and are also pictured outside speaking to a man taking notes, possibly a reporter. The group is then pictured outside a more ornate urban building, chatting, smiling at the camera and smoking.[46] These are scenes common to conflict – the upper classes shown relatively unaffected, trying to assist 'victims' amongst the working classes who continue, throughout history, to constitute the true casualties of war. The report produced by the visiting delegates attributed widespread destruction to Irish property and industry by British military forces and pledged financial support for families in economic distress.[47] Just as in the newsreels, the context and complexities of the War of Independence were not explored.

The newsreels covered the war and the violence in their own way but all of this 'bad news' was alleviated by softer, more uplifting items. An interesting item entitled *Business as Usual* is opened by the intertitle 'enterprising baker opens shop on edge of invested area'. The baker is shown operating from an open-air counter in a street patrolled by a single soldier, who watches customers go back and forth to the makeshift bakery. A crowd of children watches both the baker and the camera. The next scenes are smoky shots of a group of soldiers, reminding the audience of the difficult area in which the baker has opened.[48] A more 'normal' version of Irish life was also featured in the newsreels. An early February Pathé issue features the meet of the Ward Union Hunt at Ratoath.[49] The footage shows a large, fully attired hunt party on a county road, a more readily acceptable image of rural Ireland than burnt-out cottages and, again, an event that due to its timetabling was easier to film than spontaneous and unexpected scenes of conflict.

The 1921 coverage of St Patrick's Day reveals an image of Ireland that was familiar and which would continue to be a common feature of newsreel representation. The item opens with the intertitle 'The Dear Little Shamrock. Gathering Ireland's emblem for St Patrick's Day',[50] accompanied with scenes of a horse and cart travelling down a country road. Six Irish colleens wrapped in shawls jump off the cart and begin gathering shamrocks into baskets. They are shown sitting on a hillside in an idyllic setting, laughing and joking as they gather the shamrocks.

At a time when the War of Independence was continuing, it was highly characteristic of the newsreels to offer a portrayal of Ireland that they were most comfortable with – simple, rural, feminine. *Ireland Solves Housing Problem*,[51] two weeks later, features the hasty construction of houses in Clontarf. The 'housing problem' is not explained and we are shown scenes of construction followed by shots of neat, relatively affluent-looking streets: the kind of positive, upbeat story that could balance all the bad news items of the recent past. In this item, there is no sign of violence or conflict. *Lord Chancellor's Easter Levee* alludes to partition by stating: 'United Irish Courts meet for last time, under a new act a court will be in Dublin and Belfast.'[52] The judges' procession is depicted in all its finery and the judges gather for a photograph to mark the occasion. An item on Viscount Fitzalan in May remarks: 'First Catholic Viceroy visits Sir Hamar Greenwood.'[53] The footage shows the party walking through gardens then posing for a photo. An item a few days later depicts Viscountess Powerscourt inspecting a troop of Dublin Girl Guides.[54] Items like these are typical of the process of normalizing life in times of conflict but they also serve to normalize British presence in Ireland. In particular, the ordered nature of inspections or the conviviality of 'visits' present a stark contrast to the pockets of violence in many parts of the country at this stage.

Treaty Negotiations

The Government of Ireland Bill, which was, in essence, the fourth Home Rule bill, was introduced on 25 February 1920 and came into effect in May 1921.[55] It partitioned Ireland into six north-eastern counties to be known as Northern Ireland, while the remaining twenty-six would be known as Southern Ireland. Each part was to have its own parliament, with ultimate sovereignty resting with Westminster. As Ireland moved inexorably towards partition, the newsreels began to cover political developments in the north with some degree of sympathy. Edward Carson resigned in February 1921, moving aside for James Craig to take his place. Pathé featured his farewell speech, introducing the item with the intertitle 'Ulster's New Leader. Sir Edward Carson makes farewell speech and Sir James Craig becomes leader of the Ulster Unionist Party.'[56] Carson is shown making his way through a large crowd following a procession featuring a large Union Jack and Lambeg drums while crowds part to let him through and cheer on either side. Carson steps onto the podium and is shown speaking to the crowd in his usual stern, gruff style. Craig led the Unionists into the first election for the Northern Ireland parliament held on May 24 and inevitably won an overwhelming victory. The new parliament was opened by King George V in Belfast City Hall on June 22 amid much pomp and ceremony. The progress towards this historic day is covered well by the weekly newsreels.

Pathé shows Northern Ireland's new government on the steps of Hillsborough Castle. Shots of James Craig (Prime Minister), Thomas Andrews (Minister of Labour), Hugh Pollock (Minister of Finance), Richard Dawson Bates (Minister of Home Affairs), Milne Barbour (Ministry of Commerce) and Lord Londonderry (Minister of Education) are not accompanied by any intertitles.[57] Pathé had also been the only company to cover the election, explaining shots of streets decorated with Union Jacks by the intertitle 'Polling day scenes. Decorated streets and open air ballot boxes are features of the Northern Ireland elections.'[58] The shots clearly associate the election solely with Unionism; no Nationalist perspective is offered. Topical Budget reported the first assembly of the northern parliament at Belfast City Hall.[59] Opening with the intertitle 'Ulster's Parliament assembles. Lord-Lieutenant attends historic ceremony at Belfast City Hall', there are shots of the exterior of the City Hall followed by close-ups of representatives leaving the main entrance and chatting outside. Gaumont provided extended coverage of the official opening on 22 June in an item four minutes long.[60] Opening with the arrival of the King and Queen on the royal yacht with naval escort at Bangor, with moving shots taken alongside the royal yacht, an intertitle announces: 'passing Belfast's famous shipyards'. The yacht arrives at Donegall Quay to be greeted with flags and decorations. Scenes of 'the progress through the city' are even more impressive. The streets, decked out with bunting and Union Jacks, are full to capacity with enthusiastic crowds while the royal procession progresses through a sea of people. The Albert Clock forms the backdrop to the shot. An inspection of the guard at the City Hall is reminiscent of the changing of the guard at Buckingham Palace and testifies to both the majestic nature of the occasion and the association with Britishness which would have placated any Unionists unhappy with a home parliament. This was the beginning of the newsreels' ongoing associations between the north and Unionism, industry, the monarch and Britishness. Indeed, panning aerial shots of Belfast City Hall appear more like the rooftops of London than the new capital of Northern Ireland. Gaumont ascribes to Belfast the status of a mini-London, a satellite of the British capital clearly associated with the Union and in no way presented as distanced due to the newly assembled home parliament. Pathé's introductory intertitle announces 'the Royal opening of Ulster Parliament. Their Majesties' State Procession.'[61] The footage is similar to Gaumont's of the yacht arriving although there are more close-ups of the royal carriage processing through Belfast. Impressive overhead shots look down on the progress of the royal party through crowded and orderly streets. We then see the royal party arrive at the City Hall and pause on the steps. Again the shots are closer to the King and Queen than Gaumont's coverage, suggesting that Pathé may have been given exclusive rights to the story.[62] George V addressed the Unionist MPs (Nationalist and Sinn Féin representatives boycotted the parliament, Sinn Féin representatives meeting at Dáil Éireann in Dublin instead). George V's speech was, however, intended to address all elected representatives, whether present or not:

> I speak from a full heart when I say that my coming to Ireland today may prove to be the first step towards an end of strife amongst her people, whatever their race or breed. In that hope, I appeal to all Irishmen to pause, to stretch out the hand of forbearance and conciliation, to forgive and forget, and to join in making for the land which they love a new era of peace, contentment, and good will.[63]

The King informed James Craig that his advisors had not encouraged him to attend. The train carrying the King's cavalry was attacked next day, resulting in four deaths.[64] Characteristically, the attack was not covered in the newsreels. June had been a violent month in Northern Ireland but a truce between the IRA and the British government was eventually called on 11 July 1921 for talks to begin on the future of Ireland. There was an upsurge of sectarian conflict in the north following the signing of the Truce, and anti-Catholic riots in Belfast claimed sixteen lives. Instead of reporting the sectarian attacks raging throughout Northern Ireland, reports on the violence were sparse. Pathé reports on *Irish Pony Show* and *Irish Pageant*, *Phoenix Park Races* and *Irish Polo Season*, while Gaumont covers *Lord Londonderry's Garden*

Party at Botanic Gardens[65] with footage of James Craig, marquees, the gardens, smiling guests and children on donkeys and in fancy dress.

Newsreel coverage from July 1921 contains more political content in Irish items. What is interesting is that the newsreels cover the political developments on a weekly basis as the truce led to talks, talks to the Treaty and the Treaty to the Civil War. Again, there is a great deal of emphasis on the personalities involved and on the painstaking moves towards a settlement but there is surprisingly scant attention paid to the escalating levels of violence in Ireland and especially to the deteriorating situation in the north of the country. The Pathé issue of July 1921, for example, contains three items out of eleven related to political events in Ireland. The first reports the historic meeting at the Mansion house in Dublin. De Valera is shown posing for newsreel cameras before entering the building. There are then panning shots of the crowds in Dawson Street, an American flag in their midst.[66] A second item in the same issue reports prayers by the crowd for those involved in the conference,[67] stating that 'crowds pray for success at the conference' and showing a medium close-up of several women in the midst of a large crowd of people blessing themselves. The women bow their heads in prayer while the camera cuts to long shot of the crowd, with everyone blessing themselves, clearly identifying the whole crowd gathered outside the Mansion House as Catholic. A third item returns again to the conference to show crowds gathered outside, further testifying to a strong interest in the results of the negotiations.[68] Just a few days later, Pathé covers a demonstration in Belfast in an item entitled 'Ulster's Great Day'. The opening intertitle states: 'Sir James Craig addresses 50,000 Orangemen after imposing demonstration in the City.'[69] Overhead shots of a large procession back up the claims of the intertitle. The usual marching with bands and banners ensues, with some of the crowds walking alongside the procession. The camera then cuts to a medium close-up on Craig and several other men on a speaker's platform. They are standing, waving their bowler hats triumphantly in the air towards the crowd. The other men sit while Craig speaks, pointing his finger aggressively at the crowd then waving both his fists. On the same date, Topical Budget boasts an exclusive interview with Eamon de Valera in *Is it the Dawn?* and claiming in its intertitle: 'Though refusing all interviews de Valera asks "Topical" exclusively to issue his peace message to the whole world.' The existing item contains no footage, only intertitles:

The message: 'Ireland is fighting solely for the right to live her own life in her own way. She loves equally all her children and she needs them all. And Oh! It were a gallant deed to show before mankind, how every race and every creed might be by love combined – might be combined yet not forget the mountains from whence they rose. As filled by many a rivulet, the stately Shannon flows.' Signed Eamon de Valera July 4 1921.[70]

Luke McKernan concludes that this item evoked a strong sympathy for de Valera and praises Topical's coverage of Ireland, describing it as 'impressive because of its thoughtfulness'.[71] In general observation of Topical's Irish coverage, which McKernan quantifies as 10 per cent of Topical's output between 1920 and 1922, rising to 20 per cent 'at high points in the crisis', he suggests that including such political content would be difficult for the newsreel without 'betraying some kind of position' and that Topical's stance was 'faith in an equitable peace settlement and the validity of the Irish Free State'.[72] McKernan's view of this, given the expense required to support filming for sustained periods, is that 'Topical's coverage is praiseworthy therefore in extent and kind.'[73] Going back to Topical's coverage of the 1916 Rising and its aftermath, there appeared a broader understanding of Irish insurgency than appeared in the other companies' newsreels, in particular when Topical showed images of Thomas Clarke and close-up shots of the Irish rebels immediately after the leaders of the rebellion had been executed. This sympathy is interesting, given Topical's official capacity during the First World War and proximity to the British Establishment. and raises the complexities associated with newsreel coverage of Ireland during this period.

Footage of de Valera arriving in London with Sinn Féin ministers in an item entitled *I Want Peace* also reflects McKernan's observations.[74] De Valera is shown sitting in the back of a car which then drives off through a dense crowd. Gaumont Graphic also covers this letter which is summarized on the NoS database:

Sir, The desire you express on the part of the British Government to end the centuries of conflict between the people of these two islands and to establish relations of neighbourly harmony, is the genuine desire of the people of Ireland. I have consulted with my colleagues and secured the views of representatives of the minority of our nation in regard to the invitation you have sent me. In reply I desire to say that I am ready to meet and discuss with you on what basis such a conference as that proposed can reasonably hope to achieve the object desired.

An intertitle reads: 'Ireland's Hour. Sinn Féin leaders leave Kingstown for England.'[75] A truce to aid further negotiation had been declared on 11 July 1921 after de Valera had several lengthy discussions with Lloyd George.[76]

After two items on de Valera, Topical follows with coverage of 1921's Twelfth of July celebrations. The intertitle reports that '100,000 Belfast Orangemen march to Ballylesson to celebrate the 232nd anniversary of the Battle of the Boyne.'[77] There are shots of the parade at Donegall Place and the City Hall. James Craig is shown speaking from a podium, sternly shaking his fist in the air. Gaumont Graphic also reports de Valera at Downing Street with similar scenes to Topical's coverage, except one shot of a member of the crowd holding a Tricolour.[78] Pathé Gazette also shows footage of de Valera in London in *Sinn Féiners in Downing Street*, predicting that 'peace prospects are bright'.[79] Shots of crowds milling around are followed by a car pulling up; de Valera gets out and goes straight into Downing Street without looking around. There are further scenes of crowds and women kneeling in the street at the front of one group. A close-up shows three well-dressed women kneeling on the ground, one policeman standing to the right of the shot while another woman behind, standing, holds up a photo. The item finishes with de Valera driving off again through a cheering crowd. The interesting aspect of this is that for all the concentration on the talks in London and seemingly peaceful pageantry in the north, the month of July was a particularly violent month, especially in Belfast. According to Bardon, sixteen Catholics and seven Protestants were killed and 200 Catholic homes were destroyed.[80] This violence was not reflected by the newsreel companies, who continued in their characteristically positive vein, depicting prayers for peace, peace talks and Orange pageantry.

In Pathé's 28 July 1921 issue, four out of eight items deal with Irish matters: *Ireland a Dominion, Pony and Donkey Races at Finglas Road, De Valera in London* and *De Valera*. The political items refer to de Valera's visit to London to meet Lloyd George in 'talks about talks' and it is obvious that the newsreels maintained a positive, up-beat mood about these negotiations. (The later negotiations involving Michael

Collins and Arthur Griffith would prove more problematic.) The first Pathé item reports an enthusiastic reception for de Valera on his return to Ireland, suggesting that the cheering crowds approve of the peace proposals.[81] The items towards the end of the newsreel, showing de Valera in Dublin, attribute equally enthusiastic sentiments in the intertitle: 'De Valera receives frenzied welcome from Irish sympathisers on arrival in London.'[82] The accompanying footage shows de Valera's car being swamped by supporters, so much so that he has difficulty opening the door of the vehicle. The pony races merely confirm that normal life carries on against the background of intense political manoeuvring.

The newsreels continue to cover negotiations regarding the Irish question in a predictable and generally non-controversial manner. After extensive debate in the Dáil it was decided that a five-man delegation, led by Arthur Griffith and including Michael Collins, would be sent to engage in negotiations in London. Collins did not relish the prospect, commenting that 'to me the task is a loathsome one. If I go, I go in the spirit of a soldier who acts against his better judgement at the orders of a superior officer.'[83] The newsreels duly reported what were always going to be very difficult and fraught negotiations in typical manner. *Irish Peace Congress*[84] from Pathé opens with its usual optimism: 'Sinn Féin and Government delegates meet and everybody hopes for a happy settlement.' There are various shots of the delegates both in a group and individually. Most look calm and relaxed. Pathé reflected an optimism at this stage that would prove misguided: Ireland was about to be plunged into another period of violent conflict.

The Treaty

Michael Collins stated uncertainty about whether the Treaty delegation was 'being instructed or confused' during its discussions with Lloyd George, adding 'the latter I would say'.[85] In a personal letter to Kitty Kiernan on the matter of signing the Treaty, Collins reveals an optimistic hope for the settlement. Writing on the morning of 6 December (the agreement had been reached in the middle of the night) he poignantly states: 'I don't know how things will go now but with God's help we have brought peace to this land of ours – a peace which will end this old strife of ours forever.'[86] Like the newsreels, Collins' optimism was misguided.

Three out of five items in Topical Budget's 8 December issue deal with Irish politics and the historic signing of the Treaty. The opening item, *Forgive and Forget*,[87] had been filmed in June and dealt with the opening of the Northern Ireland parliament by George V. The introductory intertitle featured a small picture of hands shaking underneath the title 'Forgive and Forget' and went on: 'recalling the King's noble plea at Belfast for peace, a plea which has at last borne fruit'. The film shows the royal parade down High Street, showing the Albert Clock clearly in the background on the way to the City Hall. Once again the north is depicted as aligned with Unionism, watching orderly royal parades while the film moves on to associate the south with 'terror'. It does this through its next intertitle, 'Recalling the Terror before the Truce', while accompanying scenes show Black and Tan soldiers in the back of a jeep travelling down a city street and then shots of soldiers on horseback. The next item shows the intertitle 'Irish Free State',[88] continuing: 'after centuries of strife Britain adds a contented New Dominion to the Crown'. To suggest that Ireland was now 'contented' was, again, typically upbeat newsreel style, but also perhaps a call for Irish audiences in particular to endorse the signing of the Treaty. Despite the contentment described, negotiation of the Treaty had been a protracted process and Collins certainly recognized the opposition its signing would face in the Dáil. Nevertheless the newsreel enthusiastically continues its report: 'at 2 o'clock in the morning – after a day and a night where there seemed no hope – the Dáil Éireann delegates agreed to an arrangement whereby all Ireland except Ulster – becomes a Free State. The standing of the Irish Free State will be similar to that of our other Dominions, owing allegiance to the King. Ulster may join the new State if she wishes.' Next we are introduced to 'The men who signed for Dáil Éireann. Mr Arthur Griffith left, Mr RC Barton centre.' R.C. Barton was a member of the Irish Cabinet and attended the Peace Conference in England. There is an unidentified man on the right. An item on nocturnal lighting in Brighton follows before the third Irish item, opening with the intertitle 'Peace Council at the Palace. "Splendid News!" says the King – His smile reflects the Irish sunshine.'[89] Lloyd George comes out onto a set of steps with the King and other Treaty delegates. The King is shown talking to the camera. Next we see shots of the front door of 'No. 10 where the Peace was signed' followed by a close-up on a signed copy of the Treaty. We then see 'The Irish Delegates who signed the memorable Treaty.' There are shots of Collins and two other men. The camera pans round to show Arthur Griffith. Collins is shown talking with another man, smiling and laughing heartily. The final shot is a freeze-frame of Collins, smiling and looking upwards. It is a poignant shot, given that Collins himself realized that he had 'just signed his own death warrant'.[90] Within eight months he would suffer fatal injuries in an ambush in his home county of Cork.

The exact same item appears as part of Pathé's 12 December issue. On Pathé's website it can be viewed as *Peace Council at the Palace*, but it is titled *Irish Peace* on NoS. The footage and intertitles are the same as Topical Budget's item, but *Irish Peace* appears alongside two other items of national interest, *Essex Village Elects its Boy Bishop*, *Off to Australia on the First Government Liner*, and a third for local consumption, *Internees Free* – most likely added for the Irish edition of this particular issue. Pathé's previous issue, just three days after the signing of the Treaty, shows de Valera visiting Galway. The intertitle reads: 'de Valera accompanied by Minister of Defence and Chief of Staff, visits Galway.'[91] The item shows the three men travelling around Galway by car and being met by large crowds, indicating de Valera's popularity and, given the date of this item, perhaps confirming his belief that it was a wise choice to send others as plenipotentiaries to London while he remained prominent in the Irish people's psyche at home. However, even though this item is dated 9 December 1921 on NoS, in Pathé's catalogue the clip is listed as 16 January 1922. By this stage, the Treaty had been signed and ratified and the Treaty debate was raging throughout the country. If the later date is the correct one, again the item confirms de Valera's popularity, an interesting offering from a British newsreel which would most certainly want to reaffirm support for the Treaty. Discrepancies in cataloguing offer different possibilities in the connotations of the representation of de Valera's popularity. Given that the item is labelled 'Ireland' in the 'local/special' section of NoS's production information, it is likely to have been produced for Irish audiences only and was perhaps an attempt to cover differing reactions to the Treaty for Irish audiences, themselves split in opinion as to its validity as a solution to the 'Irish question'. A different view of de Valera is produced for British audiences, as indicated by the item *Sinn Féin's Would-Be Dictator*,[92] included in the British edition (listed on NoS as fourth item in the main British edition, whereas *Internees*

Welcomed Back,[93] showing 'enthusiastic scenes' on the return of prisoners, is produced for the Irish edition). The item does not appear on British Pathé's website under this name although it is likely to have been the same footage as appeared in the above-mentioned item showing de Valera in Galway.

The information given on NoS states that 'Mr De Valera accompanied by Mr Cathal Brugha (Minister of Defence) and Mr Richard Mulcahy (Chief of Staff) reviews members of the Irish Republican Army.' De Valera has been depicted in Galway with the same two members of his government. Given that no other similar item appears on the Pathé website, it is likely that the same footage has been repackaged with different political overtones for British and Irish audiences. This offers an interesting comment on newsreel production: newsreels were acutely aware of what audiences might find controversial. The consequence of producing controversial material was that if audiences didn't 'like' the newsreels, exhibitors could end their contracts with their newsreel provider. Keeping audiences 'happy' was commercially essential to newsreel companies. What made this more complex in Ireland was the difficulty in reconciling Unionist and Nationalist viewpoints when producing material. Ultimately, the distribution circuit was a British one – and newsreels were mostly aimed at audiences throughout Britain rather than Ireland. A compromise in production for Ireland was the issue of 'local/special' items for Irish audiences – an example is Gaumont Graphic's coverage of the return of Irish prisoners in its 12 December 1921 issue.[94] An intertitle reads: 'Sinn Féin Prisoners Released – crowds outside Bank of Ireland rush to greet first Peace freed internees.' There are shots of cobbled streets and trams outside the bank; prisoners are shown on the top deck of the tram in what almost appears to be a homecoming parade. Despite the newsreels' attempts to produce items of local interest, it was still difficult to make political content acceptable to audiences which were ideologically split and whose cultural outlook would have most certainly been piqued by newsreel coverage of this period. Out of this difficulty in Irish representation, arose a pattern of differentiating between north and south in the newsreels, a pattern which would conceptualize and visualize partition for Irish audiences.

Some of the difficulties in presenting Irish content are exemplified in Topical Budget's coverage of the post-Treaty debates. No sooner had the agreement been reached than Topical was reporting 'Irish Peace Imperilled by Extremists' in an item slightly different in tone to its optimistic coverage of the signing of the treaty.[95] The first intertitle reads: 'Mr De Valera leaving the Mansion House after demonising the Treaty.' Eamon de Valera is shown getting into an open-topped car; a woman sits beside him. 'But Dublin's attitude is obvious. Mr Griffith and Mr Michael Collins who signed the Treaty were wildly welcomed home.' There is a view of Griffith walking through a crowd, followed by shots of a dense crowd. The newsreel clearly aligns itself with the treaty signatories, and in reporting de Valera's 'demonisation' of the Treaty, subtly 'demonises' de Valera himself by dubbing him an 'extremist', threatening Ireland's final chance for peace. The next intertitle reads: 'Mr Shakespeare the Prime Minister's courier who dashed to Ulster by destroyer'; there is a shot of Shakespeare followed by the intertitle 'Sir James Craig arriving at Ulster Parliament to attack the Treaty.' Craig is shown getting out of a car and walking up a set of steps. What is interesting here is the lack of address of the Ulster question in the midst of the Treaty debate. Clearly Unionists wished to maintain the Union with Britain, and the Treaty threatened that link. It would appear that the newsreel is suggesting that the Treaty is the best option and should be accepted by its critics – de Valera and Craig. Once again the complex relationship between Unionists and the British government is demonstrated alongside the newsreels' difficulties in contextualizing such political complexities.

The next intertitle confirms this viewpoint by celebrating the release of Irish prisoners: 'triumphant procession of released internees' is accompanied by footage of a group of men standing in an open horse-drawn carriage on a cobbled street. The men are cheering and waving an Irish flag. The next intertitle reads: 'And "Dear, Dirty Dublin" is at Peace' and is followed by a view down O'Connell Street, shown to be relatively quiet. Topical Budget continues its coverage of the release of Irish prisoners in another item a few days later entitled *Further Pictures of Irish Peace*.[96] The first intertitle states: 'Long, Long Trail to Freedom. 1700 Internees released from Ballykinlar Camp.' Men carrying small suitcases are shown walking down a country road. They are wearing civilian clothes. There are then shots of uniformed men also carrying cases. A large crowd is depicted beside a stationary train in the countryside. There is a close-up of men and women holding a

Tricolour; the women are holding biscuit tins. People on the platform wave as the train leaves the station. On the same day, Gaumont released *Sinn Féin Parliament*,[97] asking 'Ratify or reject? Dáil Éireann meet – Irish parliament assemble to decide the all important question.' There are shots of cars arriving and men gathered on a set of steps. Topical Budget also deals with this meeting, opening with the intertitle 'Sinn Féin members meet at Dublin Parliament House for fateful session.'[98] There are overhead shots of the Mansion House, with the familiar crowds waiting outside. An intertitle states: 'A Kiss for de Valera's Hand!' and the film shows a woman rushing to kiss de Valera's hand as he leaves the Mansion House. Pathé's footage announces 'Momentous Meeting of Dáil Éireann. Members of the Dáil meet at University College for the ratification of the Peace Treaty.'[99] The shots are almost exactly the same as Topical Budget's footage, although from slightly different angles.

January 1922 begins with Michael Collins' visit to Armagh featured in Pathé Gazette.[100] The item opens with an intertitle announcing 'Michael Collins, the IRA leader, makes his first public appearance in his constituency at Armagh.' This is followed by a panning shot of three Ford Model T cars bearing Tricolours driving through a street, preceded by marching men wearing sashes and flanked by men walking alongside. Michael Collins sits in the second car. There are shots of crowds in the street and a hotel with a Tricolour flying outside it. A car drives up to the hotel while crowds gather round it. A mainly male crowd waits outside the doorway of a building. A group of men with Michael Collins among them leaves the building and push their way through the crowd. Michael Collins, sporting a small moustache, climbs onto a platform and remains still apart from a small gesture of scratching his nose whilst there is a great deal of movement in the crowd around him. Another man makes some opening remarks while Collins looks down to read over his speech. Collins gives his speech, looking down at intervals at his script. The platform, flanked by crowds, is draped with bunting and flags. People sit or lean against a fence in the foreground, some looking towards the camera. The item finishes with a close-up of Collins making an impassioned speech. Collins frequently appears animated in the newsreels – his charisma and energy is evident on the screen. He is often shown chatting and joking in a relaxed and casual manner whether it be with potential Irish voters[101] in *Irish*

Elections or with Treaty delegates outside 10 Downing Street.[102] This depiction ties in with accounts of Collins as a passionate and emotional man; in fact, Lloyd George commented on his behaviour during the Treaty negotiations, describing him as being 'just a wild animal'.[103] The fact that Gaumont Graphic featured an item on the 'Birthplace of Michael Collins' in their last January issue of 1922 is indicative of newsreel interest in the figure of Collins. The item shows Collins at the ruins of a country farmhouse (presumably his family home which had been burned down during the War of Independence). There is an unidentified man walking towards the camera, chatting and smiling. Other shots show a man leading a white horse through a courtyard followed by a scene with a man holding hands with two children. What is most interesting about this reel is the fact that at the height of post-Treaty tension, Collins was the signatory whose background was most interesting to Gaumont, and indeed other media, at the time.[104] Pathé features an extremely charismatic Collins in an issue from March 1922 entitled *Fighting Speech by Michael Collins*.[105] An intertitle introduces the item: 'Dublin. A Fighting Speech by Mr Michael Collins to huge crowd in shadow of old Irish Parliament, opens Free State Election Campaign.' A huge crowd is depicted listening to Collins speak. He is shown in close-up, shouting passionately to the crowd and finally raising his hand in the air and bringing his fist down in a violent gesture. The image portrayed of Collins throughout the newsreels is the antithesis of the portrayal of de Valera, who is often expressionless, understated in his movements and appears to have little rapport with the camera or those around him. This image of de Valera will be further explored in examination of his relationship with the newsreels during the 1930s.

Evacuation of British Troops

Pathé begins its coverage of the evacuation of British troops in *Realising Freedom in Dublin*.[106] The item opens with the intertitle 'soldiers are removing barbed wire barricades – the prelude to departure of all British troops'. Shots of sandbagged barricades are followed by close-ups of soldiers ripping away barbed wire and occasionally glancing at the camera. Topical Budget covers *The 'Surrender' of Dublin Castle*[107] on 19 January 1922. An intertitle explains that this 'historic building which for centuries has been the stronghold of the Crown [is] formally handed over to Provisional Government of Southern Ireland'. There is a view from above looking down on a crowd-lined street with vehicles passing through. The next intertitle states: 'Provisional Government, headed by Mr Collins, arrives to take over.' There are general views inside the courtyard of Dublin Castle. The last intertitles read: 'Exit the Viceroy, Lord Fitzalan', 'The Black & Tans pack up' and finally 'The last guard of the Castle dismissed'. Gaumont Graphic covers the event on the same day in *Dublin Castle Handed Over*.[108] An intertitle offers contextual information: 'Dublin Castle – Handed over to the Free State. Provisional Government installed. The Castle has been the seat of the Govt. since about 1560.' There are shots of an officer shaking hands with troops, who are then shown lifting their caps and cheering. There are scenes of crowds, comprised of military personnel and civilians, outside the entrance to Dublin Castle watching cars and horse-drawn carriages coming out. There is a cut to shots of suited men exiting through a doorway while crowds watch. Large crowds in the street watch a tank drive past before we see a woman amongst a largely male crowd, waving an indistinguishable flag; a policeman restrains her. Topical returns to the subject matter in light-hearted manner in *British Evacuate Ireland*[109] on 23 January. The intertitle reads: 'Topical Budget. British Evacuate Ireland after Hundreds of Years of Occupation. 60,000 troops pack up the Irish trouble in their old kit bags!' An individual soldier is shown packing up his bag, before we see a long line of soldiers in horse-drawn carts travelling on a country road. The soldiers are then shown at a railway station. Pathé's coverage on the same day reads: 'The Evacuation of Ireland. Vanguard of the 60,000 British troops leave for England.'[110] Gaumont Graphic also continues the footage on the same day with *IRA Guards at Dublin City Hall*.[111] The intertitle explains: 'Dublin City Hall taken over by Civilian Guards. Flags exchanged in the presence of Alderman Cosgrave, representing the Corporation.' A Tricolour is shown being hoisted up a flagpole by two men.

A few days later Gaumont features *Troops Leaving Cork*.[112] The lead intertitle states: 'evacuating Ireland – first actual embarkation pictures: troops leaving Cork Station and going aboard City of Cork SS "Glengarriff" and arriving at Fishguard Great Western Railway.' There are shots of a commanding officer leading troops out of a gateway with two clearly visible signs saying 'IN' and 'OUT' – troops are marching from the 'OUT' exit. They are carrying rifles, some wave and smile jovially at the camera and there is a relaxed air about the march. There is a cut to some troops standing by a wall with ships in the background while a boy is chatting to troops. They are relaxed and smiling, many looking at the camera. One lifts his cap to the camera. There are then shots of troops boarding the vessel in no particular formation, lifting boxes in a casual manner. There are shots of the ship pulling into the harbour. The next intertitle states: 'Taking home a pack of hounds used for tracking delinquents.' There are shots of soldiers, each with two dogs on leashes, walking towards the camera, again smiling and acknowledging the camera. Even the dogs don't look particularly fierce or threatening. Topical Budget continues the coverage with *The Great Trek*.[113] The opening intertitle reads: 'horse and foot still pouring out of Ireland.' A group of men are shown in front of the camera, an intertitle describing them as 'men of the Irish Free State who are taking the place of British Troops'. Two men wearing civilian clothes and carrying rifles on their shoulder are shown guarding a building. Pathé's coverage on the same day refers back to connotations of the Western Front in its opening intertitle: 'home from the Irish Front. Thousands of men, horses and guns are leaving daily.'[114] This is immediately followed by a shot of a large procession of horses. There are then various shots of troops boarding ships, accompanied with another word reminiscent of wartime: 'Everyone happy, and "Tommy" not the least.' The soldiers are shown cheering and waving from the boat before moving to the intertitle 'The first soldiers of the Irish Free State – mount guard over Dublin City Hall'. Three soldiers dressed in ties, hats and trench coats and carrying rifles are depicted. Pathé's *Irish Free State Soldiers, Receiving Uniforms* again refers to the word 'Tommy' in its opening intertitle: 'soldiers of the Irish Free State – receive first uniforms which paradoxically enough, are almost identical with Tommy's'.[115] The next shots feature the interior of a uniform factory, with workers sewing clothes. There is a close-up of an expressionless soldier being fitted for a uniform while workers look on. There is then a big close-up on an individual button, clearly depicting a harp and differentiating Irish uniforms from their British counterparts. Nevertheless, Pathé attempts through its intertitle to stress the similarity of the uniforms, apparently taking some pleasure in highlighting this fact for British (and presumably Irish) audiences. The distinction between uniforms is blurred, their connotations problematic.

The troops feature further in Gaumont's *Dublin – Beggar's Bush Barracks*.[116] An intertitle states: 'Beggar's Bush. Famous Barracks in IRA hands. Auxiliary Division Headquarters taken over by Irish Free State.' Troops are shown parading through crowded streets with a pipe band. One soldier is depicted carrying a Tricolour. Beggar's Bush appears again in Pathé's 6 February issue which opens with the intertitle: 'new history is being made daily in Ireland. Crowds cheer spic and span soldiers of Republican army at taking over of Beggar's Bush barracks, lately headquarters of the auxiliaries.'[117] The same issue also features an item on border discussions between Collins and Craig.[118] The opening intertitle reads: 'Captain Craig – Ulster's Leader – comes to Dublin to confer with Mr Michael Collins on difficult problem of boundaries.' Only Craig is depicted in the newsreel – mounting a set of steps and then in front of a set of railings, looking stern and formidable and lifting his hat to the crowd. While the military forces taking over from the British certainly included members of the Irish Republican Army, they also drew upon ex-servicemen from the British Army. (Five of the Irish infantry regiments were disbanded in June 1922.[119]) A Topical Budget item from the following December appears to show the evacuation of troops still in progress, even at the end of 1922.[120] Half of the item deals with the final evacuation of British troops, the intertitle stating: 'departure of last British troops marks beginning of new era in Ireland'. The second half of the item is devoted to Tim Healy, described as 'veteran Irish patriot', becoming first Governor of the Irish Free State. The Governor-General was the King's representative in Ireland, so in this item we have the military evacuation juxtaposed with an Irish 'patriot' as acting British representative.

Civil War

The Treaty debate intensified from the beginning of 1922, the most significant vote being taken on 7 January 1922 when the Treaty was ratified by sixty-four votes to fifty-seven, leading Tim Pat Coogan to comment that 'by seven votes, the people's representatives had accepted the foundation document on which independent Ireland was subsequently to be built'.[121] Almost immediately, pro- and anti-Treaty factions were formed, particularly within the IRA which had now become a large contingent of the south's main military force. With the army split, Civil War loomed and by March 1922, opponents of the Treaty formed a separate force.[122] Evacuation of British troops was still in progress at this stage, often causing military equipment to fall into the hands of anti-Treaty factions, equipment later to be used in civil warfare. Equally confusing was the fact that both pro- and anti-Treaty forces claimed to be the 'true IRA', although they became known in local communities as 'Free State' troops (pro-Treaty) and 'Irregulars' (anti-Treaty)[123]. The splits in allegiances were complex and caused by a variety of opinions and antagonisms, but the majority of the original IRA were anti-Treaty.[124]

Once again the newsreels would prove pro-Treaty in outlook. Pathé describes Eamon de Valera as 'the irreconcilable' in its item *Mr de Valera Opens Anti-Treaty Campaign*.[125] De Valera is pictured on a makeshift platform speaking in an animated and aggressive manner to the surrounding crowd. In contrast to previous depictions by the newsreels, he is shown as more animated than usual, waving his hands and shouting, leaning over the huge crowd below. Panning shots conclude the item by showing streets filled to capacity. It is clear from the newsreel that de Valera is vehement in his anti-Treaty stance and that he has a large amount of support. Collins is shown to be speaking to an even more impressive crowd in Cork in Pathé's 20 March item entitled *Michael Collins*.[126] The opening intertitle reads: 'great Cork Treaty Meeting. Mr Collins receives enthusiastic reception from the huge gathering despite salvoes of shots from a few malcontents.' Panning shots reveal vast crowds, cheering and waving. There is a cut to a close-up on Collins; he is scanning the crowd, making an impassioned speech. He is also depicted balanced on the very edge of the platform, trying to lean as close to the crowd as possible, and is gesticulating strongly. We then see the crowd cheering and waving. Next there appear to be scuffles in the crowd as people are shown leaving.

Pathé features the item *IRA Parade* in its 16 March 1922 edition, encapsulating in its title the lack of newsreel contextualization or sensitivity to the complexity of Irish politics at this stage. The opening intertitle describes how 'Mr RJ Mulcahy, Minister of Defence, hoists the flag at interesting Beggar's Bush ceremony.' Mulcahy is shown inspecting the troops and hoisting a large Tricolour. Just a couple of weeks later, Pathé details problems within the Defence Forces, but again in simplistic terms. On 4 April Pathé opens an Irish item with the intertitle 'Irish Army Crisis. 3,000 rebellious troops of IRA hold parade in defiance of headquarters.'[127] Panning overhead shots show a large and ordered formation of troops. There is a cut to a head-on view of a car, one man standing in the car and facing to the right of shot. To the left of shot a soldier stands holding a Tricolour in front of a formation of soldiers around the car. *Wexford Treaty Meeting* a week later reports more violent Treaty-related discussions, the opening intertitle describing 'lines torn up ... trains delayed'.[128] Two signallers are shown waving flags along parallel sets of train tracks. We then see a crowd standing beside a train, staring at the camera. A close-up of the crowd reveals many of them smiling, some glancing at the train and back to the camera. Then there are scenes of people standing on damaged tracks while there are some attempts to repair them.

Northern Ireland Prime Minister James Craig's response to increasing violence was to expand the 'B' class of Special Constables to include Protestant workers and farmers in particular. Fighting became so intense along the border in June 1922 that some farmers were forced to flee their homes, leaving their farms in the hands of the Specials.[129] These evacuations were covered by a Pathé item describing 'refugees from the Ulster Border – where fighting is intense – pouring into Dublin'.[130] There are shots of people lifting cases and possessions off a cart. The camera cuts to a close-up of a young child sitting on a piece of luggage while people mill round him. Other children are then shown lifting bundles. Through its close-up on a child, Pathé seemingly sought sympathy for northern workers forced to flee their homes. There is no comment on the subsequent fate of these families, particularly as northerners were forced to seek safety in Dublin.

Topical Budget depicts *The Battle of Belleek* in June 1922.[131] The opening intertitle reads: 'Topical's exclusive pictures of the Ulster border town seized by the Sinn Féiners. Troops moving into action.' Troops are shown marching down a country lane. There is a close-up of an artillery gun being taken into action. Armoured vehicles are shown passing down the same lane. The next intertitle describes 'shelling the village', which is followed by a long shot of an artillery gun being fired in a field. There is a panning shot looking down on the town of Belleek. An intertitle states: 'General and staff watching operations'. They are depicted looking through binoculars. The next intertitle states: 'Entering the village'; it is accompanied by footage of officers walking up a hill. Men in civilian clothes enter through a passage-way in a wall. We then see a close-up of troops resting in the street accompanied by the intertitle 'Lads who took the Town'. Another Topical Budget item in the same month describes 'loyal southern Irish Regiments'.[132] The opening intertitle explains: 'and while British Troops guard the Ulster Frontier, six loyal southern Irish Regiments – disbanded under the Treaty – hand their colours to the King for safe-keeping at Windsor'. An overhead view looks down on the army parade followed by shots of soldiers carrying the Union Jack. The camera then cuts to a close-up on soldiers carrying children followed by a panning shot of a large group of children.

Pathé's *Irish Elections*[133] (mentioned above) opens with Michael Collins talking to a woman milking a cow, then talking and laughing with three men, one of them sitting on a barrel. The newsreel shows Collins talking and shaking hands with a group of women, then an elderly couple. There is a cut to Collins making an impassioned speech to a crowd. Collins, the charismatic personification of the pro-Treaty stance, is featured again in Topical Budget's *Civil War in Ireland* a week later.[134] McKernan describes this particular newsreel as 'remarkably modern in manner', pointing out that 'nothing in War Office Topical Budget took the cinema audience quite so near the fighting';[135] the pictures of shelling which follow are unusual in the context of newsreel coverage at this stage. Once again Topical Budget appears more comprehensive in its coverage of Irish affairs than some of its counterparts. The opening intertitle states: 'Civil War in Ireland. Mr Michael Collins' desperate fight against Irregulars. These remarkable pictures of the bombardment of the Rebels' stronghold in the Four Courts, Dublin, were taken by Topical's operator lying on his back under fire.' There is a long shot of the Four Courts building from the far side of the River Liffey. 'A Sniper's nest' is the next intertitle, featuring views from the top of the Four Courts building. 'Free State guns in action' is accompanied by footage of military vehicles in the street. 'Shells bursting on the Four Courts' gives way to smoky shots of shelling again at the Four Courts. There is then a view of troops manning a large gun in the street. The next scenes feature shots of gunfire followed by sandbags in position beneath broken windows. 'Snipers emptied the streets' is accompanied by a man looking down an empty street. 'Homeless!' proclaims the next title, showing adults and children seated on the pavement. 'Rory O'Connor Commandant of the Rebels and defender of the Four Courts' is accompanied by a drawing of O'Connor, and 'Later. The Four Courts go up in flames' is accompanied by a drawing of the building on fire, again testifying to the 'aftermath' of newsreel footage – in this case drawings are used as substitutes for footage of the actual event. The final shots are of smoky, damaged buildings along the Quays. Gaumont features *Bombardment in Sackville Street* on the same day,[136] showing the GPO, various buildings with sandbags in the windows, shots of Nelson's Pillar and the by now familiar smoky depictions. In fact, McKernan (1992) suggests that scenes of fighting may have appealed to audiences, which perhaps explains why there are so many smoky shots of artillery fire present in coverage of 1920s Ireland.

Hemming in the Rebels[137] in Topical Budget's 6 July issue features a view of an army van driving down an empty Sackville Street (later renamed O'Connell street) towards O'Connell Bridge, where a group of people has gathered. The next intertitles state: 'Moran Hotel after bombing attack' and 'crowds watch the fighting all day long'. A close-up view of a priest sitting in an open-topped car is accompanied by the intertitle 'Father Albert as mediator under flag of truce.' A man to the priest's right holds a white flag. The item finishes showing a fireman trying to put out a fire. Pathé also features damage to Sackville Street in an issue produced the same day. *Rounding up the Rebels*[138] offers 'scenes during the successful attack by Free State troops on rebels' last stronghold, Sackville Street'. There are shots of soldiers searching men on a bridge followed by footage of two soldiers escorting a man along an empty street. The next intertitle reads: 'three 18pdr shells were sufficient to make rebels in Moran's hotel hang out white flag'. There are shots of crowds milling around outside Moran's hotel, then a close-up on its broken windows. The next intertitle and scenes are reminiscent of First World War footage. 'The Red Cross did noble work in the battle zone' gives way to panning shots of empty streets with just a few soldiers. The next shots are of 'Father Albert – a negotiator for peace'. Father Albert is depicted in a car with soldiers. More violence is featured in Topical Budget's *Dublin's Civil War*.[139] The item opens with the intertitle 'how the Rebels were burned out of Sackville Street'. Clouds of smoke signify conflict while intertitles describe 'the first shell' and 'first shell bursting'. A building is depicted with billowing smoke and then fire coming from the ground-floor windows. This footage is remarkable in that it shows the shelling actually taking place, rather than the damage inflicted in its wake which was more typical of news-reel coverage. 'Rounded up' is followed by shots of a group of army men confronting and then surrounding a man. The intertitle 'the Red Cross' is followed by overhead shots of two men carrying white flags.

In contrast to the violence depicted in Dublin, a Pathé issue from 17 July describes a *Peaceful Twelfth*.[140] The opening intertitle read 'A peaceful "Twelfth". 50,000 Orangemen celebrate the 232nd anniversary of the Battle of the Boyne.' Shots of a relatively slow and orderly procession contrast starkly with smoky scenes of Civil War battles. The parade is shown marching towards Belfast City Hall – all buildings depicted are shown intact and the streets are full in comparison with the empty, damaged streets of Dublin's city centre. However, these shots are qualified with the explanation that 'armoured cars protected the procession'. We see the armoured cars flanking the parade before the camera cuts to scenes at Balmoral where two Union Jacks decorate the speaker's podium. A close-up on James Craig features him speaking to a large if rather dispersed crowd.

Topical Budget features the *Fall of Limerick*[141] in its 29 July 1922 issue, claiming 'Exclusive pictures taken by a Topical Staff cameraman with the National Army'. The intertitle further explains: 'These are the first pictures which show the organisation and established military system now under the supreme command of General Michael Collins.' There is an overhead view of the River Shannon followed by close-ups on damaged buildings including a church. Michael Collins appears again in a Pathé issue two days later.[142] This time Pathé claims the 'first and exclusive portrait in uniform' while showing a uniformed Collins facing the camera, smiling and chatting to the cameraman. Topical Budget's next item on Irish matters opens with the intertitle 'Irish National Army Sweeping On. Capture of another Town after brisk bombardment. Passed by Irish Censor. Topical Budget.'[143] Men are shown pushing a gun through a field followed by shots of military vehicles on a country road. One is flying a Tricolour. Soldiers are then shown getting out of vehicles. Next there is a damaged building with 'Vote Sinn Féin IRA' written in large letters.

Again Pathé claims 'unique' pictures in *Mopping Up. Battle of Adare*.[144] The intertitle reads: 'Ireland. Mopping Up – Unique pictures taken under fire – of actual surrender of band of rebels during battle of

Adare. Pathé Gazette.' Soldiers are shown marching on a wide dirt road. There are views of an armoured car and rebels surrendering. Even though Pathé captures the surrender, footage of the battle is markedly absent.

Arthur Griffith's death is featured in Pathé's 21 August issue. The item opens with the intertitle: 'Dublin mourns dead president. Remarkable demonstration of public sympathy. Impressive scenes as the Cortege wends its way through hushed streets thronged with half a million mourners.' The overall item lasts eleven minutes and features scenes of the lengthy state funeral procession, with coffin draped in a Tricolour, vast crowds lining the streets, and finishes with scenes by the graveside. Michael Collins is featured in a further Pathé item entitled 'Michael Collins at Burial of Arthur Griffith', an item obviously filmed before Collins's death but released afterwards.[145] The opening intertitle reads: 'General Michael Collins. A peculiarly melancholy interest attaches to this – the last picture ever taken of assassinated leader – at the grave-side of Mr Arthur Griffith.' The newsreel's emotional tone evokes the newsreels' general sympathy towards Collins after December 1921 as a pro-Treaty signatory. Collins is depicted in the left of the frame watching gravediggers shovel earth into the open grave. The next Pathé item is 'Ireland Mourns Passing Michael Collins'[146] which opens with the intertitle 'A nation in mourning. Irish capital struck dumb with grief at "coming home" of General Michael Collins.' There is footage of a military guard beside the coffin, followed by rows of people gathered along pavements, then people filing into a building, probably to pay their respects. Footage of the open coffin follows, with several soldiers standing guard. This Pathé issue also features *Riots in Belfast*[147] which contains no intertitles but shows footage of children sitting amidst a pile of rubble and then cuts to adults picking their way through the remains of a completely destroyed house.

Pathé provides more footage of the funeral three days later, again testifying to the huge importance of the story and the newsreels' attitude to the dead leader: 'Dublin. More than half a million mourners bid a silent farewell at passing of Michael Collins – Ireland's Soldier Statesman.'[148] There is a view of O'Connell Street packed with people. The coffin is carried out of the church by eight soldiers and placed on an open, horse-drawn carriage and draped with a Tricolour. This is followed by general views of the funeral procession and finally the lowering of the coffin at the graveyard. Topical Budget's coverage opens with the intertitle 'Let the Dublin Guards Bury Me!'[149] and then goes on to state: 'All Dublin watched the honouring of Michael Collins' dying wish.' There is footage of the coffin being carried out of church by officers. The next intertitle states that 'the only flower on his coffin was a lily from his fiancée', again attempting to evoke an emotional response in audiences with the poignant nature of the intertitle. The next shots show the coffin processing past the GPO with huge crowds lining the streets.

Pathé continues coverage of Collins's funeral into September with an item entitled 'Grave of Michael Collins'.[150] The item opens with the intertitle 'emblems of sympathy. Floral tributes from the world over on the grave of the late General Collins.' Mourners are shown beside a large amount of flowers and wreaths. The next intertitle states: 'Mr Sean Collins and his sister, Miss Johanna Collins, visit their brother's grave.' Collins's siblings are shown beside the grave, reading the floral tributes. There are then panning shots of a vast array of flowers. These humanizing depictions of Collins are interesting, given the vigour with which he conducted attacks on the British Establishment and military during the War of Independence.

A Pathé item on 16 October opens with the intertitle 'General Mulcahy (Commander-in-Chief) hoists the flag over Gormanstown Aerodrome, the former Headquarters of the "Black and Tans".'[151] A small parade of soldiers, flanked by two clergymen, is shown carrying the Tricolour. The flag is set down on an altar by one of the soldiers and blessed with incense by a priest. The flag is hoisted while the soldiers take a salute. There are then shots of a larger military parade. The item ends with a shot of the hoisted Tricolour. The nature of the relationship between Church and military is a strong feature of the newsreels in the 1930s and 1940s and will be discussed further in subsequent chapters.

In November, Pathé featured an item on Terence MacSwiney's sisters.[152] An opening intertitle rather frivolously states that 'it must be in the family! While Miss M. MacSwiney hunger-strikes inside Mountjoy Prison, her sister Annie does the same outside.' There are shots of a crowd outside Mountjoy and then a close-up of two partitions, with a gap in the middle. Through the gap we can see a bed. To the right of one partition a woman is sitting with a crucifix. There is then a close-up on Annie MacSwiney, wrapped up in bed and staring straight ahead mournfully: the visuals are clearly at odds with the flippant intertitles. An item in the same issue continues in the same dismissive and distanced vein, commenting on the execution of former British Army soldier Erskine Childers. The author of the spy novel *The Riddle of the Sands*, Childers had become interested in the nationalist cause and progressed up the ranks of the Home Rule movement, becoming secretary general of the Treaty delegation. Bitterly opposed to the Treaty, Childers joined the anti-Treaty movement and was executed by the Provisional Government in November 1922.[153] Pathé shows no mercy to the London-born Childers, who had been executed for possession of a pistol given to him by Collins,[154] in its comment: 'Erskine Childers – the Renegade – who vainly invoked aid of King he betrayed to save him from death sentence.'[155] There is a medium close-up of a suited Childers talking to camera. Pathé's coverage of both items is not only cynical, but also suggests a deeper distrust of what were seen to be Nationalist extremists, prepared to risk everything for Irish independence.

1923 – a More 'Civilized' Representation of Ireland

The footage of 1923 was to be much less condemnatory and much less violent; Collins's death in August signified the end of smoky shots of shelling and damaged buildings in the newsreels, which once again become interested in reporting on political events and figures rather than violent conflict, although it was probably practically difficult to capture footage once the conflict moved out of Dublin. Even before the end of the Civil War there is less coverage of Irish politics in general. Coverage of Ireland peaked in 1921, with 11 per cent of British newsreel stories covering Ireland, a large jump from just 3 per cent in 1920. While 1922 and 1923 both offered 6 per cent coverage of Irish items, the stories connected to Ireland in 1923 are significantly less political, returning to society events, sport and personalities. The following explorations are of some items of political interest.

Pathé's 18 January edition features an item entitled *President Cosgrave* covering the destruction of Cosgrave's home by 'Irregulars'.[156] Opening with the intertitle 'President Cosgrave visits his burnt-out home at Rathfarnham', the item shows footage of the remains of Cosgrave's home. The roof of the building is gone and the exterior walls are blackened with smoke damage. Cosgrave is shown speaking to reporters at the front door. The next intertitle reads: 'all that remains of his valuable library'. A pile of burnt and tattered books lies on the ground; some of the pages are blown away in the wind. A man with a rifle sifts through the remains of the books. Cosgrave is then depicted in the interior of the house surveying the damage. The item is sympathetic to Cosgrave, seen as a figure of authority in a violent civil war. Cosgrave is associated with books and learning in the item – the 'Irregulars' are associated with the destruction of this. Given that Cosgrave was a pro-Treaty figure, this was a convenient representation of a more 'civilized' Irish leader, victim to the anarchic anti-Treaty forces.

A new Governor of Ulster is reported in March 1923. Pathé's intertitle reads: 'Duke of Abercorn makes state entry into Belfast.'[157] A procession is shown through Belfast streets decked with Union Jacks. Abercorn is shown inspecting troops at Belfast City Hall. Pathé's accompanying intertitle reads: 'The Duke of Abercorn, Lord Pirrie, The Marquis of Londonderry, K.G., etc, etc. Pathé Gazette exclusive by special permission.' The dignitaries are pictured seated for a photograph. At a time when partition was beginning to become a normality, the north was positioned in the newsreels through iconic imagery of Union Jacks as very clearly British. There was no recognition of northern Nationalists.

The physical manifestation of a border was evident in coverage of customs operations in Pathé's *Anything to Declare* in April 1923.[158] The opening intertitle explains that 'All goods crossing "frontier" are examined by Free State's new customs.' Customs officers are shown thoroughly checking cars going across the border in a rural area. More significantly, this item recognizes the border between north and south and the necessary customs checks involved. It was the visualization of the apparatus of partition which began to implant the idea of a partitioned Ireland in both Irish and British audiences, who were still coming to terms with the practicalities of the Irish situation.

The question *Free State or Republic?* was still being asked in August 1923 by Topical Budget.[159] The item shows 'soldiers guarding Dublin polling booth in momentous election'. This election saw the first appearance of Cumann na nGaedheal, a party formed just a few months previously by pro-Treaty Sinn Féin TDs (Teachtaí Dála). The election was to prove extremely successful for Cumann na nGaedheal, although there is little detail given about its results in this item. The footage shows the counting of votes, followed by General Mulcahy, while the intertitle explains that 'General Mulcahy, Minister of Defence, whose troops captured de Valera, has been returned.' Clearly the capture of the disruptive de Valera is recognized as beneficial, and Mulcahy has been suitably rewarded by his election (and, by proxy, suitably supported by the Irish people). The newsreel then shows Mrs Despard ('Lord French's sister. A noted Republican') in St Stephen's Green in Dublin. The final figure to be depicted is Vivion de Valera, blond haired with crooked teeth and glasses and described as 'son of the Republican leader'. There is no explanation given to the shots of de Valera's son, although it may have been an attempt to humanize a figure recognized by the newsreels as 'mysterious'. For the Irish electorate, he signified his father's imprisonment and had the potential to evoke public sympathy.

Newsreel coverage of events in the south of Ireland during the 1920s eclipsed coverage of the north. The Unionist regime had not, however given up its interest in publicity and harnessing the media for propaganda. John Hill also defines film as 'a fertile ground for propaganda' in the promotion of Northern Ireland post-partition.[160] An important post-partition organization was the Ulster Association, established in April 1922 to promote the image of 'Ulster' at home and abroad and to assist the government in maintaining its links with Britain. Through offices in Belfast and London, news and favourable publicity was distributed throughout Britain, amounting to '60,000 columns of information in the world's press'.[161] The organization's publicity activities were transferred to the Ministry of Commerce in 1925, subsequent to agreement on the border issue, although much of its funding was redirected to the Ulster Tourist Development Association in 1927.[162] While 1920s newsreels were necessarily preoccupied with events in the south of Ireland, particularly during the Civil War, in the 1930s the newsreels were to serve the Northern Ireland government's desires to construct a positive image of the north. The newsreels in the 1930s began to build on their represen-tation of a violent and self-destructive southern Ireland in the 1920s and present the north as a positive alternative of an obedient, industrial Irishness which was loyal to the British government and monarchy.

In discussing Ireland's indigenous newsreel, *Irish Events*, Ruth Barton suggests that

British newsreels of the day, such as those of Topical Budget, depicted the events of 1916 and the later Civil War (1922–23) as an assault on property and propriety, with the camera lingering on burning buildings and looted shops. The defeat of the 'rebels' in 1916 was emphasized through footage of prisoners being marched off under guard and the subsequent British withdrawal represented as an act of goodwill. Sinn Féin prisoners held under martial law were, it was reported by the Pathé Gazette in 1920, treated as 'prisoners-of war' whilst sympathy for Michael Collins in his battle against the 'irregulars' was expressed in a number of newsreels. In contrast, Whitten's footage, although technically more primitive, made direct appeal to the hearts of its Irish audience.[163]

It is hardly surprising that Norman Whitten's indigenously produced newsreel series, Irish Events, differs from external British representation. However, while the general impression given by the British newsreel companies is one of an inherently violent (Nationalist) Ireland, the complexity of Irish politics is demonstrated somewhat by contradictions in the newsreel footage. Whilst there is a proliferation of smoky scenes of conflict, there is also, occasionally, a recognition of deeper historical issues which the newsreels cannot contextualize. McKernan highlights this in his praise for Topical's coverage of events in Ireland in this period and it is perhaps Topical Budget, above other companies, which may have alluded more openly to the complexity of Irish politics. Barton suggests that the defeat of the 1916 rebels is emphasized through footage of prisoners being marched off under guard and this may have been the case for British audiences. For audiences in Ireland watching this footage it is possible that sympathy is evoked for the prisoners by clearly showing their faces and the face of one of the executed leaders. The differing potential responses of audiences to this material also reflects the complex changing reactions to the Rising and the prolonged executions of its leaders.

One particular representation of Loyalist Belfast comes from an unlikely source, Norman Whitten's Irish Events newsreel. *The Agony of Belfast* features footage of children in streets littered with debris and run-down houses. Many of them stare at the camera. Some women look on, making the footage appear almost staged. The graffiti in the background reads: 'no pope here', while a panning shot of children reveals the corner of a mural of William of Orange. Overhead shots of the city centre are interspersed with more shots of children playing in debris against a backdrop mural of King William painted on the gable wall of a house. The newsreel then covers an implied eviction through panning shots of a family outside a house with furniture piled up on the pavement. The camera cuts to sandbags on the pavement with children standing alongside while well-dressed women walk past and look back at the children[164] Ironically, at a time when British newsreels were seldom representing Unionism in their items, Norman Whitten chose to film a Loyalist area for his Irish newsreel. While Whitten shows a Catholic eviction, he also depicts the poverty of Loyalist Belfast. His use of a Shakespearean quote – 'where civil blood makes civil hands unclean' – suggests a condemnation of the conflict as a whole. The play from which this quote is taken, *Romeo and Juliet*, features a tragic love story set against a background of rival factions. By the end of the play,

4.2 Irish Events: *The Agony of Belfast*, Courtesy of the IFI Irish Film Archive.

its two main protagonists are dead and the final conclusion is that 'all are punish'd'.[165] In conflict, both sides have suffered without gain and two young lives have been lost. In Whitten's newsreel, the young of both sides are depicted – the Protestant children sitting on a pile of rubble and the Catholic children outside the house from which their family has been evicted. Whitten's ultimate comment seems to be that the youth of both communities will suffer, and there is little evidence of gain through this political conflict.

A Pathé compendium piece comprising footage from various events across a number of years exemplifies the images of Ireland depicted in the newsreels during the conflicts of the early 1920s. Entitled *Riots and Revolutions*,[166] the first intertitle reads: 'crowds must be kept moving, and clashes between opposing factions are daily occurrences'. There are shots of running crowds pursued by troops while two women look on. There is a cut to soldiers lying on the ground firing rifles. The next intertitle reads: 'The New Lord Mayor of Cork, Donald O'Callaghan – the third mayor Cork has had in eight months'. This is followed by a medium close-up of the new mayor. His expression is initially serious and then he smiles as if told to by the cameraman. There is a cut to shots of a funeral cortège, and military procession, juxtaposing the mayor, a symbol of Irish politics, with a funeral cortège, a symbol of death – a stark comment on the connection between Irish affairs and violent conflict (and a particularly accurate one, given the fate of the two previous Lord Mayors of Cork). The next title has a different design and is only on the screen momentarily – possibly as a result of an earlier edit: 'Dublin, Ireland. Hundreds of victims in wake of Irish disorders – British soldiers pay final tribute to comrades killed in ambush.' Another intertitle follows: 'Reprisal raids by the "Black & Tans" continue to spread death and destruction – scenes of ruins in town of Trim.' This constructs the Black and Tans as a ruthless force, determined to stamp out Irish insurrection. It also suggests that the Irish appetite for violence is so profound that such an unruly force is needed to keep Irish rebels in check. Accompanying this message are shots of wreckage and burnt-out buildings.

The next intertitle reads: 'Fleeing with all their possessions – the Sinn Féin flag leads the way.' People are shown loading possessions into a cart outside their house. The cart moves off with man at the front holding up a Tricolour. The action then moves to 'Walls of the Four

Courts Building which tell the tale of a 5-day bombardment'. Shelling of the Four Courts is shown with smoke drifting from nearby building; the streets in these shots are virtually empty. A close-up on the Four Courts reveals the extent of the damage. 'Free State soldiers receiving medical attention after their victory ... ' is followed by a shot of a soldier having his head bandaged by another soldier while he smokes a cigarette. There are shots of barricaded streets and a row of men with their hands up being searched by a soldier: 'Barricaded windows in hotels which were used as strongholds by the Republicans'; 'Free State troops patrol almost every street in Dublin, and all the passersbys are subjected to a thorough search.' Another title reads: 'Sinn Féin demonstrations sweep Ireland – British use tanks to quell riot and seize arms at Sinn Féin arsenal'; this is followed by shots of crowds of troops around a large tank. The newsreel gallops through various scenes of ruined buildings, shelling, funeral processions and evictions, juxtaposing politics and death and presenting an anarchic and chaotic picture of contemporary Ireland. It also comments on newsreel portrayal of Irish politics at this time – full of images of violence and anarchy and void of any political analysis. Just as Aldgate claims of the newsreel coverage of the Spanish Civil war was misleading, so too were the newsreels covering Ireland's War of Independence and Civil War which lacked explanation and were highly selective in their portrayal of events for the British and Irish public.

Conclusion

There are many discrepancies with regard to dating during this period. One example is *Great Sinn Féin Round Up*, dated simply 1919 on Pathé, and not even mentioned on NoS.[167] The first intertitle reads: 'Great Sinn Féin Round Up. Armoured car and tank used in military raid on Sinn Féin "Arsenal". (Exclusive Pictures).' A tank is depicted in the bottom right-hand corner of the intertitle. The intertitle gives way to another one stating that 'Crowds cheer arrested suspects who were hurried away in lorries.' There are then overhead shots of armoured cars driving through crowds. While it is clear that the onlookers watch with interest, there are no obvious examples of cheering: hands are by sides, and there is little obvious bodily movement concurrent with cheering – no raised hands, hats or repeated movements. As the shots are overhead we cannot see facial expressions and there is nothing in the general crowd's posture to suggest cheering. Even without accurate dating, this newsreel offers an interesting insight into how intertitles could be used to suggest to audiences what was happening in accompanying footage. By the end of the 1920s, newsreels were on the brink of the greatest development of the genre, the advent of sound. Sound commentaries, as we shall see in subsequent chapters, were used differently to intertitles, but offered similar and even stronger propaganda potential in explaining and critiquing and even creating meaning for the images to which they were connected.

A great deal of the material covering Ireland's move towards partition and its immediate aftermath covers the violent political conflict within which the two states of Ireland emerged. This material, however, is punctuated and diluted by the standard 'trite' newsreel content of sports events and personalities. In particular, when 'personalities' were royals or British representatives, this served to normalize what was essentially a time of great upheaval; it also continued to make associations with all things 'British' and to integrate Ireland into British culture at a time when Nationalists were seeking out a new Irish identity, independent from all connection with Britain. The dominant ideology of the newsreels is unsurprising: given a lack of sustained indigenous production, cinema exhibitors were left with British newsreels for inclusion in their programmes.[168]

Another significant item covers internees at Ballykinlar Camp, imprisoned under the Special Powers Act of 1922, many held until 1924. The introductory intertitle opens with 'near Belfast. Martial Law in Ireland. Scenes in the first great concentration camp of captured Sinn Féiners who are treated as prisoners-of-war'. This item is significant in that it associates the north with the Irish conflict. The prisoners are being held near Belfast: this suggests that Belfast is a secure enough location to house a POW camp, again confirming its status as more orderly than the conflict-ridden south. The next intertitle states that 'some "Shinners" are camera-shy!' There are general views of the camp with its barbed wire and corrugated buildings, verifying the intertitle's evocation of a POW camp. The prisoners are shown parading in the yard and tidying their huts. Next there is a close-up of a door with the word 'church' on it. Written in chalk below this is 'Our priest is on the run', and partly rubbed out below is 'We want more food.' A man is shown writing 'Up De Valera' and then 'IRA'. In this short section, the newsreel sums up many of the associations the future 'Éire' would have, particularly during the 1930s – de Valera as undisputed leader; the Church and State intertwined; the struggle for 'food' and the economic war; the IRA as a disruptive force.

From the end of 1924, the majority of newsreel footage of Ireland for the rest of the decade covers sporting events, with the occasional dog show, royal visit or religious festival. Remnants of the conflict of the early 1920s are echoed in commemorations of the deaths of John Redmond, Arthur Griffith and Michael Collins, or coverage of reconstruction of the Four Courts. Politics is also present in stories about border issues; one in particular featuring the arrest of the 'stormy petrel',[169] Eamon de Valera, on his crossing of the border pre-empts the newsreels' attitude to de Valera in the 1930s and 1940s. It is in the mid to late 1920s that partition is evoked by scenes of loyalist rallies in the north, and military parades and drilling exercises in the south. This is exemplified perfectly by Gaumont Graphic which covers 'Memorial of the 1916 rebellion' in its 12 May 1925 edition and then 'Empire Day at Belfast' in the north in its 25 May edition. Frequent depictions of religious festivals in the south are counterbalanced with celebrations of Orangeism in the north. It is at this point that the newsreels begin to conceptualize partition and create differing identities for north and south, and this ongoing process is particularly evident in the 1930s.

NOTES

1. *Sinn Féin Parliament.* War Office Topical Budget, Issue 387–2, 27 January 1919.
2. Bardon (1992), p.465.
3. *In Memory of John Redmond.* Topical Budget, Issue 395–2, 24 March 1919.
4. *Canadians in Ireland.* Topical Budget, Issue 396–1, 27 March 1919.
5. *Nurse vs Tommy*, Pathé, 1919. This item does not appear on NoS. It appears on the Digital Film Archive, dated simply 1919. It is available for download on the Pathé website, dated 1914–19. www.britishpathe.com
6. *Dublin's Peace Day Procession.* Gaumont Graphic, Issue 870, 24 July 1919.
7. *Man of Ulster.* Gaumont Graphic, Issue 876, 14 August 1919.
8. *Irish Guards Visit to Belfast.* Pathé Gazette, Issue 416–1, 14 August 1919.
9. *Ulster Celebrates Peace.* Topical Budget, Issue 416–1, 14 August 1919.
10. *Comrades of the Great War.* Gaumont Graphic, 26 April 1919. This item does not appear on NoS.
11. O'Broin (1983), p.5
12. *The Mystery of de Valera.* Topical Budget, Issue 389–2, 10 February 1919.
13. Coogan (2003), p.75.

14. *Re-Enter de Valera*. Topical Budget, Issue 397–1, 3 April 1919.
15. *Under Martial Law*. Gaumont Graphic, Issue 845, 28 April 1919.
16. Bardon (1992), p.463.
17. *Strikers' Demonstrations in Belfast*. Gaumont Graphic, Issue 821, 3 February 1919.
18. *Great Fire in Donegall Street*. Gaumont Graphic, Issue 821, 3 February 1919.
19. *Ulster Celebrates Peace*. Topical Budget, Issue 416–1, 14 August 1919.
20. *De Valera in Boston, USA*. Pathé Gazette, Issue 593, 28 August 1919.
21. Hannigan (2008), pp.46–7.
22. Francis M. Carroll, *American Opinion and the Irish Question 1910–23* (Dublin: Gill & Macmillan, 1978) cited in Coogan (2003), p.86.
23. *American Reception to De Valera*. Gaumont Graphic Unreleased, 19 August 1919.
24. Bardon (1992), p.465.
25. *War of Reprisals*. Pathé Gazette, Issue 706, 27 September 1920.
26. *Reprisals in Ireland Condemned by Sir Hamar Greenwood*. Pathé Gazette, Issue 708, 4 October 1920.
27. Coogan (2003), p.83.
28. *General Sir Neville MacCready*. Pathé Gazette, Issue 657, 8 April 1920.
29. O'Broin (1983), p.9.
30. *Death of the Lord Mayor of Cork*. Pathé Gazette, Issue 716, 1 November 1920.
31. *Funeral of Terence MacSwiney*. Irish Events, Irish Film Archive, Dublin. Although an intertitle for this film states 'October 1921' it is actually footage from the previous year.
32. One of the men killed had been wrongly identified as a secret agent and was, in fact, an Irish vet. There were further injuries and fatalities involving men who were not part of the 'Cairo gang'.
33. Hart (2005), pp.240–1.
34. *Murdered Officers – Dublin's Tribute*. Gaumont Graphic, Issue 1011, 29 November 1920. This item does not appear on NoS.
35. *Murdered Officers Borne to England*. Pathé Gazette, Issue 724, 29 November 1920.
36. O'Broin (1983), p.9.
37. *No-One Can Insult Our Flag*. Pathé Gazette, Issue 722, 25 November 1920.
38. *Side Lights on Sinn Féin*. Pathé Gazette, Issue 723, 25 November 1920.
39. *Ireland's Agony*. Topical Budget, Issue 486–1, 16 December 1920.
40. *Reprisals by Order*. Pathé Gazette, Issue 735, 6 January 1921.
41. *Sir Hamar Greenwood Reviews and Addresses RIC Auxiliaries in Phoenix Park*. Pathé Gazette, Issue 741, 27 January 1921.
42. *Funeral of Di Tobias O'Sullivan*. Pathé Gazette, Issue 741, 27 January 1921.
43. *All's Fair In …* . Pathé Gazette, Issue 744, 7 February 1921.
44. *First Meeting of White Cross to Relieve Suffering in Ireland at the Mansion House*. Pathé Gazette, Issue 744, 7 February 1921.
45. *Lady Sykes Visits Reprisal Scenes at Sixmilebridge, Co. Clare*. Pathé Gazette, Issue 744, 7 February 1921.
46. *American Mission*. Pathé Gazette, Issue 747, 17 February 1921.
47. *Report of American Committee for Relief in Ireland*. New York: Treasurer's and Secretary's Office, 1922.
48. *Business as Usual*. Pathé Gazette, Issue 749, 24 February 1921.
49. *Meet of the Ward Union Hunt at Ratoath*. Pathé Gazette, Issue 743, 3 February 1921.
50. *The Dear Little Shamrock*. Pathé Gazette, Issue 755, 17 March 1921.
51. *Ireland Solves Housing Problem*. Pathé Gazette, Issue 760, 4 April 1921.
52. *Lord Chancellor's Easter Levee*. Pathé Gazette, Issue 762, 11 April 1921.
53. *Viscount Fitzalan*. Pathé Gazette, Issue 770, 9 May 1921.
54. *Viscountess Powerscourt*. Pathé Gazette, Issue 771, 12 May 1921.
55. Bardon (1992), p.477.
56. *Ulster's New Leader*. Pathé Gazette, Issue 745, 10 February 1921.
57. *Northern Ireland Parliamentary Representatives*. Pathé Gazette, 1921. This item appears on NI Screen's Digital Film Archive. There is no entry for the item on NoS.

58. *Polling Day Scenes*. Pathé Gazette, Issue 776, 30 May 1921.
59. *Ulster's Parliament Assembles*. Topical Budget, Issue 511–1, 9 June 1921.
60. *State Opening of the Northern Irish Parliament*. Gaumont Graphic, 22 June 1921. There is no entry on NoS for this item.
61. *State Opening of Ulster Parliament*. Pathé Gazette, Issue 781, 16 June 1921.
62. The newsreels occasionally negotiated exclusive rights to coverage of particular events.
63. Bardon (1992), p.481.
64. Ibid., p.482.
65. *Lord Londonderry's Garden Party at Botanic Gardens*. Gaumont Graphic, Issue 1070, 23 June 1921.
66. *Mansion House Conference*. Pathé Gazette, Issue 787, 7 July 1921.
67. *Prayer for Peace*. Pathé Gazette, Issue 787, 7 July 1921.
68. *De Valera and Members of Irish Republican Party Attend Meeting in Mansion House*. Pathé Gazette, Issue 787, 7 July 1921.
69. *Ulster's Great Day*. Pathé Gazette, Issue 788, 11 July 1921.
70. *Is it the Dawn?* Topical Budget, Issue 515–2, 11 July 1921.
71. McKernan (1992), p.134
72. Ibid.
73. Ibid.
74. *I Want Peace*. Topical Budget, Issue 516–1, 14 July 1921.
75. *Threshold of Irish Peace*. Gaumont Graphic, Issue 1076, 14 July 1921.
76. Coogan (2003), p.93.
77. *Ulster Day the Twelfth*. Topical Budget, 1921. This item appears on the Northern Ireland Screen's Digital Film Archive. There is no corresponding NoS entry.
78. *Mr de Valera at Downing Street*. Gaumont Graphic, Issue 1077, 18 July 1921.
79. *Sinn Féiners in Downing Street*. Pathé Gazette, Issue 790, 18 July 1921.
80. Bardon (1992), p.482.
81. *Ireland a Dominion*. Pathé Gazette, Issue 793, 28 July 1921.
82. *De Valera in London*. Pathé Gazette, Issue 793, 28 July 1921.
83. T. Ryle Dwyer, *Michael Collins and the Treaty: His Difference with de Valera* (Dublin: Mercier Press, 1981), p.46 cited in Ryan (1989), p.11.
84. *Irish Peace Congress*. Pathé Gazette, Issue 815, 13 October 1921.
85. O'Broin (1983), p.51.
86. Ibid., p.74.
87. *Forgive and Forget*. Topical Budget, Issue 537–1, 8 December 1921.
88. *Irish Free State*. Topical Budget, Issue 537–1, 8 December 1921.
89. *Peace Council at the Palace*. Topical Budget, Issue 537–1. 8 December 1921
90. Coogan (2003), p.105.
91. *De Valera, Accompanied by Minister of Defence and Chief of Staff, Visits Galway*. Pathé Gazette, Issue 831, 9 December 1921.
92. *Sinn Féin's Would-Be Dictator*. Pathé Gazette, Issue 833, 15 December 1921.
93. *Internees Welcomed Back*. Pathé Gazette, Issue 833, 15 December 1921.
94. *Sinn Féin Prisoners Released*. Gaumont Graphic, Issue 1119, 12 December 1921.
95. *Irish Peace Imperilled by Extremists*. Topical Budget, Issue 537–2, 12 December 1921.
96. *Further Pictures of Irish Peace*. Topical Budget, Issue 538, 15 December 1921.
97. *Sinn Féin Parliament*. Gaumont Graphic, 15 December 1921. This item does not appear on NoS.
98. *Sinn Féin Members meet at Dublin Parliament House*. Topical Budget, Issue 538–2. 19 December 1921.
99. *Momentous Meeting of Dáil Éireann*. Pathé Gazette, Issue 834, 19 December 1921.
100. *Michael Collins the IRA leader*. Pathé Gazette, 9 January 1922. This item does not appear on NoS.
101. *Irish Elections*. Pathé Gazette, 26 June 1922.
102. *Peace Council at the Palace*. Pathé Gazette, 12 December 1921. This item does not appear on NoS.

103. Coogan (2003), p.118.
104. *Birthplace of Michael Collins*. Gaumont Graphic, 28 January 1922. This item does not appear on NoS.
105. *Fighting Speech by Michael Collins*. Pathé Gazette, Issue 857, 9 March 1922.
106. *Realising Freedom in Dublin*. Pathé Gazette, Issue 842, 16 January 1922.
107. *The 'Surrender' of Dublin Castle*. Topical Budget, Issue 543–1, 19 January 1922.
108. *Dublin Castle Handed Over*. Gaumont Graphic, Issue 1130, 19 January 1922.
109. *British Evacuate Ireland*. Topical Budget, Issue 543–2, 23 January 1923.
110. *Evacuation of British Troops from Ireland*. Pathé Gazette, Issue 844, 23 January 1922.
111. *IRA Guards at Dublin City Hall*. Gaumont Graphic, Issue 1131, 23 January 1922.
112. *Troops Leaving Cork*. Gaumont Graphic, Issue 1132, 26 January 1922.
113. *The Great Trek*. Topical Budget, Issue 544–1, 26 January 1922.
114. *Soldiers Home from Irish Front*. Pathé Gazette, Issue 845, 26 January 1922.
115. *Irish Free State Soldiers, Receiving Uniforms*. Pathé Gazette, Issue 846, 30 January 1922.
116. *Dublin – Beggars' Bush Barracks*. Gaumont Graphic, 2 February 1922. This item does not appear on NoS.
117. *New History (Ireland) Republican Army*. Pathé Gazette, Issue 848, 6 February 1922.
118. *Captain Craig and Michael Collins Confer (Dublin) on Boundaries (North and South)*. Pathé Gazette, Issue 848, 6 February 1922.
119. Fitzpatrick, David, *Militarism in Ireland, 1900–1922*, (1997), p.406.
120. *Rebirth of a Nation*. Topical Budget, Issue 589–2, 11 December 1922.
121. Coogan (2003), p.111.
122. Beckett (1966), p.456.
123. The pro-Treaty side favoured the term 'Irregulars' when describing the anti-Treaty forces.
124. Regan (2001), p.51.
125. *Mr de Valera Opens Anti-Treaty Campaign*. Pathé Gazette, Issue 851, 16 February 1922.
126. *Michael Collins*. Pathé Gazette, Issue 860, 20 March 1922.
127. *3,000 Irish Army Rebels Hold Parade*. Pathé Gazette, Issue 865, 6 April 1922.
128. *Wexford Treaty Meeting*. Pathé Gazette, Issue 867, 13 April 1922.
129. Bardon (1992), p.489.
130. *Refugees from Ulster Border (Where Fighting is Intense) Pouring into Dublin*. Pathé Gazette Issue 883. 8 June 1922.
131. *The Battle of Belleek*. Topical Budget. Issue 564–1, 15 June 1922.
132i. *Loyal Southern Irish Regiments*. Topical Budget, 12 June 1922. This item does not appear on NoS.
133. *Irish Elections*. Pathé Gazette, 26 June 1922. This item does not appear on NoS.
134. *Civil War in Ireland*. Topical Budget, Issue 566–2, 3 July 1922.
135. McKernan (1992), p.135
136. *Bombardment in Sackville Street*. Gaumont Graphic. Issue 1177, 3 July 1922.
137. *Hemming in the Rebels*. Topical Budget. Issue 567–1, 6 July 1922.
138. *Rounding up the Rebels*. Pathé Gazette. Issue 891, 6 July 1922.
139. *Dublin's Civil War*. Topical Budget, Issue 567–2, 10 July 1922.
140. *Peaceful Twelfth*. Pathé Gazette, Issue 894, 17 July 1922.
141. *Fall of Limerick*. Topical Budget, Issue 570–1, 29 July 1922.
142. *General Michael Collins*. Pathé Gazette, Issue 898, 31 July 1922.
143. *Irish National Army Sweeping On*. Topical Budget, Issue 571–1, 3 August 1922.
144. *Mopping Up. Battle of Adare*. Pathé Gazette, 10 August 1922. This item appears on the Digital Film Archive. There is no corresponding entry on NoS.
145. *Michael Collins at Burial of Arthur Griffith*. Pathé Gazette, Issue 905, 24 August 1922.
146. *Ireland Mourns Passing Michael Collins*. Pathé Gazette, Issue 906. 28 August 1922.
147. *Riots in Belfast*. Pathé Gazette, Issue 906, 28 August 1922.
148. *More than Half a Million Mourners*. Pathé Gazette, Issue 907, 31 August 1922.
149. *Let the Dublin Guards Bury Me*. Topical Budget, Issue 575–1, 31 August 1922.
150. *Grave of Michael Collins*. Pathé Gazette, Issue 909, 7 September 1922.
151. *General Mulcahy Hoists flag*. Pathé Gazette, Issue 920, 16 October 1922.

152. *While Miss MacSwiney Hunger-Strikes in Mountjoy Prison, Her Sister Annie Does the Same Outside*. Pathé Gazette, Issue 932, 27 November 1922.
153. Kissane (2005), p.63.
154. Ibid.
155. *Erskine Childers, the Irish Renegade*. Pathé Gazette, Issue 936, 27 November 1922.
156. *President Cosgrave*. Pathé Gazette, Issue 947, 18 January 1923.
157. *New Governor of Ireland*. Pathé Gazette, Issue 959, 1 March 1923.
158. *Anything to Declare*. Pathé Gazette, Issue 970, 12 April 1923.
159. *Free State or Republic?* Topical Budget, Issue 627–1, 30 August 1923.
160. Hill (2006), p.6.
161. Ibid., p.7.
162. Ibid., pp.25–6.
163. R. Barton (2004), p.16.
164. *The Agony of Belfast*. Irish Events dated circa 1920 on Digital Film Archive, and 1922 at the Irish Film Archive.
165. William Shakespeare, *Romeo and Juliet* in *Shakespeare: The Tragedies* (New York: Smithmark, 2000), Act V, Scene III, p.116.
166. *Riots and Revolutions*. Pathé dated on Digital Film Archive as 1921, but appears to be a compendium piece including footage from both the War of Independence and the Civil War. The item does not appear either on NoS or on British Pathé's website.
167. *Great Sinn Féin Round Up*. Pathé, 1918.
168. *Martial Law in Ireland*. Pathé, 1923–24. .
169. *De Valera – Stormy Petrel*. Pathé, Issue 1133, 3 November 1924.

5

The 1930s: Culture and Politics

By the mid-1930s, the newsreels had grown to what would be the peak of their success. The newsreels of the 1930s were dominated by stories on royalty, sport and personality; characteristically, given their upbeat nature, they displayed a somewhat cavalier attitude to growing international tension in the lead-up to the Second World War. Newsreels screened in Ireland were similar in content to those screened throughout Britain, with the occasional substitution of some local stories of interest. Pathé, however, was the only company making a consistent effort to produce a local edition for Ireland, presumably because it was the largest and best equipped of the newsreel companies – often shooting two to three Irish items for substitution in their main newsreel. In terms of Irish items throughout the 1930s, the content was not dissimilar to that of British stories. According to my own estimates, a staggering 45 per cent of Irish items during the decade were concerned with sport while only 17 per cent covered politics. This was partly to do with the newsreels' consistently optimistic nature and their determination to avoid overly controversial stories.

This chapter will examine political material and the attempts by governments in the north and south to harness the newsreels to present their political messages and construct 'their' Ireland in a favourable light post-partition. It will also examine the portrayal of Ireland, north and south, in coverage of non-political items. An important case study in this chapter is coverage of Ireland by the American newsreel company March of Time, which produced two films about Ireland in 1937 and 1938 which present very differing views of Irish politics. This chapter will examine the relationship between the two films and in particular how the first sparked an attempt by the Northern Ireland government to present a propagandized film about the north in response to what was seen to be a favourable depiction of the south of Ireland. This case study will demonstrate the challenges each government faced in both self-representation and the issue of how to construct the 'other' Ireland in relation to their own while working within the generic confines of newsreel production.

Cultural Coverage of North and South

The focus here is on the way in which the newsreels covered political issues in Ireland and Northern Ireland during the 1930s, but, given the predominance of lighter items, especially sport, public events and rituals, it is interesting to establish the main thrust of newsreel coverage before looking at the political issues. One of the recurring themes in this general coverage was Ireland's sporting culture, and some significant patterns can be deciphered.

The Irish sporting items covered included hockey, rugby, soccer and motor sports, with only periodic coverage of Gaelic sports. (Around thirty items out of nearly four hundred sports-related items cover Gaelic sports.) Universal and Paramount leave the coverage of both Gaelic football and hurling to Gaumont, British Movietone News and Pathé.

In one 1938 Gaumont item covering a Gaelic match, the lack of knowledge about the subject is evident from the commentary:

> It's not quite soccer, it's not quite Rugger, it's not quite netball, it's a fight. Call out the marines as well and keep the peace. A team from Ireland beat the New York team, they beat them hollow and they beat them up. In the end there was so much red blood flowing they had to call in their girlfriends to help them paint the town white.[1]

Gaelic sports, and the Irish talent for them, are portrayed as violent and forceful – tapping into stereotypes of the Irish as aggressive and undisciplined. The feminization of the aggressive players – both through associations with netball, a female sport, and then again at the end of the commentary – also taps into the representations of the south of Ireland as more feminine than the masculine industrial north, and this will be discussed further below. British Movietone News takes a more polite, albeit quietly condescending tone in their coverage of the same match. The commentator explains that we are watching scenes of 'that comparatively rare sport Gaelic football' and then qualifies: 'I'm afraid I'm not competent to explain all the niceties of the game, but you'll observe that players use their hands as well as their feet.'[2] He goes on to comment that 'this is done in Rugger of course, but not in quite the same way' – an emphasis on 'quite' adds a patronizing tone to the statement. The use of the term 'rugger' has, in its connotations, an association with the term 'Oxford-er',[3] referring to Oxford alumni, and thus associating the sport with the middle and upper classes. From the commentator's tone it is clear that Gaelic football has no such equivalent association. There are general shots of the action of the game until a close-up on one particular tackle which turns into a brawl, with other players gradually joining in. Against the background noise of booing from the crowd, the commentator retorts: 'it seems in Gaelic football you can go on playing after the gong has gone'.[4] An undercurrent of violence is also present in other coverage of Gaelic football: a 1937 item is introduced by the intertitle 'Kerry and Cavan play Gaelic football and live to fight again', although an Irish commentator, Tony Quinn, gives a softer description of the all-Ireland Final, and suggests that 'Now there'll be some ignoramuses that'll be askin' "What is this game?" '[5] Whilst the previous British Movietone item was made for a general audience and was most likely distributed to British and Irish audiences, this item is marked 'Dublin' on the issue sheet and would have been seen only by Irish audiences. Pathé provides the most extensive coverage of the sport through the 1930s and also catered more specifically for Irish audiences. Unsurprisingly, then, the company is generally more respectful than the other companies in its coverage – often praising the skill of the players although sometimes prone to describing the game as 'wild' and the crowd as 'wild' or 'plum crazy'. There are overtones of violence in the commentary of one item, with players said to be 'fighting back, battering the Mayo goal with the force a ram'.[6]

Another item associates the sport with the Catholic Church as Canon McGuirk is pictured dedicating a new stand in Croke Park.[7] Members of the clergy feature prominently in the opening shots of the 1938 all-Ireland final,[8] while Gaumont's commentary for the same match tells us that 'the game was started by Dr Browne, Bishop of Galway'.[9] A priest throws the ball onto the pitch to begin the match in Pathé's coverage of the 1934 final.[10]

Associations with the Church are also present in coverage of hurling matches: in the 1937 all-Ireland final – according to Gaumont's commentary – several leading clergymen are present at the match, with one starting the action by throwing the ball onto the pitch – a regular occurrence, as demonstrated by other newsreels covering hurling matches. In Pathé's coverage of this event, players are even shown genuflecting to the priest before the match begins.[11] There are also associations made between the players and nature (a recurrent theme in the newsreels' portrayal of southern Ireland in particular). Gaumont's wording states: 'the Tipperary men got in their stride, and like a mountain torrent swept all before them'.[12] (The issue sheets for this item confirm that it was shown in Belfast, Dublin, Manchester and Newcastle; presumably the English locations were chosen for exhibition because of a large Irish contingent in their cinema audiences.)

The associations made between the Church and Gaelic games reflected the importance of religion in Irish public life and in Nationalist ideology which linked public life and leisure with religion and Nationalist ideals. In the newsreels, the Irish people were represented as a deeply religious people, with religion extended to all aspects of life and politics. Just as the monarchy would be associated in the newsreels with northern Unionism, so the Catholic religion would be associated with southern Nationalism through images of the religious clergy at sporting events and military parades.

Just as the clergy are present in coverage of Gaelic games, members of the royal family are often shown at rugby matches. In a February 1933 item the Duke of York watches Ireland being 'well beaten' by England. Camera shots before the match show the duke shaking hands with the English players (but not with the Irish team).[13] The language in a December 1934 'rugger' match which leaves England victorious over Ireland is somewhat evocative of battle. Ireland's 'magnificent tackling' breaks up 'nearly every English movement'. Despite England being described as the 'superior' side, the English have to 'fight every inch of the way'.[14] Undertones of Irish aggression also appear in a match between Ireland and Scotland covered by British Movietone News in February 1935. The Irish side is depicted as set to 'make a terrific fight over it', encouraged by the 'wildly excited'[15] Dublin supporters. Unusual behaviour by supporters is shown at the start of the match as a fan is depicted sliding down the sides of the goalposts. A British Movietone

News item describes fans in Belfast: 'as usual the excitement proves too great for some people who decorate the goal posts with leeks and frying pans'.[16] While this comment clearly applies to Welsh fans, there is still a slightly disparaging tone – one which extends to the Celtic nations rather than simply Ireland. What is 'other' here thus becomes what is 'not English' or at least fails to fall within the traditional English temperament of dignified reserve. The Duke of Abercorn is shown greeting the players before the match. Welsh players are described as battling 'valiantly' before succumbing to 'an heroic victory' for the Irish. There is a wildness depicted in the crowd whose 'enthusiasm takes control', forcing animated fans onto the pitch to celebrate. An element of 'craziness' (at least according to the British Movietone News database) occurs at a 1936 soccer match between Germany and Ireland. British Movietone News's database entry reads: 'crazy man on the field taken away by police'. The actual newsreel shows a lone man going on to the pitch, removing his coat, laying it on the ground and dancing over it while the commentary describes the 'display by a wild Irishman who's under the impression he's won the big sweep and bought the ground'. Eventually a policeman drags the man off the pitch.[17]

Other sporting events covered include rugby, athletics, the renowned Dublin sweepstakes and occasionally hunting. Coverage of the 1932 Los Angeles Olympics shows two Irish athletes, R. Tisdall, 'Old Cambridge Blue', winning the 400-metre hurdles, and 'Dr Patrick O'Callaghan' competing in the hammer throw. There is an elitist element to both men: to one because of his title, and to the other because of his background and the fact that he speaks to the camera in Received Pronunciation.[18]

In general, Irish sports are treated by the newsreels with a condescending air. Commentators disparagingly display a lack of knowledge about Gaelic sports, attempting to locate Gaelic football in particular in relation to the more British sports of soccer and rugby. In describing Irish participation in rugby and soccer, the tone is slightly more respectful, recognizing Irish skill in these games, but still referring to spectators as wild and excitable. What emerges from these representations is a clichéd 'Irishness' (as portrayed from a British perspective, even when addressing solely Irish audiences) of aggressive and undisciplined players and spectators. An innate 'wildness' proliferates in representations of the Irish in moving images throughout the twentieth and even the twenty-first centuries: the newsreels proffered some of the first of such non-fiction depictions.

Horses and their 'Irish' Associations

The Dublin Horse Show was covered every year throughout the 1930s (and had appeared almost as frequently in the preceding decade), with the exception of 1931. There are thirty-one items in total covering the subject and indeed there are further items shown in local southern reels on horse shows in England and America. The coverage of the Dublin show generally depicts a popular event widely attended by the Irish population. A 1930 Pathé item even suggests that the event provides an opportunity to forget political differences. An intertitle opening the item *Royal Dublin Horse Show* states that 'Irishmen, and more particularly Irishwomen, forget all differences of creed, race and class, in their common adoration of "man's noblest friend" – the horse!' There are panning shots of well-dressed spectators at Punchestown race course, suggesting that there seems to be less mixing of classes than the title would suggest. By 1933, the coverage still associates the event with women, but does not give the impression that the horse show is attended by all classes. The opening music for a 1933 British Movietone News item covering the Dublin Horse Show is Celtic and lilting in tone. We are told it is a society event, the main attraction being a military jumping competition, and we see shots of well-attired men, and women wearing elaborate hats and carrying parasols. (In these items, shots often inter-cut between the horses and glamorous spectators, particularly women powdering their faces or lighting cigarettes.) The show is described as 'probably the most famous event of its kind in the world', attracting many foreign competitors. An association between the Irish people and horses is common. The 1934 British Movietone News coverage of the Dublin Horse Show suggests that 'Dublin's world famous horse show attracts everyone involved with horses and who would there be in Ireland that is not?'[19] An August 1936 British Movietone News item asserts this again: 'everybody in Ireland is interested in horses. They are all proud of their country's reputation for bloodstock.' In most of the coverage of the Dublin Horse Show during the 1930s, horses are specifically linked with the Irish people, an association that would recur in representations of Irishness in the newsreels during the 1940s.

Tourist Trophy Races

If horses were associated with Dublin and the south, the main sporting event associated with the north in the newsreels of the 1930s was the Tourist Trophy (TT) races. The first TT races were held in the Isle of Man. While the motorcycle TTs are still held there, the car races moved to Northern Ireland in 1928. The Tourist Trophy Races took place on the Newtownards circuit from 1928 to 1936, when a fatal accident led to the deaths of eight spectators. The race was moved to Donnington for the next two years and then suspended during the war. It moved back to Belfast, to the safer Dundrod route after the war, but when the safety of this route was also questioned, it was moved again to Goodwood and then Oulton Park, Silverstone, where it gradually died out.

The main force behind the encouragement of the Tourist Trophy races was the Ulster Tourist Development Association (UTDA) which had grown out of the Ulster Association, with James Craig as president. Given the association's connection with government, John Hill concludes that 'its promotion of tourism could assume a more directly political character', suggesting that materials produced for the UTDA were decidedly Unionist in tone.[20]

The filming of the Tourist Trophy races was perceived to offer a potential springboard for the newsreel companies to show wider representations of the north. Correspondence between the Ulster Tourist Development Association and the Stormont government reveals communication with several of the newsreel companies in relation to 'the publicity we hope to obtain as a result of the visit of representatives from the various Film Corporations during the forthcoming Motor Car Race'.[21] Four newsreel companies expressed a willingness 'to take pictures in addition to the Race provided that the suggested subjects would, in their opinion, be worthy of reproduction'. The letter describes the companies in question, British Movietone News, Gaumont, Paramount and Empire News, as the 'Big Four' in the film world, who 'control, as far as news bulletins are concerned, the vast majority of picture theatres through the British Empire and the United States'. This demonstrates a strong recognition of the power of newsreel representation, and a desire by the UTDA to utilize the medium to portray Northern Ireland in as favourable a light as possible. The letter expresses particular interest in a short talk by the Prime Minister 'on Ulster generally and perhaps boosting Ulster as a holiday resort'. (Previous correspondence suggests a wariness on the part of the Governor of being 'featured on the films!' suggesting that it would not be dignified.)[22] A further list of 'Ulster items of interest' is attached, including coverage of Mount Stewart, the seat of Lord Londonderry; a film of the Ulster Cabinet; Hillsborough Castle, 'the residence of His Grace the Governor of Northern Ireland, the Duke of Abercorn, including the "Old Guards" dressed in 200-year-old uniforms; the Linen Research Institute and possibly York Street Flax Spinning Company; the Giant's causeway; Belfast Rope Works; Harland and Wolff; Belfast Corporation Gas Works; St Patrick's Grave in Downpatrick'. James Loughlin recognizes the government's ability to utilize film for political purposes: 'the occasion of the Ulster Grand Prix in 1931 was used to create an opportunity for British Movietone News, to make a film of Craigavon and his cabinet speaking about Northern Ireland'.[23] While the coverage of the race appears in the editions of British Movietone News, Universal, Paramount and Pathé, there are no further items on either Craigavon or Northern Ireland in any British Movietone News edition for that month, although Paramount did release an item featuring Craigavon, entitled *Trouble in Ireland*, in the same issue. This item covers Craigavon's meeting with his Cabinet after border riots. British Movietone News's filming of Northern Ireland and the Cabinet may have been specially distributed as a local item for addition to the standard reel.

While Gaelic sports were portrayed as parochial, violent and difficult to understand, the TT races were marketed as an exciting international event as well as associated with technological progress. British Movietone News's opening intertitle covering the 1931 race describes it as a 'thrilling 410 mile duel' while the winner comments that 'it would be impossible to find a more ideal course for a car race of this description'.[24] Universal's coverage of this race describes the competitors as 'dare-devils', emphasizing the race as a 'daring affair', while the Dundonald hairpin bend is described as 'one of the supreme tests of driving skill' and the victor ultimately takes his place as 'one of our greatest road-racing drivers'.[25] Pathé's 1933 coverage is entitled 'Speed Gladiators' Most Thrilling Duel'. Tribute is paid to Freddie Dixon's 'daring and expert cornering' as winner of the 1935 race, described as 'Britain's great international classic'.[26] The voiceover informs the audience that 'the world's leading drivers' are present in Gaumont's coverage of the 1936 race, which, due to a tragic accident, would be the last held on the Newtonards circuit. The twists and turns through the narrow streets of Newtonards become familiar scenes. Bizarrely, in this Gaumont coverage the commentator describes the fatal crash, commenting that 'Many were killed and injured in this unhappy incident' while we see survivors being helped into an ambulance. The commentator then tells us the winners of the race and their average speed with no further details given about the accident, a clear example of the newsreels' enduring capacity to ignore bad news and remain consistently upbeat. Also left out of this item, although included in British Movietone News (which also accurately reports the six fatalities), is the fact that this was the first year that female drivers participated in the TT races.[27]

Political Coverage of the South

At the beginning of the 1930s a certain sense of political and social equilibrium had been established in Ireland – the British were happy with the Cosgrave administration and as a result Anglo-Irish relations were relatively good. Kevin Rockett suggests that by the 1930s there was an increasing awareness of the importance of newsreels amongst the Irish government, borne out by Cosgrave's interaction with both Pathé and British Movietone News.[28] In a Pathé item from November 1930, lasting almost four minutes, a slightly uncomfortable, suited and coiffed Cosgrave addressed the camera directly.[29] The previous intertitle introduces him: 'President COSGRAVE grants the PATHÉ GAZETTE an exclusive talk on IRELAND and her status in INTERNATIONAL AFFAIRS.' There is only one shot throughout the film, a medium close-up of Cosgrave, speaking without notes. The appearance and subsequent disappearance of a figure behind Cosgrave and the slightly jumpy nature of the shot suggests there was some editing of the piece, perhaps to give Cosgrave time to gather his thoughts. His eyes frequently dart to the left, as if he is awaiting a prompt from the wings, and his speech is stilted and often punctuated with erratic pauses. He addresses his lack of experience with the camera in his opening sentence but acknowledges, with a wry smile, that 'the apparatus through which I am now speaking, for the first time, affords one very stimulating thought, that it gives no opportunity for the opposition to interrupt, or to tend towards pessimism and therefore I have, on a very dull morning, a field almost entirely to myself'. Thus it is Cosgrave who acknowledges the interview as a political broadcast, revealing the growing interest of the Irish government in the potential of newsreel propaganda. Cosgrave goes on to discuss a world 'full of great political and economic anxieties' and describes the leaders of the world pondering 'what hope there is for mankind, what prospects there are for peace'.

The government had achieved a certain degree of success in its international performance. The Irish delegation played a prominent role at the 1926 Westminster Conference which afforded all the Dominions equal status; the first Irish Ambassador to Washington was appointed in 1928 and Ireland won a seat on the Council of the League of Nations in 1930. However, as Lee states, 'if the international performance was diplomatically skilful, it proved electorally futile'.[30] Cosgrave went on to lose the election the following year. In reference to the world economic situation (which had been destabilized by the Wall Street Crash of 1929) he interestingly portrays Ireland in a position of near immunity: 'we here in this country, by reason of our less costly standard of living and more pastoral life are perhaps less vulnerable to the disastrous economic shocks which affect other countries and in consequence, can view with considerable detachment this serious world situation'. This rather utopian view of Ireland was far removed from the political difficulties of previous decades and Cosgrave continues to utilize his newsreel platform to paint the state in an advantageous position: 'we have, by reason of our economic structure, some advantages which other nations may possibly envy, and may subsequently come to emulate and it is then, with considerable hope for the future we face the troubled times which are affecting other countries'.

Setting up Ireland as an economic model seems somewhat naive, even despite Cosgrave's recognized interest in financial rectitude during his time as leader. The tone of the piece offers an insight into Cosgrave's intentions in the representation of Ireland for British audiences. The message here certainly seems addressed to England and the outside world, a statement that Ireland is prospering in and worthy of taking its place on an international stage. Ireland's 'new found freedom', Cosgrave further asserts, 'gives us opportunities for developing in our own way untrammelled and uninterrupted'. After establishing an independent agenda, Cosgrave describes Ireland's interaction with other Dominion governments, who 'are with us in that Great Commonwealth of nations known as the British Commonwealth of nations'. He takes a slight pause just before the word 'British', a hesitancy which alludes to the political difficulties with continued contact with what we almost expect him to call 'the British Empire' despite his relatively genial relationship with the British government.

Cosgrave then goes on to discuss the unity between 'the various self-governing dominions', stressing the formation of 'new ties and friendships' and the ultimate finding of 'much grounds for common action, great opportunities for co-operation and much hope for the future, tending towards the uplifting of mankind, general peace and general recapitulation of the world's economic forces'. The final message 'is one of peace and goodwill to all' and efforts 'towards restoring damages which have resulted from the Great War, towards repairing the fallen economic structures and towards making the world a place of peace and goodwill'. As he concludes, Cosgrave literally (and almost comically) bows out of the frame. This issue also includes another Pathé 'exclusive' of 'the first pictures taken at the Curragh – once British Army Headquarters'. The item shows pipers leading an army march along a country road while two men and a dog standing in the adjoining field watch; there are then shots of training exercises. This item appeared before Cosgrave's interview after an opening item on *Gallant Little Belgium* (celebrating the 100th anniversary of the country's 'cherished and hard fought fight for liberty') and an item on cycling in Paris. The item on the Irish Army is followed by a piece on vintage cars and 'girls' hockey' before Cosgrave's interview which concludes the newsreel. Cosgrave gave approval for the item to be shown to Gordon Lewis, Pathé's Dublin editor.[31] An encounter with British Movietone News in 1931 was to prove more problematic for the Cosgrave administration. Cosgrave was approached directly by the company in a letter dated 7 January 1931 requesting an interview for circulation in Britain, Ireland and the US, leaving 'the subject to your [Cosgrave's] discretion' and suggesting that the film 'can be made in the open air or in your residence'. The Cosgrave government viewed this as 'a very good [opportunity] from the propaganda angle'.[32] Rockett explains that 'British Movietone News's intention was for Cosgrave to place less emphasis on commercial trade with Britain, or the presentation of the Irish Free State as a separate and individual country to that of Britain, in favour of positioning Ireland within "the Commonwealth group and

closely linked in co-operation with other Dominions." '[33] In further
correspondence it was suggested by British Movietone News that
the President should make a separate speech for circulation in
America. British Movietone News's representative, Norman J.
Hulbert, met with Cosgrave and suggested two messages each on the
following subjects:

(a) For Great Britain
     on the commercial relations and trade between the two
     countries, and the trade and industrial progress of the
     Irish Free State.
(b) For America
     Irish ties with America – possibility of air routes from there
     to Ireland etc.[34]

These suggestions were further clarified by Hulbert, British Movietone
News's representative, as noted in a government memo which requested
the following:

1. Wider aspect such as could be shown with interest in any
    country.
2. A reference showing Saorstat and Great Britain not merely
    separate and individual countries but rather of the Common-
    wealth group and closely linked in cooperation with other
    Dominions.
3. The general world desire for international peace. That
    notwithstanding the horrors of the last war some nations are
    showing danger signs, and that it is imperative that the coun-
    tries of the world should dedicate themselves to disarmament
    and peace. Methods by which world peace may be attained –
    mutual understanding amongst peoples, visits to other coun-
    tries,etc. An appeal to youth who did not feel the horrors of the
    last war.
4. Saorstat policy, i.e. international outlook. So many of her
    people have settled abroad that she must necessarily have an
    international outlook.
5. Modern Anglo-Irish literature mentioning Yeats etc.
6. Trade references somewhat brief and general.
7. Mr Landau explained that what he can use with most success
    is the type of talk which is personal and intimate and appeals

to cinema going folk – too much commercial trade talk will not reach them.

8. If the speech is long they can subdivide it suitably.
9. American message (b) to remain as previously designed plus world peace.

A draft speech, not ultimately used, read as follows:

> On this, the national holiday of Ireland the message I have to send across the Irish sea is one of friendship and goodwill. The economic stress of recent years has not diminished either our political bonds of mutual respect or our commercial ties of mutual trading interest. Great Britain remains our best customer and the Irish Free State one of the best of Britain's.
>
> Those who buy our cattle, our bacon, butter and eggs, our stout, whiskey, biscuits, or tweeds may rest assured of finding those and all the other products for which we have established a name constantly improving in quality, while they multiply their demand without risk of any shortage in quantity.
>
> On the other hand British producers for the Irish market may take comfort from the fact that we have suffered less from recent economic depression than many of their other customers. The adverse balance in our visible trade continues to shrink, unemployment amongst us happily has not increased, almost alone among European countries we have been able this year to reduce our contributions to the unemployment fund. A cheap and abundant supply of electricity is now available throughout the state and is raising our standards both in comfort of living and productive capacity. Our credit stands exceptionally high. We are genuinely solvent customers for whatever we still need to buy.
>
> To those oppressed with the material problems of today who look for rest from the turmoil of city life, for sport or recreation, for beauty for the eye or a stimulus to the imagination I can, with special gladness, undertake that Ireland, if they visit her will be found to have lost none of her ancient charm, nor an Irish welcome any of its old sincerity.

The final instruction for this draft was 'short sentence in Irish'. Presumably the content of this sentence had not yet been confirmed, or was to be left up to Cosgrave's discretion.

In the finished film, Cosgrave addresses the camera directly, speaking without notes in a medium close-up shot throughout the duration of the film. The film's editor, Landau, was happy with the outcome. The only problem with the film, as he mentioned in a letter to the Department of the President, was that 'traffic noises intrude now and again on the voice, but this I am afraid was unavoidable, as we were rather near a road, and the fact that the President was speaking rather softly, necessitated our increasing the volume of sound, which naturally also increased the volume of outside noises'.

The final commentary was as follows:

> Disarmament is first and last a political question; that is, a problem which must be faced and solved by the people themselves. I have no doubt that amongst my audience in this theatre there are many for whom the horrors of war are a none too remote memory, and to those I need not emphasise the importance of preventing the recurrence of that dreadful catastrophe so memorable because so dreadful. To the youth who are listening to me for whom the World War may be no more than dates in a text book I would say: war is amongst the greatest of the scourges of mankind, concentrate and persevere in your efforts to place the organisation of peace upon sure foundations. We who are associated in the British Commonwealth of Nations have a special interest in the preservation of the peace of the world. Great Britain and Ireland are great emigrating countries: our sons in a very real sense 'inhabit the earth.' A repetition of the strife of 1914–18 would find our people engaged in armed conflict with each other and this would be so whether the struggle were a war of nations or a war of continents. It is for the youth of all countries by their enlightened and unspoiled idealism to work together for a better understanding between nations. When they are old, their children will bless the efforts which they have made; their reward will be in the happy consummation of peace and goodwill on earth.

While Cosgrave is evoking the conflict of the First World War, there are echoes here of both the War of Independence and the Civil War. The appeal he makes for 'better understanding between nations' could equally apply to Anglo-Irish relations and, indeed, Cosgrave's relationship with the British administration was a cordial one at the time.

The instructions for the American film came from the President's office in a letter dated 30 April 1931 from F.T. Cremins to Mr Jones in the Dublin office of the Fox film company:[35]

The film for the United States to contain only the portions:

(a) The portion commencing and finishing as follows:
In addressing yet again an American audience I cannot but recall once more the cordial welcome and kindly hospitality given to me as the representative of my country on the occasion of my visit to the United States three years ago. In my speech at Philadelphia during a memorable day at that great city I stated – what is so well known – that 'it is not possible to draw closer the bonds of affection between this country and mine'.

(b) The portion commencing and finishing as follows:
The first years of her career in foreign affairs find Ireland standing side by side with United States in the promotion of a policy of international peace and goodwill.

(c) The portion commencing and finishing as follows:-
I believe that the history of this generation will be an unhallowed chapter if the collective genius of its statesmen fails to solve the twin problems of security and disarmament.

The final portion of the film was the section to be exhibited in Britain. However, as Rockett tells us, 'because Cosgrave would not approve the American version, an indication of his sensitivity to Irish Americans, only the British/Irish version from which a reference to world peace was cut, was released in all countries'.[36] Clearly the comments on peace and war were sensitive and Cosgrave was acutely aware of the potential power of any message transmitted through cinema news.

Cosgrave's 'peace plea' appeared as the second item of the newsreel, which began with an item on a motor boat launch in Italy attended by the Italian writer D'Annunzio. After Cosgrave's speech there were items on the launching of the *Deutschland* in Germany, weekend cruising in New York, Buddha's birthday celebrated in Japan, a 'zoo on the move' and the Church of Scotland Assembly[37] – a typically wide-ranging newsreel edition.

Military Parades

The impressive military defence parades which would dominate Irish Movietone News during the Second World War (and will be explored in detail below) were foreshadowed by newsreel coverage of military parades in the 1930s. In *Erin on Parade* (1931), the opening intertitle describes the 'vast crowds' watching the 'impressive march past of army!' during a St Patrick's Day parade.[38] Shots of marching troops watched by crowds lining the streets precede coverage of President Cosgrave's holiday address. In contrast to the shots of large crowds, there is a medium close-up of Cosgrave, standing alone and addressing the camera directly: 'I am very pleased to be afforded this opportunity on the occasion of the feast of our national apostle, through the courtesy of the Paramount Sound company to say just a few words on Ireland.' The camera moves in for a closer shot – Cosgrave's speech is halting as he continues, looking to the side of the camera as the wind ruffles his hair: 'During the last 8 or 9 years, political responsibility has been shouldered for the first time in our history by this country and in that connection our principal concern was education, and economic conditions. New roads and reconstruction of bridges and a general [slight pause] acceptance on the part of the people of their new responsibility and citizenship.' In coverage of St Patrick's Day the following year, Church and State are linked through the opening shots of soldiers kneeling in ordered groups on the barracks' square as the commentary tells us: 'A special Mass is held for units of the Free State Army as Ireland celebrates the fifteenth centenary of the arrival of St Patrick on her shores.' The camera pans along the lines of kneeling soldiers towards the altar while 'Hail Glorious St Patrick' is played. An intertitle stating that 'All Dublin turns out as picked regiments march through city' gives way to shots of vast crowds filling Dublin streets and straining to see the military band making its way through. Over the more uplifting strains of the military band, the commentator describes the scene – 'In its spectacular parade through the city, Erin's fine little army rejoices the hearts of all Dublin's citizens' – while Frank Aiken, recently elected Minister for Defence, takes the salute.[39] Aiken had previously been an anti-Treaty IRA commander and symbolized the significant changes which had taken place in the Irish military. These scenes evoked national solidarity and security and became even more prevalent during the 'Emergency' of the Second World War.

The Election of de Valera

If the sense of equilibrium existing at the beginning of the 1930s was related to Cosgrave's relatively cordial relationship with the British authorities, this was to change with the election of Eamon de Valera in 1932. When Cosgrave called a general election in February, his main platform for re-election stood on law and order and 'the defence of religion', with the claim that a Fianna Fáil victory would bring 'irreligion' and a heightened vulnerability towards materialism and communism.[40] Fianna Fáil emphasized the abolition of the oath of allegiance and concentrated on social and economic policy, addressing the problem of unemployment in particular.

Cosgrave feared that a Fianna Fáil government would bring financial ruin, a resurgence of the IRA with official backing, and confrontation with Britain. The moment on 9 March 1932 when de Valera entered Leinster House in Dublin to take up office was tense: some Fianna Fáil deputies carried revolvers into the Dáil, one even assembling a sub-machine gun in a telephone box.[41] Sticking to his election manifesto, de Valera informed Westminister that he would remove the Oath of Allegiance and, furthermore, was to withhold the land annuities to Britain. Given that the 1931 Statute of Westminster stated that central legislation applied to dominions only with their consent, there was little the British government could do about the removal of the oath. However, refusal to pay the Land Annuities breached international agreement and sparked what would become a bitter economic war. In July 1932 Westminster imposed a 20 per cent duty on livestock and dairy produce from the Free State which was duly followed by de Valera's 20 per cent tariff on British electrical goods, cement, machinery, iron and steel.[42]

Tim Pat Coogan portrays de Valera as a master of propaganda, turning election meetings into 'pure theatre':

> He would enter a country town, studiedly late, to whet the waiting crowd's appetite, on a white horse, wearing a long black cloak, preceded by a guard of honour of men carrying lighted sods on pitchforks. His meeting would very probably be punctuated by cheering, occasional fist fights, interjections from hecklers, and an air of excitement that made his bandwagon irresistible.[43]

De Valera's command of the newsreel camera was not quite so effective and certainly not as skilful as his use of radio. Unlike Cosgrave he often read out statements with little inflection or regard for the camera, appearing sullen and abrupt as a result. Many items covering de Valera at this stage show him reading statements to camera with little expression. One example is a British Paramount News item, *De Valera Wins*,[44] subtitled 'De Valera interview in Dublin', which is less an interview than one medium close-up of de Valera reading the following from a statement: 'It will be the dawn of a new day for Ireland. Our people in the United States, in Britain, in Australia, will know a gladness there not experienced since 19 hundred and 21. The joy, born of the coming together of old friends long divided has set the youth of the country on fire.'

Even as the camera moves closer for the next shot there is little sense of 'fire' in de Valera's expression as he continues, monotone:

> The problem of unemployment, vexing the industrialised countries, can be solved in our peculiar conditions here. We have only to set out to produce for our own home market and we can provide work for a number greater than that of our unemployed. To my mind, the hope for the world today is in each country making itself as economically self-sufficing as possible, each confining its produces from outside to what it is all together incapable or clearly quite unfitted to produce. I am happy to send greetings to the friends all over the world who are so interested in our success.

After his election win, a Paramount News item excitedly states in its opening intertitle: 'All Eyes on Ireland! Dublin – No quarrel with Britain!'[45] The first shot of de Valera, wearing his characteristic black overcoat, carries little of the enthusiasm of the intertitle. De Valera reads slowly from a piece of paper held in both hands, occasionally looking up at the camera:

> The present government of the Irish Free State has been elected by a large majority for the purpose of putting into execution a programme based on the deep national instincts of the Irish people. This programme aims at restoring the unity of this island and creating an independent Ireland living its own cultural, economic and national life. We do not wish to seek quarrels with any country. We wish well to our neighbour, Great Britain, and to all other countries. We want our liberty so our co-operation with

Great Britain may be one of harmony and friendship and to remove every obstacle to the natural growth of good relations between the Irish and British people.

The suggestion here is that any opposition to Ireland's 'liberty' would in itself be an impediment to building good relations to Britain. Although Paramount's intertitle concludes for itself that Ireland has 'no quarrel' with Britain, there is a veiled threat in de Valera's speech that good relations can only flourish if Ireland is allowed to strengthen her own national and cultural identity without British interference. De Valera finishes with a direct look at the camera, while his words complement an almost prophetic glance towards his future policy by the end of the 1930s with the outbreak of war.

De Valera's policy of ratcheting up the harder Republican stance, however, was well caught in another Paramount item from March 1932, on a memorial service for the 1916 leaders, which carries a reminder of previous strains in Anglo-Irish relations. An opening intertitle states: 'Free State Remembers. Dublin mourns dead leaders of 1916 rising. Thousands march to Republican Army's memorial service at Glasnevin.' Large numbers of marching men, dressed in overcoats and hats and watched by vast crowds are described as 'Republican sympathisers' by the commentary, commemorating the 1916 Rising in which 'so many Irishmen lost their lives'. The commentator continues, in almost a hushed voice: 'wending its way through streets which were once the scene of conflict, the procession moves towards Glasnevin cemetery'. A large Tricolour fills the screen before the camera cuts to scenes at the cemetery where 'the great throng gathers around the Republican plot, the huge grave of Republicans killed in the struggle from 1916 to 1923'. Prayers in Irish are audible while the camera pans the crowd scene which is peppered with Tricolours. Maurice Twomey, described as 'the veteran Republican army leader', addresses the crowd, reading a message issued by the IRA Army Council which was to be read at all simultaneous commemorations throughout the country. A close-up of two men – one older with moustache and bowler hat, one young and wearing glasses – sums up the range of the crowd as Twomey commences: 'comparatively few of those men whose remains lie here were known to us personally. The proclamation of the Republic of 1916 will remain for us the fundamental declaration of the right and authority of our nation to fight for its inalienable right to sovereign independence.'

The Eucharistic Congress – June 1932

5.1 Pathé Super Gazette: *A Million Kneel in Worship*, Copyright British Pathé Ltd.

Soon after de Valera's election in 1932, a huge national event was to occur in Ireland in the form of the Eucharistic Congress, a Catholic gathering of clergy and lay people in adoration of the Eucharist. It is an international event still held in cities throughout the world since the first congress was held in Lille in 1881. In 1932, with Dublin as its chosen location, it offered de Valera a chance of reconciliation with the Catholic Church which had excommunicated anti-Treatyites during the Civil War. Lee suggests that it might have been to Cosgrave's benefit to have post-poned the general election until after the Eucharistic Congress, 'where he could have been photographed incessantly with the papal nuncio for the edification of the plain people of the Free State',[46] while Tim Pat Coogan recognizes that it 'proved an important milestone in the respectabilisation of de Valera and Fianna Fáil'.[47] The British Movietone News item *Papal Delegate Steps Ashore in Dublin* covers, as we are told in the opening intertitle, the 'great Eucharistic Congress Ceremony'.[48] The item begins with shots of Cardinal Lauri's arrival, to be met by the

Archbishop of Dublin and representatives of the government. Cheering crowds can be seen (and heard) gathered at the docks for his arrival. The coverage continues the following week in *Millions at Phoenix Park Mass*.[49] The commentator describes the attendance at Mass in Phoenix Park, the climax of the Eucharistic Congress, as reaching one million people, 'twice the normal population of Dublin'. At this point there is a short extract of the actual Mass, celebrated by Cardinal Lauri, followed by the singing of Count John McCormack, a papal count and internationally celebrated tenor, to accompany the offertory procession. In shots of the altar a large military cohort can be observed lined up immediately in front of the congregation.

Paramount's coverage of the event contains the famous footage of Count John McCormack singing 'Panis Angelicus' while various dignitaries and politicians line up to kiss the Papal ring. The event is a symbol of Irishness and Catholicism coming together and, in the symbolism of members of government kissing the Papal ring as Cardinal Lauri sits enthroned, a statement of state subservience to the Catholic religion. (The footage also demonstrates the Irish Free State's capacity to host such an event.) What further cements the religious connection in the Paramount newsreel is the depiction of de Valera at the Cardinal's side as he arrives in Kingstown. In the concluding shots of the newsreel, Benediction is shown and the procession of the Sacrament through the streets of Dublin, the Cardinal accompanied by a military escort.[50] In further coverage, Paramount, like Movietone, emphasizes the sheer size of attendance for Mass in Phoenix Park in its opening intertitle: 'a million at prayer! Mighty congregation gathers for Pontifical High Mass in Phoenix Park.'[51] The vast crowds are shown kneeling, heads bowed reverently. Universal's commentary describes the thousands of diverse people gathering 'to partake of this mystic beneficence dispensed by the spiritual ruler of Christendom through his chosen representative Cardinal Lauri'. The newsreel also refers to the technology used: 'loudspeakers carry the reverent voice to the farthest edges of the kneeling crowds and indeed across to other countries of Europe. The emotion of millions is excited by this service ... This week religious fervour has turned Dublin into a city of prayer.'[52] Observers certainly picked up on the religious fervour of the event. Jonathan Bardon cites T.J. Campbell (former editor of the Irish News, and MP for Belfast Central at the time of the Congress), who in his book *Fifty Years of Ulster 1890–1950* describes scenes at the Congress as 'amongst the most impressive and joyful ever witnessed among the Irish nation ... The procession was like a swiftly-flowing, never-ending stream of humanity ... Rapt adoration, amid breathless stillness, was around.'[53] Archive footage of the Eucharistic Congress was used in Cathal Black's controversial documentary *Our Boys* (1981) which explored Catholic education in the 1960s. Martin McLoone suggests that the use of images of the Eucharistic Congress 'provides the context for the film's exploration of Catholic education, itself a unique synthesis of religion and Nationalism'. These iconic images immediately conjure up images of the relationship between Church and politics in Ireland, thus quickly contextualizing this relationship for viewers. In fact, McLoone states that they provide 'a rather graphic illustration of how closely intertwined Irish civil authority and Catholic church authority were in the period after independence'.[54] The images of the Eucharistic Congress shown in the newsreels to both British and Irish audiences were to become iconic in evoking the high point of Catholic Ireland and significant in marking the increasing divergence of north and south, particularly in the psyche of northern Unionists who responded to the furore of the Congress with suspicion.

De Valera saw the Eucharistic Congress as a means of addressing the suspicion with which he was regarded by the Catholic Church. He had been perceived as a communist and blamed for the Civil War after refusing to accept the Anglo-Irish Treaty of 1921. The newsreel images of de Valera at the side of Cardinal Lauri during the celebrations meant that the Irish people saw these attempts to ingratiate himself again with the religion so closely associated with Irish Nationalism.

The 1933 Elections

When he came to power in 1932, de Valera commanded only a small majority, and to continue with his policy of reinvigorating Nationalist and Republican values into Ireland's political culture he needed to secure a bigger majority. Consequently, in January 1933 he called a surprise election, gambling on the fact that his policy of wooing the Church, standing up to the British and playing the statesman on the world stage (especially at the League of Nations) would give him an advantage over an ill-prepared opposition. In contrast to newsreels in which he had to address the camera directly, de Valera was a formidable presence at the hustings and his election rally prowess is captured in a Paramount item entitled *Irish Rush Election*[55] on the snap election de Valera called in 1933. An intertitle contextualizes: 'Leitrim – Mr De Valera, urging his government's re-election on "No-annuity-payments-to- Britain" policy.' We are told by the commentator of de Valera's 'whirlwind tour of the whole electorate'. The small streets of Drumshambo are filled with people, some leaning out of windows to hear de Valera speak. He mounts the speaker's platform amidst cheering and applause. In this item it is the crowd he addresses, not the camera. He is animated and without notes, scanning the crowd as he reminds them of his pledge to tackle the land annuities imposed on farmers. There are cheers as he moves on to discuss the Oath of Allegiance – 'a fulsome source of division' which had been held up by the Senate but which de Valera promises on his return to abolish 'over their heads'.

De Valera went on to win the election with an increased majority, and in an item called *De Valera Triumphs*[56] an affable and magnanimous William Cosgrave is shown with his wife, chatting to the camera about his loss to de Valera in the election:

> The last few days of the general election, were, of course, very much more interesting than the earlier days. The meetings were sometimes late, there were bonfires, there was great enthusiasm. But in any case, the contest has taught us to consider all the points that were at issue in the election. I think that people generally will be satisfied with the result.

A more serious de Valera characteristically reads the following statement to the camera:

> The programme of Fianna Fáil has now been definitely adopted as the national policy of the Irish people. That programme aims at restoring the unity of Ireland and securing its independence, at placing as many families as possible on the land, and building up our industries so that the food we eat, the clothes we wear, the houses we live in, the articles in common daily use in the lives of our people may all, as far as is reasonably possible be produced by Irish labour from Irish materials. The friends of Ireland will rejoice with us that we have seen this day and that, as in the past, they will sustain us with their aid and attend our efforts with their thoughts and prayers.

The Blueshirts

De Valera's attitude towards the IRA became increasingly strict throughout the 1930s, but if he faced challenges on the left from the IRA, he
faced equal opposition from the right in the form of the Blueshirts.
(There were frequent disputes between the IRA and the Blueshirts
during this period.) As head of the army and then Chief Commissioner
for the Garda Síochána, General Eoin O'Duffy had repressed the anti-
Treaty Republicans with great vigour. After his second, decisive election
victory in January 1933, de Valera dismissed O'Duffy and in July he
became leader of the Army Comrades' Association, an organization of
ex-servicemen from the Free State Army who had fought for the Treaty
against the Republicans in the Civil War. This organization was hostile
to de Valera and grew in numbers as a reaction to his election victories.
By this stage the movement had already associated itself with continental
fascism, its members parading in their characteristic blue shirts which
gave them their popular name. O'Duffy renamed the movement the
National Guard and organized marches where the salute 'Hail O'Duffy'
could be heard. O'Duffy had been expected to lead a coup during the
annual Griffith, Collins and O'Higgins demonstrations but de Valera's
swift and decisive security measures hampered his political aspirations.[57]

Newsreel coverage of the Blueshirts was sparse, probably due to their
controversial association with fascism. During the 1930s there are only
four items in total dealing with the Blueshirts, two produced by
Paramount and two by Movietone. The fascist movement was ignored
by the other companies. Equally, Paramount and Movietone are the only
two companies to undertake coverage of Oswald Mosley's fascist
demonstrations in Britain during the1930s, the other companies leaving
them untouched due to the controversy courted by the inclusion of such
items. Strikingly, these two companies also lead the way in coverage of
the growth of National Socialism in Germany. A startling 73 per cent of
the coverage of events in Germany from 1930 to 1939 was provided by
Paramount and Movietone, the remainder being almost equally split
between Pathé, Universal and Gaumont.[58] Paramount was controlled by
the American Paramount company, while British Movietone News was
jointly owned by 20th Century Fox and Associated Newspapers[59],
publishers of the *Daily Mail*, the newspaper in Britain which most
closely associated itself with the fascist position until the war drew it
into a patriotic stance. Paramount would also court controversy when

it included an item critical of appeasement in the run-up to the Second World War, which will be explored in the next chapter.

In a Paramount news item from August 1933 entitled *Gen. O'Duffy Explains*,[60] the opening intertitle reads: 'Dublin – National Guard leader denies dictatorship aim! Asserts Guard is unarmed civil organization, non-political and independent.' We then see O'Duffy, dressed in civilian clothes, against a backdrop of leafy trees, with one hand behind his back and in the other a piece of paper from which he reads:

> The National Guard of Ireland is a civil organization, its members are unarmed. The principle objects of the organization are to promote the re-union of Ireland, to oppose Communism and kindred societies, to uphold Christian principles, to promote and maintain social order, to lead the Irish youth in a movement of constructive national action, to set up machinery for the prevention of strikes and lockouts by harmoniously composing industrial differences, to reduce unemployment by the provision of useful and economic public work.

The camera moves in as O'Duffy refutes claims that the National Guard's main aim was to set up a dictatorship: 'The National Guard is strongly opposed to anything flavouring of a dictatorship or a coup d'état and was brought into being to assist the people in their efforts to oppose any departure from democratic and representative governments.' The camera moves closer again as O'Duffy's tone becomes graver: 'During these days when the names of our three great leaders are on everyone's lips I very earnestly appeal to the Irish people at home and abroad to support the National Guard in reaching the goal of Griffith, Collins and O'Higgins, an Ireland united peaceful, prosperous, free and honoured by our own children and by all nations.' O'Duffy rarely looks at the camera throughout his speech and, perhaps because of having to squint due to sunlight, has an almost shifty demeanour. Like de Valera, his one-to-one on-camera personality is lacklustre, but a later Paramount item covering O'Duffy's speech to a large rally portrays a more bombastic and theatrical character. Entitled *Gen. O'Duffy defies de Valera*,[61] the item covers an 8,000-strong Blueshirt rally at Clonmel. The opening intertitle explains that the 'leader of opposition parties (on parole pending trial by Military) rouses big United Ireland meeting'. The camera pans the crowd cheering and waving their hats to welcome

O'Duffy as he steps out onto a balcony of the Ormond Hotel while the commentator informs us that 'the eyes of all Ireland centred on Clonmel' where crowds gathered to hear 'de Valera's dynamic opponent' and leader of the United Ireland Party. O'Duffy is much more animated as he apologizes to the crowd for having to read his speech as he is 'to appear in the dock next Tuesday and I have to be very careful that I am not taken up by some local secretary of Fianna Fáil for contempt of court'. The amused crowd cheers as he begins to read his speech, in which he accuses Fianna Fáil of 'pilfering' fourteen million pounds from the Irish people.

Movietone's first item covering the Blueshirts offers the following opening intertitle: '600 Irish Blueshirts conceal uniforms. Warned by Civic Guards, paraders don overcoats on Inchicore march to Bluebell cemetery.'[62] Light-hearted and fast-paced music precedes the next intertitle: '600 members of the Young Ireland Association or "Blueshirts" are on parade at Inchicore County Dublin.' It tones down any potential trouble and concludes the item by ensuring the audience is aware that the parade passed off 'without ... incident.' A large number of uniformed Blueshirts are shown in conversation with the guards before continuing their parade with their overcoats on. Bizarrely, the commentary sounds as if it is describing a fashion item as it informs the viewer that 'women also wearing the forbidden colour form a large section of the parade, marching along in great style following the male division'. Through associating the threatening Blueshirt uniform with women, a symbol of potential conflict is feminized and made less threatening; the newsreels frequently feminized the dangerous or subversive as a means of implicitly condemning anti-Establishment or anti-British behaviour.

The next Movietone coverage is in 1937 and reports the Blueshirts' involvement in the Spanish Civil War. The IRA had been proclaimed an illegal organization on 18 June 1936 and the Spanish Civil War offered the possibility of getting rid 'of some of her wild men of both varieties':[63] some Blueshirts joined Franco's National Front while many IRA members volunteered for the International Brigade to fight for the Spanish Republic. The tone is less sympathetic in this newsreel, presumably as international conflict was mounting at this stage. The commentary reports:

> Home from the war, and back to old Ireland come Franco's Irish volunteers, 633 of them. A few injured but the big majority

> unscathed. The Irish brigade was raised by General O'Duffy, who for a welcome home had to submit to a rigid customs examination. The brigade had six months' service in Spain and marched through Dublin decked with some of their souvenirs, the rest of their trophies had been left behind with the customs.

There are scenes of O'Duffy's suitcase being checked at customs, followed by shots of a relatively subdued parade through Dublin. The scanty coverage overall reflected the newsreels' reluctance to engage with controversial material and it is significant that the only two newsreels to cover these fascist associations with Ireland included a company that would become even more controversial in its Irish coverage during the Second World War and a company with more right-wing associations.

A British Movietone News item in February 1936 covered the funeral of de Valera's son, Brian, killed in a riding accident. Opening with the intertitle 'De Valera Bereaved' and footage of de Valera, without expression and surrounded by family, the commentator reads the intertitle. The next shot is of a tree with a large protruding branch dividing the screen horizontally as the commentator continues 'an overhanging branch cut short the life of his son Brian as he galloped his horse in Phoenix Park Dublin'. Shots of the coffin being carried out of the house are followed by the funeral procession shown entering Glasnevin cemetery as the voiceover comments 'what a terribly tragic way for the Irish President's son to meet his death'. Over shots of mourners following the flower-laden coffin before it is lowered into the ground, condolences are offered: 'Mr de Valera and his other sons follow the coffin to the graveside at Glasnevin cemetery. Their grief is bitter and with their grief Britain and the Empire sympathises, mourning with the Irish Free State, shocked at the poignant tragedy.'[64] The reverential tone of the newsreel is significant in its diplomacy, given the increasing tensions in relations between Britain and the Irish Free State at this stage.

While a degree of deference is awarded to de Valera at this time, there are occasional hints of his complex relationship with Britain. Later in 1936, de Valera is shown at the Irish Games in a British Movietone News item released in September. Over shots of de Valera (wearing sunglasses), we are told, with a familiar sense of condescension, 'Mr de Valera attends the Irish national sports, some of which are most peculiar.'

We are shown a marching band and then what appears to be a shot-putter hoisting a large weight over a line while the commentator continues: 'they swing 56lb weights through their legs and they swing them over a sort of high jump breaking records and everything'. The next shots are of a pole-vaulter making the jump, then forward rolling to his feet while the voiceover comments: 'when it comes to pole-vaulting, you can be assured there'll be quite a spot of originality displayed by someone'.[65]

A 1938 British Movietone News item covering *St Patrick's Day in Éire* suggests the dominant British attitude to de Valera: acknowledging his electoral authority but seeking to find in the situation those familiar elements of a general 'Irishness' that weakened that authority somewhat. The commentator begins with a mock Irish accent – 'sure and begorrah it's St Patrick's Day and there's a fine parade of the Irish army in Dublin'. He then reverts to Received Pronunciation to continue: 'Well, no matter if Ireland is now called Éire, it's the same place with the same institutions and St Patrick is still its patron saint.' Military parades are shown throughout the streets of Dublin while Minister for Defence Frank Aiken presides. After a shot of young children, the camera cuts to marching officers while the commentary tells us that 'among the young officers in the parade is Captain Vivion de Valera, furthest from the camera, son of the Taoiseach, that's the ex-president's new title'. De Valera's car is depicted driving through the crowds 'The Taoiseach himself drives by car to the Pro-Cathedral. We don't see him but he has an appropriate escort of cavalry.'[66] The political complexities in Ireland were never too far away and one of the most telling examples of the interplay between the newsreels and these realities was provided by the American March of Time newsreel when it turned its attention to Ireland.

March of Time – an American Perspective

De Valera's 1937 constitution laid claim to the six counties of Northern Ireland, provided for an elected president and acknowledged 'the special position of the Holy Catholic and Apostolic and Roman Church'.[67] The new constitution was approved by a referendum on 1 July 1937, the same day as the general election which confirmed de Valera as Taoiseach, a change in his title commented on in typically light-hearted manner in the 1938 St Patrick's Day item discussed above. Bardon suggests that northern Catholics felt alienated by de Valera, and argues that in fact the new Taoiseach

> had chosen to create a twenty-six county state that seemed to close off the few remaining routes to reunification – a state verging on the theocratic, with rigid censorship and a constitutional prohibition on divorce and family planning; a state compelling every child to learn Irish and turning its back, like Northern Ireland, on the cultural diversity of its people; and a state with one of the most highly protected economies in the world.[68]

The constitution supplies the basis for an interesting episode in newsreel coverage, and one which characterizes the representation of Ireland, north and south, during the 1930s. This case study also exemplifies some of the difficulties in dating newsreel coverage.

In October 1936, *Kinematograph Weekly* reported that the March of Time camera crew had been recently filming in Ireland and had visited Drogheda, Dundalk, Galway, Connemara and Limerick, 'where they spent some time filming the giant hydro-electric plant at Adnacrusha'. H.W. Lancaster, the March of Time representative, 'said that although they had only been a short time in the Free State they were very much impressed by the work carried on and the beauty of the country'.[69] The article suggested that the scenes would be released in about three months' time. However, the following month the Marquess of Donegall wrote (on 17 November) to the Northern Ireland Ministry of Commerce about being invited to a press screening of what he called March of Time's 'fifth edition'. Both *Kinematograph Weekly* and *Today's Cinema* report a screening in Dublin for de Valera, members of the Cabinet, Diplomatic Corps, representatives of foreign governments and 'other leading people in Dublin'. This was probably the screening to which Donegall was invited. *Kinematograph Weekly* reports that 'there is general praise for the film, and the unanimous opinion is that the section of "March of Time" which deals with the Free State is going to do the country good'.[70] *Today's Cinema* also describes praise for the film from de Valera and the Lord Mayor of Dublin, who considered the film very valuable for attracting tourist trade. The film's director, H.W. Lancaster (who had visited the previous month for filming), is reported to have 'said that the picture was primarily made for the people of America, with whom he believed it would go over "really big" '.[71] The film had been briefly reviewed in *Today's Cinema* on 21 November, in an article which identified it as appearing alongside an item on American politics. The review describes 'a generous study of the Irish Free State, its rise to economic independence and the creation of national industry and renaissance of Gaelic culture which have marked the past fifteen or so years'.[72] Two more detailed reviews appear in *Monthly Film Bulletin* and *Film Weekly* in December. *Film Weekly*'s article identifies two American items alongside what it describes as 'Ireland's New Deal'. It describes the Irish items as 'both dramatic and enthusiastic' and 'a glowing account of national prosperity, very pro-de Valera but not unduly prejudiced'. Further approval of de Valera is manifest in the next paragraph – 'his quiet manner and dreamy scholastic speech are impressive and surprising' – while the article goes on to sympathize with the depiction of 'farmers' efforts to smuggle cattle into Northern Ireland and so evade the former exorbitant English cattle tax'. Finally, the review describes 'the contrast between the romantic pastoral Ireland of everybody's dreams, and the burgeoning factories of the modern industrial state which is growing up'. The *Monthly Film Bulletin* review will be discussed below as its detailed description of content is pertinent to the edition of the film examined in this chapter.

A file in the Public Record Office of Northern Ireland entitled 'Inclusion of Northern Ireland in the Series of Films "March of Time" ' details that while a film featuring the Irish Free State had been completed, there was no record of its exhibition as of 1 July 1937.[73] This delay in distributing the edition until after that date followed a general distribution pattern of films being exhibited first in America and then in other countries. (The film was, as has already been confirmed, made for American audiences.) A later film made by March of Time covering Irish neutrality during the Second World War was shown in London in June 1944, but it was not released in Ireland until the following October.[74] As a result, distribution in Ireland, even for items containing content pertinent to Irish audiences, was often delayed due to local factors, including censorship. However, further investigations have suggested that there may have been two versions of the film – the first being the one previewed in the November screening mentioned above, the second being a similar version but with added content, which appears, according to records in the US National Archives, to have been released in May 1937.

I would argue that Donegall saw the first version of what subsequently was released as *Irish Republic* (the problematic nature of this title will be discussed below). Donegall's viewing of this item sparked his interest in making a March of Time film about Northern Ireland. Prior to the screening, Donegall expressed a wish, 'without being too controversial', to the Ministry of Commerce, 'to show the other side of the picture as related to Northern Ireland' and demonstrate 'that Northern Ireland has done much better by remaining loyal to the Crown than the Free State has done by adopting the machinations of Mr de Valera'. Given that Donegall was writing from the offices of the *Sunday Dispatch*, it is likely that he wished to include an article on the film in the next edition of the paper. In order to do this, he requested some information and data, which would facilitate what he described as 'a bit of a counter-blast' in the following Sunday's edition. W.D. Scott replied on behalf of the ministry with a document entitled 'Progress of Northern Ireland as compared with that of the Irish Free State'.[75] The document described a rise in Northern Ireland's external trade while alleging that there was a decrease in southern trade. It illustrated the North's favourable trade relationship with Britain while reporting on a 50 per cent decrease in agricultural exports from the south to Great Britain. People from Northern Ireland were said to invest more than twice as much in savings than southerners, they had better access to electricity and telephones, and received higher unemployment benefits.[76] The provision of this information anticipated a favourable portrait of developments in the south in the March of Time film. The film and Donegall's reaction to it marked the beginning of a process to harness the powerful representative powers of March of Time in the propaganda war to present the north as a loyal and valuable asset to the United Kingdom.

Irish Free State/Irish Republic

The item outlined in the articles above is referred to as 'Ireland's New Deal', 'Irish Free State', 'Irish edition of March of Time', 'Free State Edition'. The only related film currently referenced in the March of Time collection in the US National Archives is called *Irish Republic*. One of the most obvious difficulties with *Irish Republic*[77] is its title. While the 1937 Irish constitution replaced the original Constitution of the Irish Free State, Ireland did not become a republic until 1949 when the Republic of Ireland Act was introduced. Thus the title of the film is not just misleading, but constitutionally, if not politically, incorrect. There are further discrepancies in the dating of the film. The above articles describe a film exhibited in November 1936, whereas the National Archives record the film as released in May 1937. *Monthly Film Bulletin*'s December 1936 review of *Irish Free State* offers evidence to suggest there were two versions of the film. The version still in existence (according to records in the March of Time collection) is *Irish Republic* and its content will be discussed below. *Monthly Film Bulletin* offers a detailed description of the content of *Irish Free State*. Much of this content appears to be the same as *Irish Republic* apart from the movement of Irish families under the land settlement scheme; the Dairy Science School in Cork; America as a market for Guinness, the Ford factory and the success of Irish maternity hospitals. These sections appear to have been replaced with content on the upcoming Irish constitution when *Irish Republic* was released on 14 May 1937. Also, *Irish Free State* is identified as appearing in an edition with one or two items on American politics, one of which related to Roosevelt. *Irish Republic* appears alongside *Puzzle Prizes* and *U.S. Unemployed*. Furthermore, while Northern Ireland is mentioned in *Irish Republic* there are no reports that it was dealt with in *Irish Free State*. The first version of the film does not appear to be in existence, so only *Irish Republic* will be discussed below.

The film opens with scenes of O'Connell Bridge, the Custom House and other easily identifiable shots of Dublin streets, while the famous American commentator, Westbrook Van Voorhis (known as 'the voice of Time') contextualizes for the audience: 'Peaceful today and bustling with trade are the streets of Dublin where not long ago Irishmen were fighting bloody battles against British rule.' The camera cuts to shots of Trinity College, a recognized historical symbol of Protestant learning, while the commentator continues: 'in the orderly Georgian city of today, only a few relics testify that here the British crown once held sway'. The next feature of the film was an unusual one in standard newsreel production – the inclusion of maps. The first map is one of the United Kingdom, clearly identifying England, Scotland, Wales and Ireland, without partition. In the top right-hand corner of the shot there is a crown presiding over the United Kingdom. There is a brief intercut of a Union Jack flapping in the wind before a second map appears, showing

Ireland partitioned into 'Northern Ireland' and the 'Irish Free State'. The camera moves in for a close-up on the map of Ireland; the overall commentary accompanying this section is as follows:

> For eight centuries Great Britain and Ireland together comprised the United Kingdom. But save in the six loyal counties in the North, it was only the British army in Ireland that kept the kingdom united. Fifteen years ago Britain yielded to the twenty six Catholic counties, set them up as the Irish Free State with Dominion status. But loyal Northern Ireland remained in the kingdom.

The section with the maps, as we shall see, also appears in the later March of Time feature, *Ulster vs Éire*, the follow-up film released in 1938 ultimately to counteract the images of the south presented in *Irish Republic*. The commentary is almost exactly the same, although spoken by a British commentator.

To continue with a comparison between the two films it is necessary to complete a full description of *Irish Republic*. After the above introduction, the commentator continues: 'this year in its constitution the Free State proclaims all Ireland a sovereign and independent nation the Republic of Eirse' (sic). Accompanying the commentator's clumsy mistake, the camera moves from the map of Ireland to a mock-up of the Irish Constitution with the following visible: 'The Constitution of the Republic of Éire. Preamble. In the name of the Most Holy Trinity, we the people of Éire hereby adopt, enact and give to ourselves this constitution.' Attention is then placed on Eamon de Valera:

> Father of this new nation, framer of its constitution, commander-in-chief of its patriotic army is New York born Eamon de Valera. Not since Parnell has any leader so completely held the trust of the Irish people as this Mathematics professor turned statesman who, through five years as head of the Free State, has worked for the single purpose, to free Ireland from the last traces of British dominance.

The exterior of Leinster House is depicted, followed by scenes of the interior showing de Valera and his Cabinet. The Tricolour is intercut before the next shot, a close-up on de Valera, much in the same way that the Union Jack has been intercut earlier in the film, each flag operating as a convenient pictorial symbol of political polarity. We then see de Valera inspecting a large and impressive military parade.

At this point an intertitle interrupts with the caption 'Raw indeed were the materials Irish leaders had to work with in fashioning their new nation.' The commentator goes on to describe Ireland's agricultural position over shots of a small cart careering down a country lane – shots in thematic and visual opposition to the large military parade directly preceding the intertitle. We then see a shawled woman pushing a cow into a thatched cottage, scenes which March of Time would repeat in its 1944 film *The Irish Question*, which explored the issue of Irish neutrality during the Second World War. The commentator explains: 'On Ireland's farmland, live 60% of her population, many of them medieval in their simple poverty.' Shots of spinning and weaving are accompanied with the comment that 'into the rural community, ideas of progress, of altered living standards, have filtered slowly'. A man is shown walking a donkey, overburdened with hay, down a country lane while the commentator continues: 'from one generation to the next, there has been little change in the peasant's barren routine of hard work, for the most meagre returns. The leading industry of the farmland has long been cattle-raising for export to England.' Cattle and sheep are shown walking through the streets of a small town. The commentator goes on to describe Éire's economic war with Britain:

> Many a farmer faced starvation when de Valera's Nationalist policies lead to a tariff war. For as Britain and the Free State began piling up customs barriers against each other's goods, 90% of Ireland's markets were completely choked off. Many a farmer took to smuggling cattle across the border to markets in Northern Ireland but even though self-preservation drove them to trade with the enemy, farmers remained staunch de Valera men.

After shots of customs, a single farmer is depicted pushing cattle through a field, then the ruins of what appears to be an old castle. The Economic War had come about with the suspension of land annuities which Irish farmers had been paying to the British Exchequer. The British government reacted by imposing tariff restrictions on Irish goods which had a crippling affect on the Irish economy. In this section of the film, Northern Ireland is defined as the 'enemy', only to be traded with in times of severe economic crisis.

A second intertitle is accompanied by the Irish national anthem – 'in a national plebiscite, de Valera asks the Irish people to ratify what he has done, and what he further proposes for Ireland'. The commentator states: 'undoubted first choice for the Irish people for their first President as provided for in the constitution will be de Valera himself'. There is a medium close-up of de Valera, seated, reading the following statement: 'the present Irish government, was elected on a programme with very clearly defined national aims. The economic aim is to make the country as self-sufficing as is reasonably possible.' The next images are of money and bank tills and clean, organized, advanced-looking schools while the commentator describes de Valera's policies: '1937 finds de Valera's programme for Ireland already underway, a nation already functioning with its own coinage, its own system of raising state revenue, a growing school system where children are learning to speak Gaelic, Erin's ancient tongue, no longer a dead language, but an official language of a living state.' A page of text is shown in Gaelic along with shots of signs in English and Irish. The next section deals with agricultural machinery: 'On its farms, modern methods of livestock raising, as Ireland begins to supply its own market with its own Irish bacon and ham in the face of imported meat, to deal profitably on a large scale in dairy products.' There are shots of a large pig farm followed by close-ups on machinery being inspected by dairy workers in white coats, looking more like scientists conducting experiments than farm employees. The next scenes are of fields being ploughed and hay gathered while we are told '250 acres of former grazing land, newly turned over to wheat, making Ireland almost independent of wheat imports. Peat cutting machines, developing the possibility of domestic fuel, which, made into hard briquettes, is now competing with British coal.' Large peat-cutting machines are shown in the fields before a cut to a mechanized assembly line of peat briquettes, a juxtaposition of men's work in the fields with use of advanced production techniques in a factory. A close-up on one of the peat briquettes shows an imprint of a harp, an enduring symbol of Irishness. The next comment is accompanied by urban scenes – unloading at a large set of docks, shots of a city panorama with factory stacks clearly visible: 'Every form of commerce and industry is being encouraged for de Valera's goal is national self-sufficiency through industrialisation. Irish energies are being turned to manufacturing as Ireland seeks economic salvation in the power of the machine and mass production.' There are images of a boot production line, then men working on the body of a car, a series of shots testifying to the diversity of Irish industry. The film evokes the success of Irish produce: 'in stores everywhere, shoppers buy Irish and imported British goods lose out in competition with home products'. This statement is illustrated by a close-up of a sign stating 'assembled in Ireland'; the camera then locates the sign alongside electrical goods in a shop window. Various products are accompanied by similar signs, some saying 'Irish manufacture' and 'Finest selected Irish', while the commentator tells us that 'cutting down on her imports, jacking up her export trade, Ireland is edging into a more favourable position in world markets'.

Housing is the next topic to be dealt with: 'for city working men and their families, the government is financing a rehousing programme aimed at eventual replacement of slum districts by model homes'. There are shots of terraced houses and scenes of rebuilding. Next the coverage of industrial Ireland reaches a climax with impressive shots of both exterior and interior of the Shannon hydro-electric department. The staff at the facility are depicted alongside huge and intricate machines, conveying to the viewers the impressive nature of the plant's technology. The commentator maximizes the dramatic power of these shots:

> Focus of the industrialisation movement is on the river Shannon, a vast hydro-electric development whose immense turbines throb like the very heart of the new Ireland. Already 700 new factories, sprung up during the past five years, are taxing the capacity of the Shannon power network and with thousands of peasants learning for the first time about the benefits of electricity, plans are being made to tap other water power areas to provide more power for more people.

The final shots of this section are on three women with a food mixer, followed by close-ups on an iron, waffle-maker (an appliance much more familiar to American audiences) and a toaster. While Irish men are shown to be harnessing technology to forward national self-sufficiency, women are shown to be embracing more advanced equipment in the home.

This is one of the few newsreels that shows a more developed, more technological and more urbanized view of Ireland; when March of Time returned to Ireland seven years later to film *The Irish Question*, southerners were depicted as poverty-stricken peasants working the land and preferring independence to technological progress. In *Irish Republic*,

Irishmen are similarly described as 'peasants' but are shown to be taking control of their country's self sufficiency and willing to appropriate technology in order to do so.

The final section of *Irish Republic* deals with the difficult question of conflicting politics north and south. It begins with the intertitle 'to the support of his Constitution, de Valera leads an immense following – but his inclusion of all Ireland in the new nation brings furious opposition'. The accompanying commentary explains: 'In Northern Ireland, more hotly loyal to the British Crown than England itself, are 800,000 Ulstermen of Protestant ancestry, most implacable haters of their neighbours across the Free State border.' The familiar map appears, this time with a glowing crown in Northern Ireland to visualize the 'heat' of Ulster loyalty. In a staged scene characteristic of the March of Time series, men drinking in a pub are shown discussing the election. One of the party – ironically, speaking with a hint of a southern brogue – shouts 'Republic is it? Let them try and get us into the Republic if they want a fight on their hands. Ulster's loyal to the King, God bless him!' Interestingly, this scene also appears in *Ulster vs Éire* and will be discussed again below. Next there are scenes of Orange marches, complete with impressive banners, as the commentator continues:

> Far outnumbered by the two million Free State voters, Ulstermen bristle at the thought of becoming a helpless political minority in the new republic. Loudly they parade their loyalty to the long line of Britain's kings and queens from William of Orange on down through good Queen Victoria on down to the new George VI. Angrily they flaunt their Orangeman banners at the Free State while police stand by alert to suppress bloody rioting.

To back up these comments, we see shots of armoured vehicles and policemen. There is then a marked change in pictorial focus with a return to rural imagery as the commentator concludes: 'but the new republic is confident that nature is stronger than politics, that natural laws of geography and economics must some day make Ireland north and south, one indivisible nation. Time marches on.'

The words used here to describe Orangemen are 'loud' and 'angry', with the suggestion of bloody rioting at marches: the north is shown aggressively protesting while the south is shown to be flourishing. The final conclusion that is drawn is that the solution lies in the creation of

what the commentator calls 'one indivisible nation'. It could be argued
here that it is the north that appears aggressive and backward, preferring
to celebrate the historical victories of the past, while the south is
embracing change and development as part of the quest for successful
self-sufficiency. All these representations change drastically in the later
film *Ulster vs Éire*.

Ulster vs Éire *(1938)*

Ulster vs Éire was undoubtedly inspired by *Irish Republic*. Donegall's
viewing of the film sparked correspondence and discussion surrounding
the possibility of producing a similar film on the position of Northern
Ireland. Mr Goldstein, identified simply as 'a local film correspondent'
in the files pertaining to MOT (March of Time) production in PRONI
(Public Record Office of Northern Ireland) was enlisted, due to his
MOT contacts, to encourage the company to film in the north, a process
which gathered momentum in the summer of 1937. A letter dated 14
July to James Stewart in the Ministry of Commerce from W.S. Magill,
secretary and organizer of the Ulster Tourist Development Association,
outlines that a Mr Goldstein suggests that March of Time is interested
in filming in Northern Ireland and queries what cooperation can be
supplied by the government, stating that financial assistance is not being
sought.[78] The reason for this is relayed in an informal talk between
Goldstein and Magill; it is that the March of Time promoters 'did not
seek official assistance of a financial character as they desired to be
perfectly free in arranging their editorial matter but he wished to be
assured that, if the idea of a Northern Ireland film matured, the
promoters would receive official assistance in every other way possible'.[79]
The assurance of official help was given and a meeting between Magill
and a Mr Swingler, a representative from March of Time, was set up. In
the subsequent meeting, Goldstein and Magill were informed of March
of Time's intention. Swingler, 'in describing the type of film which was
produced by his Company, stated that their main object was to get away
from the sentimental and usually unreal picture portrayed in such films
as *The Wee Blue Blossom*'. *Wee Blue Blossom* was a short film made in
1933 to promote the Irish linen industry. It opens with scenes of landscape, children sitting on a stone wall being nuzzled by a goat while the
commentary describes in lilting and musical tones 'the emerald isle, isle

of blue lakes and kindly hills, whose soft green slopes roll down to the sea. Land of smiles and tears, of laughter and song.'[80] This was the kind of representation Swingler and March of Time wanted to distance the company from in 1937 but, as we shall see, it is exactly the kind of picture it was guilty of painting of Ireland in the 1940s, in particular in *The Irish Question* (1944) which will be discussed below.

Swingler's four essential points in relation to the film were that it would have:

1. News value
2. Drama
3. Historical treatment if necessary to the drama.
4. A hint of future developments.

He also suggested that he would be interested in filming the Cabinet in session or at least some of the ministers[81] (presumably because the earlier film showed de Valera with his Cabinet). It was established that a March of Time cameraman would visit Northern Ireland on Monday 7 February for one or two days to take shots of the election, with a full camera unit to follow towards the end of March.[82]

The completed film opens with exactly the same footage (and negligible differences in commentary) as *Irish Republic*. What is inserted into the introduction in *Ulster vs Éire* is archive footage of King George's opening of the Northern Ireland parliament in 1920, at the same point where *Irish Republic* begins to discuss Eamon de Valera. The commentary states: 'In Belfast in 1920 King George V opened Northern Ireland's first parliament. Elected to office was a government uncompromising in its hatred of Irish independence.' A symbol of 'uncompromising Unionism' is then provided in the form of James Craig, shown at home in Stormont Castle (not to be confused with the parliament buildings). We are reminded that 'Lord Craigavon, as Prime Minister has held power throughout Northern Ireland's eighteen year history. This year he prepares for his eighth general election.' Craig is handed election posters while seated comfortably in an armchair. The *Daily Express* suggested in February 1938 that Craig was 'the one politician who can win an election without leaving his fireside', an image which is backed up by these shots of Craig at home (indeed, Craig was confined to his home throughout the election campaign due to a bout of flu).[83] The next intertitle reads: 'As Ulster's political parties make leisurely plans for the distant election, the Free State government suddenly develops a lively interest in Ulster affairs.' Shots of de Valera speaking to two men follow the intertitle, while the commentator continues: 'confident that Britain, disturbed by problems of national defence, would prefer to be neighboured by a friendly United Ireland, de Valera carries to Downing street an offer of a more co-operative policy toward the crown. In return he seeks English help in persuading Northern Ireland to join his Republic.'

We see de Valera arrive at Downing Street before another intertitle qualifies the previous comment: 'but British ministers know from long experience that Northern Ireland will decide her future allegiance for herself'. The subsequent shots show a close-up on a newspaper article with the heading 'Irish Unity Sentiment Gains. Entry of North into National Parliament is Regarded as a Possibility'. The commentator contextualizes the debate, showing scholars reading *Value of Imports and Exports, Northern Ireland 1934*: 'as British observers look for signs of lessening Ulster antagonism towards the Free State they weigh her economic arguments for and against joining the Republic.' The same error in classifying Ireland as a 'Republic' occurs in *Ulster vs Éire* as in March of Time's previous Irish coverage.

The next shots are of workers in the shipyard while the commentary continues: 'Benefiting from the union with England are Belfast's shipyards which receive a small share of British rearmament orders and in the future hope for more.' From scenes of busy workers in the shipyards, the camera cuts to shots of men milling around on a street while attention is turned to unemployment: 'yet Ulster's industries leave one third of her insured workers unemployed, worse unemployment than in the Free State'. We are quickly directed back to the world of work when we are shown a variety of tasks in York Street Mill while the commentary continues: 'Ulster's world famous linen industry is adversely affected by tariffs imposed by the Free State, tariffs which would disappear once Ulster became part of Eamon de Valera's republic.' Moving away from the industrial, we see rural scenes of thatched cottages and sheep grazing: 'Ulster's farmers are well satisfied with the union with England, for they have increased their exports to the mother country at the expense of Free State farmers handicapped by de Valera's trade war with England.' The next shot is of Stranmillis teacher training college in Belfast, followed by scenes of children in the exterior of a large school. The commentary states 'Ulstermen, proud of their advanced educational system, fear that Irish unity might bring Catholic interference in their schools.'

The next intertitle focuses attention on the election: 'Knowing that Ulster's forthcoming election will be regarded in Dublin and London as a crucial test of his anti-Republican power, Lord Craigavon takes action.' There are further shots of Craig in his armchair; over his shoulder we can read a poster featuring the campaign slogan 'You must help keep Ulster in the Empire. Vote Loyalist.' The accompanying commentary states: 'taking advantage of the alarm which de Valera's plan sends sweeping across all Ulster, Lord Craigavon catches his opponents unprepared, by giving only four weeks' notice of the pending general election'. A headline reads: 'Ulster General Election. Mr De Valera's "partition" challenge accepted by Lord Craigavon.' We then see shots of Sir Wilson Hungerford, secretary of the Ulster Unionist Council, speaking to a large crowd of subdued-looking men as the commentator explains: 'Craigavon's Unionist candidates stomp the country, calling for Loyalist critics of his veteran administration to sink their differences in the face of the common Free State enemy.' We see further shots of candidates speaking to crowds: 'They represent loyalty to the British flag as the only vital question before the electors.' Close-ups of the crowds show cheering faces and many people are waving Union Jacks: 'To the hot-headed Ulster folk, economic arguments for and against unity with the Free State dwindle into insignificance.'

Heightened music introduces the same staged scene in a bar which appears in *Irish Republic*, with the same actor pledging allegiance to Ulster in a southern accent and again stressing Ulster's loyalty to Britain. An interesting feature of the film, and perhaps a dramatic device employed by the film-makers rather than an accurate portrayal of events, is the build-up of tension through leading comments such as 'as voters stream to the polls, Great Britain awaits what may prove to be a new answer to the ancient Irish riddle for the defeat of Craigavon's government well may mean the eventual end of Irish partition'. This highly unlikely possibility is undermined by a shot of polling booths, with a large car adorned with Union Jacks right outside the door; in reality, Craig's Unionist majority was secure because it had been built into the very structure of partition. Yet the film still alludes to the results as if they were uncertain: 'but with the declaration of results comes proof of the shrewdness of Craigavon's estimate of his countrymen. His candidates sweep the polls returning him to power and amidst hysterical excitement celebrate a majority greater than ever before.'

Accompanying shots of newspaper headlines read: 'Belfast Telegraph: "Ulster Premier's Election Triumph" and "Great Loyalist Victory"', while the commentary further stresses: 'Ulstermen rejoice that they have delivered once more their traditional answer to Irish Republicanism. Eamon de Valera has failed.' The triumphant tone becomes quieter, almost reverential, when returning, one final time, to the seat of power in Northern Ireland – Craig's armchair. 'Ageing Lord Craigavon', the audience is told (he is pictured patting his dog, the implicit loyalty inherent in the visuals – home, hearth and constancy), 'is within two years of achieving his declared ambition of giving Northern Ireland twenty years of steady Loyalist government.' At this point the film once again borrows scenes and commentary from *Irish Republic*: the same shots of Orange parades are included, as well as the same sentences used to describe Orangemen as in the previous film. The terms 'loudly and angrily' are still used, but the tone is softer, less aggressive, and the commentary is spoken by a British commentator, with different modulation and inflection. The commentary also changes in its ultimate conclusion. There are no shots of tanks and no mention of bloody rioting in *Ulster vs Éire* as there had been in *Irish Republic*. In this film the Orange parades are juxtaposed with scenes of election victory, linking images of the Orange Order with celebration of current victories rather than commemorations of a restrictive past. These remarks conclude the film; there is no suggestion as in the earlier film of 'one indivisible nation'. Rather, it is instead a celebration of Unionism, leading James Loughlin to describe the film as 'a major media coup'[84] for the Unionist government, despite March of Time's documented request to remain perfectly free in arranging their editorial matter. Sir Wilson Hungerford wrote to Craigavon, on the film's screening in London, that the film was 'exceedingly pro-Unionist'. Hungerford also predicted opposition to the film, stating that 'our opponents will not like it'.[85] John Hill also describes a screening of the film in Belfast for members of the Northern Ireland government, including Craig 'who commented that the film had dealt with the subject "in a very fair manner" '.[86] Hill's comment on the film recognizes the admission of the high rate of unemployment in Northern Ireland, but critiques the lack of interrogation of the north's electoral system and the lack of representation of any opposing political side within Northern Ireland. Thus the film's analysis of 'Ulster' and 'Éire' lacks complexity.

What *Irish Republic* and *Ulster vs Éire* offer is an insight into the representation of Ireland by an outside news agency and, in particular, the ideological forces behind two very different depictions. As has already been mentioned, due to a lack of sustained indigenous production, at least until the 1950s, Ireland was catered for and covered by 'external' news producers. While most of this coverage was by British-based companies, there was also interest shown by American newsreels. Thus the representations that Irish audiences viewed of their country and themselves were, in essence, offered to them by foreign producers. In some cases, as in *Ulster vs Éire*, local forces interacted with the newsreels, often affecting the connotations associated with depictions of Ireland, further complicated by the political tensions between north and south, and each part's relationship with Britain. *Irish Republic* was primarily geared towards American audiences and presumably in particular towards Irish Americans. It offers a positive and optimistic account of Ireland's progress under de Valera's leadership and points towards a prosperous future. Its production and screening began the chain of events which led to *Ulster vs Éire*, a film that, despite sharing much common footage, was vastly different in tone, this time prioritizing the position of Ulster. Its aim was to counteract the forward-looking representation of Éire in *Irish Republic* and explain the political differences between north and south. The involvement of Northern Ireland's Unionist government undoubtedly affected the film's ideological orientation. The fact that these two films, made only a year apart by the same company, offer almost contradictory renderings of the Irish political question, testifies to the manipulability of the newsreel industry by forces of authority. They also mirror a growing tendency in the newsreels to separate north and south and present each as a unique entity. This 'partitionist' mentality was growing in the 1930s and would become more pronounced during the Second World War. The construction of north and south in the newsreels was significant for Irish and British audiences as Ireland, both north and south, gradually came to terms with two distinct identities emerging from a partitioned state.

Political Coverage of the North

The election of de Valera in 1932, and the political crescendo that this caused in Irish–British relationships, had particular significance in Northern Ireland. The political climate in the north is captured well in an interesting letter sent to the Ulster Tourist Development Association from Robert Maxwell, from Maxwell's North of Ireland tours in Liverpool. Maxwell raises concerns that 'a very large percentage of the English people do not understand the separate functions of north and south'. Maxwell referred to 'the Political Crisis in Free State' in the heading of his letter, stating that 'the dispute is causing injurious reflections to fall on the north of Ireland tourist traffic'.[87] Maxwell urges the UTDA to 'look into this matter at the earliest possible moment'. This confusion between north and south would continue, not least due to a confusion in terminology related to Ireland. A letter from the Unionist Cabinet Minister, W.D. Scott, to Blackmore, Private Secretary to the Prime Minister, refers to a complaint made about the *Daily Express* 'deliberately' using the term 'Ireland' when referring to the Irish Free State. The letter reveals that recent communication with all the leading UK newspapers invited 'their co-operation in removing the misapprehension which exists in regard to the position of Northern Ireland'.[88]

The proliferation of images of the Eucharistic Congress in the newsreels would also have angered the Unionist establishment in the north and again reinforced the divide between north and south. The overall reaction to the Congress in the south was seen as hysterical by the Northern Ireland government which concluded that the congress had created 'excitement amounting almost to frenzy'.[89] Trains and buses returning to the north with pilgrims were attacked, while during the ensuing marching season 'resolutions were carried denouncing "the unchanging bigotry of Rome" and, in particular, "the arrogant, intolerant and un-Christian pretensions fulminated by Cardinal MacRory" '.[90] During 12 July celebrations, Prime Minister Craig declared that 'Ours is a Protestant government and I am an Orangeman', while a year later his future successor Basil Brooke warned his fellow Protestants about employing Catholics, insisting, as reported by the *Fermanagh Times*, that 'he had not a Roman Catholic about his place' and pointing out that 'Roman Catholics were endeavouring to get in everywhere and were out with all their force and might to destroy the power and constitution of Ulster.'[91] Interestingly, while there was a large degree of coverage of the Eucharistic Congress, the annual 12 July celebrations were not covered by the newsreels at all in 1932. In fact, the Orange commemorations, a topic of considerable interest for the newsreels in the past, were paid scant attention throughout the 1930s.

An event associated with the north which did receive as much coverage by the newsreels as the Eucharistic Congress was the visit by the Prince of Wales to Northern Ireland to open the new parliamentary buildings at Stormont. British Movietone News's *Northern Ireland hails Prince on first Visit*[92] shows scenes of the Prince arriving at Belfast docks to be greeted by cheering crowds, clearly audible as the commentary tells us that '*all* Belfast is awaiting' the arrival of the Royal visitor (emphasis added). While the Unionist community certainly eagerly awaited the Prince's arrival, given that royal visits had a 'tendency to crystallize for Ulster Unionists their British national identity in terms of myth',[93] the Nationalist community was naturally less enthusiastic. The IRA protested the visit through a series of attacks on border posts and government installations but this opposition is not alluded to in the typically upbeat and exaggerated commentary. The Prince is greeted at Stormont by large crowds and a military band playing 'Danny Boy'. After the opening of Stormont the Prince travels to City Hall where shots of huge crowds, and buildings covered with Union Jacks, verify the commentator's remarks that 'dense masses of people have assembled to give him the greatest welcome of the day'.

Although the visit was eagerly anticipated by Unionists, there was some controversy surrounding the Prince's attitude to visiting Northern Ireland. Loughlin suggests that the fact that the Prince ignored cheering crowds on his drive through Belfast made the visit an 'uncomfortable experience for those who had awaited it so enthusiastically'.[94] The *Derry Journal* summed up the event: 'There was a noticeable lack of warmth about the entire proceedings ... Although the populace joined in the cheering all along the route to Stormont, the fact was commented upon that there appeared to be little sign of reciprocal enthusiasm shown from the official car leading the procession'[95] – even from Lady Craigavon, who noted in her diary that despite the 'great ovation from the crowds ... the Prince looked like thunder'.[96] Given the significance that Unionists attached to royal visits it is, perhaps, surprising that her speculations as to the reason for the Prince's coldness should focus on Nationalist scheming to turn the Prince against the Ulster Protestant people:

we knew he never wanted to come over but the King said he must. He had ... [heard] frightful tales about Ulster, the people, and the Government put into him for some time by his entourage with southern sympathies and had been given a completely wrong idea about everything ... It was hardly to be wondered at that he was cross ... [97]

The Prince's sullen behaviour was not unique to Ulster and would suggest that his future abdication to marry the divorced Wallis Simpson was a welcome escape from the burdens of monarchy.

One gesture towards the Nationalist community was the Prince's visit to the Catholic Mater Hospital – 'something long remembered by the Catholic community'.[98] The Prince did, however, cause controversy when he casually picked up a Lambeg drum and began playing. The incident was seized upon by the press as a sign of the monarchy's association with Orangeism. Ironically, with hindsight Edward saw the incident as a plot hatched by Unionists 'to make party use of his visit',[99] and it discouraged him from making future visits to Northern Ireland.

5.2 Pathé Super Gazette: *Cheers – All the Way*, Copyright British Pathé Ltd.

Loughlin concludes: 'had Edward retained his crown, therefore, it is possible that the demonstration of national identity based on the fulsome expression of homage and its acknowledgement between subjects and monarch, could have become problematic for Ulster Unionists.[100] Indeed, after the abdication there were incidents of Belfast cinemagoers booing and walking out when Edward's picture was shown on screen during the playing of the national anthem.'[101]

Characteristically, any controversy associated with the Prince's visit is absent from the newsreels, which covered the event with energy and enthusiasm. Pathé's coverage opens with the intertitle 'Cheers – All the Way'. The strains of 'Danny Boy' also open Pathé's item on the Prince's visit, accompanying an intertitle stating 'Cheers all the way ... greet the Prince of Wales on his first visit to loyal Ulster to open the Parliament of Northern Ireland.' The strains of 'Danny Boy' can be heard in the background, giving way to loud cheers from the crowd as the Prince's cavalcade arrives at Stormont. The Prince steps out of a car and inspects a group of soldiers while huge crowds look on. The camera then cuts to scenes of crowds and military singing the national anthem. There are further shots of the Prince inspecting the military, and tipping his hat as loud cheers break out from the crowd. He makes his way through a break in the crowd to the entrance of Stormont, saluting the cheering onlookers several times. There are no shots of the Prince inside Stormont, but there are panning shots of the crowd and Stormont buildings accompanying the audio of the Prince's speech:

> My Lord Duke, my lords, ladies and gentlemen, His Majesty the King, being unable to be present himself, has charged me, as his representative, to perform today's ceremony of opening the building which is to be the home of your parliament. No-one can fail to be touched by the nobility and bounty of fabric and the spanning of the site dominating a great part of your beautiful countryside here at the capital city of Belfast of which you are justly proud. In the name and behalf of His Majesty the King, I declare this building to be open. May the blessing of almighty God rest upon it and those ministers, magistrates and other public servants who labour therein.[102]

The content of the speech is a celebration of unionism, in contrast to the King's speech to open the Northern Ireland parliament in 1921 which addressed all Irish people 'whatever their race or creed'. The Prince celebrates the urban north through his praise of Belfast, and focuses on the northern administration, whereas the King had appealed to 'all Irishmen to pause, to stretch out the hand of forbearance and conciliation, to forgive and forget, and to join in making for the land which they love a new era of peace, contentment, and good will'. The coverage of both of these events in the newsreels demonstrates a growing partitionist perspective, a burgeoning awareness of the increasing separation of north and south. Bardon suggests that the King's opening of Parliament in 1921 was a key moment in ending the war of independence.[103] The Prince's visit in 1932 reflects back to the moment when his father visited a decade earlier and, just as the former visit was a crucial moment in the process of partition, the Prince's visit, too, signifies the expanding differences between north and south.

Indigenous Production in Northern Ireland

One indigenous effort at newsreel production was also associated with the UTDA. The cinemagazine *Ulster Movie Sound News* was established in 1937, with its first screening taking place in May and covering Coronation week. A second edition covered the Trooping of the Colour at Ballykinler, RUC sports at Balmoral and the motor race at Ballyclare, while a third dealt with the royal visit of the new king, all of these items clearly associating representations of the north with unionism. A monthly 'Ulster Movie News Journal' was planned by Louis Morrison, a photographer who subsequently got involved with local film-making. Morrison sought assistance from the Ministry of Commerce. The ministry was attempting to attract new industries to Northern Ireland under new legislation, but, unsure that film would fall within the realm of their remit, Morrison was referred to the UTDA and the Ulster Industries Development Association, which had been formed in 1929 to promote the production and purchase of Ulster goods. Unfortunately for Morrison, W.D. Scott, Permanent Secretary at the Ministry of Commerce, had viewed an edition of *Ulster Movie Sound News*, commenting that the camera work was 'atrocious' and the sound effects 'moved a large audience to laughter'. There were no further editions of the newsreel, and no completed footage is thought to still be in existence, although Morrison did go on to collaborate with Richard Hayward on travelogue films.[104]

The End of the 1930s: *The 1939 IRA Bomb Attacks*

The IRA carried out a bombing campaign in Britain from January 1939 which left seven dead and nearly two hundred wounded.[105] All of the main newsreel companies covered the bombings. In what appears almost as a homage to March of Time, Movietone's 19 January item on the Southwark bombs opens with an intertitle stating that 'the mystery grows deeper and deeper', against the backdrop of a close-up of a telephone.[106] In a dramatic reconstruction there are shots of a phone being dialled and then a voice says: 'Is that the police? There's been an explosion in Southwark.' The camera then cuts to damaged buildings and debris in the streets while the commentary moves almost seamlessly back into that of normal newsreel fare: 'that's where the bomb burst there, and here's the CID[107] searching for debris'. Men in suits and bowler hats are shown scraping the ground while the commentator continues: 'you can tell they're CID by their wristwatches'. After various shots of the damage, the commentator says: 'someone suspects Irish Republicans for wanting to blow up the city of London power station and they're searching for traces of Irish newspapers in the gutter'.

Shots through a window from the interior of a damaged building are accompanied with the explanation that 'they smashed in the windows of the Queen's head pub too, it's a crying shame'. Cutting back to the CID operatives still searching through debris, the commentator informs the audience that they haven't found anything yet and flippantly concludes: 'send for Sherlock Holmes'. Pathé's coverage is less offhand but equally as dramatic, opening with the proclamation: 'terrorism in England, it has a strange ring, but unfortunately it's true'.[108] The camera pans down a damaged building while the commentator continues: 'a series of bomb outrages occurred in many parts of the country, London, Manchester, Birmingham and Liverpool'. Next there is similar footage to Movietone's coverage, showing CID operatives searching through debris, while the audience is informed that 'where these pictures were taken, a bomb had exploded near the control room of the central electricity board at Southwark. Windows of whole streets were wrecked, but happily no-one was hurt. However, Scotland Yard is on the job. May success attend their efforts to track down the authors of these outrages.' The next shots of patrolling policemen are contextualized with the information that special guards are on patrol at power stations throughout the country.

The newsreel then moves to Manchester where 'tragedy enters the story, for at the corner of Newton and Hilton streets a man was hurled into the air and died from his injuries'. The commentator's dramatic tone is matched with scenes of wreckage before the item reaches its conclusion: 'police activity in all these districts leads us to hope that the perpetrators will soon be called upon to answer for their crimes at the bar of British justice'. Pathé covers two more bomb attacks in their 6 February issue.[109] Opening with shots of bombed tube stations, the commentator states that 'once again London has been shocked by two more deliberate attempts to destroy property and endanger life'. We see shots of the interior of one of the affected stations while the dramatic tone of the commentary continues: 'two underground stations have to be temporarily closed, a station foreman lies in hospital seriously injured'. The commentator informs us that close-ups of severe wreckage in the interior of the station 'give you an idea of the force of the explosion'. The commentary continues: 'the police appear to be convinced that these latest outrages are again the work of politicians of the underworld. Every right thinking man and woman will condemn this insolent insane attempt at terrorism which strikes at the very root of the freedom and safety of democracy.' Even though the attacks are not specifically attributed to the IRA, most audiences would have prior knowledge, through press and radio, of their involvement. The characterization of these 'politicians of the underworld' is that of insane and violent agents set to tear at the foundations of democratic society.

The campaign was not confined to England. Movietone reports, in its 23 January issue, an attack on a hotel where Frank Chamberlain, the Prime Minister's son, was staying.[110] The commentary plays down the attack, describing its location, Tralee, Co. Kerry, as 'the latest scene of mystery'. Over a couple of confined shots of rubble at the back of the hotel, the commentator states that the bomb 'didn't cause much damage as you can see from these pictures'. The commentator then adds that 'the Prime Minister's son was awakened, but otherwise unconcerned'.

In coverage of the bombing campaign, the newsreels did not specifically blame Republicans but alluded to them, drawing on audiences' prior knowledge of the attacks to condemn, often with strong language, the 'politicians of the underworld'. On the outbreak of the Second World

War the newsreels would initially deal with neutrality in a similar manner, but became much more condemnatory of Irish politics as the war progressed.

The Growing Differences in Representation Between North and South

Certainly there is a suggestion that while the world looks towards mounting international conflict, Ireland is either subversive or at play – a view that would continue throughout the war. In a Gaumont item on a *Carnival Parade in Tipperary*,[111] the commentator states: 'for the moment international worries melt away before the tide of gaiety and abandon which is a fitting climax to the light-hearted note of the day'. The ability to remain unaffected by international events is one often associated with the Irish people in the newsreels, and will become even more apparent in the next chapter's coverage of wartime Ireland.

Two major news events of the 1930s, and specifically 1932, perhaps most appropriately sum up the newsreels' ultimate representation of a growing partitionist mentality in Ireland. The Eucharistic Congress in the south and the opening of Stormont in the north act as catalysts for partition on either side of the border, reflecting the relationship between the southern government and the Catholic faith in the northern government and the monarchy respectively. The representation of both events in newsreel coverage symbolizes the increasing alienation of southern Nationalists from northern Unionists.

The newsreels both reflect and construct partition in their differing representations of north and south. This would become even more evident (and in some cases more partisan) during coverage of Ireland during the Second World War. Northern Unionists and southern Nationalists regarded each other with suspicion and attempted to police the representation of north and south – as can be seen in both governments' courting of the newsreels for propaganda purposes. There was an increasing tendency within the newsreels to split north and south into very separate entities, reflecting the growing sense of partition in contemporary audiences' minds. This separation between the two states would become even more apparent in the war years, as de Valera made his most stubborn and most determinedly independent stance, a stance facilitated by the end of the Economic War and return of the Treaty ports in 1938. While the 1930s had been a difficult time for Ireland financially, de Valera's dismantling of the Treaty had been successful in increasing the political distance between Britain and Éire.

NOTES

1. *Gaelic Football in America*. Gaumont British News, Issue 463, 6 June 1938.
2. *Irish Football in America*. British Movietone News, Issue 470, 6 June 1938.
3. Partridge (1984), p.966.
4. *Irish Football in America*. British Movietone News, Issue 470, 6 June 1938.
5. *Ireland: Description by Tony Quinn*. British Movietone News, Issue 434A, 30 September 1937.
6. *Gaelic Football Championship*. 18 September 1939, no issue number available on NoS.
7. *Kerry v. Laois* (spelled 'Leix' on British Movietone News database). August 1938, no entry available on NoS.
8. *Kerry v. Galway*. British Movietone News, 27 September 1938, no entry available on NoS.
9. *Kerry v. Galway in Gaelic Football Match*. Gaumont British News, Issue 496, 29 September 1938.
10. *Football Final in Dublin*. Pathé Super Sound Gazette, Issue 1328, 27 September 1934.
11. *Irish Hurling Final at Killarney*. Pathé Super Sound Gazette, Issue 37/72, 9 September 1937.
12. *All Ireland Hurling Final*. Gaumont British News, Issue 386, 9 September 1937.
13. *England Secure Fine Win at Twickenham*. British Movietone News, Issue 193, 13 February 1933.
14. *England beat Ireland 13–3*. British Movietone News, Issue 245, 12 December 1934.
15. *Irish XV Win Great Rugger Victory by 12–5 over Scots*. British Movietone News, Issue 299, 25 February 1935.
16. *Ireland v. Wales Rugby Match*. British Movietone News, Issue 301, 3 November 1935.
17. *Soccer*. British Movietone News, Issue 385A, 22 October 1936.
18. *British Isles Share Olympic Victories*. British Movietone News, Issue 167, 15 August 1932.
19. *First Snapshot is Judging and Jumping Competition at World Famous Show Held in Dublin*. British Movietone News, Issue 270A, 9 August 1934.
20. Hill (2006), p.7.
21. Letter from C.W.S. Magill, UTDA, to Blackmore, Private Secretary to the Prime Minister, 13 August 1931, Public Record Office of Northern Ireland, Belfast [hereafter PRONI] CAB 9F/114/1.
22. Letter from Oscar Henderson to Blackmore, 24 February 1930, PRONI CAB 9F/123/1.
23. Letter from Norman Hulbert, British Movietone News, to Craigavon, 24 August 1931, PRONI CAB 9F/123/1.
24. *British Victory in Ulster TT Races*. British Movietone News, Issue 116. 24 March 1931.
25. *International TT Belfast*. Universal News, Issue 14, 28 August 1930.
26. *Ulster Tourist Trophy Race is Won by Freddie Dixon*. British Movietone News, Issue 327, 9 September 1935.
27. *TT Car Race at Newtownards Won by Freddie Dixon and Charlie Dobson – Chambers Crashes through Barrier*. Gaumont British News, Issue 281, 7 September 1936.
28. Rockett (2004), p.18.
29. *President Cosgrave*. Pathé Super Sound Gazette, Issue 30/51, 24 November 1930.
30. Lee (1989), p.156.
31. Rockett (2004), p.318.
32. Ibid.
33. Ibid.
34. 'Talking Film' March 1931. British Movietone News, NAI, File S2366.
35. Ibid.
36. Rockett (2004), p.318.
37. *President Cosgrave Adds Voice to Peace Plea*. British Movietone News, Issue 102A, 21 May 1931.
38. *Erin on Parade*. British Paramount News, Issue 7, 23 March 1931.

39. *Erin Go Bragh*. British Paramount News, Issue 112, 24 March 1932.
40. Lee (1989), p.157.
41. Bardon (1992), p.535.
42. Ibid., p.536.
43. Coogan (2003), p.183.
44. *De Valera Wins*. British Paramount News, Issue 103, 22 February 1932.
45. *All Eyes on Ireland*. British Paramount News, Issue 113, 28 March 1932.
46. Lee (1989), p.168.
47. Coogan (2003), p.183.
48. *Papal Delegate Steps Ashore in Dublin*. British Movietone Gazette, Issue 125A, 20 June 1932.
49. *Millions at Phoenix Park Mass*. British Movietone News, Issue 160A, 30 June 1932.
50. *Acclaim Pope's Envoy*. British Paramount News, Issue 138, 23 June 1932.
51. *A Million at Mass*. British Paramount News, Issue 140, 30 June 1932.
52. *Eucharistic Congress*. Universal News, Issue 206, 30 June 1932.
53. Campbell (1941), cited in Bardon (1992), p.537.
54. McLoone in Hill, McLoone and Hainsworth (1994), p.166.
55. *Irish Rush Election*. British Paramount News, Issue 197, 16 January 1933.
56. *De Valera Triumphs*. British Paramount News, Issue 202, 2 February 1933.
57. Bardon (1992), p.542.
58. I have provided these figures through statistical analysis of 251 items covering Hitler's rise to power and government of Germany during the 1930s.
59. Aldgate (1979), p.29.
60. *General O'Duffy Explains*. British Paramount News, Issue 259, 21 August 1933.
61. *O'Duffy Defies de Valera*. British Paramount News, Issue 298, 4 January 1934.
62. *600 Irish Blueshirts Conceal Uniforms*. British Movietone News, Issue 234A, 30 November 1933.
63. Bardon (1992), p.542.
64. *De Valera Bereaved*. British Movietone News, Issue 349A, 13 February 1936.
65. *De Valera Attends Irish Games*. British Movietone News, Issue 370A, 7 September 1936.
66. *St Patrick's Day in Éire*. British Movietone News, Issue 465A, 21 March 1938.
67. Bardon (1992), p.542.
68. Ibid., p.544.
69. ' "March of Time": Ireland's Beauty Spots', *Kinematograph Weekly*, 15 October 1936, p.37.
70. Ibid.
71. 'Time's Irish March', *Today's Cinema*, 47, 3481 (7 December 1936), p.6.
72. 'The March of Time', *Today's Cinema*, 47, 3468 (21 November 1936), p.6.
73. Minute 3, 1 July 1937, in file entitled 'Inclusion of Northern Ireland in the Series of Films "March of Time" ', PRONI COM 62/1/614.
74. *The Irish Question*. March of Time, Issue 11 – 9th Year, 12 June 1944.
75. Letter from W.D. Scott (Ministry of Commerce) to Lord Donegall, 19 November 1936, PRONI COM 62/1/614.
76. Ibid.
77. *Irish Republic*. March of Time, Vol. 3, No. 10, 14 May 1937 (as referenced in the US National Archives).
78. Letter from James Stewart (Ministry of Commerce) to W.S. Magill (Secretary and Organizer of the Ulster Tourist Development Association), 14 July 1937, PRONI COM 62/1/614.
79. Minute 12, 31 July 1937, PRONI COM 62/1/614.
80. *Wee Blue Blossom*. Irish Linen Guild, 1933. This film can be viewed on the Digital Film Archive.
81. Minute 16, 8 September 1937, PRONI COM 62/1/614.
82. Minute 27, February 1938, PRONI COM 62/1/614.
83. Bardon (1992), p.544.
84. Loughlin (1995), p.108.
85. Letter from Hungerford to Craigavon, 27 April 1938, PRONI CAB9F/123/3A. See Hill (2006), p.190.

86. *Kine Weekly*, 30 June 1938, p.26, cited in Hill (2006), p.100.
87. Letter from Robert Maxwell to UTDA, 9 April 1932, PRONI CAB/9F/123/1.
88. Letter from W.D. Scott to Blackmore, Private Secretary to the Prime Minister, 7 June 1932, PRONI CAB/9F/123/1.
89. Barton (1988) in Bardon (1992), p.537.
90. Kennedy (1988) in Bardon (1992), pp.537–8.
91. Bardon (1992), p.538.
92. *Northern Ireland Hails Prince on First Visit*. British Movietone News, Issue 2111, 21 November 1932.
93. Loughlin (2002), p.114.
94. Loughlin (1995), p.111.
95. *Derry Journal*, 18 November 1932, cited in Loughlin (1995), p.111.
96. Craigavon diary, 16 November 1932, PRONI P1415/6/38, cited in Loughlin (1995), pp.111–12.
97. Ibid.
98. Loughlin (2002), p.112.
99. Ibid., p.112.
100. Ibid., p.112.
101. Ibid, p.114.
102. *Cheers – All the Way!* Pathé Super Gazette, Issue 32/93, 21 November 1932.
103. Bardon (1992), pp.480–2.
104. Hill (2006), p.108.
105. Lee (1989), p.220.
106. *The Mystery Grows Deeper and Deeper*. British Movietone News, Issue 502A, 19 January 1939.
107. Criminal Investigation Department.
108. *Bomb Outrages*. Pathé Gazette, Issue 39/6, 19 January 1939.
109. *More Bomb Outrages*. Pathé Gazette, Issue 39/11, 6 February 1939.
110. *Bomb in Ireland*. British Movietone News, Issue 503, 23 January 1939.
111. *Carnival Parade in Tipperary*. Gaumont British News, Issue 560, 11 May 1939.

6

Viewing in Éire, Northern Ireland and Britain during the Second World War

While audiences in Northern Ireland, as part of the United Kingdom, watched the upbeat, rallying newsreels designed to improve morale and increase production in the war effort, cinemagoers just across the border in the south saw no evidence whatsoever of global conflict on their screens. Irish audiences were presented with 'a radically different world to that shown to their British counterparts, a world into which the tribulations of their near neighbours and the war in Europe did not impinge'.[1] This was due to the fact that the Irish government set up a strong censorship regime to deal with wartime entertainment and information flow. The Censorship of Films Act was amended through an Emergency Powers Order extending the powers of the Official Film Censor to cover propaganda emanating from or referring to *any* of the belligerents. News films had to be free from war news: images of war were only to be permitted if the identity of the protagonists was indistinguishable and the commentary was objective.[2]

The Emergency

Éire was the only dominion in the Commonwealth to choose neutrality, and its decision was heavily criticized by the British media. Although Irish neutrality was friendly towards the Allies, as the war progressed the British government, and particularly Winston Churchill, was increasingly irritated by Ireland's lack of compromise on the issue.

Kevin Rockett qualifies the policy of neutrality adopted by the Irish government: 'in practice the Irish state embarked on what the Minister for the Co-ordination of Defensive Measures, Frank Aiken, described as a form of "limited warfare", which allowed the Irish government to steer a middle-course between conflicting strains within Irish society'.[3] Entering the war on the side of the Allies would have demonstrated support for Britain and therefore an implicit recognition of partition, anathema to many Irishmen. From the government's viewpoint, neutrality was the option that divided the Irish people least and there was also the threat of a German-backed IRA revolt to contend with if Éire had entered the war.[4] To those who may have questioned it, de Valera suggested:

> I know that in this country there are sympathies, very strong sympathies in regard to the present issues, but I do not think that anybody, no matter what his feelings might be, would suggest that the Government policy, the official policy of the State, should be other than what the Government would suggest. We, of all nations, know what force used by a stronger nation against a weaker one means. We have known what invasion and partition mean; we are not forgetful of our history, and as long as our own country or any part of it is subject to ... the application of force by a stronger nation, it is only natural that our people ... should look at their own country first and should ... consider what its interests should be and what its interests are.[5]

De Valera went on to appoint his government 'guardian of the interests of our people' and passed the Emergency Powers Act which described Irish neutrality as a state of 'Emergency'. Aware of the implications of neutrality, he called on the Irish people to remain firm and determined in the face of potential pressure.

Neutrality was overwhelmingly supported by the Irish people, so much so that when the deputy leader of the Fine Gael party advocated joining the war on the side of the Allies in the Dáil, he was forced to resign.[6] However, in practice, Éire offered a policy of 'friendly neutrality' to Britain, and Ó'Drisceoil suggests that Irish assistance to the Allies promoted its neutral status to that of a 'non-belligerent'.[7] There was also a considerable degree of assistance for Britain from Irish citizens. One hundred thousand Irish men and women worked in

British munitions factories and over 60,000 enlisted in the war effort. In total, 780 decorations, including eight Victoria Crosses, were awarded to southerners for their courage during the war.[8]

Other features of assistance to the Allies during the war included the repatriation of Allied airmen while German military personnel were interned, the exchange of weather reports, and permission, from 1941, for aircraft to fly over a portion of Co. Donegal. Southern firemen also provided valuable assistance during the Belfast Blitz, for which the Northern Ireland authorities were to find themselves hugely unprepared. This increasing assistance to the Allies had no place, however, in de Valera's public campaign, fuelled by diligent censorship, to assert Ireland's 'illusion of strict impartiality'.[9] It was most important in this age of still-emerging independence that Ireland was not seen to be consorting with the 'old enemy'.[10]

Winston Churchill recognized that the violation of Irish neutrality in a war that set out to protect the rights of small countries would provoke vilification of Britain worldwide. He also saw the vital strategic advantages of having Éire enter the war on the side of the Allies. If he could not invade Éire by force, the one persuasive technique he had at his disposal was the bargaining of Irish unity. It was an offer that would be difficult to stomach for Northern Unionists, but surely too tempting for the Irish government to turn down. Even before war had been declared, de Valera was aware of potential bargaining for Ireland's assistance in the war effort, commenting on the hypothesis of exchanging neutrality for a united Ireland as bartering 'our right to freedom in order to secure our right to unity'.[11] He was equally suspicious of the proposed declaration in favour of a United Ireland, offered on the condition of Ireland joining the war effort on the side of the Allies.[12] Entering the war, he argued, would be expected immediately, whereas unification would occur sometime in the future. Also, the reoccupation of Irish territory by the inevitable presence of British troops would have been difficult to stomach for many Irishmen whose memories of the War of Independence were still fresh. De Valera himself was well aware that his government might not survive an attempt to bring Éire into the war and was also concerned about the potential German bombing of Ireland as an example to other neutrals. Also to be taken into account as the war progressed was the growing belief among some Irish ministers that Britain was losing the war. In addition, de Valera was only too aware of the response of the Northern Ireland government to possible reunification. Predictably, the Prime Minister of Northern Ireland, Lord Craigavon, was horrified at the suggestion of such a treacherous move by the British government without prior consultation with the NI government. Craig's suggestion was military occupation of the south immediately, as de Valera, he believed, would stall negotiations until the arrival of German troops. Interestingly, the relationship between the intelligence agencies of Britain and Ireland was a more cordial one than that between the two governments, and there is some documentation to suggest that MI5 regarded Irish neutrality as an advantage.[13] Pitted against the implications of defending Ireland, a friendly intelligence exchange was seen as preferential to full-blown inclusion in the war.

The Treaty Ports

Desire for Irish assistance in the war was most closely associated with access to the Irish ports of Berehaven and Cobh (Co. Cork) and Lough Swilly (Co. Donegal). These ports had been used by the British military until 1938, when they were handed back to Ireland as part of the Anglo-Irish agreement which ended the Economic War.[14] This was bitterly opposed by Winston Churchill, who described the ports as 'the sentinel towers of the western approaches' and, even more crucially, England's 'life defences'. Churchill recognized that 'the ports might be denied to us in the hour of need' and that by handing them over could seriously compromise British security.[15] De Valera was equally vehement in holding onto the ports, claiming 'they are ours' and that any attempt to take them 'can only result in bloodshed'.[16] The invasion of Ireland by Britain was most certainly desired by members of the British Cabinet and of the Stormont government in Northern Ireland. The implacability of de Valera in relation to the Treaty Ports is borne out by a 1938 Gaumont British newsreel covering talks between de Valera and Chamberlain. Not surprisingly, de Valera declined an interview, leaving the newsreel to proclaim: 'But the Prime Minister wouldn't talk, reserving his comments for the British Prime Minister.'[17] In the printed commentary, 'British' is heavily underlined, firmly instructing the commentator where emphasis should lie.[18] Neglecting to use the Irish word 'Taoiseach', the commentator must differentiate between the two leaders, his stress on

'British' suggesting that the swing of power (and sympathy) lies with the latter. The original typed comment – 'The Prime Minister smiled, but wouldn't talk' – is also changed by handwritten notes to 'But the Prime Minister, he wouldn't talk', thus removing any images of a smiling and perhaps, by association, a more friendly de Valera. Instead, the commentary highlights his taciturn nature, a representation which seems to sit more comfortably with standard newsreel depictions of de Valera.

Propaganda and Use of Film in Wartime

Given the crucial nature of maintaining morale during wartime, the cinema was not only viewed as a useful propaganda tool but also regarded with a cautious eye to policing information released to the public. If, as Philip Taylor suggests, 'censorship and propaganda are really different sides of the same medal: the manipulation of opinion',[19] then both the British and Irish governments were ultimately concerned with controlling audience response to images of war. De Valera felt that he had to protect his electorate from harmful British propaganda, but he was equally concerned that this propaganda should not be inherently anti-de Valera. Still haunted by the war-torn images of the 1920s, de Valera felt it was important his countrymen should stand united in their independence from Britain, at least in relation to the question of neutrality. He seemed acutely aware of the potential power of real images of war tapping into collective sympathies.

Propaganda is perhaps the most effective way to manipulate public opinion and build morale through displays of apparent national strength and confidence. In turn, public morale is a vitally important aspect of successful warfare. In such a state of 'Emergency', governments at war are often tempted to use whatever means necessary to protect the 'interests' of their people, interests usually defined by those at the top of hegemonic structures. The use of powerfully persuasive propaganda is typically recognized as a necessary and excusable means of over coming the enemy. Philip Taylor suggests that the use of powerful rhetoric only becomes problematic when persuasion is eclipsed by manipulation, both in relation to the information shared *and* the information withheld from the public: 'it is not just a question of what, how, why and when you say something, and to whom, but also of what you decide to leave out. In propaganda, omission is just as significant as commission.'[20]

The propaganda potential of film had been recognized and thoroughly utilized in Britain during the First World War: the precedent had been set for the cinema as an effective producer of entertainment in depressing times and a useful vehicle for wartime propaganda. By the outbreak of the Second World War, all facets of potential propaganda were re-evaluated for their most efficient exploitation in what became 'a total war fought on a global scale in the age of modern communications'.[21] The Ministry of Information considered film a vital element of the 'Fourth Arm'[22] of defence. Within this, the newsreels played a significant part in preparing the British psyche for an upcoming war. As Taylor suggests, 'the newsreels, through their skilful injection of persuasive and supportive items into their usually entertaining issues over the previous five years had played a significant role in achieving this goal amongst the very people who would be expected to fight the coming Total War'.[23] Film was now an essential wartime propaganda weapon. Given the new campaign of 'total propaganda' and the idea that concepts became all the more persuasive when they frequently reappeared in various forms, the role of the newsreels was to reinforce ideas already expressed by the press and radio.[24] Newsfilm was thus saturated with war footage: the Mass Observation social research organization estimated that less than 15 per cent of newsreel coverage dealt with non-war items.[25] The Second World War was clearly not just a 'war of words', it was also an audiovisual war, a war of powerful imagery.[26]

In order to be 'good' propaganda, the films had, of course, also to take the form of good entertainment. Even bad news had to be repackaged as cheerful entertainment for cinemagoers watching news on a night out. This was second nature to the newsreels – their standard form was well recognized as consistently upbeat, even when covering the most depressing items.

Wartime Cinemagoing in Ireland

Belfast was well equipped in terms of cinema facilities. It boasted thirty-five cinemas by the late 1930s, with a capacity of 28,000 people, almost the same number of seats per capita as London.[27] Cinemagoing was equally popular in the South, with 220 cinemas in operation throughout

the country by 1939, forty-seven of them located in Dublin. Through-out Britain, nearly 4 million cinema seats between 1934 and 1939 catered for an average weekly audience of between 18.5 and 21 million. By 1945, this figure had risen (from 19 million in 1939) to 30 million people attending the cinema every week – which was more than half of the population. There were 4,000 cinemas in operation during the war, showing 3,000 newsreel issues and nearly 2,000 official films produced by the Ministry of Information (MoI).[28] To set wartime viewing in context, there were 14.5 million sales of daily newspapers in 1939 in Britain and 9 million radio sets, while the newsreels were reaching an audience of around 20 million weekly. Even the smallest of the five main newsreels (Universal News) reached a greater audience than the circulation of the largest national newspaper, the *Daily Express*.[29] Cinemagoing was not only a highly popular public pastime; it was also a very effective way of tapping into the public psyche. Maintaining morale during wartime was crucial and the cinema had a significant role to play in wartime propaganda. It was also regarded with a cautious eye, given the powerful potential of propaganda, and, as a result, the images appearing in wartime cinema screens were heavily policed.

Censorship in the UK

Censorship in Britain was not only expected to prevent the publication of information useful to the enemy, but also to ensure that information produced by the Ministry of Information for British consumption was to be believed. As the British public had 'long been accustomed to a pluralistic press', it was important that there was no obvious deviation from this journalistic style.[30] It was thus decided to censor news at source, and distribute censored news items from the 'ticker tape' lo-cated in the Press Association building in central London. This fed both the printed press and the BBC and, through this type of censorship of news at its 'origin', newspapers were able to use the bulk of news issued to them, as they had done in peacetime. Editors were obliged to clear news items which weren't issued from the 'tape' with the Censor. Newsfilm was also provided to the various newsreel companies through the Ministry of Information. This was different from the situation in the First World War, during which the Cinema Propaganda Department took on little production of its own but instead utilized the current film industry for official purposes. During the First World War, for newsfilms, official 'War Office Cinematographers' were nominated from amongst the main newsreel cameramen by a committee. The committee was initially a trade-based organization which gradually acquired official status. Its first chairman was Sir Max Aitken – later Lord Beaverbrook – and the profits from the War Office Topical Budget were largely given to wartime charities.[31] It was agreed before the Second World War broke out that uncensored newsreels would not be exported during wartime. The newsreels would be given some guidelines to the material that would prove unfavourable and a list of 'sensitive stories' was released on 8 September 1939. Newsreel companies were informed that they would be updated by the distribution of a daily 'stops' and 'releases' list.[32] The British Board of Film Censors continued to have nominal responsibility for censorship on the outbreak of war, with the assistance of a panel of advisers taken from each of the three defence departments within the Ministry of Information.

Wartime Newsreels

Gaumont British News began every item with a screen divided into four images at each corner showing different scenes and a town crier in the middle. Gaumont's tagline proclaimed that it was 'presenting the world to the world'; this was altered later in the war to 'This is the Gaumont British News, presenting the truth to the free peoples of the world.' This was characteristic of the newsreels' unashamed claims that they were objective and unbiased. Gaumont reels, like others, were often accompanied by Ministry of Information trailers. These films covered subjects of a practical nature, such as what to do on discovering a crashed aircraft, and more general war information such as female enlistment in the Armed Forces or the public's need not to waste resources during wartime. One particularly amusing item features Alastair Sim, playing the role of Nero in a museum, speaking in poetry to a student who is played by a young George Cole.[33] Nero boasts about his evil deeds, only to be met with the retort by Cole that 'your ugliest deed was just chicken feed compared with the actions of Hitler'. The final intertitle is an allusion to Nero's suspected involvement with the fires of Rome: 'Don't be like Nero, be a good citizen and save fuel.'

Pleas for help in the war effort often appeal to personal sensibilities by stressing the role each person can play individually. Another Gaumont item, showing vast numbers of tanks, stressed: 'And every worker in every British factory can feel that he or she is taking a leading part in that grim drama. Every nut is a bullet for victory, every war machine completed is a day nearer triumphant peace.'[34] Each viewer is appealed to on an individual level, and through the commentary is linked to the front line of battle by his or her efforts on the home front: 'in the great days of struggle to come, millions of factory workers, dockers and seamen will have the satisfaction of knowing that they too shared the heat of battle'.

Wartime newsreels concentrated on boosting morale, playing down losses and encouraging production in the war effort. Another feature was demonization or bestialization of the enemy, or, on occasion, using humour to deconstruct portrayals of military prowess. An example of this is the British film *Germany Calling*, which repackaged the work of Leni Riefenstahl to create 'a hilarious and biting parody to the tune of the Lambeth Walk'.[35] In the film, which was released on Christmas Day in 1941, quick cut shots of Hitler gesticulating wildly and the German Army marching are played backwards and repeated, turning the well-recognized German military order into a comical dance routine, while the Hitler salute comes across as a childish game.[36] Thus the newsreels use humour in an attempt to disperse wartime tensions and weaken the perceived threat of Nazi Germany.

Portrayals of the enemy are usually much harsher than this. The newsreels' vocabulary in describing victory over the Axis powers often includes 'battering', 'hammering', 'shattering', 'smashing' and 'pounding'. The tone is often patronizing and condescending. Accompanying scenes of large numbers of prisoners of war, one Gaumont item states: 'presently you'll notice something very strange about these prisoners. The strange thing is that they have lost their sullen, contemptuous superiority. They even smile. They're getting ready to tell us they really loved us all the time, like they did when they lost the last war.' On the commentary sheet, there is one sentence crossed out: 'Obviously, they're not quite so sure these days that their Führer is going to win.'[37]

Roosevelt calls Germany an enemy of 'all law, of all liberty, of all morality, of all religion' in an item dealing with German firing on submarines.[38] In an item covering military pageants throughout Britain, paying tribute to the Red Army, Anthony Eden addresses vast crowds against a backdrop of a huge Soviet flag: 'There is only one way in which this man can save mankind. Let him lead this monstrous Nazi machine which he has created to utter destruction and let him become for his own Germany, and to the world, such an awful monument to evil-doing and evil thinking that man will forever be warned to combine in time to prevent the rise of such another.'[39] It is not only Hitler facing demonization in these newsreels, but also the German people. In one item covering the defeat of German troops at Stalingrad, scenes of bodies, starved and freezing, lying on snow-covered ground, followed by soldiers coming out of buildings and walking through the streets, carrying white flags, are accompanied by the following commentary:

> When they are losing, the Nazis turn to make war upon their own people. These men were told that if they surrendered their families at home would be shot. What a country to fight for. Between January 10th and February 2nd 1943, over 90,000 prisoners were taken in and around Stalingrad. If that threat to families is carried out till the end of the war, the Nazis will themselves solve the problem of Germany's future.

Later, accompanying scenes of prisoners hobbling in snow, some inching along the ground because they cannot walk, the voiceover states remorselessly: 'What do you think they are thinking of as they shuffle past? What do you think their memories are? Home and family? No, they never worried about that. They were the legion of lusty hooligans shouting "Sieg Heil" at Nuremburg in 1938 and roaring for the Reich and the Führer.'[40] There is no recognition in the commentary of the suffering of the prisoners, clearly visualized by the images. We are invited to celebrate the fact that 'Axis troops are being killed, starved or battered into surrender.' In the commentary sheet for this item, an even harsher comment has been crossed out and ultimately cut from the voiceover: 'the blood – these bones will decay to fertilize the rich soil of Russia, a worthy future for men who died in so unworthy a cause'. The imagery used to portray the Japanese is even more bestial. In an item providing coverage of Papua New Guinea, the commentary describes the Buna battle zone as 'the area where every leaf conceals a rat-hole – and every rat in it is a Japanese'. In contrast, the newsreel camera is elevated to omniscient levels, described as 'the historian that marches alongside and in step with history while it's being made. It's the modern Homer that tells an Australian Iliad.' Film is personified as omniscient observer, while its subject is bestialized as a demonic race. The Australian soldiers are portrayed as Trojan warriors channelling all their 'courage, tenacity ... and solid skill' towards 'driving the grinning little bandits of the Orient out of this land from which they threaten our cousins in the Commonwealth'.[41] If any viewers are feeling sympathy when confronted with images of bodies in the water, the voiceover forcefully reminds them that 'scores of Australians have been killed trying to take prisoners or help wounded Japanese. Now they take no chances: a 36 grenade in a rat-hole makes no sentimental mistakes.' This falls into line with Donal Ó'Drisceoil's observation that Allied propaganda encouraged its audience to view the Japanese as 'apes in uniform'.[42] The audience is reminded that 'each advance carries its record of casualties' but the commentary qualifies this statement by raising doctors to epic levels, doing 'the work of heroes with the strength and willpower only of men'. This followed the general news-reel pattern of recognizing and then immediately playing down Allied losses. Another Gaumont item covering American raids on Germany carries just a hint of the losses incurred, immediately qualifying the ac-companying pictures of injured pilots being stretchered out of planes with reassurance of future victory: 'The mounting offence in the air is not achieved without cost but each raid is playing its part in weakening German fighting power and paving the way for the armies of the United Nations.'[43] The newsreels were careful about the information they released to the public and forceful in their demonization of the enemy, or perceived enemy. This would extend to Ireland in newsreels critical of neutrality, which will be discussed in more detail below.

Northern Ireland's Wartime Preparations

While Éire chose a neutral stance on the outbreak of war, its neighbours in the North, as part of the UK, had little choice in the matter. On the declaration of war, Northern Ireland set about steeling itself for impending conflict – queues of volunteers gathered at army recruit-ment offices, transport vehicles dimmed their lights, and gas masks were distributed. Belfast Corporation ensured that kerbs, lamp posts and telegraph poles were painted white in preparation for the blackout, which was, for the most part, only implemented to prevent Northern Ireland being used as an enemy guide to targets in Britain. It was strongly felt that due to distance from Germany, Northern Ireland could not be easily attacked, and despite the country's reputation as an industrial centre, a fact confirmed by the German media,[44] the threat of invasion was seen as remote. By April 1941, in spite of the Luftwaffe's current access to airfields in occupied France (which considerably shortened their potential flights to Northern Ireland) there were only twenty-two anti-aircraft balloons, light balloon barrage, no fighter squadrons available for night raids, and air raid shelters for just 25 per cent of the city's population, which explains the devastating consequences of the Belfast Blitz. Belfast suffered just four raids during the war, all during April and May 1941. In these four raids it bore more casualties than Portsmouth did in sixty-seven raids. Half of the victims were women and children who would ordinarily have been evacuated. After the bombings, 15,000 Belfast citizens were left homeless and a further 100,000 temporarily homeless while repairs were carried out.[45] Mass evacuations into the countryside after the raids also brought into the open the extreme deprivation of those who had lived in congested streets and suffered unemployment and poverty. The overall house construction rate in Northern Ireland was half the British average and there was inadequate maintenance of community dwellings. Events had exposed a country somewhat different to the 'enterprising' land portrayed in some of the wartime newsreels which will be discussed later in this chapter. While the imagery shown to the workers of Northern Ireland in many of the factories throughout the country was carefully constructed to maximize production for the war effort, the defensive measures put in place to tackle any potential attack were less organized. The consequences of the Northern Ireland government's lack of action were sorely felt in the aftermath of the Blitz. There is no coverage of the bombings in Belfast in 1941 – in fact the only newsreel coverage of the North for the year is a series of reports on army training exercises in Northern Ireland – all of which are released between 27 October and 3 November. All five main newsreel companies cover the training exercises. The newsreel coverage stresses the competence of troops and the thorough training being undertaken. Northern Ireland is identified as the training location by the commentaries, but the footage could be from anywhere; no significance is attributed to the fact that this training is occurring in Ireland. In wartime, emphasis on the strength of military was much more crucial newsreel content than coverage of the devastation of the Blitz.

Newsreels Covering Northern Ireland

The coverage of Northern Ireland mentioned above is no exception – the number of newsreels covering Northern Irish stories during the war is relatively small. The funeral of Lord Craigavon in November 1940 is covered only by Paramount and Movietone, while Pathé is the only newsreel to report that J.M. Andrews is his successor. The arrival of American troops in Ulster is one of the biggest stories to preoccupy the newsreels, with considerable coverage of the American forces during 1942. There is the occasional sporting item, coverage of the Home Forces and coverage of royal visits in 1942 and 1945. Beyond this, newsreels shown in Northern Ireland mostly contained the same items as those shown throughout Britain, with much less local flavour than the 1930s newsreels and a strong prevalence of international (and mostly war-related) news.

Items covering Northern Ireland's contribution to the war effort were congratulatory in tone – these depictions were celebrated by the Unionist regime, particularly in its attempts to enhance Ulster's reputation as a successful wartime producer and an important strategic part of the UK. So, for example, in 1940, tribute is paid to Ulster's appropriation of agricultural technology in *Dig for Victory*.[46] Against the opening rousing music and scenes of a line of tractors watched by a large crowd, we are told that 'Northern Ireland is making a superb war effort.' Basil Brooke, Minister for Agriculture and the future Prime Minister of Northern Ireland, looks on and then tries one of the new tractors for himself. In addressing the setting for the demonstration – which appears to be a large field – the commentator qualifies: 'you might think these pictures were taken far out in the country, but actually they're just in front of Government House, Belfast'. Then there is a cut to a shot of rows of tractors ploughing ground in front of the Stormont buildings. This seems, to the commentator, to be a more suitable setting for a demonstration of 'the mechanized farming of the 20th century'. Ulster is described as 'ploughing her way towards victory' with industrial prowess and the utilization of the most up-to-date and advanced technology.

Later that year, tribute is paid to the Ulster Home Guard in a Gaumont issue about the home forces. It opens with the appropriately iconic imagery of Carson's statue with Stormont looming behind it, while we are informed about the Ulster Home Guard, whose 'one aim' is 'to make life very unhealthy for any invader that might get as far as Ulster'.[47] While the audience watches shots of rifle practice, it is informed that 'these work while most of us are asleep'. We then see footage of military boats, with the slightly patronizing comment: 'that's why we seldom see this little navy of yachts and cabin cruisers and speedboats'. The Home Guard, who 'supplement the work of the army', is depicted almost as an army-in-waiting, and described in less heroic terms than the mainstream armed forces. However, they are still described as an important part of the 'defence of Britain' as rousing music reaches a crescendo.

Ultimately, the majority of newsreel coverage was upbeat, encouraging the public to participate in the war effort in order to speed up victory. Brian Barton contends that this type of news function may have incited the suspicion that the real story was hiding behind propagandistic 'good news', and the bearers of news in general were treated with some degree of distrust.[48] Nevertheless, audiences throughout Britain and Northern Ireland watched the upbeat, rallying footage expected to motivate the public in the war effort and keep up morale. Some newsreels even transcended the cinema circuit to end up being exhibited in the workplace. One example is *Ulster at Arms* (Warwork News, 1944), a tribute to Northern Ireland's contribution to the war effort, which was shown in the majority of NI factories.[49] (Warwork News was a series of newsreels produced between 1942 and 1945 by Paramount for the Ministry of Supply.) The film opens with a low-angle shot of Carson's statue, in defiant pose, his outstretched arm reaching skywards. He towers above the Stormont buildings behind him, painted black during wartime to protect against potential bombing. Interestingly, at odds with many portrayals of industrial Ulster set against rural Éire, Ulster, 'for all its industrial strength', is described as 'an agricultural country'. As will be discussed below, it is often the south which is characterized as rural and agricultural, as opposed to the urban and industrial north. In this film, Ulster's agriculture is defined by the advanced nature of its technology, shown to be fuelled by the most efficient and up-to-date machinery available. The commentary tells us: 'Bursting beyond the bounds of town and city, the wartime industry of Ulster has invaded the countryside.' Ulster's agriculture has been industrialized with modern technology in this representation, cementing what emerges in the newsreels as a pattern of industrial images of the north in opposition to rural and less modern images of the south. There are images of women walking through a courtyard followed by cattle; the camera then cuts to the rows of workers in the interiors of the dairy farm, which has added incendiary bullet production to its normal function. Several newsreel depictions of Éire suggest that peasant workers serve the land, as will be discussed below; in this film, Ulstermen are shown to strategically utilize agricultural resources to full advantage. Words like 'invaded' evoke the memory of the colonizer, appropriating local resources and using them for the purposes of the empire. Ulster, 'quick to improvise', is shown to mobilize its industrial and agricultural resources 'in the most practical way possible'.[50]

In describing the wartime production of linen, particular tribute (albeit patronizing) is paid to Ulster's female workforce, producing parachutes and military clothing. 'Every airman who has safely bailed out', we are told, 'owes their lives to the deft fingers of girls.' One young worker is shown including a note in the shirt she has just completed: 'This shirt was made by an Ulster lass whose lips were made for kissing, so hurry up and win the war, you don't know what you're missing.' It is stressed that high-grade linen is 'a luxury which there's no time to produce' and that certain factories have been adapted to produce munitions. One example is given to illustrate Ulster's enthusiastic initiative in upping wartime production: 'today this factory has changed over to war production and is making tail fins for Stirling bombers'. Frequently the real effects of wartime production are evoked; we are reminded of the forefront of battle and the incendiary bullets 'which have shot down many a Nazi plane'; the flax of Ulster 'serving the lives of men who bomb Berlin and fight the Luftwaffe to defeat'; and the troopships conveying 'matchless fighting men into the forefront of the battle'. With each of these statements the camera alternates between rows of diligent workers and close-ups of individuals, apparently unaware of the camera, ploughing through their work. Ulster's loyalty and practical nature is stressed in the opening scenes and reinforced at the end of the newsreel, with close-ups of individual workers juxtaposed with shots of the huge vessels they are working on. The commentator reminds the audience: 'Loyalty to the British Commonwealth nowhere burns more fiercely than in Ulster. To that loyalty Northern Ireland gives practical expression.' Before cutting to large troopships docked at Harland and Wolff we are shown scenes of welding. One welder in the foreground is illuminated in flashes – the sparks lighting up his mask. We see the individual, masked and unknown, representing the universal worker in his anonymity and then through shots of the troopships we see the huge work fuelled by the efforts of thousands like him. The message is clear – the work of individuals on the home front is borne directly to the front line and essential in the Allied war effort. The film ends with impressive scenes of the Harland and Wolff shipyard, and the factory workers viewing this newsreel are left to contemplate their vast and selfless loyalty to Britain in her current crisis.

As John Hill points out, while the film was produced in 1943, planning for a film on the war industries in Northern Ireland had begun in 1941, when Ernest Cooper, then at the Ministry of Commerce, visited the Ministry of Supply Films Division in London to discuss the possibility of making such a film. The Ministry of Supply organized travelling projection units for factories in Northern Ireland from April 1943 and it was through this apparatus that *Ulster at Arms* was ultimately screened. The Northern Ireland government was consulted on the film only at editing stage, at which time they requested the removal of a shot of a donkey and cart, 'presumably because of its suggestion of "primitiveness" '.[51] (As will be examined below, this is exactly the imagery employed by the newsreels to depict southern Ireland.) Opening shots of Carson and Stormont buildings immediately associate the film with a 'pro-Unionist discourse',[52] an ideological leaning reinforced by repeated use of the word 'loyalty' to describe Northern Ireland's relationship with Britain. However, Hill suggests that the film's voiceover 'indicates Northern separation from Britain' through phrases like 'exported to Britain' and the lack of the use of the first person plural: 'in this respect, the film does not employ a rhetoric that incorporates Ulster into a British "we" '.[53] Nevertheless, the Unionist government 'was delighted with the film and sought to ensure its widespread distribution' which ultimately stretched to an estimated total of

145,000 workers in 720 factories throughout the UK,[54] constituting a significant propaganda victory in the Northern Ireland government's bid to represent the North's contribution to the war effort in a favourable light. The government did not, however, have control over other sources of representation of Northern Ireland, many of which presented less approving depictions of the North.

Changing Attitudes to Irish Neutrality

The newsreels faced a challenge in their representation of neutral Éire for viewers in Northern Ireland. Throughout Britain, up to 1940, the newsreels were not hostile in their portrayal of Éire's neutrality, but as the Treaty Ports became increasingly strategically important, the tone began to change. Initially, the main concern of British newsreel companies was to convince the public that Ireland was ready to defend herself against the threat of German invasion. As usual, skilful manipulation of image and commentary served the newsreels' propagandistic purposes. When covering a pro-neutrality rally in Dublin in 1940, Pathé's commentary suggested that the panning shots depicted vast crowds supporting defensive measures against Germany.[55] The commentary reminds the audience that 'Britain and Éire may not always have seen eye to eye in the past, but today all that is forgotten in the common danger'. The newsreel attributes pro-defensive sentiments to the three main political leaders, sharing a platform to address huge crowds and standing united 'as a symbol of Éire's unity as she faces the danger of aggression'. This suggests complete political support for the bolstering of Irish defences, thus fulfilling the newsreels' current main objective – to convince the British public that Éire was more than eager to defend herself against Germany and offered friendly and supportive sentiments towards Britain. A *Times* newspaper article offers a broader picture of the events depicted in the newsreel. Cosgrave is reported to have stated: 'let none of the people be so foolish, so misguided as to give countenance and encouragement to any belligerent to invade the country', while de Valera encouraged the Irish people to stand united behind the government, 'ready to meet aggression from whatever quarter it may come'.[56] This demonstrates how newsreel commentary framed and manipulated images: the main emphasis of this rally was not on defensive measures and a close wartime relationship with Britain, as the newsreel suggests,

but was in fact a declaration of Ireland's full political support for
neutrality and preparation for defence against an attack from *any* of
the belligerents, including Britain.[57]

A 1940 Pathé issue entitled *Outposts of Peace – Irish Army Manoeuvres*
recognized that 'Among the small nations of Western Europe, there are
very few which have so far avoided being drawn into war. But one
at least has so far been able to maintain her national integrity.'[58] An
almost flattering portrayal of Ireland reminds us that the 'romantic
green isle of the west is still at peace'. We are reassured that Ireland has
'no illusions as to the security of her position', and scenes of large
organized military parades, training exercises and various shots of tanks
and equipment assure us that Ireland's 'small but efficient' army is in a
state of 'constant readiness'. Ireland is depicted as optimistically hoping
for the best but preparing for the worst. Nature is evoked in the depiction
of Ireland's current state in the 'dark clouds rolling over her skies' and
the country is repeatedly referred to as 'she'. In describing the Irish
military there is a hint of surprise when faced with the images of 'what
modern cavalry looks like in Ireland, the traditional home of the horse'.
In order for the item to assure that Ireland can defend her shores, the
newsreel attempts to show that 'the mechanization of the artillery is
complete – a sure sign of the advance of modern warfare'. The final
line of the commentary cements the portrayal of modern Ireland, looking forwards instead of holding on to old arguments with Britain: 'The
young army of Ireland rides into the future, facing its destiny with hope
and confidence.' The final shots are of an open road stretching across
a flat plain. A long line of motorcycles travels past the camera while
planes fly in formation overhead.

This is typical of the attitudes towards Ireland early in the war, transferred onto the screen – it was important that Ireland was seen as able
to protect herself, in the eyes of the British public. In the coverage of
Ireland's First Air Raid the tone is one of sympathy with Ireland and
outrage at Germany – 'the outrage occurred in broad daylight so no
excuse is possible. Not only do Hitler's bombers strike at civilians in
Britain but also in neutral Ireland.' We are told that three people have
lost their lives and are shown scenes of soldiers cleaning up the debris
wearing gas masks, due to escaping ammonia fumes.[59] As the war
continued and increased losses were incurred, and as the Treaty Ports
became more and more strategically important, the newsreels became

harsher in their portrayal of neutrality. Two Pathé newsreels covering
the bombing of Dublin illustrate this. The first, in January 1941, shows
scenes of bombed houses in Rathdown Park which the commentary
tells us 'fell victim to Hitler bombs'. It had been thought that these
bombings in Dublin on 2 and 3 January 1941 had occurred because
the Germans had mistaken Ireland for the west coast of Britain, or
alternatively that the planes had just been offloading bombs before their
return home. Handwritten notes accompanying the newsreel commentary
sheet read: 'an unidentified bomber – presumed German – bombed
the Rialto District of Dublin'. The corresponding commentary is
much more dogmatic in informing the audience that 'the Nazi raiders,
deliberately, unloaded their bombs on these houses in Éire' (emphasis
added). The item finishes with the question: 'is this another case of
Germany threatening Nazi "protection" to a neutral State?'[60] Presumably the Irish government could not have omitted such an important
local incident from cinema news, but Pathé's report was extensively cut
before being shown in Irish cinemas. Cuts to the commentary included:
'They have since proved to be of German origin'; 'murderous attack
from the sky'; 'shooting attack'; and 'strong protests have been sent to
Berlin by the Irish government'.[61] Clearly there was an attempt to remove comment or information on belligerents, as was the policy of
'Emergency' censorship. Rockett concludes that 'such treatment clearly
went beyond a reasonable interpretation of what it meant to be neutral
and suggests an almost hysterical fear of informing cinemagoers of the
reality of war and its devastating impact in Ireland, as elsewhere'.[62] A
Gaumont issue covering the same incident shows scenes of damaged
houses, stating: 'The bombs were subsequently proved, of course, to
come from Germany.' The camera cuts to a close-up of a bath blown
out onto the street by the force of one such explosion, while the
commentator threatens: 'We need say no more about this further violation of neutrality, but that doesn't mean we stop thinking it.'[63] This
item was not shown in Ireland; instead, Gaumont's Irish items for this
edition included *American Diving Stars*, *Holy Island Wedding* and
Springfield College Gym Team. The fact that such trivial reports were
included when Ireland had been attacked testifies to the intense policy
of censorship adhered to by the de Valera administration, which sought
to purge war news from the newsreels.

The next bombing of Dublin occurred in May 1941. Thirty-four

6.1 Pathé Gazette: *Germans Bomb Dublin*, Copyright British Pathé Ltd.

people were killed, nearly 100 injured, and there was damage to 300 houses.[64] By this time, frustration with Irish neutrality was beginning to filter through, with increased shipping losses in the Atlantic. A much more dramatic and graphic Pathé newsreel showed vast damage to houses, women sitting on the wreckage, and large numbers of armed services clearing the rubble; in one scene a corpse is shown on a stretcher. The commentary has a much more biting tone in its opening: 'The Germans respect nothing! Latest evidence of this is in their bombing of NEUTRAL Éire.' In the commentary sheet, the capitals for the word 'neutral' firmly remind the commentator where his emphasis should lie. He goes on to take a chastising tone, particularly stressing the italicized words in the following: 'The Éire Government has protested to Berlin against the wanton attack on their *professed* neutrality, but unfortunately, *protests* will not bring back the dead, or heal the wounds of the injured. Maybe this is the price Éire has to pay for "sitting on the fence".'[65] Robert Fisk suggests that 'the gratuitous tone of the commentator's script was deliberately offensive, with its suggestion that Éire had adopted her policy of neutrality – "sitting on the fence" out of cowardice rather than necessity'.[66] This item was still deemed too politically sensitive to show even after the Emergency Power Order had been lifted in 1945.[67] A less controversial item was produced by British Movietone News. Accompanying scenes of devastating wreckage in the North Strand area, the commentator states: 'The most serious bombing yet to be delivered upon Éire occurred recently in Dublin. Over thirty people were killed, many more were injured, and some hundred were rendered homeless. All this in spite of the fact the country has observed strict neutrality and its towns haven't even been blacked out.' The film goes on to show Mrs Clarke, Mayor of Dublin, visiting North Strand, and concludes simply: 'The Éire government has protested to Germany.' Extensive cuts were also ordered for this newsreel before exhibition.[68]

Paramount's *Ireland – the Plain Issue*

One particularly controversial newsreel was *Ireland the Plain Issue*, intended solely for British audiences, which was produced by British Paramount News in 1942. Historian Robert Fisk suggests that the film 'sounded – and looked – as if it was intended to prepare the British public for an Allied invasion of Éire'.[69] The film shows houses overrun with animals and children entering schools barefoot, with the commentary stating that 'Irish peasants – sharing their cottage with the pig, living on potatoes – are freer than the English artisan.' It went on to accuse their leader of being a 'dictator', leading a Catholic state which disliked 'Protestant England'. Not surprisingly, it caused great controversy on its release. Fisk suggests that the newsreel depicts the Irish as 'unclean, weak, idle and cowardly' and their political motives as 'naïve and selfish'. Fisk even compares the film with Nazi propaganda, with all the racist connotations that such a comparison implies, concluding that the newsreel 'was both provocative and deeply disturbing'. Another offending feature of the film was its stereotyping of the backward, rural south in contrast with the industrial, hard-working and loyal north. The people of Northern Ireland, the commentary claims, are 'wealthier than the southern Irish, more enterprising, better businessmen' and ultimately closer to English ideals of industry and progress. To visualize this opposition, the shots of Northern Ireland depict the impressive building of Stormont, the shipyards, and the interior and exterior of a large linen mill. These scenes evoke Unionism and modern industry in contrast with the images which represent the south in a rural capacity – shots of rivers and countryside, fields being ploughed and pipe-smoking men and women.

Despite what the newsreel suggested, the reality was somewhat different. At the outbreak of war, Northern Ireland was the most economically disadvantaged region in the UK – it had the highest unemployment and death rates and its educational services were far behind England and Wales (probably due to a lack of generosity from a Westminster government that favoured other areas in Britain).[70] Although Northern Ireland's contribution to the war effort was significant, it was consistently lower than any other region in the UK.[71] There were claims from the Ministry of Aircraft Production that Short and Harland was working at 65 per cent efficiency and that levels of morale were low and absenteeism high.[72] Even though strikes were illegal in Northern Ireland from 1940, there were 270 throughout the war, suggesting that the sentiments expressed by Craigavon – 'we are the king's Men and we shall be with you to the end'[73] – were not passionately adhered to in all quarters, and certainly not to the extent suggested in this particular newsreel, which firmly stated that no Ulsterman desired neutrality. There were also several incidents of protest against the war in the North including households defying the blackout. Slogans such as 'ARP for English slaves, IRA for the Irish' reminded local and national government that public backing for the war was split in Ulster.[74] While Basil Brooke could claim, as the war was drawing to a close, that he hoped Britain realized 'that we are necessary to you'[75] – and certainly British ministers were grateful for Northern Ireland's input – its contribution was not quite as ebullient as portrayed in the newsreels.

Equally, the wartime atmosphere in Northern Ireland was observed by Tom Harrisson, founder of the Mass Observation social survey organization, as profoundly different to the rest of Britain. He commented on the overall 'slackness of the atmosphere' and the 'irritation and resentment' caused by the war. He was overcome by the laid-back attitude of the community in general: 'people thought nothing of asking me to lunch and taking the whole afternoon. Being half an hour late for an appointment did not matter in the slightest.' He was particularly disturbed by the daytime sight of men lounging and sleeping in the grounds of Belfast's City Hall, commenting that 'in Britain the whole tempo has changed from peacetime and anyone who behaved in a peacetime way now in London or Liverpool would at once be noticeable and might even cause a riot'.[76] Government minister John McDermott acknowledged that Northern Ireland was 'only half in the war'.[77] Tom Harrisson believed this apathy to be due to a lack of conscription, given the huge part it had played in influencing the British wartime psyche.[78] Such an observation was simplistic, given the intense debate that potential conscription had generated even before Ireland had been partitioned in the First World War. Not surprisingly, there was more than indifference felt towards the war in west Belfast – manifest through a shortage of volunteers from the Falls Road. Before the war had even started, local Republicans held a mass protest, building bonfires out of government-issued gas masks.[79] Harrisson also found in his survey that Protestants welcomed American troops as a deterrent to Nationalist trouble, whereas Catholics were much more antagonistic towards the US forces.[80] Overall, Northern Ireland's contribution to the war effort was much more complex than *Ireland – the Plain Issue* indicated.

The Irish situation was so complicated for Paramount that there are a number of inaccuracies in the newsreel, as Fisk points out:

> To talk about the 'long memory' of the Irish may have had considerable justification, but even a short memory should have advised the film's makers that the Anglo-Irish Treaty was signed in 1921 – not 1920 – that Kevin O'Higgins was not one of the Treaty negotiators, that the chairman of the Treaty delegation was named Griffith and not 'Griffiths', and that Collins was not the only one of the three Irishmen mentioned to be assassinated; O'Higgins was shot dead in Dublin in 1927. The newsreel commentary continued with little more respect for accuracy than it had already shown.[81]

Further inaccuracies occurred in Paramount's treatment of 'Éire's pocket army – 7,000 strong', whose training, the film claimed, was US based and whose uniform consisted of German-style helmets in order to save them 'from the embarrassment of looking British'. In fact, there were around 250,000 regular and volunteer troops in the Irish armed

6.2 Pathé Gazette: *All for Defence*, Copyright British Pathé Ltd.

forces in 1942, and the German-style helmets (also used by Norwegian Allied troops) had been replaced by a British model.[82] While German-style helmets had been used from 1927 (after being purchased from the British company Vickers), they were withdrawn in 1940.[83] The shots of troops drilling in the film show soldiers wearing German-style helmets.

The commentary also states: 'The IRA – a body not always helpful to the de Valera Government and other volunteers are doing Home Guard duty; less to stop two million Nazis dropping from the sky than to raise Cain should a British destroyer stray within territorial limits.' As Robert Fisk points out, the Home Guard did include members of the old IRA, but to suggest that its current members made up the Home Forces was 'ridiculous'.[84] The Dublin government had devised a defence plan based on the possibility of a German invasion occurring in conjunction with a Republican rising. This internal threat prompted stern measures towards the IRA. By August 1942, six members of the organization had been executed, two volunteers shot dead while resisting arrest and three more dead after a hunger strike. Brian Barton sums up treatment of the IRA during the war: 'over 1,000 detention orders were made for IRA members, 400 were sentenced to terms of imprisonment and roughly 1,100 were taken into custody – 600 was the largest number at any one time'.[85] The IRA was certainly not de Valera's choice as an ideal Home Guard.

The final comment of the film accompanies a head-and-shoulders shot of de Valera (almost like a mug shot), expressionless, looking directly at the camera while the commentary advises: 'The time has come to say to Éire: "forget your trouble with England – at least till after the war." Éire like the rest of us will go under if the Nazis win. Don't let history say that de Valera unknowingly helped Hitler to fill the bloodbath of the New Order.' Such a controversial attack was not standard newsreel style, but Paramount was less likely to shy away from controversial fare than the other newsreel companies, as it demonstrated in its coverage of Oswald Mosley's fascist demonstrations in the 1930s. Initially Paramount defended the film, stating to the press: 'we attempted to present the full facts of the case. We do not believe that in doing so we gave grounds for offence. We have not the slightest desire to give offence to Catholics in Ireland or elsewhere.'[86] Kevin Rockett suggests that *The Plain Issue* 'does not seem to have been submitted to the Irish Film Censor because of its openly anti-Irish bias'[87] and so would not have been shown in the south. It is possible, however, that it may have been exhibited in some first-run cinemas in the north. Screenings of the newsreel in Britain led to a complaint by John Dulanty, High Commissioner for Éire. It was subsequently withdrawn, with apologies from Paramount and the excuse that both the chairman and managing director had been in the US at the time of its release. Those responsible for the film, Paramount claimed, had been censured.[88]

This was not the first time Paramount had caused controversy in its coverage of international affairs for local audiences. The company had been reprimanded by the British government in September 1938 when they included an item openly critical of appeasement, which was hurriedly withdrawn on the day of release. While Paramount claimed that the decision to withdraw the item was their own, Liberal MP Geoffrey Mander claimed in the House of Commons that the government had officially requested its withdrawal. The government, concerned about the effect that the item might have on Chamberlain's negotiations with Hitler, had asked Paramount to contact all its cinema exhibitors and request them to remove the item from the newsreel. The ensuing debate in the House of Commons raised interesting views on the responsibility of the newsreel industry to be aware of producing controversial newsreels in such tense times.[89] The trade journal *The Cine-Technician* asked for clarification on the issue of censorship, given that in this case the Home Secretary claimed 'there was no censorship and no undue pressure' for the British newsreel industry, yet the news-reel was still conspicuously withdrawn.[90] This particular article also reminds its readers that as the newsreel companies were, for the most part, pro-government there was little need to censure them for including controversial material. Given that there had never been an official censorship system in place for the British newsreel industry, there was a general self-censorship, adhered to at a national level. This was based on an unwritten code of newsreel ethics which editors hoped would help them avoid the censorship inflicted on feature films. It was gener-ally accepted by the Newsreel Association of Great Britain and Ireland – an organization (running from 1937 to 1960) set up to discuss policy and issues related to the five largest newsreel companies – that if the newsreels avoided controversy they could keep the privileged position they held outside the realm of the censor. However, British newsreels did not escape censorship during the war – every single film exhibited to the public had to have government approval. As Taylor states, 'film propaganda was clearly too serious a business to be left solely to the film-makers'.[91] Film was too effective a war weapon to be utilized without government sanction.

British Paramount News tackles Irish neutrality again in the 1944 newsreel *Britain, US Isolate Éire*.[92] The commentary describes a 'decision taken by the President and Mr Churchill to isolate Éire as far as possible'. The film was ultimately a reaction to de Valera's rejection of an American request to close the Axis ministries in Dublin, particularly when the use of transmitters from the German legation to send weather reports and other information to Berlin was discovered. De Valera eventually confiscated the transmitters, but the whole episode caused much concern for the British government.

The film's initial portrayal of the Irish 'frontier' shows images of a rural road, with two Ulster policemen checking the papers of a man travelling through in a small lorry, and then a second man on a horse and cart. The camera focuses on a sign for vehicles travelling into Éire which reads: 'WD and RAF out of bounds USA off limits'. The camera then cuts to a sign stating: 'Fork left for Dublin', while the commentary tells us that there are still German and Japanese embassies there. The underlying message carries the suggestion that while British and American troops are not welcome across the border, German and Japanese spies are constantly at work.

The familiar stereotyping of north and south is once again portrayed through the juxtaposition of images of the rural south with the industrial north. Shots of Irish farmhouses complete with animals are followed by pictures of the shipyard with large numbers of men working. Once again Paramount pays tribute to 'Ulster's famous shipyards' and the 'whole industrial power of the six Northern counties' providing consistent support for the war effort. The one chink in Ulster's armour, according to the newsreel, is its easily compromised strategic position. Intelligence, it is claimed, was leaking to the neutral south and immediately spirited off to the Axis powers through their diplomatic representatives in Dublin. One example given here is immediate knowledge that American reinforcements have arrived in the North. Other information leakage could 'be fatal in the early days of the Second Front' and could potentially 'cost the allies thousands of lives'. A close-up of a group of soldiers presents the potential victims of this breach of intelligence.

The tone is one of irritation with Ireland, depicted as callously looking after its own interests while global war wages throughout the world. The commentator stresses the word 'legal' in describing Éire's right to remain neutral and pits this against Britain's right to prevent the flow of axis information through Éire as 'fully justified'.

In *Britain, US Isolate Éire*, through skilful inflection, the commentator prioritizes the 'just' over the 'legal' in the sentence: 'no-one disputes that Éire is perfectly within her legal rights in remaining neutral; no-one disputes that Britain and America are fully justified in preventing the Nazis getting information which might cost the Allies thousands of lives'. The audience cannot avoid a comparison with what the newsreel clearly suggests is Ireland's refusal to accept its global responsibility to enlist in the struggle against what Paramount's *The Plain Issue* described as a 'bloodbath of the new order'. The newsreel qualifies these comments through its imagery of vast lines of military vehicles, thus reassuring the British viewer that the Allies' military prowess is working to assuage Ireland's treachery. The ultimate message cannot be one of defeat – while Ireland is condemned vocally for its interaction with the enemy, the viewer is reminded visually of British military strength. After an accumulation of images of aerial, naval and ground forces we are told that 'as the war material accumulates in Northern Ireland, Ulster and the military keep extra watch on the border'. The commentary comes dangerously close to suggesting that Allied downfall might still be imminent, even at this late stage in the war, and that defeat could easily scapegoat Ireland's compromising position. Ulster becomes the bastion of defence, the potential saviour in the face of implicit Irish treachery. The newsreel is upbeat in its conclusion: images of identity cards being searched are matched with rousing music, reaching a crescendo with the conclusion that the 'leak has been pretty well blocked. Ulster, Britain and America are now going to keep the military secrets from going over the border.' On the newsreel's accompanying commentary sheet, last-minute changes had been made to this final sentence. Previously it read: 'Ulster, Britain and America are keeping the military secrets from going over the border.' With the slight changes to suggest that this will now happen in the future, instead of currently, it is intimated that leaks were only being blocked at this late stage (July 1944). The viewer is left comfortable in the belief that no further intelligence leaks will occur, but wondering just what price may have been paid for Ireland's staunch neutrality.

In the Pathé item *News from the Éire Border*, some of the same footage is used with a different commentary:

> Germany and Japan are no respecters of neutrality. Slipping their spies over the border was far too easy. The Allies are much too close to big moves to permit Éire to jeopardize the success of our operations. The North–South border is sealed ... credentials have to be right. Britain and America take this step to safeguard the lives of their forces. It puts an end to the situation where we work while others peep.[93]

In his victory broadcast after the war had ended, Churchill would remind the British and Irish public of these risks, suggesting that whilst avoiding invading Ireland and enforcing a change to its neutral status, the British government 'left the de Valera government to frolic with German and later Japanese representatives to their hearts' content'.[94]

Coverage of American Forces in Northern Ireland

Clair Wills suggests that when America entered the war, 'a diplomatic crisis loomed' in Ireland. Given Ireland's historical ties with the United States, Irish neutrality was no longer secure in the fact that its powerful friend, America, was also neutral. When American troops began arriving in Northern Ireland in January 1942, there was increasing fear of invasion of Éire, and rumours that the Americans had come to take the Treaty Ports were rife. Also implicit in the stationing of troops in the north was a recognition of partition. Although American troops were confined to the north in their official capacity, they often travelled to Dublin for leave and 'Dubliners became used to seeing trains unload their cargoes of GIs seeking twenty-four hours of indulgence'.[95] Thus the north was associated with war and the south became a place of entertainment and escapism.

While de Valera viewed the arrival of American troops in Northern Ireland as the occupation of a foreign force (and even sent a protest to the American government),[96] the 'Dough boys' offered another useful propaganda outlet for the newsreels. Gaumont used the opportunity to present 'another picture that speaks louder than words of Anglo-American solidarity' in its 29 January 1942 issue.[97] Accompanying shots of troops arriving by boat, the commentator continues:

> The arrival in Northern Ireland of the first contingent of the United States army to stations in the United Kingdom. Within seven weeks of the declaration of war on Germany, President Roosevelt has sent to Britain this token of true alliance between the English speaking nations. Numbers of course are secret, but there were several thousands in this first landing of well equipped American troops. Thousands more will grow to millions as Uncle Sam's huge plan for victory is fulfilled. Twenty-five years ago the fathers of these Americans crossed the Atlantic to fight as our Allies. We both know now to our cost that the job was left half done. The 1942 generation has no illusions left. This time we mean to finish it.

There are shots of troops waving enthusiastically, accompanied by rousing music. Similar energetic and cheerful music is used by Movietone in its item *Dough Boys in Ulster*.[98] The commentary is light-hearted to begin with, describing how 'the first film of American troops in Northern Ireland, since their arrival that is, finds them in

good heart in spite of the British climate. Rain, slush and mud have
been making their exercises anything but a picnic and I wouldn't be
surprised to hear some pretty hard things from them about this phase
of their activities.' There are shots of the soldiers tramping through wet
muddy fields, feet sinking right down into the mud as the commentator
qualifies: 'all the same they're in good heart, all determined not only
to win the war, but also to make their quarters a home from home'.
The camera cuts to a single soldier, smoothing back his thick, curlyish
black hair in a doorway. A makeshift sign over the doorway reads:
'Hollywood'. The soldier dons his cap and there is a cut to a shot of five
soldiers, arms round each other, laughing and smiling at the camera.
They are also located in front of a doorway, probably leading into their
barracks. The sign above them, with slightly more elaborate lettering
reads: 'Waldorf Astoria. Society Boys'.

Next, the audience is introduced to General Hartle, the American
troops' commanding officer, shown with General Franklyn, 'his British
opposite number'. Hartle, we are told, is 'determined that his force shall
not only enjoy exercises in the mud, but also display the maximum
of smartness and discipline on parade'. The commentator places
particular stress on the word 'enjoy', suggesting that the soldiers will
tolerate the change in climate whether they like it or not, and likewise
adapt to other cultural differences. 'British nurses' are depicted on a
balcony, watching the soldiers' parade, and 'respirator drill' during
which soldiers are shown donning gas masks with great haste. The
commentator's final remark is: 'the first use of gas by the Germans in
October 1914 proved somewhat of a boomerang but maybe they'll try
it again. As for the bayonet, the infantryman apparently still knows
what to do with that.' Strong emphasis is placed on the final word,
while the last shots are of soldiers with bayonets running towards the
camera. Apart from the mention of Northern Ireland at the beginning
of the newsreel, this could have been located in any part of Britain; the
emphasis is on Britishness – the nurses are British, General Hartle is
General Franklyn's 'British' opposite number.

The newsreels' coverage of the Home Forces in Northern Ireland
takes a similar tack, one item covering an inspection of the ATS 'somewhere in Northern Ireland'. Another item entitled *Tough Training by
the Army* shows military training exercises. We are told that cameramen
in Northern Ireland have taken the footage but beyond this there is no

further mention of location. Instead the commentator concentrates on 'an army of highly skilled specialists' on the 'newest assault course'. Northern Ireland is almost portrayed simply as a training ground in these items, with no particular patriotic association with the war. At such an emotive time, it is typical that the newsreels do not cover Northern Irish participation in the war, or Irish neutrality with any depth or complexity. As is often the case with newsreel coverage of Ireland, what is omitted is as significant in defining the newsreels' attitude to Ireland as the types of stories which do make the final editions.

After the decline in industry in the 1930s, the Second World War was seen as a turning point for Northern Ireland, offering the opportunity for renewed industrial vigour in war production and increased employment (despite the fact that unemployment was still higher in Northern Ireland during the war than in other regions in the UK). While Northern Ireland's contribution to the war effort strengthened its relations with Britain, there was insecurity in the Unionist government surrounding the fact that Britain had been willing to surrender the North to de Valera in return for Irish support on the side of the Allies. After this, Unionists were determined to improve the war effort and make Northern Ireland be seen as an integral part of the UK. Generating good publicity for Ulster and policing the images created of Northern Ireland was seen as an effective way of doing this. Newsreel images played a part of this process, despite the fact that Northern Ireland was generally under-represented in newsreels and official film-making during the war, 'and certainly out of step with the claims made for its economic and military importance'.[99] While films depicting Northern Ireland's contribution to the war effort were seen as successes by the Unionist administration, there were attempts to produce more of this type of film, testifying to an awareness of the importance of producing favourable images of the North and, by doing so, strengthening its links with the Union. The Northern Ireland government had little to fear in representations of the North by British newsreel companies, who generally portrayed Ulster as a loyal, hard-working and an effective wartime producer.

During the war, significantly more stories covering the south were produced, compared to those covering the north. Many of these stories were not connected to the war and were produced to cater to Irish audiences at a time when censorship prohibited inclusion of war stories in newsreel editions exhibited in Ireland. Coverage of Ireland in stories produced for Britain and Northern Ireland was preoccupied with Irish neutrality – firstly to reassure that it would not affect Allied successes or prove unable to withstand German invasion; secondly, later in the war, to condemn the lack of Irish assistance to Britain, particularly surrounding the Treaty Ports.

What is significant, in examining the material discussed above, is that these portrayals of Ireland, north and south, were only accessible to viewers in Northern Ireland (and throughout Britain). Viewers in the south were not exposed to these representations, and their criticisms of Éire's neutral stance. Instead, audiences in Éire watched coverage which was highly sanitized when it came to details of global conflict, and more in keeping with peacetime newsreel content.

Emergency Newsreels in Éire

Fencing in Ireland,[100] *Baby Boxers*[101] (covering an infant boxing match) and *Balloon Houses* ('inexpensive igloos while you wait!')[102] were just some of the titles which appeared as part of specially edited cinema newsreels produced for Irish audiences during the Second World War. While trivial, quirky items like these were typical of the standard news-reel at the height of its popularity in the 1930s, the content was to change considerably for audiences throughout Britain and Northern Ireland on the outbreak of war, but not for viewers in the south of Ireland. This split in viewing mirrored the widening gap between north and south, and was itself a manifestation of the growing partitionist mentality in the Irish public's psyche.

Wartime viewing in Éire was profoundly different to that in Britain. De Valera's sentiments and policy were to be reinforced through a strict censorship campaign. In the interwar period there were discussions between Britain and Ireland about a possible censorship scheme for Ireland in the event of war. Ultimately a report based on British censor-ship policy was produced for the Irish government in 1938. The powers of wartime censorship were included in the Emergency Powers Act, which was introduced when war broke out and amended in 1942 (when printers could be required to submit material for censorship prior to publication). This covered all publications, press, communications and film. The only broadcasting station, Radio Éireann, was already state controlled and so operated self-censorship. Film censorship was carried out under the existing film censor. In Éire, the general aim of the censor was to prevent public consumption of any material that could prove a threat to neutrality. Joseph Connolly, who became Controller of Censorship on the outbreak of war, stated in a memo to de Valera that this may include 'suggestions (a) that we are not really neutral, (b) that we cannot continue to be neutral, (c) that we are wrong in being neutral, (d) that the big majority of the people are supposed to be the enemies of Britain'.[103] Connolly advocated a strict censorship of the press, refusing publication of any pro-belligerent article. He included in this any report in the newspapers of the speeches of TDs outside the Dáil in favour of the Allies.[104] Connolly suggested to the film censor, at that time James Montgomery, that the following would have to be eliminated from cinema screens:[105]

> 1. All films dealing with war preparations, parades, troop movements, naval and aircraft movements, Defence preparations, pictures of shelters, sandbagging etc.
> 2. All references for or against any of the countries involved as their mode of living, culture, etc.
> 3. All films dealing with Imperial, Colonial or Dominion activities which tend to glorify the Empire or British rule
> 4. All news films – Pathé Gazette – Movietone etc. must be free from war news or anything of a propagandist or partisan nature. [Frank Aiken, Minister for the Co-ordination of Defensive Measures, clearly felt that the effect of cinema propaganda was much more dangerous than that carried by the press:
> it has been agreed that newsreels showing war pictures will be stopped for the duration of the war. The reason is that we do not want any trouble in the picture houses. If a newsreel is shown in which one belligerent or the other is prominent, somebody may start to 'booh' and somebody may start to cheer, and we do not want that sort of competition to start ... We allow war pictures to appear in the newspapers simply because they are in cold print, and if a man gets a newspaper in the morning he will not start either cheering or booing the paper.[106]]
> 5. References such as 'Our King and Country' – 'This Little Island of Ours' [meaning Great Britain], 'We' [meaning the British people] – 'Our troops' and the like must be eliminated.

It was decided that film censorship would fall within the realm of the department of justice, rather than within that of the controller of censorship, and that ultimate responsibility would lie with Frank Aiken, Minister for the Co-ordination of Defensive Measures. This remained the case until 1942 when a new order gave any minister the power to reject a film on 'Emergency' grounds.[107] Montgomery's first action was to inform the cinema owners of Irish censorship policy with regard to film – they were told that the 'rulers, statesmen, warriors and flags of the belligerents' were not acceptable and that war news should 'not be accompanied by titles or commentary of a propaganda nature'.[108] Given that the Mass Observation social research organization estimated that 85 per cent of newsreels contained war news,[109] this presented a problem with regard to newsreel distribution to the south of Ireland. All references to war were banned in the hope that viewers in southern Ireland would live in a cocoon untouched by wartime propaganda, and particularly the pro-British propaganda that was inherently critical of Irish neutrality. Newsreels were scrutinized, edited and completely cleansed of any mention of the war. In fact, British newsreels commonly shown in Irish cinemas were so heavily edited that there was very little footage left. Three companies, Pathé, Gaumont and Movietone, produced Irish editions, combining international items (particularly from America) on non-war matters with items of local interest. These newsreels were much more in line with the trivial, upbeat, bland newsreels that had been popular in the 1930s. These specifically packaged Irish editions were distributed up to 1943, when a shortage of film stock stopped their production.

Donal Ó'Drisceoil offers the example of a Gaumont newsreel issued in May 1940. During a week when Rotterdam and Canterbury were bombed, the items in Gaumont's Irish edition included: the New York World Fair; US polo stars playing for charity; a carnival in Zurich; the opening of the US baseball season; and torrential floods and storms in America.[110] So while audiences in the North of Ireland followed every detail of the war with keen interest, cinemagoers just across the border in the south saw no evidence whatsoever of global conflict on their cinema screens.

Some belligerent propaganda films were exhibited in Éire for private consumption, but this was strictly monitored and the material was mostly of British origin.[111] The fact that general public consumption was free from belligerent propaganda during the war did not dampen down concerns about threats to Irish ideology through the cinema from other sources. A 1942 report for the Irish government on the film industry expressed concern about the interests of 'foreign nationals' in cinema exhibition in Ireland.[112] Particular concern was raised about a Dublin cinema which threatened to be the first in a potential British chain of first-run houses. The report indicated that other Dublin cinemas already felt threatened by this particular cinema due to its 'cross-channel affiliations' and recommended that 'measures be taken to restrict alien penetration'. In a particularly racist and anti-Semitic section of the report, concerns were raised:

> [that] a service such as the cinema, which nowadays plays so large a part in the social and cultural life of the community, should be controlled to such an extent as at present by persons whose ideas and general outlook are alien to those of the majority of our people. It was held that to leave such persons free to prescribe cinema programmes was to allow them too important a measure of influence over the minds, culture and social habits of our people, and was tantamount to giving them partial control of our public education.[113]

In a paradoxical qualification of these statements, this section concludes that no legislation could be introduced against Jews, 'surreptitiously or otherwise', as many Jews 'are in fact Irish nationals'. The next section moves on to describe how the complete content of films shown in Irish cinemas was produced by American and British cinema. Given the lack of a national cinema there appears an increasing concern about the lack of Irish input into such an influential medium. Perhaps the stringent wartime censorship of the cinema belied a more deep-rooted wariness towards cultural elements threatening the fabric and diffusion of accepted Irish tenets.

Irish Movietone News

The most comprehensive 'neutralized' newsreel exhibited to Irish audiences during the war was Irish Movietone News, produced by the British Movietone company with some help from the Irish Army. Items were suggested and filmed by the Irish Army from 1940 until May

1943 when production ceased due to a shortage of raw film stock. The army's involvement explains the preponderance of military items included in these newsreels, which tirelessly return to Local Defence Force (LDF) parades. Other subjects include sporting events, religious processions, and the usual newsreel trivia. Pathé and Gaumont also used some of the footage from Movietone for their Irish editions – pooling of footage was a common newsreel practice during wartime. A principal liaison figure between the Irish Army and Movietone was Captain Seamus MacCall. Dermot O'Donovan, in his thesis on 'Neutral Éire on the Screen 1939–45', suggests that MacCall had input into the commentaries.[114] However, post-production was undertaken by Movietone and, as such, the final product was edited and completed by the newsreel company rather than the army.

Military parades throughout the country were featured in Irish Movietone News, assuring audiences that Ireland was well defended against any potential enemy in the midst of what was described as 'a time of gravest danger' in one item showing characteristic reluctance to use the word 'war'.[115] The subject of international conflict hovers over these displays of national unity but emphasis is concentrated on internal defensive measures rather than outside events. Repeated scenes of huge rallies are described as: 'gigantic'[116] in Drogheda; the 'biggest military parade ever to be seen in the city'[117] of Cork; the 'largest known march in Wexford';[118] 'huge crowds' packing the streets of Tralee;[119] 'impressive scenes in Dundalk'.[120] The superlative nature of the commentary is bolstered by pictures of orderly volunteers watched by large crowds, presided over by the imposing figure of de Valera, attired completely in black, often in contrast to a sea of white-uniformed nurses. In speeches by their leader, the volunteers are often praised for their service to their country, and appeal is usually made for more volunteers, supplies of clothing and money. A priest often blesses military colours and the troops are inspected by de Valera or an appropriate representative in his absence, visualizing for the audience the inextricable link between Church and State. The Taoiseach frequently barges through lines of military in some cases with an almost comic lack of interest – he never looks directly at the troops he is inspecting. Having to acknowledge the defence preparations necessary in the face of war, even for a neutral, appears almost an irritation, an interruption in the ongoing struggle to establish Ireland as an independent and self-sufficient entity. In one item he rushes along a line of troops so quickly that he almost stumbles.[121] Conversely, when the vast lines of military personnel march past de Valera – who is usually positioned on a raised platform – we can often see their faces turn upwards to gaze at their leader, the consistent symbol of unfaltering Irish determination. The feature of large demonstrations of defence forces is hardly unusual in times of war. What *is* unusual is the lack of reference to the actual war! Commentaries skilfully gloss over the war, concentrating instead on playing up the strength of Ireland's military should it be necessary to call upon these defences.

Military training exercises also appear in the *Irish Movietone News* series. Such training includes – to quote the newsreels – 'mock' or 'imaginative bombing attacks',[122] Army medical training where 'occasionally there's a genuine casualty, by accident perhaps',[123] and scenes of Marine Service exercises proving that it is 'in a constant state of readiness to defend Ireland's shores'.[124] Often the volunteers training are shown having tea or meals after their work, since, we are told, 'Irishmen are notoriously fond of their cup of tea.'[125] These scenes serve to highlight the fact that these are merely training exercises, and Ireland is not suffering the reality of war. One item shows the Construction Corps enjoying their outdoor work in the sunshine. At lunchtime they eat what is shown in close-up to be a hearty meal, even though the commentary tells us 'today's Friday, a fast day, but it looks pretty good for a fast day'.[126] After lunch the men, on their half-day off, are shown playing rounders and swimming. In another item dealing with 'holiday training' for the Citizen Army, the commentary states: 'and now to the more serious business of getting rifles. What's the use of a soldier without a gun?' At this point, shots of a soldier handing out guns from the back of a truck are juxtaposed with a scene of seated soldiers peeling potatoes while the commentary describes 'activity of another kind' – namely, 'a course in potato peeling'. 'Wait', the commentator gushes, 'till their wives and mothers see these.' Immediately attention is drawn away from the rifle, the masculine weapon of war, to the preparation of food, highlighted by the commentary as a feminine pastime. The juxtaposition of rifle with food appears in another item covering Local Defence Force training, which cuts quickly from scenes of snipers taking part in an exercise to a shot of an ice-cream seller offering 'Kavanagh's Pure Ices' to the soldiers who are smiling and, as the commentary states, 'fraternising round the ice cream barrel'. The concluding remark sums up the British view of the work of the Irish military – 'it's a grand life'.[127]

Food is featured again in an item covering the opening of a new soldiers' club in Dublin, where 'soldiers can get satisfying meals for less than you would pay anywhere else in town, with sausage, bacon, eggs and chips, a pot of tea and plenty of bread and butter, all for a shilling'. The commentary is accompanied with scenes of soldiers seated in pleasant surroundings with flower-filled tables and waitresses bringing large plates of hot food. 'Then after a good meal you can retire to one of the recreation rooms for a brisk game of chess.' The camera cuts to two soldiers at a chess board; one rests his head on the table, apparently asleep, while the other is propped up but dozing, while the commentator suggests that these two 'future generals' are learning strategies and planning future wars on the chess board. Religion appears once again through the presence of the club's chaplain, supervising table tennis games and offering advice on books. The item ends showing a soldier wakening up in a comfortable dormitory with breakfast in bed!

In one Irish Movietone News item covering training and manoeuvres of 'local defence volunteers still full of zeal and energy', the accompanying notes for the item read 'LDF and Éireann army co-operate. Patrols are sent out, bridges blown up and a good time had by all. Typically Irish and mostly out of focus.'[128] The connotations of these notes suggest an implicit view of the Irish as enjoying 'playing' at war without having to endure the responsibility or harsh conditions of actual warfare. There is a slightly disparaging tone detectable in the comment on the actual filming of this item – 'typically Irish and mostly out of focus'. The Irish camera crew (also part of the Irish military) were not producing competent, professional films and there is the hint that this attitude to Irish film-making perhaps extends to other military activities.

Even in the portrayal of fleets of Dublin motorcyclists, formed to keep communications open in the event of air raids, the cyclists are pictured training in the countryside rather than the city. These cyclists are being trained 'to ride through debris, bomb craters and all the other things which air raids bring'.[129] Yet their training takes place through open country and rough hillsides. The trainee shown in this particular shot looks very unsteady; the bike falls and he has to clamber off, trying to regain his balance and control of the vehicle. The training is deemed 'intensive' but the shots of unsteady riders compared to concurrent shots of American troops training looks amateurish. Further shots show more competent riders training on rough, stony ground 'approximate to the same as that which might be expected during a raid'. As with many of the newsreels showing army training, refreshments feature in the newsreel. The cyclists are given tea from the mobile canteen, 'the first of its kind in Éire'. From the shot of the mobile van, with food being handed out through the side, we cut to the first women to be featured in the clip, pouring tea for the officers, amongst them the commander – who 'welcomes his share' – seated cross-legged on the ground and accepting the beverage being poured for him. He turns and smilingly acknowledges the camera. He looks relaxed and casual. The newsreel concludes with shots of two different riders delivering an important message from Dublin Castle.

In portrayals of Irish defence forces, emphasis is often placed on food or rest alongside work. In one item entitled *Irish Army Helps Increase Fuel Production* the newsreel opens with scenes of men washing and shaving outside their tents, 'ready for another strenuous day'.[130] After breakfast, they 'march off to work, a whole battalion of them. They're not armed with rifles and machine guns, their weapons are spades and wheelbarrows. For these soldiers are waging war against winter.' Once again the Irish are associated with the land, happier waging war with the elements than entering the conflict employing the time of their British counterparts. In close-ups of the men working, they are wearing civilian clothes, and some are smoking while they work – only the commentary associates the scene with the military. After some brief scenes of turf-cutting we are informed: 'But today's a short day anyway. Back in camp again it looks as though there's something special up. Yes, it's a gala day, a turf gala too.' We are shown scenes of the turf-cutters enjoying themselves in the sunshine with races, music and dancing while the commentary sums up: 'This is what digging turf does for you.'

Ireland's youth is not ignored in the newsreels' portrayal of the defence effort. One item covers 'a great rally of youth organisations' which included Catholic Boy Scouts, Irish Girl Guides, and Boys' Brigade taking their rightful place in Ireland's defence effort.[131] The young people's parade follows the same format as adult services parades

– good training for young people in preparation for future services to the
state. The same item moves on to cover an Air Raid Precautions services commemoration for the first anniversary of those killed in the
North Strand bombing of 31 May 1941 (coverage of which was not
shown in Ireland, as discussed above). No details are given of the bombing, as the commentary states simply that 'the procession swung along
from the bombed area to the Central Model School'.
Attention is diverted from the bombing to the movement of the troops
– there is no explanation of why the bombing occurred, or casualties or
damages inflicted. This is perhaps the most overt reference to war, but
the details given are sketchy. The tragedy is glossed over quickly and
the newsreel's ultimate emphasis is placed upon the youth in training
and the current civil defence organizations. Shots of marching female
officers complete the image of man, woman and child bolstering
Ireland's defences, while the accompanying commentary reminds us
that 'the parade was an indication of the growing strength, dignity and
capacity of the various civil defence organisations'.

The next item in this edition covers a parade of the Dublin division of
the Red Cross.[132] The male members of the division are shown marching
through a grey, rainy day – there are fewer spectators than normal and
some carry umbrellas. The Red Cross nurses are the next to parade
through, resplendent against the murky day in their white uniforms and
headdresses bearing the recognizable emblem of the Red Cross. The
commentary makes no specific reference to the nurses – in fact, while these
images are shown, we are told, rather comically, that 'the First Aid section
of the Irish Catholic Boy Scouts were also represented in the parade'.
Presumably members 'other' than the male officers are suitably evoked
through the shots of the Red Cross nurses. After being visually presented
with marching officers, then marching nurses, our attention is drawn to
five soldiers in triangular formation, the first carrying a Tricolour; their
background is a sea of angelic, almost nun-like white uniforms. The
accompanying commentary tells us that 'a picturesque element in this
impressive scene was the raising of the Tricolour to general salute'. The
vast array of uniforms merges into the ultimate symbol, the Tricolour, and
the message of compliance and servitude to the state is clear – that it is the
duty and responsibility of every Irish man and woman to be on the alert,
ready to defend his or her country if necessary. If there are any dissenters,
they are not visible in these newsreels.

As with the representation of Irish soldiers in military items, in the depiction of meals, entertainment and a less than professional-looking army, an underlying 'othering process' can also be detected in non-military depictions of the Irish. In an item on a Cross Country Championship at Finglas, some interesting preconceptions are alluded to by the commentator.[133] Alongside scenes of the runners powering through the countryside, the commentator tells us that they run 'well in form and jump like well trained hurdlers'. The association here is that it is quite an achievement for these untrained Irishmen to run like 'proper' hurdlers. What gives this suggestion further weight is that we are told that the runners are barefoot. However, even in close-ups of the runners' feet over a particular jump we can see that the shots accompanying this comment testify otherwise. By the end of the item, the commentator's uncharacteristic slowing down of his speech cements the item's patronizing tone as he articulates each syllable of 'Well done Claremont!' carefully, as if praising a child.

This sense of 'otherness' is also demonstrated in an item covering a Christmas Day swim at Clontarf outside Dublin.[134] Highlighting himself as a foreigner in his pronunciation of Clontarf (with cumbersome emphasis on the first syllable) it becomes clear that the commentator regards this as a strange event for Christmas Day: 'some hardy people like spending the festive season this way. And well, if they like it, why not?' The commentator emphasizes the word 'like' as if he is surprised anyone should enjoy such a pursuit. This again is the Irishman comfortable with the elements of nature, in fact preferring them to a civilized meal by the fire. The newsreels traditionally qualify the use of less than perfect pictures; this case is no different. The foggy, unclear shots of the outdoor bathers are accompanied with the comment: 'This is the O'Reilly cup; unfortunately there was a thick sea fog which made photography a little difficult.' The apology is unnecessary as the blurry pictures convey the cold and foggy nature of the day, as if the camera has captured the temperature as effectively as the thermometer it shows in the opening shots. Clearly the harsh conditions portrayed highlight the unusual nature of this Irish event. Another contributing factor to the evocative nature of the shots is the contrast between audience and competitors – the competitors thrash through the water enveloped with misty air while the onlookers watch, wrapped up in the comfort of hats and overcoats. In his concluding remarks, the commentator once again stresses the 'otherness' of this event by stressing the syllables 'my' and 'they' in his comment 'This isn't quite *my* idea of spending Christmas but *they* all seem quite happy about it.' The Irish remain close to the earth, choosing the outdoors even on Christmas Day, while the 'civilized' commentator infers that his idea of Christmas Day is quite the opposite.

The patronizing tone and sense of 'otherness' which appears in Irish Movietone News is interesting, given that these newsreels were produced for Irish audiences. These newsreel commentaries demonstrate deep-seated British attitudes to Ireland's desire for independence and policy of neutrality. (In particular, the condescension that is clear in coverage of the military is reminiscent of the attitudes present in coverage of Gaelic sports in the 1930s, as discussed in the previous chapter.) The fact that these attitudes have been allowed to infiltrate material produced for Irish audiences suggests that there was an underlying hope that perhaps these might – in a subtle way, given censorship restrictions – sway Irish people in their support for neutrality. In this sense the newsreels were not just fulfilling a distribution issue (in supplying material for a state still on the British distribution circuit) but also performing a propagandistic function – one which they were careful not to make overt.

Northern Ireland is seldom referred to in Irish Movietone News, most probably since its market was southern Ireland; Northern Ireland – as part of the UK and a country involved in the war – was becoming ever more separate from the southern state. The increasing manifestation of partition is, however, evident in one religious item covering the consecration of the Bishop of Clogher – a man, the commentary tells us, with a difficult diocese to deal with, as 'half of it's in the six counties and half in Éire and the administration of it is a task for which Monsignor O'Callaghan is well suited'.[135] There is no further qualification of this statement, although we are told in the next sentence that Bishop O'Callaghan shares a 'quiet gentleness and strength in repose' with his predecessor. This is the only clue we are given as to how he might be suited to deal with a difficult diocese. Despite this lack of clarification, the commentary later states: 'Bishop O'Callaghan has our best wishes and sincerest prayers in the difficult task which he now assumes.' Clearly the 'difficult task' mentioned refers to overseeing a diocese which bridges the divide between north and south. The newsreel thus recognizes the difficulties in overseeing two distinct communities, testifying to the growing dichotomy of north and south in cultural representation of Ireland. Bishop O'Callaghan is pictured beside an older bishop, their sceptres framing them. Crowds full of admiration look on, held back under the watchful gaze of a soldier. The newsreel enforces the link between Church and State through its shots of de Valera juxtaposed with images of clergy. The link between the two is further emphasized through scenes of the lines of priests in the procession flanked by stationary soldiers presiding over the procession. Church and State are clearly intertwined through the images, and this conjugation is visually approved by the large crowds outside the cathedral, framed with a background of countryside – a perfect summing up of the newsreels' depiction of (southern) Ireland – Church and State conjoined, and all men part of the land, a rural community that is inward-looking rather than forward-thinking. But while the three are linked, they are not equal.

After the service, the bishops are filmed coming out of the church, de Valera following close behind. An interesting shot shows the bishops in procession while soldiers stand in formation behind them, their rifles protruding onto the background. Through the rifles we see the crowds, kept back from the clergy by the soldiers. The dynamics of the shot are also significant – the bishops move forward, slowly, regally. The soldiers are stationary; the greatest movement is through the applauding crowd, but even that is in unison, each man behaving like the others in his allotted group. The military punctuates and frames the proceedings. The final remark tells us 'To conclude the proceedings, here are the Monaghan and District LDF who had formed the guard of honour.' The last shot shows us the cathedral in the left background, while the foreground is made up of marching soldiers moving toward the camera. Trees line the middle of the shot, mirroring the marching soldiers moving towards the camera. A powerful Irish image – Church, military and nature.

For the large part, the Irish Movietone items concern themselves with military matters – hardly surprising, given the involvement of the Irish Army in their production. However, the fact that those who filmed much of the content had no control over the final commentary is clear in the patronizing tone of much of the material. Although the slightly disparaging tone is hard to ignore, it is never overtly suggested in these newsreels that Irish defences are slipping: some of these scenes would have appeared in British newsreels to help persuade the British public that Ireland could resist attack against Germany if necessary. Most of the footage provided by the army would, however, have been viewed only by audiences in the south of Ireland. Out of twenty-three reels of Irish Movietone News in the British Film Institute, dated between 1940 and 1943 (comprising 120 items), a third of the material deals with items of a military nature. The rest includes local sporting events, religious parades, society weddings and general trivia. There is occasionally a portrayal of Ireland enjoying itself while the rest of the world is at war, particularly in some commentaries. In one Pathé item we are told that Irish cabbies in Dublin 'all go for a joy ride';[136] another item shows comically dressed pantomime players in Dublin playing hockey: 'it's a riot', the commentator tells us.[137] Another almost ridiculously trivial item shows the film censor, Ian Montgomery, and Mr Justice Hanna, High Court Judge (although on his day off!) looking on as 'a party of pretty puppy Pointers pose for a perfect picture'.[138]

While coverage of such events seems absurd during times of intense international warfare, these newsreels really have more in common with peacetime coverage which was consistently upbeat and light-hearted. In general, these 'neutralized' stories allowed the cinema-going public to view news similar in shape and content to that of the pre-war era. However, Kevin Rockett writes of the relief felt by cinema exhibitors when these newsreels ceased due to a shortage in film stock in May 1943. The Irish public, it seemed, had long tired of the inane nature of wartime cinema news.[139]

March of Time's *The Irish Question*

De Valera's rejection of the American request to close the German and Japanese ministries was dealt with in a twenty-minute March of Time issue entitled *The Irish Question*.[140] After the propaganda successes of *Ulster*[141] and *Ulster at Arms* for the Northern Ireland government, March of Time's representation of Ireland in *The Irish Question* was to prove vexing for the Unionist regime.[142] After their successful commandeering of March of Time to produce *Ulster vs. Éire* in 1937, the Northern Ireland government was disappointed in what it believed to be a relatively favourable depiction of Éire in a film made with the full sanction of the southern government. Particular objection was raised towards one section of the commentary suggesting that the Irish people would only feel completely free with the abolition of partition.[143]

The newsreel begins not with footage of Ireland, as would be expected from the title, but with scenes of the Houses of Parliament and shots of London buses. The accompanying commentary begins: 'even in wartime, Britain and the rest of the world can never ignore the Irish. As a nation – neutral; as individuals – Irish.' The footage then cuts to images of the BBC's overseas office and a commentator reading news. One of the main stories focussed upon is the controversial issue of the will of the wife of George Bernard Shaw. True to March of Time style, a staged scene of the reading of Mrs Shaw's will follows, in which we are told she has provided £100,000 'to teach the Irish self-control, elocution, deportment, the art of personal contact and social intercourse'. Her will describes her belief that 'awkward manners' 'vulgarities of speech and other defects' prevent many Irish people from gaining appropriate employment. Emphasizing objections to these comments from the wife of 'one of the most famous living Irishmen', shots of newspaper headlines highlight some of the backlash caused by the content of the will, one headline describing it as 'a slur on race whose culture has enlightened the world'.

The next scene confirms the average Irishman's anger with these comments, showing a typical Irish couple, seated in front of a fire. The man smokes his pipe while his wife knits; the Sacred Heart picture, a standard relic in Catholic homes at the time, is clearly visible on the wall. In anger the man recounts to his wife Shaw's approval of the will: throwing his paper to the ground, he spits: 'and that man calls himself an Irishman'. His wife placidly retorts: 'I wouldn't wonder Mrs Shaw knew the value of self-control after living with him for near fifty years.' The camera moves to another typical Irish scene – the local pub. A heated discussion ensues about just who should undertake teaching the Irish manners. 'The English?' one customer retorts before banging his fist on the bar counter and challenging 'let 'em try'. He then offers a sample of his own manners by demanding of the barman that 'you give me another beer you', to which the barman replies: 'mind you keep a civil tongue in your head'. Just like the support for de Valera and Irish neutrality, the opinion of Mrs Shaw's will seem unanimous. (Interestingly, Dermot O'Donovan suggests that this section was cut from the version of the film screened in Ireland, probably as it was deemed offensive by the Irish censor.)[144]

Satisfied with its depiction of the average Irishman, the next intertitle describes 'the proud and sensitive people of Ireland'. An Irish commentator further explains life in the 'lovely and sorrowful land of St Patrick'. The scenes are agricultural – of rugged landscape and picturesque farms, a land of 'magical' place names that 'live in the laments of poets who have sung to sweeten Ireland's wrong'. The language used by the commentator is musical and poetic and in stark opposition to the framework set up by the official March of Time commentary. Even so, we are reminded that few would swap places with an Irish farmer. Life is depicted as rural and strangely fascinating, an existence to be marvelled at by the newsreel voyeur in the comfortable distance of the urban cinema. Irish farmers, we are told, spend their life toiling to 'till the soil that bore them'. There is no suggestion of leaving native soil; the Irishman seems inextricably bound to his birthplace, and firmly intent on maintaining his existence from within, free from external forces, having 'fought again and again to set it free'. Independence cannot be taken for granted and must be conserved 'for the children of Ireland and the generations to come'. The children of Ireland are shown going to school: many are barefoot. Freedom, we are told, 'has not brought riches to Ireland. We have lived too long and too intimately with poverty to be rid of it in a few short years.' But, the narrator explains, 'if this land is poor, it is still ours to make or mar'.

Perhaps this sums up one of the most crucial perceptions of Éire's decision to remain neutral: the Irish were seen to be stubborn followers of independence, despite the potential economic and social consequences. To opt out of a world war rather than compromise independence was typically Irish. The juxtaposition of this suggestion with the exploration of Irish Catholicism can hardly be seen as coincidental. Religious faith in Ireland, it is stated, 'is no mere conviction, for deep in the Celtic nature is a hunger for the things of the spirit'; vocations to the priesthood bring honour upon Irish families, as 'there is no higher calling among the young men of Ireland'. Men of God help 'to form the character of the Irish people, their faith, their culture and their way of life'. In a section of notes on dope sheets, commentary not ultimately included in the film further explores the role of the priest through the figure of 'Father McMahon', called 'a great man' by his parishioners. Father McMahon, we are told in the notes, is a figure of modernization in his home parish of Lusk. Having 'pestered the electric power people' until his village was given electricity, he then turned his attention towards 'agitating for a cinema in Lusk'. This representation of Irish Catholicism as a force for progress with the community would have addressed some of the anti-Catholic bias which appeared in Paramount's *Ireland – the Plain Issue* but the section was not included in the final film, perhaps due to time constraints.[145]

Having firmly established its context, the film begins to explore its central theme of Irish neutrality. One concern raised about the film was that it would show Ireland at play while the rest of the world is at war. David Gray, the US Ambassador to Ireland, wrote: 'Many Irish hate to be displayed before the world as enjoying themselves extravagantly while the rest of the world is at war.'[146] Certainly this concern seems to be justified when the commentary, overrunning scenes of men playing cards and gambling in the streets, tells the viewer: 'Dublin is one of the few cities of Europe in which men can feel secure in the pleasant and diverting ways of peacetime.' The narrator asks why should this privilege be given up and argues, in a comment tinged with religious undertones: 'after too many bitter years of fighting for its own causes and principles, Ireland had us lead not into war'. Cementing the images of Ireland at peace, the film moves to Leopardstown race track and other sports which 'have gone on undisturbed in Ireland while the rest of the world has been at war'. Images of Gaelic football matches further mirror Irish unanimity about the issue of neutrality: large watching crowds are described as feeling 'a sense of our unity and our nationality'. The seal is then set on the insular Irish people whose 'nationalism is still too much in our thoughts to make worrying about the rest of the world a major concern of ours'. The final restriction of Irish liberty is the Northern Ireland question: 'no Irishman will ever feel his people are truly free until Northern Ireland, still under the British crown, is restored to Éire, and all Ireland is made one'. Crucially, 'resentment of partition has strengthened our determination to remain neutral ... For Ireland today independence and neutrality have become one indivisible cause.' A cause, the commentary explains, that Ireland is prepared to fight for again. The Irish commentator finishes on a positive note, explaining that trade has continued between Britain and Ireland during the war and 'since the British have never violated our neutrality, the war years have brought better feeling between our two nations'.

The next section of the film is bridged with an intertitle describing the US demand for Éire to suspend relations with the Axis. The March of Time official commentator takes over the story, describing Irish neutrality as 'a serious handicap'. The film's visuals change tack with a map showing strategic weakness for American forces due to Irish neutrality, followed by intercutting scenes of American and Irish commentators, arguing Éire's position in relation to the war. Various accusations are calmly presented by the American figure and defiantly refuted by his Irish counterpart. Cutting to scenes of Dublin, we are told that while the US had been 'Éire's greatest friend', still its diplomatic requests were rejected. This criticism is qualified by reassuring descriptions of Éire's assistance to the Allies in terms of labour and military volunteers. The potential consequences of neutrality, however, cannot be ignored: over scenes of turf-cutters, the commentary prophesies: 'economic sanctions and the loss of British markets can bring unemployment and hard times but the Irish will face that possibility. They will get along with what they have. For this is the way they have chosen and if it's a hard way, they are determined to stick to it.' Perhaps the film's ultimate stereotyping lies in its subsequent comment: 'Those who seek the answer to the Irish question of today or the Irish question of tomorrow, must look not to logic, but to the poetry of the Irish.' The film returns to the Irish commentator for a short burst of poetry and ends with rural scenes of thatched cottages, horses and carts, and images of the landscape. The lines quoted are:

> The world wears down to sundown,
>   And love is lost and won,
> But he recks not of love or gain,
>   The King of Ireland's son.
> He follows on for ever, when all your chase is done
> He follows after shadows –
>   The King of Ireland's son.[147]

The poem quoted is 'The King of Ireland's Son' by Nora Hopper, an English poet, daughter of an Irish officer in the British Army. Ireland is a main concern of her poetry, which draws comparisons with the early work of Yeats. Martin Williams suggests that the imagery in the poem, while drawing on Irish myth, suggests that the hero must reach the 'promised land' alone and with great difficulty – certainly connotations already suggested in the newsreel of the Irish struggle for independence. Williams also suggests that the final lines of the poem 'apply to some contemporary Irish Republicans as pertinently as to their grandfathers'. It was this type of mythologizing which was used by Nationalists 'to elevate the whole struggle against the British – a process which began before 1916 and was greatly accelerated afterwards'.[148] In this newsreel, the evocation of this imagery is used to bolster imagery of the Irish as obsessing with myth, poetry and ideological struggle at the expense of progress, economic success and involvement with real international issues.

The Irish government expressed concerns prior to the film's production about the ultimate depiction of neutral Éire, and Major Guilfoyle from Military Intelligence (G2) accompanied the film crew during production. Only one major concern was raised. Notes on dope sheets relating to shots of champagne being served at a dance in the Gresham Hotel in Dublin called for the deletion of the scene due to the authorities' fear that it may have given 'a derogatory inflexion on their attitude on neutrality in a world at war'.[149] The scene was not included and no further objections to the film were made. As Donal Ó'Drisceoil points out, in contrast to official priorities, no concern was expressed about scenes of barefoot children entering schools or the 'stereotypically patronizing approach to the commentary'.[150] Concerns about the final film were also raised in advance by the film's director, experimental British film-maker Len Lye, who was employed by March of Time on a freelance basis to complete the film. In a letter to G2, Major Guilfoyle suggested that Lye

> [was] not enamoured with March of Time methods in film commentary ... Lye reminded me on more than one occasion that he could take no responsibility for the eventual sub-editing and commentary. All he could do was to cover such aspects of the normal life of the country as would be of interest to the general body of cinemagoers in America. The subsequent editing and commentary by over emphasis, understatement or deletion could give any film an undesirable slant.[151]

Despite the concerns expressed, the film was exhibited in both the north and south of Ireland, and indeed throughout the world. Its publicity described the film as 'the latest of a series of films in which the March of Time has dealt with neutral nations, and many will find this one the most attractive for its tolerant understanding and humour'. It goes on to describe the Shaw incident as 'an example of the kind of tea-cup tempest which is ever bursting about the Irish, and which makes them the most difficult people in the world to ignore'. We are told that the average Irishman, 'when he is not working ... is reciting poetry, talking politics or cheering a race horse. And working or playing, he is a Catholic all the time.'[152] The publicity, if faintly condescending, evokes the main tone of the film: one of distanced observation of the 'otherness' of Ireland – poetic, rural, Catholic and neutral.

Conclusion

It was only at the end of the war that films and newsreels banned by the Irish censor appeared in abundance in the cinemas; it was the first time in six years that war footage was readily available to audiences. Even then, however, newsreels covering the conflict were still contentious. Rockett gives the example of a Pathé item submitted in June 1945, covering bombing of the North Strand Road in Dublin, which was removed due to 'sarcastic' remarks which 'would undoubtedly have caused offence'.[153] In this light, Rockett describes 'an almost hysterical fear of informing cinemagoers of the reality of war and its devastating impact in Ireland, as elsewhere'.[154]

A report was produced between 1938 and 1942 by the Inter-Departmental Committee on the Film Industry in Éire, which addressed concerns that the cinema could influence the 'minds, culture and social habits' of the Irish people.[155] Similar concerns had appeared in 1936, in the report of the Committee on Cinematograph Films in Britain which recognized the cinema's potentialities 'in shaping the ideas of the very large numbers to whom it appeals' as 'almost unlimited'.[156] While there was most certainly a common awareness between Irish and British governments of the power of newsreel propaganda, there was equally a common desire to utilize the newsreel to support national policy. Through the use of carefully constructed propaganda newsreels, viewers in the North were exerted to fully engage in the war effort to increase valued industrial production. In the south, de Valera felt that he had to protect his electorate from harmful British propaganda, and he was equally concerned that that propaganda would be inherently anti-de Valera. One of the most interesting features in the case of the Second World War and Éire was what was omitted in de Valera's remarkable denial of wartime onscreen news for southern audiences. He seemed acutely aware of the potential power of real images of war tapping into collective sympathies.

Pronay suggests that the viewing of news in the cinema 'could evoke a greater degree of rapport and emotional involvement from the audience than printed words and pictures could'.[157] If, as le Goff suggests, 'the mass media are the primary vehicles for the expression and ordering of mentalities',[158] then the newsreels' role in everyday life could be viewed as pivotal in influencing, forming and moulding opinion in a systematic way, given their homogeneity and regularity. It was for this reason that the policing of national images, particularly during wartime, was so crucial for the governments of both the north and south of Ireland.

Through the purging of war news in the southern newsreels, audiences were reminded that while they must rally to the defence of their country in time of 'Emergency', the Second World War should not feature in their daily lives or places of entertainment. What we have in terms of newsreel coverage of the Second World War is not just varying representations of north and south but also a reflection of the consolidation of partition, mirrored by the differences in the news and propaganda offered to northern and southern audiences. The physical split of cinema viewing during wartime, with the prevalence of war news for one audience and the lack of it for another, typified the growing recognition of partition in Irish consciousness. This would be cemented in the psyche of Northern audiences through newsreel contextualization of a diplomatic action of the southern government.

As the war drew to a close, the newsreels were visibly at a loss in facing the dilemma of how to portray the horrific images their cameramen captured at the liberation of Nazi concentration camps, but audiences were, nevertheless, granted access to these images. The fact that the public in the North of Ireland viewed images of obscene cruelty unparalleled in contemporary cinema exhibition meant that de Valera's expression of condolence on the death of Hitler in May 1945 was seen as an unspeakably repugnant act, and historian Jonathan Bardon suggests that 'the wave of disgust that swept across the majority in Northern Ireland served as a reminder of how far the war had

widened the gulf between north and south'.[159] Ian Wood describes de
Valera's decision to call on Hempel, the German Minister, in Dublin on
2 May 1945, just two days after Hitler's suicide, as 'disastrous', suggesting that 'de Valera gave to the world a signal of what could only be
interpreted as his country's moral myopia'.[160] De Valera's actions were
not quickly forgotten. Writing in 1995, Kevin Myers reminds us that, for
the Irish people, 'de Valera's wretched visit to the German ambassador
to offer his condolences upon the death of Herr Hitler still causes an
exquisite embarrassment'.[161] On the sixtieth anniversary of VE day,
Henry McDonald writes of 'the lengths to which the then Taoiseach
and his ministers went as they tried to portray revelations about the
concentration camps as Allied propaganda'. The article covers the
research of Patrick Maume into de Valera's criticism of the *Sunday
Independent*'s coverage of the liberation of Bergen-Belsen as 'anti-
national propaganda'.[162]

Just as broadcasting would be used to 'copper-fasten' what Martin
McLoone describes as a 'partitionist mentality',[163] the split in wartime
newsreel viewing symbolized the division in Ireland's political positioning
within an international conflict. By the end of the war, any possibility of
a United Ireland had gone. Northern Ireland's contribution to the war
effort improved relations between its government and Westminster – in
fact, 'it was the important strategic role played by Northern Ireland
during the war that proved the decisive factor in reinforcing Northern
Ireland's position in the UK'[164] (just as Éire's neutrality and failure to
offer the strategic advantage of the Treaty Ports increased the distance
between the Éire government and Westminster). Kevin Rockett states
that 'while World War One had served as a catalyst for action among
those seeking a separate Irish nation-state, World War Two helped to
reinforce independent Ireland's isolation from the rest of the world'.[165]
Ireland's neutral stance, a separation from Britain's wartime involvement,
had not only established its political independence from its colonizer
but, by proxy, from the rest of the world. Against this backdrop, it is
possible that Éire's neutrality in the Second World War, its failure
to participate in a globally accepted war, did more to construct it as
'other' in Britain's psyche than any previous conflict.

NOTES

1. Ó'Drisceoil (1996), p.33.
2. Rockett (2004), p.338.
3. Ibid., p.334.
4. Ó'Drisceoil (1996), p.3.
5. Dáil Éireann, 2 September 1939, cited in Moynihan (1980), pp.418–19.
6. Reid (unpublished thesis, 1996), p.18.
7. Ó'Drisceoil (1996), p.7.
8. B. Barton (1995), p.111.
9. Ó'Drisceoil (1996), p.7.
10. Ibid.
11. B. Barton (1995), p.39.
12. Bardon (1992), p.558.
13. O'Halpin (2003), p.31.
14. Girvin (2006), p.xix.
15. *The Times*, 6 May 1938, in B. Barton (1995), p.88.
16. *The Irish Times*, 8 November 1938, in B. Barton (1995), p.88.
17. *De Valera Arrives in England*. Gaumont British News, Issue 423, 17 January 1938.
18. Commentary sheet available for viewing on NoS.
19. P.M. Taylor (1999), p.153.
20. Ibid., p.45.
21. Thorpe and Pronay (1980), p.48.
22. P.M. Taylor (1999), p.176.
23. Ibid., p.112.
24. Ibid., p.177.
25. Mass Observation File Report 22, *Content of Newsreels*, 28 January 1940.
26. P.M. Taylor (1999), p.189.
27. B. Barton (1995), p.13.
28. P.M. Taylor (1999), p.180.
29. Pronay (1982), pp.175–6.
30. Thorpe and Pronay (1980), p.8.
31. Ibid., p.14.
32. Reid (unpublished thesis, 1996), p.27.
33. *Nero Trailer*. Gaumont British News, Issue 954, 25 February 1943.
34. *The World at War*. Gaumont British News, Issue 873, 18 May 1942.
35. Thorpe and Pronay (1980), p.42.
36. Listed on NoS as *Hock Der Lambeth Valk*. Pathé Gazette, Issue 41/103, 25 December 1941.
37. *Victory in Africa*. Gaumont British News, Issue 977, 17 May 1943.
38. *Roosevelt's Speech*. Gaumont British News, Issue 804, 18 September 1941.
39. *All Britain Pays Tribute to Red Army*. Gaumont British News, Issue 954, 25 February 1943.
40. *Stalingrad. Destruction of the German Sixth Army*. Gaumont British News, Issue 955, 1 March 1943.
41. *Tanks Rout out Buna Japs*. Gaumont British News, Issue 968, 15 April 1943.
42. Ó'Drisceoil (1996), p.125.
43. *Flying Fortresses in Action*. Gaumont British News, Issue 965, 5 April 1943.
44. B. Barton (1995), p.79.
45. Ibid., p.72.
46. *Dig for Victory*. Pathé Gazette, Issue 40/7, 22 January 1940.
47. *Ulster Home Guard*. Gaumont British News, Issue 689, 12 August 1940.
48. B. Barton (1995), p.6.
49. Letter from Jock Henderson to Ernest Cooper, Director of Information Services, 7 March 1944, PRONI, CAB9F/123/3B.
50. *Ulster at Arms*. Warwork News, Issue S15/39, January 1944.
51. Hill (2006), pp.94–5.

52. Ibid., p.95.
53. Ibid.
54. Ibid., p.96.
55. *All for Defence*. Pathé Gazette, Issue 40/50, 29 June 1940.
56. 'Party Unity in Éire' (1940).
57. Fisk (1983), p.336.
58. *Outposts of Peace – Irish Army Manoeuvres*. Pathé Gazette, Issue 40/54, 4 July 1940.
59. *Ireland has First Air Raid*. British Movietone News, Issue 587, 2 September 1940.
60. *Éire Bombed*. Pathé Gazette, Issue 41/4, 13 January 1941.
61. Rockett (2004), pp.338–9.
62. Ibid., p.339.
63. *Nazi Bomb Damage on Dublin*. Gaumont British News, Issue 733, 13 January 1941.
64. Coogan (2003), p.257.
65. *Germans Bomb Dublin*. Pathé Gazette, Issue 40/54, 4 July 1940.
66. Fisk (1983), p.338.
67. Rockett (2004), p.339.
68. Ibid.
69. Fisk (1983), p.338.
70. B. Barton (1995), p.2.
71. Bardon (1992), p.580.
72. Ibid., p.581.
73. Ibid., p.581.
74. Ibid., p.555.
75. Fisk (1983), p.470.
76. B. Barton (1995), p.16
77. PRONI, CAB 4/473, 15 May 1941, cited in B. Barton (1995), p.24.
78. B. Barton (1995), p.24.
79. Ibid., p.124.
80. Ibid., p.124.
81. Fisk (1983), p.339.
82. Ibid., p.340.
83. Wood (2002), pp.85–6.
84. Fisk (1983), p.340.
85. B. Barton (1995), p.37.
86. 'Éire Objects to Film' (1942), p.3.
87. Rockett (2004), p.455n.
88. Ó'Drisceoil (1996), p.43.
89. *House of Commons Debates*, vol. 342, cols 1261–319, 7 December 1938, cited in McKernan (2002), pp.121–33.
90. Elvin (1939), pp.141–6.
91. P.M. Taylor (1999), p.179.
92. *Britain, US, Isolate Éire*. British Paramount News, Issue 1364, 27 March 1944.
93. *News from the Éire Border*. Pathé Gazette, Issue 44/25, 27 March 1944.
94. Bardon (1992), p.585.
95. Wills (2007), p.6
96. Coogan (2003), p.266.
97. *First American Troops in Ireland*. Gaumont British News, Issue 842, 29 January 1942.
98. *Dough Boys in Ulster*. British Movietone News, Issue 663, 16 February 1942.
99. Hill (2006), p.105.
100. *Fencing in Ireland*. Pathé Gazette, Issue 41/82, 13 October 1941.
101. *Baby Boxers*. Gaumont British News, Issue 871, 11 May 1942.
102. *Balloon Houses*. Pathé Gazette, Issue 41/97, 4 December 1942.
103. Fisk (1983), p.140.
104. Ibid., p.140.
105. See Rockett (2004), pp.335–6.

106. Ibid., pp.339–40.
107. Ó'Drisceoil (1996), p.33.
108. Ibid.
109. Mass Observation File Report 22, *Content of Newsreels*, 28 January 1940.
110. Ó'Drisceoil (1996), pp.33–4.
111. Private Exhibition of Belligerent Propaganda Films, National Archives of Ireland, Dublin [hereafter NAI], DFA238/167.
112. *Report of Inter-Departmental Committee on the Film Industry*, March 1942, NAI, R303 3/5.
113. Ibid.
114. O'Donovan (unpublished thesis, 1996), p.6.
115. *Colours for the LDF*. Irish Movietone News, Story No. 42809A, 1942.
116. *LDF Recruiting Parade at Drogheda*. Irish Movietone News, Story No. 45205A, 1942.
117. *Army Parade – Dublin, Cork*. Irish Movietone News, Story No. 42891, 30 September 1942.
118. *Big Parade at Wexford*. Gaumont British News, Issue 816, 30 October 1941. Due to the absence of Irish Movietone News stories on NoS, the references given are from the British Film Institute's catalogue. Many of Gaumont's Dublin issues used the same footage as Irish Movietone News – the pooling of footage between newsreel companies was common practice during wartime. When this has occurred I have used NoS's references for Gaumont material, for the purposes of more accurate dating.
119. *De Valera at Tralee*. Irish Movietone News, Story No. 41560, 11 October 1941.
120. *LDF Parade*. Irish Movietone News, Story No. 42965, 16 October 1942.
121. *Mr de Valera at Mullingar*. Gaumont British News, Issue 813, 20 October 1941.
122. *De Valera Reviews ARP Parade*. Irish Movietone News, Story No. 39847, 10 March 1940.
123. *Army Medical School – Ireland*. Irish Movietone News, Story No. 41731, 22 December 1941.
124. *Marine Service*. Irish Movietone News, Story No. 42756, 24 August 1942.
125. *An Army Marches on Its …* . Irish Movietone News, Story No. 41596, 20/11/1941.
126. *Construction Corps at Work in Éire's Forest*. Irish Movietone News, Story No. 204581A, 1941.
127. *Éire's Cavalry on Wheels*. Irish Movietone News, Story No. 41266, 9 May 1941.
128. *LDF and Army Manoeuvres*. Irish Movietone News, Story No. 45210A, September 1941.
129. *Dublin Cyclists Train to Keep Open Communications*. Irish Movietone News, Story No. 204550A, 7 April 1943.
130. *Irish Army Help Increase Fuel Production*. Irish Movietone News, Story No. 45280A, 5 September 1941.
131. *Youth Safety First Parade*. Irish Movietone News, Story No. 206508A, 1942.
132. *Red Cross Procession*. Irish Movietone News, Story No. 206508A, 1942.
133. *Cross Country Championship at Finglas*. Irish Movietone News, Story No. 204512A, 1943.
134. *Xmas Morning at Clontarf Baths*. Irish Movietone News, Story No. 204512A, 23 March 1942.
135. *Bishop of Clogher Consecrated at Monaghan*. Irish Movietone News, Story No. 204550A, 7 April 1943.
136. *Irish Cabbies Meet in Phoenix Park, Dublin*. Pathé Gazette, Issue 40/4, 11 January 1940.
137. *Fancy Dress Hockey at Kimmage, Dublin*. Pathé Gazette, Issue 40/7, 22 January 1940.
138. *Irish Kennel Club Show*. Pathé Gazette, Issue 40/25, 25 March 1940.
139. Rockett (2004), p.341.
140. *The Irish Question*. March of Time, 9th year, No. 11, 12 June 1944.
141. *Ulster* (1940) was a short film, produced with the assistance of the Ulster Tourist Development Association, showing Northern Ireland's contribution to the war effort. John Hill suggests it was 'a selective, and implicitly partisan imagining of "the people of Ulster" that suppresses the problematic relationship of the Northern Ireland Parliament to the whole of its "people", as well as the social and religious divisions that characterise the Northern Irish "community" ' . See Hill (2006), p.86.
142. Ibid., p.100.

143. Ibid.
144. O'Donovan (unpublished thesis, 1996), p.24.
145. Undated dope sheet for roll 88, from file titled 'Film – March of Time', Irish Military Archives, Dublin, G2/X/1504.
146. Cole (2006), p.152.
147. From the poem 'Daluan' by Nora Hopper (1894).
148. Williams (1983), pp.307–28.
149. Undated dope sheet for roll 96, from file titled 'Film – March of Time', Irish Military Archives, Dublin, G2/X/1504.
150. Ó'Drisceoil (1996), pp.44–5.
151. Letter from Major Guilfoyle to CSO, G2 Branch, 10 December 1943, from file titled 'Film – March of Time', Irish Military Archives, Dublin, G2/X/1504.
152. March of Time publicity sheet for *The Irish Question*, 9th Year, No. 11 12 June 1944.
153. Rockett (2004), p.339.
154. Ibid.
155. Report of Inter-Departmental Committee on the Film Industry, March 1942, NAI R303 3/5.
156. *Film Censorship Consultative Committee reconstituted as Cinematograph Advisory Committee*, PRO (Britain)), HO45/24945.
157. Pronay in P. Smith (1976), p.98.
158. Sorenssen in Smither and Klaue (1996), p.44.
159. Bardon (1992), p.583.
160. Wood (2002), p.61.
161. Myers (1995), p.13.
162. McDonald (2005).
163. McLoone in McLoone (1996), pp.20–34.
164. Hill (2006), p.79.
165. Rockett (2004), p.334.

7

Conclusion: The 1950s –
The Advent of Television and
Decline of the Newsreels

Attitudes to the newsreels after the propaganda onslaught of the Second World War were increasingly sceptical and the public's cynicism towards the genre, coupled with the advent of television, signified a crisis for the newsreel industry in the 1950s.

A *Times* article from November 1958 outlined Rank's attempt to produce a cinemagazine to replace Gaumont British and Universal news, 'both of which will cease'. The aim, as reported by the article, was to present entertainment which would 'have a more lasting impact than the present newsreel content'.[1] Two years previously, the Newsreel Association (NRA) was clearly aware of the threats to the future of the genre, as outlined in a letter from Sir Gordon Craig, Chairman of the NRA, to Mr R.C. Bryant, Under Secretary of the Films Division, Board of Trade, which suggested the newsreels might be saved if a quota system was implemented. The letter highlights the economic problems facing the newsreel industry with the growth of television, coupled with the fact that 'newsreel production and print costs have risen by over 100% since pre-war times'.[2]

Clearly the newsreels were struggling to compete with the immediacy of television news and sought to highlight their important function of 'exporting' news abroad. In relation to Ireland, during the 1950s the newsreels attempted to cater for Irish audiences in a more sustained way than in any previous decade. Irish stories were frequently added on to mainstream newsreels distributed to Ireland. Two particular case studies are worth noting.

Universal Irish News

Universal Talking News (latterly known as Universal News) took up
the sound reins from its silent precursor Empire News Bulletin on 14
July 1930 and ran until 31 December 1959. It was taken over by Gau-
mont-British News in 1949, and although the content produced for
each newsreel was essentially the same, they kept the separate names.[3]
Universal Irish News, a separate local edition, appeared alongside the
main edition from January 1952 and ran until 1956. Local Irish items
were substituted for items of a 'more British' interest.

On some occasions the items produced for southern Irish audiences
followed exactly the same format as the British National newsreel, but
in other cases there are interesting differences. On the issue sheets of
Universal News, there are often notes as to which items should be
removed or substituted in local reels for Scotland, Manchester and
Liverpool, Leeds, West of England and even Belfast. Universal Irish
News is denoted in the bottom half of the issue sheet, with clear
listings of each item to be included. While local items are produced for
the other areas only occasionally, Universal supplied southern Ireland
with two specifically Irish issues per week, while viewers in the North
watched the main issue supplied to the rest of the UK, with occasional
local stories substituted (such as royal visits to the North). Again there is
a split here in viewing for northern and southern audiences. A significant difference between the main Universal issues and its Irish editions
are the multitude of religious items which appear in the Irish editions but
are not included in the main issue. Just as religious items are numerous
in Universal Irish News, royal items are equally popular in the main
British issues, though are seldom included in the Irish editions[4]. Viewers
in Northern Ireland, however, would, like other viewers in the UK,
have watched the plethora of royal stories. When it came to the Coronation, the entire main issue was dedicated to Coronation coverage, while
the Irish issue comprised 'Irish Fashions in America'; 'Shoe Fashions
Display'; 'Consecration of Airplanes'; 'Minister Visits Technical
School'; 'Sailing Boats Launched at Skerries'; 'Sailing Season Opens'.[5]
If anything demonstrates the cultural gap in post-partition Ireland, this
difference in newsreel coverage for June 1953 does so amply. British
sporting events are, however, often included in the Irish reels –
Wimbledon is always covered extensively in British and Irish reels, as
well as boxing, motor racing, rugby and soccer events, although Irish

sports are seldom mentioned in either edition. There is no GAA (Gaelic Athletic Association) coverage, and only one item covering the 1952 'Hurling Final',[6] which is a departure from previous newsreel coverage of Gaelic sporting events. For the most part, Universal Irish News contained the same types of stories included in the main edition, but with a more local interest. An example of this was the An Tostal Festival, an Irish Festival which took place each spring and which is frequently covered in Irish editions, often appearing in several issues and usually mentioned at least once in the main edition. In one particular item covering the opening of An Tostal in 1955, the newsreel commentary demonstrates a markedly more progressive attitude towards the south of Ireland than had been demonstrated in previous decades.[7] The item depicts Seán T. O'Kelly, the second President of Ireland, wearing top hat and tails and inspecting troops whilst the commentator describes 'a great festival of springtime revealing the culture and charm and no less the achievement of a republic that was born on this spot less than four decades ago'. We see a parade of armoured cars and overhead shots of perfect formations of marching men, watched by huge crowds, while the commentator reels off a list of the defence weapons on parade: 'equipment that makes up the all round strength of a mobile striking force. Every vantage point is filled, every eye feasts on the great panorama of colour enriching a great day in the history of our modern republic.' The reason this comment is interesting is twofold – firstly, the commentator describing 'our modern republic' is English; secondly, given the newsreels' previous stereotyping of backward Ireland, this comment is significantly progressive. Further images of Ireland's future are evoked through imagery of the rebirth of the nation. Ireland is described in utopian terms as 'a young country, a young nation, marching towards its day of golden achievement'. The violent and complex construction of that nation is absent: once again there is little room in the newsreels for explanation as to why Ireland is a country supposedly in her youth. The British edition of this issue does not feature this footage, instead opting for 'The Queen in Lancashire'.

Universal Irish News ceased in 1956, the same year that Gael Linn's Amharc Éireann was launched. From 1956 to 1959, Amharc Éireann ran a monthly Irish edition attached to the main Universal News edition until the demise of Universal News. From 1959 to 1964, Gael Linn issued weekly editions of Amharc Éireann.

Amharc Éireann provides an important insight into how Ireland was represented by indigenous producers after having been catered for and covered by outside news producers for most of the newsreel era.[8] It was the first sustained attempt to offer weekly local news for Irish audiences which was actually filmed and edited in Ireland. Usually, four items were covered each week and each issue lasted four minutes in total. Commentaries were entirely in Irish. For the first three years of production, the films 'were explanatory in nature and didactic in tone', seeking to present various aspects of Irish culture to the Irish people. At a time when emigration in Ireland was high, Mairéad Pratschke suggests that 'The films aimed to inspire a confidence in Ireland and its capacity to produce valuable goods, to promote its own industrial development, to compete internationally, to sustain its population, and to reassure the Irish of their collective self-worth at a time when depression had taken its toll on the national psyche.'[9] Given this agenda, the films cover the development of Irish industry, the Irish landscape (almost in the form of travelogues or tourist-based material), Irish culture, women and work. The films from the period 1959–64 'differ in tone, style and content', recording 'the dramatic transformation that Ireland underwent in economic development, international affairs, and social and cultural life'. There are a number of commemorative items in this series, and coverage of the armed forces and examination of the disaporic community, as well as the common newsreel preoccupation with sporting events. While the British newsreels often took a disparaging and patronizing tone towards Irish sports, such as Gaelic football and hurling, in comparison with soccer, in Amharc Éireann these sports are prioritized, while soccer is excluded as essentially an English game. The content of these films offers a fascinating insight into Ireland's first sustained indigenous newsreel and how its tone and aims differed from the external production to which audiences before the 1950s had become accustomed. Drawing upon these two instances of newsreel production it becomes clear that the newsreels' attitudes to Ireland became slowly more progressive only when the newsreel industry was in decline.

Conclusion

This book set out to interrogate the newsreels' relationship to Ireland in terms of both content and representation. It began by examining the newsreel genre and then sought to explore coverage of Ireland through three main historical periods of Irish history – the turbulent War of Independence, Civil War and partition era; the more peaceful 1930s; and the Second World War. The central hypothesis here is that the newsreels contributed to the development of a 'partitionist' mentality in Ireland. The focus of this study has been on textual analysis of newsreels covering Irish stories for British and Irish audiences between 1910 and 1945, with a brief reflection on the decline of the newsreel industry in the 1950s. This period offered the chance to examine the newsreel genre from its establishment, through the height of its popularity, and culminating in its significant and propaganda-fuelled coverage of the Second World War. Thus the genre has been scrutinized from its beginnings, through its popular peacetime coverage and its interaction with official sources during wartime. This detailed examination suggests that the newsreels contributed to the embedding of partition in the psyche of both the Irish and the British public, addressing fluid variations in location, opinion and allegiances. This is particularly manifest in how the newsreels covered north and south during the relatively peaceful but politically turbulent 1930s, at a time when the distance between north and south was growing, a process that concluded with the cementing of partition in the differing states of north and south during the Second World War. While the basis of this study has been textual analysis of the newsreels themselves, historical accounts have also been drawn upon, as well as government documents and related production information, where available. There are no audience studies detailing the Irish public's reception of British newsreels and there is scant information on distribution practices. Where possible, I have drawn on newsreel issue sheets and cameramen's dope sheets to gather information on story listings, changes in commentaries and substitutions of particular items for local editions, although this information is not consistently available in relation to Irish content. Existing newsreel research has provided a context to produce what is the first study of coverage of Ireland within the current body of academic work.

As a genre the newsreels were in essence a pro-Establishment, non-controversial medium. They were consistently upbeat, cautious in choosing content and eager to please audiences and exhibitors. They sought to reinforce hegemonic norms and preferred to avoid conflict or overtly political material. Given the nature of their form, coverage of Ireland as a site of conflict and shifting identities and allegiances posed an ongoing dilemma. Content, coverage and representation for and of Ireland presented the newsreels with unique challenges.

The coverage of the era of the Home Rule debate (1910–23) coincided with the birth and development of the newsreel as genre and industry. The beginning of this era saw the growth of the Home Rule movement and Unionist opposition to any form of self-government for Ireland. Even before Ireland was divided, the newsreels were exhibiting a 'partitionist mentality' in their differing representations of north and south. A strong association of the north with Unionism is set up through iconic imagery of Orange marches, meetings bedecked with Union Jacks and displays of solidarity such as the signing of the Covenant. Nationalism is seldom demonstrated in newsreels covering the north during this time; it is firmly confined to the south. The newsreels seemed prepared for partition even before it became an historical fact. In both pre- and post-partition coverage, the newsreels desperately attempt to present the conflict in their characteristic upbeat manner. This is demonstrated in the cheerful and optimistic coverage of the Treaty negotiations. This coverage, however, gives way to smoky scenes of the War of Independence and then the Civil War, in particular in the violent 'aftermath' scenes of 1922. The south of Ireland is shown fighting against itself in a brutal civil war (only years after Britain had been involved in a world war), confirming it as 'other' to the orderly military displays and royal items which represent Britain in the newsreels of this era. In fact, a steady stream of items covering royal visits and military parades attempt to normalize British presence in Ireland, particularly to invoke loyalty during the First World War and subsequently after partition, to associate the new Dominion with an ongoing 'Britishness'.

Aldgate suggested that the newsreels covering the Spanish Civil War were deliberately selective in their coverage in order to prevent the situation from being fully understood by British audiences. Similarly, in covering events in Ireland the newsreels were sometimes misleading and on occasion failed to include information, or else were guilty of serious errors. A clear example of this is the newsreels' coverage of the activities of the Black and Tans. They do not condemn the violent and anarchic incidents which proliferated during the War of Independence – in some cases they do not even identify the Black and Tans as perpetrators, falling in line with Irish Secretary Hamar Greenwood's tendency to ignore any misdeeds. The newsreels happily supported the Establishment, avoiding controversy by doing so. Instead of exploring the violent nature of the British military forces, they evoke sympathy by showing how Ireland is affected by war, implicitly suggesting that the war should end – that the suffering depicted is not something the Irish people could possibly want. Similarly, when the newsreels covered the Blueshirts in the 1930s, the movement is feminized in order to appear less threatening. (There is also the use of light-hearted music, a characteristic newsreel trait, and reassurance that parades have passed off peacefully.) Crucially, there was no explanation of Irish involvement in the Spanish Civil War. While incidents like these may have simply misled British audiences, Irish audiences would have recognized discrepancies in the misrepresentation of events. Nationalists, in particular, may well have objected to the 'Ireland' portrayed by the British and, on occasion, American newsreels. Nevertheless, in the absence of sustained indigenous production, these were the only onscreen news images available to Irish audiences.

The 1930s began with the Cosgrave administration, which maintained a reasonably good relationship with Britain. Britain's relationship with de Valera would prove more problematic. In their treatment of de Valera, the newsreels aim to strike a balance between deference to him as a political leader and assurance that his strongly Nationalist agenda will be kept in check. The newsreels amply covered two of the major events which epitomized the nature of partition in the 1930s. The Eucharistic Congress clearly associated the government of the south with the Catholic religion and the Nationalism of Eamon de Valera, while the opening of the Stormont parliament building clearly associated the north with the monarchy and Unionism. Further polarization between the two states was set up in the American representations of the March of Time series. These cemented the newsreel tendencies to show the south as agricultural, rural and feminine, and the north as industrial, urban and masculine. The feminization of the south can be traced back to early representation of Irish colleens picking shamrock for St Patrick's Day. The association of the south with the rural feminine was one which the newsreels were comfortable with: rural femininity was non-threatening and easily controlled. Images of the north as progressive and diligent sat more easily with the 'British' ideals of industry, masculinity and progress.

These images would be further consolidated by the newsreels' coverage of the politics of Ireland's relationship with the Second World War. While the south remained neutral, the north was firmly involved in the war effort. These physical differences spoke volumes about the growing nature of partition. While the newsreels initially portrayed Ireland as a plucky neutral, ready to defend itself against German invasion, a tangible frustration with Éire's inaction in the war effort can be traced as Allied losses grew and the Treaty Ports became more significant as a potential strategic weapon. Representations of the north show loyalty to the Crown and enthusiastic production in the war effort. The most dogmatic representation occurs in Paramount's *The Plain Issue* which depicts Ulster as an industrially powerful asset to the Allied war machine, while Éire languishes in a state of insular apathy. The newsreels' ultimate representation of Ireland was of an industrialized, loyal, masculine and hard-working north in opposition to a backward, rural, feminine south.

The newsreels were essentially pro-British and pro-Establishment in outlook. They sought to portray British normality as the status quo – as can be seen by the amount of British military or royal items which occurred in coverage of Ireland during various times of crisis in the first half of the twentieth century. These items normalized British presence in an Ireland which was rebelling against these hegemonic norms and seeking to carve out an independence for itself. This kind of political complexity was never manifest in the newsreels, since they were subject to the British hegemony they sought to perpetuate and confined by the practical production restrictions of the genre. While Ireland struggled with its new partitioned identity, the newsreels sought to convey a political world which was simultaneously subversive and loyal, British and anti-British, same and 'other'. This huge paradox proved to be one of the newsreels' greatest challenges. They struggled to construct 'two Irelands' for audiences still coming to terms with partition. In the dichotomy they created in constructing Ireland for contemporary viewers, it could be argued that the newsreels came to terms with partition more quickly than the Irish people and that their representation contributed to the growing construction of partition in the Irish public's psyche. Their response to the Irish situation and the ultimate complexity of their portrayal of Ireland exemplifies the difficulties which existed in representing Irish culture, difficulties which continue to be manifest in the cultural representation of twenty-first-century Ireland.

NOTES

1. 'Rank to Produce Cinema "News Magazine" ', *The Times*, 19 November 1958.
2. Letter from Sir Gordon Craig, Chairman of the NRA, to Mr R.C. Bryant, Under Secretary of the Films Division, Board of Trade, 11 September 1956, National Archives, Kew, INF 12/623.
3. See the British Universities Newsreel Database for a brief account of the history of each newsreel; the section on Universal News is available at http://www.bufvc.ac.uk/databases/newsreels/history/newsreels.html#universalnews.
4. As an example, the issue sheet for Universal's Issue 492, 15 October 1956: 'As Universal above, Omit Royal Journey, Add Pope Innocent beatified.'
5. Universal Irish News, Issue 142, 4 March 1952.
6. *Railway Cup Final*, Universal Irish News, Issue 17, March 1952
7. *Irish News Highlights*, Universal Irish News, Issue 337, 18 April 1955.
8. Pratschke (2005), pp.17–38.
9. Ibid., p.21.

Filmography

All newsreels described in the text are referenced as endnotes. The following filmography details all stories with content related to Ireland and does not include other content which may have been screened as part of Irish 'LOCAL/SPECIAL' produced for distribution in Ireland. Not all of the items below are described in the text. Much of this research has drawn upon the British Universities Film and Video Council Database, News on Screen (hereafter NoS). http://bufvc.ac.uk/newsonscreen

Movietone
British Movietone News
Some of the following items appear as both part of British Movietone News and British Movietone Gazette. Where a story appears in both issues, the number given is the British Movietone News Issue Number.

Dublin Grand Prix. Issue 7, 22 July 1929.
Kissing the Blarney Stone. Issue 8, 29 July 1929.
A Glimpse into the Heart of Ireland. Issue 27, 9 December 1929.
Ireland v. Wales. Issue 40A, 13 March 1930.
Kingsford Smith. Issue 55A, 26 June 1930.
Dublin Sweepstake for Fabulous Prize Money is Drawn. Issue 42A, 20 November 1930.
See what All Sweep Was About. Issue 77, 24 November 1930.
Glorious Devon is Blessed by Winners of Dublin Sweep. Issue 77S, 27 November 1930.
England Subdued by Ireland at Rugby. Issue 89, 16 February 1931.
British Victory in Ulster TT Races. Issue 116, 24 March 1931.
President Cosgrave Adds Voice to Peace Plea. Issue 102A, 21 May 1931.
Eucharistic Congress. Issue 109A, 9 July 1931.
Irish Sweepstake is a Popular Draw. Issue 128A, 19 November 1931.
Royal Meath Meet at Drumree X–Roads. Issue 95, 23 November 1931.
DIL Dissolved for Irish Elections. Issue 139A, 4 February 1932.
Free State in Grip of General Election. Issue 142, 22 February 1932.
Irish Sweepstake is Nearly Won. Issue 143, 29 February 1932.
Fianna Fáil Party Release Prisoners. Issue 145, 14 March 1932.
Dublin Sweep Draw Eclipse Politics; Irish Republican Army Come Out into Open at Dublin. Both in Issue 145A, 17 March 1932.
IRA Marches past 1916 Headquarters. Issue 147A, 31 March 1932.
Irish Hurling Teams Give London a Treat. Issue 154A.
De Valera Sets Foot in England Again. Issue 158, 13 June 1932.
Papal Delegate Steps Ashore in Dublin. Issue 159A, 20 June 1932.

Millions at Phoenix Park Mass. Issue 160A, 30 June 1932.
Mollison Steps Off for Ireland. Issue 166A, 11 August 1932.
British Isles Share Olympic Victories. Issue 167, 15 August 1932.
Mollison Crowns his Aerial Career. Issue 168, 22 August 1932.
Irish Army Holds Field Manoeuvres. Issue 170, 5 September 1932.
De Valera Makes Call to League. Issue 173A, 29 September 1932.
Sweepstake Fever Reaches its Climax. Issue 175, 10 October 1932.
Armistice Day. Issue 180, 14 November 1932.
Northern Ireland Hails Prince on First Visit. Issue 181, 21 November 1932.
Cosgrave Promises to Restore Market. Issue 188, 9 January 1933.
De Valera Opens Election Campaign. Issue 188A, 12 January 1933.
Cosgrave Hits Out in Irish Election. Issue 189A, 19 January 1933.
Irish Free State Goes to the Polls. Issue 190A, 26 January 1933.
De Valera Outlines Fianna Fáil's Policy. Issue 191A, 2 February 1933.
Irish Couple Receive Medieval Welcome. Issue 192, 6 February 1933.
England Secure Fine Win at Twickenham. Issue 193, 13 February 1933.
Italian Air Armada in Ireland. Issue 213A, 6 July 1933.
Dublin Horse Show Draws Big Throng. Issue 218A, 10 August 1933.
Quietness of Dublin Confounds Rumour. Issue 219A, 17 August 1933.
Puck Fair is Held in County Kerry. Issue 220A, 24 August 1933.
Irish Sweepstake is Drawn in Dublin. Issue 229, 23 October 1933.
Lindberghs Depart on Mystery Flight. Issue 229A, 26 October 1933.
600 Irish Blueshirts Conceal Uniforms. Issue 234A, 30 November 1933.
Movietone Reviews 1933. Issue 238A, 28 December 1933.
*First Snapshot is Bevy of Black Cats Vying in Dublin for Honour of Posing at Sweepstake
    Model.* Issue 244, 5 February 1934.
Dublin – Rugby Union. Issue 245, 12 February 1934.
Dublin – Ireland v. Belgium Soccer. Issue 247A. Issue 247A, 1 March 1934.
Dublin – Pilgrim's Sail for Rome. Issue 249, 12 March 1934.
Irish War Veterans March to Cenotaph. Issue 249A, 15 March 1934.
Irish Sweepstake is Drawn in Dublin. Issue 250A, 22 March 1934.
King and Queen Pay Visit to Aldershot. Issue 255, 23 April 1934.
US–To–Rome Flyers Are Down in Ireland. Issue 259, 21 May 1934.
*First Snapshot is Judging and Jumping Competition at World Famous Show Held in
    Dublin.* Issue 270A, 9 August 1934.
Dublin – The Irish Sweep Draw. Issue 282, 20 October 1934.
Ireland – Beet Factory Opens. Issue 287A, 6 December 1934.
England beat Ireland 13–3. Issue 245, 12 December 1934.
English XV. Beat Ireland by 14–3. Issue 297, 11 February 1935.
Irish XV. Win Great Rugger Victory by 12–5 Over Scots. Issue 299, 25 February 1935.
Ulster Tourist Trophy Race is Won by Freddie Dixon. Issue 327 9 September 1935.
Ireland v. Wales Rugby Match. Issue 301, 11 March 1935.
The Dublin Plaza is Burnt Out by a Disastrous Fire; Jubilee. Both in Issue 308, 29 April
    1935.
Jumping Contests Are the Highlight of Dublin Show. Issue 322A, 8 August 1935.
Crowning King of Dalkey is Just an Old Irish Custom. Issue 323A, 15 August 1935.
Lithuanian Flier Crashes in Ireland. Issue 26 September 1935.
Duke of Abercorn in Northern Ireland Opens New Reservoir. Issue 21 November 1935.
All Blacks v. Ireland. Issue 340, 9 December 1935.
Uniforms. Issue 345A, 16 January 1936.

Ireland Beat England 6–3 at Rugger (also titled *Rugger International Ireland v. England*). Issue 349, 10 February 1936.
De Valera Bereaved. Issue 349A, 13 February 1936.
Farming. Issue 350, 17 February 1936.
Wales v. Ireland. Issue 354, 16 March 1936.
Cork Motor Show. Issue 363A, 21 May 1936.
De Valera Attends Irish Games. Issue 370A, 9 July 1936.
Dublin Horse Show. Issue 374A, 6 August 1936.
Ireland v. Germany Soccer. Issue 385A, 22 October 1936.
Irish Ploughing; *Rugby.* Both in Issue 402, 15 February 1937.
Rugby. Issue 404, 1 March 1937.
March Snow. Issue 406, 15 March 1937.
George VI. Issue 408, 29 March 1937.
O'Duffy's Men Back from Spanish Civil War. Issue 420A, 24 June 1937.
Atlantic Conquest. Issue 422A, 8 July 1937.
The Dublin Horse Show. Issue 426A, 5 August 1937.
Erin. Issue 427, 9 August 1937.
The King's Cup Air Race. Issue 432, 13 September 1937.
Ireland: Description by Tony Quinn. Issue 434A, 30 September 1937.
Ireland's Constitution Day. Issue 448, 3 January 1938.
Cabbies Derby in Dublin. Issue 448A, 6 January 1938.
Éire–Britain Conference. Issue 450, 17 January 1938.
Mr De Valera in London for Talks. Issue 450A, 20 January 1938.
Mr De Valera Goes Back. Issue 451, 24 January 1938.
Ulster Unionists Win Election. Issue 454, 14 February 1938.
St Patrick's Day in Dublin. Issue 459, 21 March 1938.
St Patrick's Day in Éire. Issue 465A, 21 March 1938.
Cork Motor Races; Britain–Éire Agreement. Both in Issue 464A, 28 April 1938.
New President of Éire Elected. Issue 466, 9 May 1938.
Irish Football in America. Issue 470, 6 June 1938.
All Quiet During Irish Elections. Issue 472, 20 June 1938.
Installation of New President of Éire. Issue 473A, 30 June 1938.
Evacuation of Spike Island. Issue 475A, 14 July 1938.
Douglas Corrigan Flies the Atlantic; Dublin Steamer in Collision in Fog. Both in Issue 476A, 21 July 1938.
Aviation: Departure of the Mayo Composite. Issue 477, 25 July 1938.
Corrigan Flies to England. Issue 477A, 28 July 1938.
Mercury's Pilot Talks of Flight. Issue 478, 1 August 1938.
Kerry v. Laois [spelled 'Leix' on British Movietone News database]. August 1938, no entry available on NOS.
Dublin Wedding. Issue 497A, 15 December 1938.
Movietone's Review of the Year. Issue 499A, 29 December 1938.
The Mystery Grows Deeper and Deeper. Issue 502A, 19 January 1939.
Bomb in Ireland. Issue 503, 23 January 1939.
Rugby International. Issue 510, 13 March 1939.
The Crime of the 'Athenia'. Issue 536, 11 September 1939.
Far Victorious. Issue 545A, 16 November 1939.
Cab Sir? Issue 553, 8 January 1940.
Jack Chaucer Wins Great Irish 'Chase'. Issue 556A, 1 February 1940.
American Citizens Leave Eire for Home. Issue 574A, 6 June 1940.

Nazis Prey on Neutrals. Issue 558, 12 February 1940.
Irish Parties Unite on One Platform. Issue 576A, 20 June 1940.
Ireland Keeps Close Watch on Coasts. Issue 579, 8 July 1940.
Ulster is Ready if Trouble Comes. Issue 538A, 8 August 1940.
Ireland Has First Air Raid. Issue 587, 2 September 1940.
Funeral of Lord Craigavon. Issue 600A, 5 December 1940.
Bombs on Neutral Free State. Issue 606, 13 January 1941.
Dublin Bombed. Issue 627, 9 June 1941.
Stiff Training for Our New Model Army. Issue 647, 27 October 1941.
The Yanks are Here. Issue 660A, 29 January 1942.
Dough Boys in Ulster. Issue 663, 16 February 1942.
Safe Passage to Ulster. Issue 668, 23 March 1942.
Yanks and Tanks Land in Northern Ireland. Issue 677, 25 May 1942.
Sir Alan Brooke Visits 'America–in–Ireland'. Issue 678, 1 June 1942.
Royal Guests for US Troops. Issue 682A, 2 July 1942.
Baseball May Capture Northern Ireland? Issue 685A, 23 July 1942.
British Army v. Ireland. Issue 714, 8 February 1943.
Éire Border Check Up. Issue 773, 27 March 1944.
Royal Visit to Northern Ireland. Issue 842A, 26 July 1945.
RAF Sink U Boats. Issue 865A, 3 January 1946.
Rineanna – Atlantic Terminus. Issue 873, 25 February 1946.
Are You Backing Prince Regent? Issue 874, 4 March 1946.
Money is the Subject. Issue 879A, 11 April 1946.
Military Jumping at Dublin Show. Issue 904A, 3 October 1946.
Seeking the Elusive Leprechaun. Issue 914A, 12 December 1946.
Britain's Shipbuilding Boom; FA Cup Sixth Round. Both in Issue 926A, 6 March 1947.
Ireland – National Winner Welcomed Home. Issue 913A, 10 April 1947
British Win at Dublin Show. Issue 949A, 14 August 1947.
Ship Launched by Radio. Issue 951, 25 August 1947.
Clonard Confraternity Jubilee. Issue 952A, 4 September 1947.
Progress in British Shipyards. Issue 959, 10 October 1947.
Fianna Fáil Heads Poll in Eire Elections. Issue 975A, 12 February 1948.
Sport – Grand National Horses Fail; Ireland's Rugby Victory. Both in Issue 976A, 19 February 1948.
Éire Changes its Government. Issue 977, 23 February 1948.
St Patrick's Day in New York and Dublin. Issue 981A, 25 March 1948.
Classic Jumping at Dublin's Show. Issue 1000A.
Scotland v. Ireland Football. Issue 1016, 22 November 1948.
Rugger – Scotland Fail to Hold Ireland. Issue 1030A, 3 March 1949.
Sport – Ireland Wins Triple Crown. Issue 1032A, 17 March 1949.
Éire Becomes a Republic. Issue 1038, 25 April 1949.
International Horse Show. Issue 1052, 1 August 1949.
Galway Bay Air–liner Rescues; International Sports – Barry's Great Title. Both in Issue 1054A, 18 August 1949.
Refugees Break Journey at Cork. Issue 1062, 10 October 1949.
England's Runaway Victory. Issue 1068, 21 November 1949.
A White Christmas – May Be! Issue 1071A, 15 December 1949.

Irish Movietone News (1940–43)

As the Irish Movietone News series does not appear on (NoS) I have used the story numbers used in the British Film Institute's (hereafter BFI) collection of Irish Movietone News as references.

De Valera Reviews ARP Parade. Story No. 39847, 10 March 1940.
Construction Corps at Work in Éire's Forests. Story No. 204581A, 1941.
Éire's Cavalry on Wheels. Story No. 41266, 9 May 1941.
LDF and Army Manoeuvres. Story No. 45210A, September 1941.
Army Help Increase Fuel Production. Story No. 45280A, 5 September 1941.
De Valera at Tralee. Story No. 41560, 11 October 1941.
An Army Marches on Its ... Story No. 41596, 20 November 1941.
Army Medical School – Ireland. Story No. 41731, 22 December 1941.
Youth Safety First Parade. Story No. 206508A, 1942.
Red Cross Procession. Story No. 206508A, 1942.
Colours for the LDF. Story No. 42809A, 1942.
LDF Recruiting Parade at Drogheda. Story No. 45205A, 1942.
Xmas Morning at Clontarf Baths. Story No. 204512A, 23 March 1942.
Marine Service. Story No. 42756, 24 August 1942.
Army Parade – Dublin, Cork. Story No. 42891, 30 September 1942.
LDF Parade. Story No. 42965, 16 October 1942.
Dublin Cyclists Train to Keep Open Communications. Story No. 204550A, 7 April 1943.
Bishop of Clogher Consecrated at Monaghan. Story No. 204550A, 7 April 1943.

British Paramount News

Erin on Parade. Issue 7, 23 March 1931.
Irish 'Sweep' Draw. Issue 21, 1 June 1931
Irish Grand Prix. Issue 30, 11 June 1931.
Artic 'Subs' Arrives [sic]. Issue 34, 25 June 1931.
Ulster TT Thrills; *Trouble in Ireland*. Both in Issue 51, 24 August 1931.
Money to Burn. Issue 61, 29 September 1931.
Test Night Eyes. Issue 68, 2 October 1931.
Egypt Next Stop. Issue 70, 29 October 1931.
Manchester 'Sweep'. Issue 76, 19 November 1931.
Irish 'Sweep' Draw. Issue 77, 23 November 1931.
New London Air–port. Issue 84, 17 December 1931.
Bell Rope Goes. Issue 87, 28 February 1931.
Sweep Envoy off; *De Valera Wins*. Both in Issue 103, 22 February 1932.
Mix 'Sweep' Fortunes. Issue 109, 14 March 1932.
Is It Car or Boat? Issue 110, 17 March 1932.
Erin Go Bragh. Issue 112, 24 March 1932.
All Eyes on Ireland. Issue 113, 28 March 1932.
Free State Remembers. Issue 114, 31 March 1932.
Mighty Tune Up. Issue 120, 21 April 1932.
Woman Flies Atlantic. Issue 129, 23 May 1932.
Meet the Other Half. Issue 130, 26 May 1932.
Acclaim Pope's Envoy. Issue 138, 23 June 1932.
A Million at Mass. Issue 140, 30 June 1932.
Irish Talk Fails. Issue 145, 18 July 1932.
Mollison All Set. Issue 152, 11 August 1932.

Mollison Gets There. Issue 155, 22 August 1932.
9 Hp Wins Ulster TT. Issue 156, 25 August 1932.
Jim Mollison Home. Issue 161, 12 September 1932.
Shuffle of Fate. Issue 168, 6 October 1932.
£2,378,939 at Stake! Issue 169, 10 October 1932.
Rosie Beats Shamrock! Issue 172, 20 October 1932.
Ulster Greets His Royal Highness! Issue 181, 21 November 1932.
Irish Rush Election. Issue 197, 16 January 1933.
Cosgrave Stirs Dublin. Issue 198, 19 January 1933.
De Valera Triumphs. Issue 202, 2 February 1933.
Ulster Railways Idle. Issue 203, 6 February 1933.
Mariners in 'Battle'. Issue 210, 2 March 1933.
Airmen Cross Swords. Issue 212, 10 March 1933.
Honour St Patrick; *Your Ticket's Here*. Both in Issue 215, 20 March 1933.
Baseball Goes East. Issue 230, 11 May 1933.
Italy's Sky-fleet on Way. Issue 246, 6 July 1933.
Mr De Valera Speaks Out. Issue 258, 17 August 1933.
General O'Duffy Explains. Issue 259, 21 August 1933.
Crack Speedsters Clash. Issue 263, 4 September 1933.
O'Duffy Defies de Valera. Issue 298, 4 January 1934.
Biggest Dam Finished. Issue 308, 8 February 1934.
Fortunes Galore. Issue 320, 22 March 1934.
New Airline 'Christened'. Issue 325, 9 April 1934.
Atlantic Flown Again. Issue 337, 21 May 1934.
Ocean Flyers Crash. Issue 364, 23 August 1934.
Forty Aces Race Ulster TT. Issue 367, 3 September 1934.
England Beat Ireland. Issue 413, 11 February 1935.
No Trams, No Buses. Issue 423, 14 March 1935.
All Quiet on Irish Front. Issue 434, 25 April 1935.
Freddie Dixon Wins TT. Issue 473, 9 September 1935.
Two Flights – Two Crashes. Issue 478, 26 September 1935.
Farewell, Lord Carson. Issue 487, 28 October 1935.
No Title. Orangemen celebrate Battle of Boyne anniversary. Issue 577, 7 September 1936.
Lost Airmen Rescued from Jaw of Death. Issue 587, 12 October 1936.
Refugeees Fill Valencia as Cortes Meets. Issue 605, 14 December 1936.
RAF Disaster. Bombers Crash in Fog, Three Dead. Issue 606, 17 December 1936.
England Beat Ireland, 9–8. Issue 623, 15 February 1937.
Atlantic Planes Complete Test on Schedule. Issue 664, 8 July 1937.
Border Terror Fails to Shake Ulster Loyalty. Issue 670, 29 July 1937.
Mr De Valera Arrives to Start Talks. Issue 719, 17 January 1938.
De Valera Puts His Case to Government. Issue 720, 20 January 1938.
Ireland Scotched. Issue 732, 3 March 1938.
New Cruiser for Britain. Issue 737, 21 March 1938.
Irish Pact Ends Feud. Issue 748, 24 August 1938.
Yates Wins Golf Title. Issue 758, 2 June 1938.
Dr Hyde Installed as First President of Eire. Issue 766, 30 June 1938.
Air Hero by Accident. Issue 772, 21 July 1938.
Runaway Ship Brings Tragedy at Launch. Issue 885, 21 August 1939.
Lord Craigavon Laid to Rest. Issue 1019, 5 December 1940.
Invasion Begorra? Ulster is Ready. Issue 1114, 3 November 1941.

Ireland the Plain Issue. Issue 1140, 2 February 1942.
Doughboys Settle Down in Northern Ireland. Issue 1144, 16 February 1942.
Ambassador Winant Visits US Troops in Northern Ireland. Issue 1148, 2 March 1942.
Allies Plan More Shocks for Nazis. Issue 1164, 27 April 1942.
Tanks on All Sides Mass Against Nazis. Issue 1172, 25 May 1942.
The Yank in Ulster Please General Brooke. Issue 1 June 1942.
US Army in Ulster Impresses the King. Issue 1183, 2 July 1942.
Breeches Buoy Joins Army. Issue 1193, 6 August 1942.
Britain, US, Isolate Éire. Issue 1364, 27 March 1944.
Ulster Fetes King and Queen. Issue 1503, 26 July 1945.
Captive U–Boats Provide RAF Sitting Target. Issue 1549, 3 January 1946.
Princess Names Latest Carrier. Issue 1572, 25 March 1946.
Farmer Wins Manx Trophy. Issue 1620, 9 September 1946.
Air Crash Kills Twelve. Issue 1653, 2 January 1947.
These Planes Bring News. Issue 1728, 22 September 1947.
Princess Margaret Launches Liner. Issue 1736, 20 October 1947.
France and US Tie in Dublin Horse Show. Issue 1826, 30 August 1948.
Morecambe Picks National Beauty. Issue 1828, 6 September 1948.
King Reviews Eight Thousand Territorials. Issue 1845, 4 November 1948.
Scots Snatch Victory in Last Minute. Issue 1850, 22 November 1948.
Éire Severs Crown Link. Issue 1853, 2 December 1948.
Irish Bill Signed. Issue 1862, 3 January 1949.
Northern Ireland Premier's Son Weds. Issue 1881, 10 March 1949.
Ireland Beat Wales, Keep the Triple Crown. Issue 1883, 17 March 1949.
Independent Éire Celebrates St Patrick's Day. Issue 1884, 21 March 1949.
Ireland Inaugurates Republic. Issue 1894, 25 April 1949.
Ulster Acclaims Princess. Issue 1905, 2 June 1949.
Soccer International – Goal Glut Swamps Ireland. Issue 1954, 21 November 1949.

Warwork News (subsidiary of British Paramount News)
Ulster at Arms. Issue S15/39, January 1944.

Empire News Bulletin
Battle of the Boyne. Issue 23, 19 July 1926.
Shamrock Day. Issue 93, 21 March 1927.
President Cosgrave. Issue 184, 2 February 1928.
Irish Civic Guards in Paris. Issue 261, 29 October 1928.

Gaumont
When no issue numbers are available for the following items, they have been viewed at the BFI but are without corresponding details on NoS.

Royal Visit to Ireland. Issue 38, 12 July 1911
The King Reviews in Phoenix Park, Dublin, Ireland. Issue 39, 20 July 1911.
The Titanic Leaving Belfast Lough for Southampton. Issue 112, 18 April 1912.
Ireland's New Lord Lieutenant Arrives. Issue 425, 19 April 1915.
The Funeral of the Victims of the Lusitania Disaster. Issue 432, 13 May 1915.
The Lord Lieutenant of Ireland Inspects a Good Muster of Boys' Brigade at Dublin. Issue 434, 20 May 1915.
The Irish Derby. Issue 447, 5 July 1915.

Sergeant Mike O'Leary, VC. Dublin's Welcome to Our Famous Hero. Issue 448, 8 July 1915.
Sinn Féin Released and Return to Dublin. Issue 652, 21 June 1917.
Countess Markievicz Returns to Dublin. Issue 652, 21 June 1917.
Ulster Division Fund, 2 July 1917.
Orange Day Demonstrations in Belfast, 14 July 1917.
'Hesperian' Another Victim to Piracy. Issue 466, 9 September 1915.
Sale of M Edmund Blanc's Racehorses at Kenilly. Issue 487, 22 November 1915.
National Dances by Schoolchildren at Leyton School. Issue 572, 14 September 1916.
Sole Survivor of Irish Sea Collision Between 'Connemara' and 'Retriever'. Issue 588, 9 November 1916.
Lt John Holland Married Frances Grogan at Queenstown, Cork. Issue 609, 22 January 1917.
Dublin's Red Cross Inspected. Issue 653, 25 June 1917.
Lady Carson's Ulster Fund. Issue 656, 5 July 1917.
Young Ireland, Lady Wimborne with the Prize Winners at the Dublin Baby Show. Issue 657, 9 July 1917.
The Irish Convention. Issue 663, 2 August 1917.
Salmon Fishing in Ireland. Issue 665, 6 August 1917.
Gala for Service Charity, Blackrock Dublin. Issue 674, 6 September 1917.
Runaway Engine, Dublin. Issue 677, 17 September 1917.
Troops Inspected in Ireland. Issue 685, 15 October 1917.
America v. Canada. Baseball Match Played at Dublin. Issue 695, 19 November 1917.
Meet of the Irish Harriers at Fermoy. Issue 696, 22 November 1917.
At Fortwilliam Park. Issue 719, 11 February 1918.
Mr John Dillon, MP. Issue 729, 18 March 1918.
St Patrick's Day. Issue 730, 21 March 1918
Ireland Refuses Conscription. Issue 733, 1 April 1918.
An Irish Wedding. Issue 754, 13 June 1918.
Inspection of Girl Guides at Dublin. Issue 765, 22 July 1918.
Recruiting in Ireland. Issue 772, 15 August 1918.
Off to France. Issue 773, 19 August 1918.
Visit to Inter–Allied Exhibition, Dublin. Issue 774, 22 August 1918.
Red Cross Pageant, Dublin. Issue 794, 31 October 1918.
Dublin School Cadets Inspected. Issue 800, 21 November 1918.
Strikers' Demonstrations in Belfast. Issue 821, 3 February 1919.
Great Fire in Donegall Street. Issue 821, 3 February 1919.
Comrades of the Great War, 26 April 1919.
Under Martial Law. Issue 845, 28 April 1919.
Lord French Visits a Garden Fete at Phoenix Park, Dublin. Issue 859, 16 June 1919.
Dublin's Peace Day Procession. Issue 870, 24 July 1919.
Man of Ulster. Issue 876, 14 August 1919.
Royal Dublin Society Horse Show; Consecration of St Colman's Cathedral. Both in Issue 881, 1 September 1919.
Welsh Rugby Fifteen. Issue 938, 18 March 1920.
Royal National Lifeboat Institution. Issue 949, 26 April 1920.
Sinn Féin in London. Issue 950, 29 April 1920.
Launch of the 'Dorsetshire'. New Bibby Liner Leaves the Slips at Harland and Wolff's Yards, Belfast; Ladies International Hockey; Royal National Lifeboat Institution. All in Issue 950, 29 April 1920.
Jockey's Football Match. Issue 94, 13 May 1920.

Louth After Floods. Issue 960, 3 June 1920.
Holywood Regatta (Ireland); *Irish Jumpers.* Both in Issue 981, 16 August 1920.
Sinn Féiners Demonstration. Issue 982, 19 August 1920.
Murdered Officers – Dublin's Tribute. Issue 1011, 29 November 1920.
Sinn Féin Outrage in Liverpool. Issue 1012, 2 December 1920.
Jockeys Play for Charity. Issue 1018, 23 December 1920.
RIC Auxiliary Cadets Inspected by Sir Hamar Greenwood. Issue 1028, 27 January 1921.
Ireland Honours Her Brave. Issue 1033, 14 February 1921.
Rugby International at Twickenham. Issue 1034, 17 February 1921.
International Hockey. Issue 1042, 17 March 1921.
Epidemic of Arson Believed to be the Work of Sinn Féiners. Issue 1046, 31 March 1921.
Scotland International Champions. Issue 1050, 14 April 1921.
State Opening of the Northern Irish Parliament. 22 June 1921. Story not released.
Launch of the Craigavon. Issue 1061, 23 May 1921.
Dublin's Custom House Ablaze. Issue 1063, 30 May 1921.
Northern Ireland Parliament. Issue 1066, 9 June 1921.
Royal National Lifeboat Institution. Issue 1069, 20 June 1921.
Lord Londonderry's Garden Party at Botanic Gardens. Issue 1070, 23 June 1921.
Threshold of Irish Peace. Issue 1076, 14 July 1921.
Mr de Valera at Downing Street. Issue 1077, 18 July 1921.
Royal Dublin Horse Show. Issue 1084, 11 August 1921.
Irish Jumpers. Issue 1085, 15 August 1921.
Irish Peace Plans Wrecked. Issue 1095, 19 September 1921.
Mr de Valera. Issue 1095, 19 September 1921.
Sinn Féin Delegates Leave for London. Issue 1102, 13 October 1921.
Ulster Honours Heroic Dead. Issue 1114, 24 November 1921.
Sinn Féin Prisoners Released. Issue 1119, 12 December 1921.
Sinn Féin Parliament (also entitled *Mr Darrell Figgis* on NoS with accompanying notes:
    'taken as not released'). 15 December 1921.
Irish Free State: Men Who Will Govern Ireland Pose for Gaumont Camera. 11 January
    1922. Story not released.
Dublin Castle Handed Over. Issue 1130, 19 January 1922.
IRA Guards at Dublin City Hall. Issue 1131, 23 January 1922.
Evacuating Ireland. Issue 1132, 26 January 1922.
Birthplace of Michael Collins. 28 January 1922. Story not released.
Troops Leave North Wall, Dublin, for England. Issue 1133, 30 January 1922.
Requiem Mass for the Late Pope at Dublin; *Dublin – Beggars' Bush Barracks.* Both in
    Issue 1134, 2 February 1922.
International Hockey. Issue 1136, 9 February 1922.
£50,000 Fire Ruin of Printing Works – Dublin. Issue 1137, 13 February 1922.
Irish Anti–Treaty Plan; *Dublin, England XV Rallies 12 v. Ireland 3.* Both in Issue 1138,
    16 February 1922.
IRA Take Over Bank of Ireland. 28 February 1922. Story not released
Ladies Hockey International; *St Patrick's Day. Presentation of Shamrock 1st Battalion
    Irish Guards at Windsor.* Both in Issue 1147, 20 March 1922.
Irish Cross Country Championship. Issue 1149, 27 March 1922.
1st Irish Postal Van to be Built by Provisional Government. Issue 1152, 6 April 1922.
Ireland 8 v. France 3 at Dublin. Issue 1154, 13 April 1922.
Civil War in Ireland. Surrender of the Four Courts; *Bombardment in Sackville Street.*
    Both in Issue 1177, 3 July 1922.
Dublin's Battlefield. £3,000,000 Damage. Sightseers. Issue 1180, 13 July 1922.

Ulster's Territorial Force. Issue 1180, 13 July 1922.
Call to Arms. Recruiting for Free State Army – Dublin. Issue 1181, 17 July 1922.
Aeroscope Camera Test. 19 July 1922. Story not released.
With the Nationalist Army in Ireland. Issue 1185, 31 July 1922.
Impressive Scenes at the Funeral of Mr Arthur Griffith, First President of the Irish Free State. Issue 1190, 17 August 1922.
The RIC's Successors. Parade and March Past of the New Civic Guard at Dublin. Issue 1191, 21 August 1922.
Dublin in Mourning. The Lying in State of the Late General Michael Collins. Issue 1193, 28 August 1922.
Rebel Activity in Ireland. 2 October 1922. Story not released.
Farewell Scenes. Last British Military Ceremony in Dublin. Issue 1226, 21 December 1922.
Dublin Explosions. Issue 1239, 5 February 1923.
International Rugby. Issue 1242, 15 February 1923.
The Duke of Abercorn. Ulster's Enthusiastic Welcome at Historic State Entry of First Governor into Belfast; International Rugby. Both in Issue 1246, 1 March 1923.
Lord Derby in Belfast with Royal Ulster Constabulary. Issue 1258, 12 April 1923.
The Duke of Abercorn. Issue 1265, 7 May 1923.
Fleet at Bangor. Issue 1271, 28 May 1923.
Pilgrimage Up Croach Patrick, Mayo. Issue 1291, 6 August 1923.
Northern Ireland Constabulary Tournament – Belfast. Issue 1292, 9 August 1923.
Royal Dublin Horse Show. Issue 1295, 20 August 1923.
Troops of Free State Army Parade Through Dublin in Memory of Michael Collins. Issue 1297, 27 August 1923.
Lord Carson Cuts First Sod of New Waterworks in Silent Valley, Newcastle. Also in Ulster. Issue 1311, 15 October 1923.
Rugby Centenary. Issue 1317, 5 November 1923.
Opening of the Ulster Parliament by His Grace the Duke of Abercorn. Issue 1355, 16 March 1924.
Hurling Match. Issue 1357, 24 March 1924.
Londonderry's Royal Visitors. Issue 1393, 28 July 1924.
As I Was Saying. Mr De Valera, the Irish Republican Leader, Continues the Speech Broken by His Arrest. Issue 1400, 21 August 1924.
Loyal Ulster. Issue 1411, 29 September 1924.
Scotland v. Ireland. Issue 1374, 22 May 1924.
The Rugby International. Issue 1460, 19 March 1925.
Memorial of the 1916 Rebellion. 13 May 1925. Story not released.
Empire Day at Belfast. 25 May 1925. Story not released.
Orange Day. 12 July 1925. Story not released.
The Grand Prix of Ulster. Issue 1510, 10 September 1925.
Gaumont Graphic 15 Years Review. Issue 1523, 26 October 1925.
Ireland Wins! Issue 1549, 25 January 1926.
Robert Yates. Issue 1567, 29 March 1926.
Still Going Strong. Issue 1568, 1 April 1926.
Memorial Unveiling. Issue 1595, 5 July 1926.
Inter–league Soccer. Issue 1621, 4 October 1926.
International Football. 21 October 1926. Story not released.
River (Bann): Head of the River Race. 13 December 1926. Story not released.
Copper Quarry Opened. Issue 1645, 27 December 1926.

England Beat Ireland. Issue 1659, 14 February 1927.
Ireland v. England. Issue 1732, 27 October 1927.
Impressive Scenes at Armagh. Issue 1733, 31 October 1927.
Another Transatlantic Attempt. Issue 1721, 19 September 1927.
Royal Inniskilling Fusiliers. Issue 1896, 30 May 1927.
Great Liner Aground! Issue 1850, 13 December 1928.
Wales Beat Ireland 2–1. Issue 1762, 9 February 1928.
Sir Granville Ryrie in Northern Ireland. Issue 1772, 15 March 1928.
Bravo 'Bremen'! Issue 1781, 16 April 1928.
Ireland Gets There First! Issue 1785, 16 April 1928.
Hello, Belfast! Issue 1798, 30 April 1928.
New Motor Vessel. Issue 1864, 31 January 1929.
Building a 27,000 Ton Liner. Issue 1887, 22 April 1929.
Greyhound Point to Point. Issue 1887, 22 April 1929.
Launch of 'Ulster Prince'. Issue 1889, 29 April 1929.
Gaelic Football at Dungannon. Issue 1894, 16 May 1929.
Northern Ireland Parliament; Gallant SOS Men. Both in Issue 1899, 3 June 1929.
Rallyo. Issue 1902, 13 June 1929.
Current for County Antrim. Issue 1924, 28 August 1929.
Four Nations Rugby Battle. Issue 1935, 7 October 1929.
'Southern Cross' Atlantic Flight. Issue 2010, 26 June 1930.
Carnival Day at Balmoral! Issue 2012, 3 July 1930.
Shopping Joys! Issue 2010, 26 June 1930.
Imperial Parade at Belfast. Issue 2000, 22 May 1930.
She's Britain's Fastest! Issue 2068, 15 January 1931.
England V. Ireland Rugby Match at Twickenham. Issue 123, 16 February 1931.
Opening of Belfast Union. Issue 204, 26 November 1931.
Extension of Belfast Union. Issue 2159, 30 November 1931.
Springboks v. Ireland at Dublin. Issue 212, 24 December 1931.
England v. Ireland Rugby. Issue 228, 18 February 1932.
Readman Funeral in Ireland; Opening of Abercorn Bridge by Duchess of Abercorn. Both
    in Issue 247, 25 April 1932.
Funeral of Mrs Pearse at Rathfarman. Issue 249, 2 May 1932.
Opening the Industrial Fair in Cork. Issue 253, 16 May 1932
Miss Amelia Earhart Makes Lone Flight from Newfoundland to Ireland. Issue 255, 23
    May 1932.
Atlantic Flown Again. Issue 2210, 26 May 1932.
Atlantic Flight. Issue 281, 22 August 1932.
J.A. Mollison Leaves Ireland for his Atlantic Flight. Issue 2235, 22 August 1932.
J.A. Mollison and Aeroplane in Ireland. Issue 2236, 25 August 1932.
Mr Cosgrave Meeting at Trim, Ireland. Issue 286, 8 September 1932.
Scotland V. Ireland Football. Issue 290, 22 September 1932.
All Ireland Football Match. Issue 292, 29 September 1932.
'Motorcycle Steeplechase'. Issue 2260, 17 November 1932.
Prince of Wales Opens New Government Building in Ireland. Issue 307, 21 November
    1932.
England v. Ireland Rugby. Issue 331, 13 February 1933.
Railway Strike Scenes from Ireland. Issue 332, 16 February 1933.
Launch 'Diogenes' from Harland and Wolff's Shipyard – Belfast. Issue 1144, 9 March 1933.
International Rugby. Issue 340, 16 March 1933.

Scotland v. Ireland Rugby. Issue 345, 3 April 1933.
Pontypool Carnival; Australian School Regatta. Issue 374, 13 July 1933.
Ireland v. Wales Soccer. Issue 308, 9 November 1933.
Review of Fascists; Spirit of Erin. Both in Issue 12, 8 February 1934.
Scotland v. Ireland Rugby. Issue 18, 1 March 1934.
Belfast Fire; Ireland v. Wales Rugby. Issue 21, 12 March 1934.
Irish Ex–Servicemen. Issue 22, 15 March 1934.
Mixing Counterfoils. Issue 23, 19 March 1934.
Burning Irish Sweep 'Voodoo' on the Liffey; Irish Sweep Draw in Dublin; Irish Pilgrims in Rome. All in Issue 24, 22 March 1934.
De Valera at Mullingar. Issue 26, 29 March 1934.
De Valera at Clonmel. Issue 32, 19 April 1934.
Atlantic Flyers in Ireland. Issue 49, 18 June 1934.
Irish Sweep Winners. Issue 49, 18 June 1934.
Dublin Fusiliers at Low. Issue 52, 28 June 1934.
Belfast Fire (Hillsborough Castle). Issue 64, 9 August 1934.
Ulster Grand Prix. Issue 68, 23 August 1934.
Ulster TT Race. Issue 71, 3 September 1934.
De Valera in London. Issue 73, 10 September 1934.
Irish Sweep Procession. Issue 86, 26 October 1934.
Irish Sweep Draw. Issue 87, 29 October 1934.
American Irish Sweep Winners. Issue 91, 12 November 1934.
England v. Ireland. Issue 117, 11 February 1935.
Garda Police Ball. Issue 123, 4 March 1935.
Ireland v. Wales Rugby International. Issue 125, 11 March 1935.
Irish Guards Presented with Shamrock on St Patrick's Day. Issue 127, 18 March 1935.
New York Celebrates St Patrick's Day. Issue 132, 4 April 1935.
Dublin Plaza Fire. Issue 139, 29 April 1935.
Germany Beat Ireland (Soccer). Issue 144, 16 May 1935.
RUC Sports at Belfast. Issue 154, 20 June 1935.
Dublin Horse Show. Issue 169, 12 August 1935.
Kilkenny Beat Limerick at Hurling at Croke Park. Issue 176, 5 September 1935.
Felix Waitkus. Issue 182, 26 September 1935.
De Valera Speaks at Ennis. Issue 186, 10 October 1935.
England Defeat Ireland in Soccer International at Belfast. Issue 189, 21 October 1935.
Cambridgeshire Irish Sweep Procession and Mixing of Counterfoils. Issue 191, 28 October 1935.
American Irish Sweep Winner. Issue 195, 11 November 1935.
Duke and Duchess of Gloucester in Ulster. Issue 204, 12 December 1935.
Wales Defeat Ireland in Rugby International. Issue 231, 16 March 1936.
St Patrick's Day Celebrated in Dublin. Issue 232, 19 March 1936.
Irish Sweep Procession and Mixing in Dublin. Issue 223, 23 March 1936.
Irish Sweep Draw at the Mansion House, Dublin. Issue 234, 26 March 1936.
St Patrick's Day Celebrated in New York. Issue 236, 2 April 1936.
Linfield Defeat Derry at Belfast. Issue 239, 13 April 1936.
Motor Racing at Cork. Issue 249, 18 May 1936.
Cork Motor Racing. Issue 250, 21 May 1936.
Mixing of Counterfoils for Derby Irish Sweepstake. Issue 251, 25 May 1936.
Olympic Diving Hopes Practise at Uxbridge. Issue 265, 13 July 1936.
Dublin Horse Show. Issue 272, 6 August 1936.

TT Car Race at Newtownards Won by Freddie Dixon and Charlie Dobson – Chambers Crashes Through Barrier. Issue 281, 7 September 1936.
International Car Race at Phoenix Park. Issue 287, 28 September 1936.
Mayo Defeats Leix in All Ireland Football Match. Issue 288, 1 October 1936.
Irish Sweep Draw in Dublin. Issue 294, 22 October 1936.
Scotland Defeat Ireland. Issue 298, 5 November 1936.
Snow Scenes in Scotland and Northern Ireland. Issue 308, 10 December 1936.
Mr De Valera in London En Route for Zurich. Issue 316, 7 January 1937.
England Defeat Ireland in Rugby International. Issue 327, 15 February 1937.
Ireland Defeat Scotland in Dublin Rugby International. Issue 331, 1 March 1937.
Ireland Defeat England in Hockey Match at the Oval. Issue 335, 15 March 1937.
Ireland Defeat Wales in Belfast Rugby Match. Issue 341, 5 April 1937.
Cork Car Racing Won by Prestwich. Issue 356, 27 May 1937.
The 'Caledonia' Arrives at Foynes from Newfoundland. Issue 371, 19 July 1937.
King George and Queen Elizabeth Visit Ulster. Issue 374, 29 July 1937.
Dublin Horse Show. Issue 376, 5 August 1937.
Second Day of Dublin Horse Show. Issue 377, 9 August 1937.
Ulster Motor Cycle Grand Prix. Issue 381, 23 August 1937.
All Ireland Hurling Final. Issue 386, 9 September 1937.
Launch of the 'Capetown Castle' at Belfast. Issue 391, 27 September 1937.
All Ireland Hurling Match in Dublin; Dublin Horse Show. Both in Issue 417, 26 December 1937.
De Valera Arrives in England. Issue 423, 17 January 1938.
De Valera Calls at No. 10 Downing Street. Issue 424, 20 January 1938.
De Valera Leaves London. Issue 425, 24 January 1938.
Ulster Election Scenes in Belfast. Issue 431, 14 February 1938.
England Defeat Ireland at Rugby. Issue 432, 17 December 1938.
Scotland Defeat Ireland. Issue 436, 3 March 1938.
Wales Defeat Ireland in Rugby International; De Valera in Downing Street. Both in Issue 439, 14 March 1938.
HMS 'Belfast' Launched at Belfast by Mrs N. Chamberlain. Issue 441, 21 March 1938.
St Patrick's Day Parade in Dublin; St Patrick's Day Ball at the Albert Hall; Ireland Defeat Wales in Soccer. All in Issue 441, 21 March 1938.
De Valera Arrives in London to Sign Agreement with Britain. Issue 452, 28 April 1938.
Éire's New President. Issue 453, 2 May 1938.
Sydney Celebrates St Patrick's Day. Issue 456, 12 May 1938.
Gaelic Football in America. Issue 463 6 June 1938.
President of Éire Installed in Dublin. Issue 470, 30 June 1938.
Joe Kennedy in Éire. Issue 473, 11 July 1938.
Spike Island and Cork Harbour Defences Handed Over to Éire by Great Britain. Issue 474, 14 July 1938.
Dublin Horse Show. Issue 481, 8 August 1938.
Irish Open Amateur Golf Final. Issue 491, 12 September 1938.
Mr De Valera Honoured by the League of Nations. Issue 493, 19 September 1938.
Kerry v. Galway in Gaelic Football Match. Issue 496, 29 September 1938.
Scotland Defeat Ireland in International Soccer Match at Belfast. Issue 500, 13 October 1938.
Launch of the 'Pretoria Castle' at Belfast. Issue 501, 17 October 1938.
England v. Ireland Soccer. Issue 510, 17 November 1938.
Twenty–Two Bridesmaids in Dublin Wedding. Issue 518, 15 December 1938.

Bomb in Ireland. Issue 503, 23 January 1939.
New Primate of All Ireland. Issue 531, 30 January 1939
Ireland Defeat England in Rugby International. Issue 13 February 1939.
Ireland v. Scotland in Dublin. Issue 539, 27 February 1939.
Mr De Valera in London En Route for Rome. Issue 542, 9 March 1939.
Ireland v. Wales at Belfast. Issue 543, 13 March 1939.
St Patrick's Day in New York. Issue 548, 30 March 1939.
Irish Sweep Winners in US. Issue 550, 6 April 1939.
Irish Grand National. Issue 552, 13 April 1939.
Irish Cup Final. Issue 556, 27 April 1939.
Irish Ballroom Championships. Issue 558, 4 May 1939.
Irish Cup Final Replay. Issue 559, 8 May 1939.
Carnival Parade in Tipperary. Issue 560, 11 May 1939.
Irish Sweep Draw. Issue 563, 22 May 1939.
Sweep Winner in New York. Issue 567, 5 June 1939.
Dublin 'Old Crocks' Car Race. Issue 574, 29 June 1939.
Irish Varsity Sports. Issue 576, 6 July 1939.
Irish Open Golf Championship. Issue 581, 24 July 1939.
Army Sports at Phoenix Park Dublin. Issue 586, 7 August 1939.
Dublin Horse Show. Issue 586, 10 August 1939.
Ulster Grand Prix. Issue 589, 21 August 1939.
Ulster Grand Prix Won by Serafini. Issue 590, 24 August 1939.
Irish Cambridgeshire. Issue 603, 16 October 1939.
The Irish Cesarewitch. Issue 609, 6 November 1939.
Cole and Cook in Dublin; Farr v. Abrew in Dublin. Issue 612, 16 November 1939.
Ireland's Largest Bullock on Show. Issue 625, 1 January 1940.
Christmas Swimming Race in Dublin. Issue 626, 4 January 1940
Irish Cabinet Meet in Phoenix Park. Issue 628, 11 January 1940.
Irish Red Cross Sweepstake. Issue 632, 25 January 1940.
New Dublin Airport Opened. Issue 633, 29 January 1940.
Irish Red Cross Steeplechase. Issue 634, 1 February 1940.
Motor Torpedo Boat for Ireland. Issue 635, 5 February 1940.
Irish Ploughing Championships. Issue 636, 8 February 1940.
Irish Hockey. Issue 650, 28 March 1940.
Soccer League of Ireland v. Irish League. Issue 650, 28 March 1940.
St Patrick's Day in America. Issue 651, 1 April 1940.
Éire Ministers in London. Issue 660, 1 May 1940.
Irish Trade Delegation for London; *Scotland v. Ireland Soccer in Ireland*; *Punchestown Races*. All in Issue 661, 6 May 1940.
Big Timber Fire in Dublin. Issue 662, 9 May 1940.
Irish Fencing Championships. Issue 663, 13 May 1940.
US Polo Stars Play for Charity; *Feria Fete in Seville*; *Carnival in Zurich*; *Baseball Season Opens in US*. All in Dublin Issue 664, 16 May 1940.
Dublin's Great Spring Show at Ballsbride. Issue 665, 20 May 1940.
Irish Golf Tournament. Issue 669, 3 June 1940.
Society Wedding in Dublin. Issue 672, 13 June 1940.
Ireland's Call to Arms. Issue 675, 26 June 1940.
Irish Army Manoeuvres. Issue 678, 4 July 1940.
Éire Stands Guard on Her Coasts; *Golf Tournament at Lucan*. Both in Issue 679, 6 July 1940.
Éire Has Mined Her Coast Line. Issue 682, 18 July 1940.

Mine Laying on Ireland's Coast. Issue 683, 22 July 1940.
Tramway Sports in Dublin. Issue 687, 5 August 1940.
Galway Races. Issue 688, 8 August 1940.
Ulster Home Guard. Issue No. 689, 12 August 1940.
Training Motorcyclists for Irish Army. Issue 693, 26 August 1940.
De Valera with Southern Command. Issue 695, 2 September 1940.
Air Raid on Éire. Issue 696, 5 September 1940.
Limerick Horse Show. Issue 697, 9 September 1940.
Irish Hurling Finals. Issue 698, 12 September 1940.
De Valera with Local Security Force. Issue 701, 23 September 1940.
Ireland's Local Security Force. Issue 702, 26 September 1940.
Petrol Destroying Device in Ireland. Issue 703, 30 September 1940.
Irish Army Engineers Manoeuvres. Issue 705, 7 October 1940.
De Valera at ARP Parade. Issue 707, 14 October 1940.
Camogie Match in Ireland. Issue 711, 28 October 1940.
C. McCarthy Joins the Army. Issue 712, 31 October 1940.
Kerry v. Meath Charity Soccer Match. Issue 713, 4 November 1940
De Valera with the Local Security Force. Issue 716, 14 November 1940.
Sale of Looo Irish Castle; *Eire's New Construction Corps.* Both in Issue 720, 28 November 1940.
First Dublin Nursery Centre Open. Issue 772, 5 December 1940.
De Valera in Waterford. Issue 726, 19 December 1940.
Mr De Valera Reviews Construction Corps. Issue 728, 26 December 1940
Irish Agriculture Maintains High Standard; *Commissions for IRA Veterans*; *Bomb in County Dublin.* All in Issue 731, 6 January 1941.
New Archbishop of Dublin. Issue 732, 9 January 1941.
Nazi Bomb Damage on Dublin. Issue 733, 13 January 1941.
Bomb Damage in Eire; *Carman's Derby in Ireland.* Both in Issue 735, 20 January 1941.
Mr Willkie Visits Éire; *Parland Cup in Ireland.* Both in Issue 743, 17 February 1941.
Irish Ploughing Contest; *Dublin Blood Transfusion Service.* Both in Issue 749, 10 March 1941.
Irish Guards Celebrate St Patrick's Day. Issue 752, 20 March 1941.
Spring Tide Comes Early to Dublin's Zoo; *Irish Guards Celebrate St Patrick's Day.* Both in Issue 752, 20 March 1941.
Funeral of Canadian High Commissioner in Eire. Issue 753, 24 March 1941.
Wings Over Ireland Part 1; *Gaelic League Procession in Dublin*; *St Patrick's Day Soccer Match.* All in Issue 755, 31 March 1941.
Archbishop of Dublin Blesses Church. Issue 756, 3 April 1941.
Dublin's Sportsmen's Show; *Dublin Indoor Tennis School*; *Wings Over Ireland Part 2.* All in Issue 758, 10 April 1941.
Opening New Soldiers' Club in Dublin. Issue 761, 21 April 1941.
De Valera Presents Medals to Men in 1916 Rebellion. Issue 762, 24 April 1941.
Spectacular Parade in Dublin. Issue 763, 28 April 1941.
Bridging a River by Éire's Army. Issue 764, 1 May 1941.
Irish Ballroom Dancing Championships. Issue 767, 12 May 1941.
Head of River Race Through Dublin. Issue 770, 22 May 1941.
University College Dublin Sports; *Cycling at Limerick.* Both in Issue 776, 12 June 1941.
Premiere Handicap at Hollywood Park. Issue 778, 19 June 1941.
Shield Presented to Best Irish Speaking School. Issue 779, 23 June 1941.
Corpus Christi Procession in Bandon Éire. Issue 781, 30 June 1941.

Irish Wreath Laying Ceremony. Issue 782, 3 July 1941.

Irish Derby. Issue 783, 7 July 1941.

New Lord Mayor of Dublin. Issue 785, 14 July 1941.

Horse Show in Dublin. Issue 785, 14 July 1941.

Dublin Society Show; *Hurling Semi Finals.* Both in Issue 797, 25 August 1941.

Irish Construction Corps Lumbering. Issue 800, 4 September 1941.

Picturesque Wedding in Dublin; *Éire's Army Increases Fuel Production.* Both in Issue 803, 15 September 1941.

Sports Day at Phoenix Park; *All Ireland Gaelic Final*; *Roosevelt's Speech.* All in Issue 804, 18 September 1941.

Harvesting in Dublin; Irish Cavalry on Wheels. Issue 806, 25 September 1941.

Presentation of Colours in Dublin. Issue 807, 29 September 1941.

Fencing in Ireland. Issue 811, 13 October 1941.

American Religious Mission in Dublin; *Éire's Marine Service.* Both in Issue 812.

Mr de Valera at Mullingar. Issue 813, 20 October 1941.

Parnell Week in Dublin. Issue 815, 27 October 1941.

Big Parade at Wexford; *Dublin's Lord Mayor Opens New Bridge*; *Inspection of ATS in Northern Ireland.* All in Issue 816, 30 October 1941.

Éire's Port Control Service. Issue 818, 6 November 1911.

Irish Cattle Arrive at British Port. Issue 819, 10 October 1941.

Irish Army Commissioning; Tralee Defence Parade. Issue 17 November 1941.

An Irish Stud Farm; *Army Field Kitchen in Ireland.* Both in Issue 824, 27 November 1941.

Rugby in Ireland. Issue 826, 4 December 1941.

Mr De Valera Visits Limerick. Issue 829, 15 December 1941.

Beauty Contest Winners in Phoenix Park; *Irish Anti–Aircraft Unit Cross Country Race.* Both in Issue 830, 18 December 1941.

Éire's Progress – 1941. Issue 833, 29 December 1941.

Christmas in Ireland; *Ireland's Medical Service*; *Cabbies Derby in Ireland.* All in Issue 836, 8 January 1942.

Bakery Fire in Dublin; *Post Officer Workers Hold Protest Meeting in Dublin.* Issue 839, 19 January 1942.

First American Troops in Ireland; *Wedding in Dublin*; *Hockey in Dublin.* All in Issue 842, 29 January 1942.

Wedding of Irish King's Descendant; *Further Pictures of the Arrival of the First American Expeditionary Force in Ireland.* Both in Issue 843, 2 February 1942.

Red Cross Steeplechase Cup in Ireland. Issue 845, 9 February 1942.

Irish Cross Country Races. Issue 848, 19 February 1942.

Wicklow Wins Ploughing Match. Issue 850, 26 February 1942.

Irish Soldiers Lumbering. Issue 851, 2 March 1942.

Dublin Film Conference. Issue 853, 9 March 1942.

Dublin ARP at Work; *Snow in Dublin.* Both in Issue 854, 12 March 1942.

Eireann Bull Show. Issue 857, 23 March 1942.

Eireann Junior Cross Country Championships. Issue 860, 2 April 1942.

Tulip Time in County Dublin; *Mullingar National Defence Week.* Both in Issue 863, 13 April 1942.

LDF Parade in Dublin; *FAI Cup Semi Final.* Both in Issue 865, 20 April 1942.

Baby Boxers. Issue 871, 11 May 1942.

May Processions in Dublin. Issue 872, 14 May 1942.

AEF Infantry Training in Northern Ireland; *The World at War.* Both in Issue 873, 18 May 1942.

Bicycles in Dublin; No Title. US Reinforcements in Northern Ireland; *Royal Dublin Horse Show*. All in Issue 875, 25 May 1942.

No Title. General Brooke Inspects US Army in Northern Ireland. Issue 877, 1 June 1942.

LDF on Parade at Limerick. Issue 878, 4 June 1942.

Re–naming Bridge in Dublin. Issue 879, 8 June 1942.

New Cathedral in Ireland; *LDF Parade in Ireland*. Both in Issue 883, 22 June 1942.

Corpus Christi in Dublin. Issue 884, 25 June 1942.

Dublin Regatta. Issue 885, 29 June 1942.

No Title. The King and Queen in Ireland. Issue 886, 2 July 1942.

Irish Pig Market; *College Races in Dublin*; *GBS Gymnastics in Dublin*. All in Issue 887, 6 April 1942.

Episcopal Jubilee Mass in Dublin; *East of Ireland Golf*; *Irish Derby*. All in Issue 889, 13 July 1942.

Step Together Week in Éire; *LDF Sports at Waterford*. Both in Issue 893, 27 July 1942.

Liffey Swim; *Regatta at Black Rock*; *Irish Oaks*. All in Issue 896, 6 August 1942.

Swimming Championship at Black Rock. Issue 898, 13 August 1942.

Church Parades in Dublin. Issue 899, 17 August 1942.

Byrne White Wedding in Dublin; *The Phoenix Plate*. Issue 902, 27 August 1942.

Irish Air Service Opened; *Mr De Valera at Innisnungret*. Both in Issue 905, 7 September 1942.

Harvesting in Ireland; *Enniscrone Show*; *Cork v. Dublin Hurling*. All in Issue 908, 17 September 1942.

The Irish Marine Service; *Irish Hurling Finals*. Both in Issue 911, 28 September 1942.

Irish Army 'On the Way'. Issue 914, 8 October 1942.

Field Mass Held in Phoenix Park. Issue 915, 12 October 1942.

Irish Defence Force Manoeuvres. Issue 916, 15 October 1942.

Mr De Valera Reviews Troops; *Big Parade in Cork*. Both in Issue 917, 19 October 1942.

LDF Parade in Dundalk. Issue 920, 29 October 1942.

Éire Remembers Thomas Davies. Issue 921, 2 November 1942.

Defence Minister at LDF Parade at Arklow. Issue 922, 5 November 1942.

Local Defence Force Parade; *Irish Army Communication*. Both in Issue 923, 9 November 1942.

University College Dublin Rag. Issue 926, 19 November 1942.

Irish Apple Harvest. Issue 932, 10 October 1942.

Irish Review of the Year. Issue 938, 31 December 1942.

Kids go to Cinema; *Irish Heavyweight Championships*; *Christmas Day Swim in Contare*. All in Issue 941, 11 January 1943.

New Arrivals at Dublin Zoo. Issue 944, 21 January 1943.

Irish Artillery in Action. Issue 947, 1 February 1943.

Dublin ARP Practice and British Army v. Ireland Rugby. Issue 950.

4 Mile Cross Country at Dunleer. Issue 954, 25 February 1943.

Famous Horse Show. Issue 955, 11 February 1943.

LDF Parade; *Bull Show in Ireland*. Both in Issue 959, 15 March 1943.

LDF Parade. Issue 965, 5 April 1943.

Archbishop Spellman in Éire. Issue 968, 15 April 1943.

Dublin Motorcyclists Train to Keep Open Communications. Issue 971, 26 April 1943.

The King and Queen Visit Northern Ireland. Issue 1206, 26 July 1945.

De Valera Arrives. Issue 1431, 22 September 1947.

De Valera at Downing Street. Issue 1432, 25 September 1947.

Rugby – Ireland v. England. Issue 1474, 19 February 1948.
US Plane Disaster in Ireland. Issue 1491, 19 April 1948.
Scotland v. Ireland. Issue 1553, 22 November 1948.
Scotland v. Ireland Rugby. Issue 1582, 3 March 1949.
De Valera in Britain. Issue 5 May 1949.
Royal Visit to Northern Ireland. Issue 1608, 2 June 1949.
Spectacular Rising in Dublin Horse Show. Issue 1628, 11 August 1949.
Skymaster Disaster off the Irish Coast. Issue 1630, 18 August 1949.
England v. Ireland. Issue 1657, 21 November 1949.
Snow in Ireland. Issue 1664, 15 December 1949.

March of Time

Irish Republic. Vol. 3, No. 10, 14 May 1937.
Ulster Versus Éire. 3rd Year, no. 11, May 1938.
The Irish Question. 9th Year, No. 11, 12 June 1944.

Pathé

Where there were no details for these items on NoS, dates have been taken from www.britishpathe.com unless otherwise stated. In some cases, monthly release dates are unavailable. Where the letters NSP appear, this indicates an edition of the Pathé cinemagazine, New Series Pictorial (1918–69).

Suffragettes Calling for Arrest of Bonar Law and Carson. Pathé, circa 1913. This appears
    on the Digital Film Archive. No corresponding entry on NoS.
Dear Little Shamrock. 1914–18
Waterford Election. Issue 472B, 23 March 1918.
Conscription in Ireland. To Be – or Not to Be? Issue 476B, 25 April 1918.
Field Marshal Viscount French Has Been Appointed Lord–Lieutenant of Ireland. Issue
    478B, 9 May 1918.
Great Sinn Féin Round Up. 1918.
Lord French at Dublin Horse Show. 1918.
Irish Guards Visit to Belfast. Issue 416–1, 14 August 1919.
There Was an Old Woman. Issue 570, 9 June 1919.
De Valera in Boston, USA. Issue 593, 28 August 1919.
Attempted Assassination – Irish Viceroy. Issue 627, 25 December 1919.
Nurse vs Tommy. 1919.
England v. Ireland. Issue 643, Issue 643, 19 February 1920.
Funeral Lord Mayor of Cork. Issue 653, 25 March 1920.
General Sir Neville MacCready. Issue 657, 8 April 1920.
Mount Joy Prison. Issue 659, 15 April 1920.
Aftermath. Issue 674, 7 June 1920.
Sinn Féin Riots. Issue 680, 28 June 1920.
Dublin Horse Show. Issue 694, 16 August 1920.
Irish Demonstrate. Issue 695, 19 August 1920.
IRA Leader McSwiney. Issue 697, 27 August 1920.
War of Reprisals. Issue 706, 27 September 1920.
Reprisals in Ireland Condemned by Sir Hamar Greenwood. Issue 708, 4 October 1920.
Death of the Lord Mayor of Cork. Issue 716, 1 November 1920.
Terence McSwiney Laid to Rest. Issue 717, 4 November 1920.
Lloyd Inspects RIC. Issue 718, 8 November 1920.

No One Can Insult Our Flag – Sinn Féiners Tear Down Union Jack. Issue 722, 25 November 1920.

Side Lights on Sinn Féin – May Connelly Punished. Issue 723, 25 November 1920.

Murdered Officers Borne to England. Issue 724, 29 November 1920.

Sinn Féin Outrages in London. Issue 725, 2 December 1912.

Death is now the Penalty for Carrying or Concealing Arms; Reprisals by Order. Both in Issue 735, 6 January 1921.

Sir Hamar Greenwood Reviews and Addresses RIC Auxiliaries in Phoenix Park. Issue 741, 27 January 1921.

Funeral of Di Tobias O'Sullivan. Issue 741, 27 January 1921

Auxiliaries at Revolver Practice; Bloodhounds are Being Used and Trained to Trace Fugitives. Both in Issue 742, 31 January 1921.

Meet of the Ward Union Hunt at Ratoath. Issue 743, 3 February 1921

All's Fair In … . Issue 744, 7 February 1921.

First Meeting of White Cross to Relieve Suffering in Ireland at the Mansion House. Issue 744, 7 February 1921.

Lady Sykes Visits Reprisal Scenes at Sixmilebridge, Co. Clare. Issue 744, 7 February 1921.

Ulster's New Leader. Issue 745, 10 February 1921.

France v. Ireland; Irish Ladies v. Gents at Hockey, and the Ladies Won. Both in Issue 746, 14 February 1921.

American Mission to Relieve Distress in Ireland Visit; Honours Even. Both in Issue 747, 17 February 1921.

A Thrilling Race at First Meeting on Famous Irish Course; MR Gerrard – Famous Spokesman. Both in Issue 748, 21 February 1921.

Business as Usual; Dublin County Harriers; All–Ireland Final. All in Issue 749, 24 February 1921

Trotting and Whippet Racing; Second Annual Bull Show. Both in Issue 750, 28 February 1921.

Scotland Beats Ireland; With the Bray Harriers. Both in Issue 751, 3 March 1921.

A Good Run with the Famous Bray Harriers in the Beautiful Wicklow Mountains Country; World's Largest Motor Boat Launched at Harland & Wolff's Yard; Scotland Defeated in Rugby International. All in Issue 752, 7 March 1921.

Ruas Spring Shows. Issue 754, 14 March 1921.

The Dear Little Shamrock; 20,000 people on their knees; Naas Harriers Point to Point. All in Issue 755, 17 March 1921.

Ireland Solves Housing Problem. Issue 760, 4 April 1921.

On the Liffey. Issue 757, 24 March 1921.

Junior Schools' Cup Rugby Final. Issue 758, 28 March 1921.

Irish Grand National. Issue 759, 31 March 1921.

Ireland Solves Housing Problem; Louth Hunt Point–to–Point Races. Both in Issue 761, 7 April 1921.

Ireland Defeat West of Scotland Ladies at Hockey International; Dublin University Defeat University College. Both in Issue 761, 7 April 1921.

Lord Chancellor's Easter Levee; A Race Course on a Mountain. Both in Issue 762, 11 April 1921.

Universal Sorrow; Lord Mayor Inaugurates Motorboat Service on the Liffey. Both in Issue 763, 14 April 1921.

Irish Society Wedding; Punchestown Races; Late Archbishop of Dublin. All in Issue 764, 18 April 1921.

Co. *Dublin GAA Championship*; *Phoenix Park Races*. Both in Issue 765, 21 April 1921.
Salmon Fishing on the Liffey; *The Curragh Races*. Both in Issue 766, 25 April 1921.
The Curragh Races; *Opening of Irish Polo Season; Whippet Racing*. Both in Issue 767, 28 April 1921.
Animals Take Advantage of Sunshine; *Irish Cricket Season*. Both in Issue 768, 2 May 1921.
May Day Procession. Issue 769, 5 May 1921.
Viscount Fitzalan. Issue 770, 9 May 1921.
Viscountess Powerscourt; *Irish Amateur Golf Championship*. Both in Issue 771, 12 May 1921.
Irish Cinema Trade Football; *Coal Strike*. Both in Issue 772, 16 May 1921.
Irish Amateur Athletic Championships; *Leinster Motor Club*. Both in Issue 773, 19 May 1921.
Baldoyle Derby. Issue 774, 23 May 1921.
Metropolitan Chase; *Irish Pageant Play*. Both in Issue 775, 26 May 1921.
Irish Trotting Races; *Polling Day Scenes*. Both in Issue 776, 30 May 1921.
Irish Pony Show. Issue 777, 2 June 1921.
Inter–Varsity Sports. Issue 779, 9 June 1921.
Irish Pageant. Issue 780, 13 June 1921.
State Opening of Ulster Parliament; *Phoenix Park Races*. Both in Issue 781, 16 June 1921.
Donkey and Pony Parade. Issue 782, 20 June 1921.
Golf; Irish Polo Season. Issue 783, 23 June 1921.
Open Air Dancing. Issue 787, 4 July 1921.
Mansion House Conference; *Prayer for Peace*; *High School Sports at Landsdowne Road*; *De Valera and Members of Irish Republican Party Attend Meeting in Mansion House*. All in Issue 787, 7 July 1921.
Ulster's Great Day. Issue 788, 11 July 1921.
Sinn Féiners in Downing Street. Issue 790, 18 July 1921.
The Curragh, Lawn Tennis; *Golf Meeting in Ireland*. Both in Issue 792, 25 July 1921.
Ireland a Dominion. Issue 793, 28 July 1921.
Pony and Donkey Races at Finglas Road; *De Valera in London*; *De Valera*. All in Issue 793, 28 July 1921.
Dominion or Republic – Peace or War? Issue 799, 18 August 1921.
Pretty Dublin Wedding. Issue 794, 1 August 1921.
Boisterous Weather; *Shipbuilding in Dublin*. Both in Issue 796, 8 August 1921.
Galway Race Prize. Issue 797, 11 August 1921.
Royal Dublin Horse Show Includes a Display by Irish Peasants. Issue 798, 15 August 1921.
Ulster Parliament Opened by the Viceroy; *Swimming Race on the Liffey*; *Dominion or Republic – Peace or War*. All in Issue 799, 18 August 1921.
Phoenix Park Plate, Won by 'Bridge Mount'. Issue 800, 24 August 1921.
Motorcycle Racing in Ireland; *Edwards and Healy Wedding*; *Open Polo Cup*. All in Issue 801, 27 August, 1921.
Lord Mayor Opens Fete in Aid of Comrades of the Great War; *An Irish War Romance*. Both in Issue 803, 3 September 1921.
Dublin Camera Club; *Back from USA*. 7 September 1921.
Roab. Issue 805, 10 September 1921.
Football Association of Ireland. Issue 806, 14 September 1921.
City of Waterford Races; *Horse Racing in Ireland*. Issue 807, 17 September 1921.

All Sports Carnival, in Aid of the Royal Hospital for Incurables. Issue 808, 21 September 1921.

Steeplechasing at Mullingar. Issue 809, 24 September 1921.

Ecila Cup Tournament; *Navan's New Racecourse*. Both in Issue 810, 28 September 1921.

SS Kyleber Lunched at Alexandra Yard, Dublin; *Commandant McKeon Starts Game at Croke Park*. Both in Issue 811, 1 October 1921.

Tiny Tots Races at Rathmines. *Polo Final at Phoenix Park*. Issue 812, 3 October 1921.

Northern Ireland Parliamentary Representatives. 1921. This appears on the Digital Film Archive but not on NoS or www.britishpathe.com.

In the Hills: The IRA. Issue 813, 6 October 1921.

Irish Peace Congress. Issue 815, 13 October 1921.

Marriage at Milltown; *National Fete*. Both in Issue 816, 17 October 1921.

Rugby. Issue 818, 24 October 1921.

Rebel Flags on Nelson's Column, Two Days After Trafalgar Day!; *Rory's Glen*; *Catholic Truth Society Conference*. All in Issue 819, 27 October 1921.

New Archbishop of Dublin, Dr Byrne. Issue 820, 31 October 1921.

Never Shall Their Glory Fade; *New Archbishop of Dublin*; *The Rev. Michael O'Flanagan*; *Coursing Season Opens*; *Second Worcesters 'Troop the Colour'*. All in Issue 821, 3 November 1921.

Dublin Union Affairs. Issue 822, 7 November 1921.

A New Experience for Female Students; *Degrees, Flour and Music*. Both in Issue 823, 10 November 1921.

Gaelic Football; *Internees Return Home*. Both in Issue 824, 14 November 1921.

Leopardstown Autumn Meeting; *Rugby*. Both in Issue 825, 17 November 1921.

The Curragh. Issue 826, 21 November 1921.

De Valera as University Chancellor; *Patriot's Last Journey*; *Erin Remembers*. All in Issue 828, 28 November 1921.

Ragging and Charity; *Queen's University and Lansdowne*. Both in Issue 829, 1 December 1921.

Dublin Blue Terrier Show. Issue 830, 5 December 1921.

De Valera, Accompanied by Minister of Defence and Chief of Staff Visits Galway. Issue 831, 9 December 1921.

Internees Free. Issue 832, 12 December 1921.

Sinn Féin's Would–Be Dictator; *Internees Welcomed Back*; *State Opening of Parliament*; *Presidential Tour Ends in Peace*. All in Issue 833, 15 December 1921.

Momentous Meeting of Dáil Éireann; *Cancer Research Fund*; *Dáil Éireann in Session*. All in Issue 834, 19 December 1921.

Dublin University's Victory. Issue 835, 22 December 1921.

Now Worth Real Money; *INA Western Division Under Review*. Both in Issue 836, 26 December 1921.

Chiefs of the INA Visit Limerick. Issue 837, 29 December 1921.

Riots and Revolutions. Dated on Digital Film Archive as 1921, but appears to be a compendium piece including footage from both the War of Independence and the Civil War.

Irish Elections. A compendium piece dated on Digital Film Archive as 1921.

Michael Collins the IRA leader. 9 January 1922.

The Treaty. Issue 840, 9 January 1922.

Realising Freedom in Dublin. Issue 842, 16 January 1922.

Evacuation of British Troops from Ireland. Issue 844, 23 January 1922

(A) Soldiers Home from Irish Front (Dublin and Belfast) (B) Irish Free State Soldiers Guard Dublin City Hall. Issue 845, 26 January 1922.
Irish Free State Soldiers, Receiving Uniforms; De Valera and Members of the Republican Party Attend at Mansion House. Both in Issue 846, 30 January 1922.
Maas Plays Hockey at Dublin. Issue 847, 2 February 1922.
New History (Ireland) Republican Army. Issue 848, 6 February 1922.
New History (Ireland) Republican Army; Captain Craig and Michael Collins Confer (Dublin) on Boundaries (North and South). Both in Issue 848, 6 February 1922.
Ireland Defeats Wales at Hockey. Issue 850, 13 February 1922.
International Rugby; Mr de Valera Opens Anti–Treaty Campaign. Both in Issue 851, 16 February 1922.
Fighting Speech by Michael Collins. Issue 857, 9 March 1922.
IRA – Occupation of Beggars' Bush Barracks. Issue 859, 16 March 1922.
Michael Collins; Launch of Giant Caisson, Dublin. Issue 860, 20 March 1922.
3,000 Irish Army Rebels Hold Parade. Issue 865, 6 April 1922.
Wexford Treaty Meeting. Issue 867, 13 April 1922.
Curragh Camp Handed over to Free State Troops. Issue 878, 22 May 1922.
The Tailteann Games, Ireland. Issue 879, 25 May 1922.
Refugees from Ulster Border (Where Fighting Is Intense) Pouring into Dublin; Funeral of Mr McGuinness. Both in Issue 883, 8 June 1922.
Dublin Coalition Campaign; British Troops Hold Review in Phoenix Park, Dublin; Tailteann Trials. All in Issue 885, 15 June 1922.
Refugees from Belfast. Issue 886, 19 June 1922.
Photographic Society of Ireland. Issue 889, 29 June 1922.
Rounding Up of Refugees, Dublin. Issue 891, 6 July 1922.
Peaceful Twelfth. Issue 894, 17 July 1922.
Rallying to the Nation's Aid. Issue 895, 20 July 1922.
Irish National Championships. Issue 896, 24 July 1922.
General Michael Collins. Issue 898, 31 July 1922.
Michael Collins Secretly Brings Troops by Sea and Turns Rebel Flank. Issue 900, 7 August 1922.
Mopping Up. Battle of Adare. Issue 901, 10 August 1922.
A Martyr to Duty: Ireland Mourns Arthur Griffith, Her First President; Dublin Horse Show. Both in Issue 903, 17 August 1922.
Dublin Mourns Dead President. Issue 904, 21 August 1922.
Michael Collins at Burial of Arthur Griffith. Issue 905, 24 August 1922.
Ireland Mourns Passing Michael Collins; Riots in Belfast. Both in Issue 906, 28 August 1922.
More than Half a Million Mourners. Issue 907, 31 August 1922.
Grave of Michael Collins. Issue 909, 7 September 1922.
Speeding on Sands at Portmarnock. Issue 910, 11 September 1922.
Irish St Leger. Issue 914, 25 September 1922.
Motorists at Golf; Unique Train Ferry on the Liffey, Dublin. Both in Issue 915, 25 September 1922.
Dublin Zoo. Issue 918, 9 October 1922.
General Mulcahy Hoists Flag. Issue 920, 16 October 1922.
Irish Grand Prix. Issue 921, 19 October 1922.
Dublin Students' Protest; Irish Cesarewitch. Both in Issue 923, 26 October 1922.
Phoenix Park – British Troops Parade; Ireland v. France; Dublin Wedding. All in Issue 924, 30 October 1922.

Dublin: Scene of Recent Attacks at Wellington Barracks. Issue 929, 16 November 1922.

A Pretty Dublin Wedding. Issue 931, 23 November 1922.

While Miss MacSwiney Hunger–Strikes in Mountjoy Prison, her Sister Annie Does the Same Outside; Erskine Childers, the Irish Renegade. Both in Issue 932, 27 November 1922.

Ireland a Dominion. Issue 936, 11 December 1922.

Late Brigadier Sean Hales and Members of the Government, Leaving High Mass in Dublin. Issue 937, 14 December 1922.

Irish and British Armies Take the Salute; Ireland, The Governor General is Now in Residence. Both in Issue 938, 18 December 1922.

Dublin City Harriers; Holiday Gathering at Fox Rock; Christmas Swimming Race at Clontarf; Trinity Defeat Oxford; Leopardstown Racing. All in Issue 941, 28 December 1922.

Holiday Racing. Issue 942, 1 January 1923.

Howth Train Smash; Fashionable Dublin Wedding. Both in Issue 944, 8 January 1923.

Paris in Dublin; Thrills and Spills. Both in Issue 945, 11 January 1923.

Cross Country Run. Issue 946, 15 January 1923.

President Cosgrave. Issue 947, 18 January 1923.

Cinderella. Issue 952, 5 February 1923.

Hockey International; Gormanstown Camp Wedding. Both in Issue 953, 8 February 1923.

Their First Defeat. Issue 956, 18 February 1923.

New Governor of Ireland. Issue 959, 1 March 1923.

Horse Jumping Competitions. Issue 960, 5 March 1923.

Mike McTigue Arrives. Issue 961, 8 March 1923.

Battling Siki Arrives in Cork; Ireland Defeats Wales. Both in Issue 963, 15 March 1923.

Hurling Match. Issue 964, 19 March 1923.

Ireland's Own Champion; Mike McTigue Who Won World's Title. Issue 965, 22 March 1923.

Rabbits and Badgers. Issue 967, 29 March 1923.

Irish Guards all over the World Receive Irish Shamrock. Issue 968, 5 April 1923.

French Footballers in Dublin. Issue 969, 9 April 1923.

Anything to Declare. Issue 970, 12 April 1923.

Ulster's Guardian of the Peace. Issue 971, 16 April 1923.

Rebel Spoil Sports Defied. Issue 972, 19 April 1923.

Dr Esposito. Issue 974, 26 April 1923.

Pretty Anglo–Irish Wedding. Issue 976, 3 May 1923.

State Visit to Derry. Issue 978, 10 May 1923.

Bray – Ireland's Future White City; Landslide at Bray Head. Issue 979, 14 May 1923.

May Day Procession. Issue 980, 17 May 1923.

Dublin Spring Show. Issue 982, 24 May 1923.

20 Rounds Draw. Issue 984, 31 May 1923.

KC and Novelist; University College Sports. Both in Issue 987, 11 June 1923.

Drilling Display; Ladies Golf Final. Both in Issue 989, 18 June 1923.

Senior Tourist Trophy. Issue 995, 9 July 1923.

The Irish Derby; Irish Military Sports. Both in Issue 996, 12 July 1923.

The Knock Out; The Marchioness of Aberdeen. Both in Issue 997, 16 July 1923.

Croke Park Boxing. Issue 998, 19 July 1923.

International Lawn Tennis. Issue 1000, 26 July 1923.

Irish Oaks. Issue 1002, 2 August 1923.

Sandycove Gala and Dun Laoghaire Regatta. Issue 1005, 3 August 1923.
Irish National Foresters Procession. Issue 1006, 16 August 1923.
De Valera. Issue 1008, 23 August 1923.
A Popular Innovation; Irish Presidential Hustle. Issue 1009, 27 August 1923.
Clontarf Gala. Issue 1010, 30 August 1923.
Ulster Grand Prix. Issue 1011, 3 September 1923.
Inter Command Contest. Issue 1013, 10 September 1923.
Polo Match; Opening of the Dáil. Both in Issue 1014, 13 September 1923.
Irish Tenor Honoured. Issue 1015, 17 September 1923.
Kilkenny Wins. Issue 1016, 10 September 1923.
President Cosgrave. Issue 1017, 24 September 1923.
Ulster Grand Prix; Opening of the Dáil. Both in Issue 1018, 27 September 1923.
Football Finals. Issue 1019, 1 October 1923.
Racing on the Strand. Issue 1021, 8 October 1923.
Hockey and Rugby Season Opens; President Cosgrave at New Bridge. Both in Issue 1025, 22 October 1923.
Catholic Truth Conference. Issue 1026, 25 October 1923.
Dublin Football Derby. Issue 1027, 29 October 1923.
Minniement Wins Irish Cezarewitch. Issue 1028, 1 November 1923.
Leopardstown Steeplechase; Degree Day Rag. Issue 1032, 2 November 1923.
Remembrance Day. Issue 1034, 26 November 1923.
The Ding Dong Game. Issue 1035, 26 November 1923.
In a Fog; Dublin University Motor Cycle Club. Both in Issue 1036, 29 November 1923.
Great Maori Demonstration. Issue 1039, 10 December 1923.
Ploughboy to Premier. Issue 1040, 13 December 1923.
Dublin's Water Supply. Issue 1042, 20 December 1923.
Rugby Hospital Cup. Issue 1045, 31 December 1923.
Review of Irish Events 1923. Issue 1045, 31 December 1923.
Martial Law in Ireland. 1923–24. This appears on the Digital Film Archive. It also appears as an undated item on British Pathé's website.
Dublin's Horse Show. Issue 1046, 3 January 1924.
Bohemians v. Linfield. Issue 1047, 7 January 1924.
Baldoyle Races. Issue 1049, 14 January 1924.
Gaelic Football. Issue 1050, 17 January 1924.
Ward Union Hunt; Phoenix Park. Issue 1051, 21 January 1924.
Floods in Ireland. Issue 1053, 28 January 1924.
Ireland Expects. Issue 1054, 31 January 1924.
A Thrilling Match. Issue 1055, 4 February 1924.
Badminton. Issue 1057, 11 February 1924.
England v. Ireland. Issue 1059, 18 February 1924.
Curragh Stable Lads Strike. Issue 1060, 21 February 1924.
Demobbed Irish Soldiers. Issue 1061, 25 February 1924.
Students at Play; Scotland v. Ireland; A Record Crowd; Horse Jumping. All in Issue 1063, 3 March 1924.
North Kildare Harriers. Issue 1064, 6 March 1924.
Leinster Motor Cycle Club; For the First Time in 25 Years. Issue 1067, 17 March 1924.
Wexford's Commemoration to Mr John Redmond. Issue 1068, 20 March 1924.
Dublin's Great Dog Show. Issue 1070, 27 March 1924.
Ireland Win Triple Crown. Issue 1071, 31 March 1924.
Sunshine; Ulster's Defeat Royal. Issue 1075, 14 April 1924.

Sportman's Races. Issue 1076, 17 April 1924.
Mullingar Races. Issue 1077, 21 April 1924.
Tancy Lee. Issue 1079, 28 April 1924
Fairy House. Issue 1081, 5 May 1924.
Galway's Choice. Issue 1084, 15 May 1924.
Clonmel Dog Show. Issue 1085, 19 May 1924.
Dublin Spring Show. 22 May 1924.
Galway's Religious Festival. Issue 1092, 12 June 1924.
Great Temperance Rally. Issue 1093, 16 June 1924.
Dublin University Harriers. Issue 1094, 19 June 1924.
American Footballers. Issue 1095, 23 June 1924.
Nature's Freak. Issue 1096, 26 June 1924.
Aonic Tailteann. Issue 1100, 10 July 1924.
Sunshine and Fashions. Issue 1103, 21 July 1924.
Tennis – Gibson Challenge Cup. Issue 1103, 21 July 1924.
De Valera and Austin Stack; *Polo*; *Golf.* All in Issue 1104, 24 July 1924
Visit of the Duke and Duchess of York to Ulster. Issue 1105, 28 July 1924.
Olympic and Tailteann. Issue 1107, 4 August 1924.
World's Largest Athletes and Record Breakers at Olympics Games. Issue 1108, 7 August 1924.
Dublin Horse Show; *Royal Irish Academy*; *Boundary Conference.* All in Issue 1110, 14 August 1924.
Anoch Tailteann Continues. Issue 1112, 21 August 1924.
Tailteann Athletes. Issue 113, 25 August 1924.
The Rodeo in Dublin. Issue 1114, 2 August 1924 (on NoS). This is listed as *Ireland's Rodeo*, Issue 1113, 25 August 1924, on www.britishpathe.com.
Water Polo. Issue 1115, 1 September 1924.
Leinster 100. Issue 1116, 4 September 1924.
Gala Day; *International Golf*; *Football.* All in Issue 1118, 11 September 1924.
Ulster Grand Prix. Issue 1119, 15 September 1924,
300,000 at Demonstration. Issue 1124, 2 October 1924.
Motor Cycling – Irish Championships. Issue 1125, 6 October 1924.
All Ireland Football Carnival; Seat of the Trouble. Issue 1126, 9 October 1924.
Tally Ho. Issue 1127, 7 October 1924.
Irish Athletic Boom. Issue 1131, 27 October 1924.
Polish Patriot. Issue 1132, 30 October 1924.
De Valera – Stormy Petrel; New Irish Courts. Issue 1133, 3 November 1924.
Removing the Remains. Issue 1134, 6 November 1924.
Thrilling Rugby. Issue 1135, 10 November 1924.
Degree Day is Joy–Day; Bobbed Bachelors. Issue 1136, 13 November 1924.
Armistice Day in Dublin. Issue 1138, 17 November 1924.
Clonespoe; The Cardinal Ireland Loved. Issue 1140, 24 November 1924.
Rugby – Ulster Defeats Munster. Issue 1144, 8 December 1924.
Solving Boundary Question. Issue 1146, 15 December 1924.
Clontarf FC. Issue 1151, 1 January 1925.
The Big Gale. Issue 1152, 5 January 1925.
Boxing; *Hockey.* Issue 1155, 15 January 1925.
President Cosgrave; *Executive Council.* Both in 1157, 22 January 1925.
Lent Bumping Races; Connemara's Appeal. Issue 1164, 16 February 1925.
Hard Luck – Ireland. Issue 1165, 19 February 1925.

Title missing (Leinster Motor Club). Issue 1167, 26 February 1925.
Disastrous Fire. Issue 1173, 19 March 1925.
Ireland's Premier Dog Show; *Free State Army.* Both in Issue 1174, 23 March 1925.
International CC Championships. Issue 1178, 6 April 1925.
Punchestown Races. Issue 1186, 4 May 1925.
First of Great Agricultural Shows. Issue 1190, 18 May 1925.
The Good Old Elizabethan Days! Issue 1198, 15 June 1925.
Corpus Christi. Issue 1199, 18 June 1925.
Title missing. Proclaiming Assembly of Parliament. Issue 1205, 9 July 1925
Bonny Babies; Tennis Novelty. Issue 1212, 3 August 1925.
Dublin Horse Show; Renters Defeat Exhibitors. Issue 1214, 10 August 1925.
Cossacks in Dublin. Issue 1215, 13 August 1925.
Ireland Remembers. Issue 1217, 20 August 1925.
Longford War Memorial. Issue 1222, 7 September 1925.
Motor Cycling at over 72 miles an Hour; Irish Free State Army. Issue 1223, 10 September 1925.
Ireland 'Healing her Wounds'. Issue 1236, 26 October 1925.
Armistice Day in Dublin. Issue 1242, 16 November 1925.
Rugby Rough? Issue 1248, 7 December 1925.
A Battle of Giants. Issue 1253, 24 December 1925.
To 'Our Lady of Lourdes'; Light Plane's Triumph. Both in Issue 1256, 4 January 1926.
New Irish Industry; Colours v. Whites. Both in Issue 1258, 11 January 1926.
Cardinal Feted. Issue 1260, 18 January 1926.
Shamrock Rovers. Issue 1262, 25 January 1926.
Ireland Defeat France. Issue 1263, 27 January 1926.
Clever Animals; *A Storm Victim.* Both in Issue 1268, 15 February 1926.
Ireland's Great Victory over England in Rugby International; *Speeding the Plough.* Both in Issue 1269, 18 February 1926.
Hockey International. Issue 1271, 25 February 1926.
To Add to His Collection. Issue 1273, 4 March 1926.
Mr Winston Churchill in Belfast. Issue 1274, 8 March 1926.
Ryan's Easy Victory. Issue 1275, 11 March 1926.
Hard Luck Ireland. Issue 1276, 15 March 1926.
Wales v. Ireland. Issue 1277, 18 March 1926.
St Patrick's Day Celebrations; *Unveiling War Memorial to Memory of Michael Hogan & 13 Others Shot at Croke Park*; *Irish Dancing Display.* All in Issue 1278, 22 March 1926.
Ireland's Premier Dog Show. Issue 1279, 25 March 1926.
Big Holiday Crowd. Issue 1284, 12 April 1926.
Northern's Jubilee Cup Victory. Issue 1285, 15 April 1926.
Sodality Observances. Issue 1286, 19 April 1926.
Bray Harriers Point to Point. Issue 1287, 22 April 1926.
First of the Irish Classics. Issue 1288, 26 April 1926.
Archbishop of Dublin; *Irish National Forresters.* Both in Issue 1291, 6 May 1926.
Punchestown Races. Issue 1295, 20 May 1926.
Dublin Spring Show. Issue 1296, 24 May 1926.
2,000 Guineas; *Lawn Tennis.* Both in Issue 1297, 27 May 1926.
Bishop of Ossary Inspects Dublin Boys' Brigade. Issue 1298, 31 May 1926.
Clever Drill Display. Issue 1299, 3 June 1926.
His Eminence Cardinal O'Donnell; *St Dunstan's*; *Degree Day Rag by Trinity Students.* Both in Issue 1301, 10 June 1926.
Cinema Golf Match. Issue 1302, 14 June 1926.

Embargo Wins Irish Derby. Issue 1307, 1 July 1926.

A Tennis Lesson. Issue 1310, 12 July 1926.

Flight of Moth Aeroplanes; Douglas Gymkhana; Motor Racing Phoenix Park. All in Issue 1311, 15 July 1926.

For Valour. Issue 1313, 22 July 1926.

Athletic Championship at Lansdowne Road. Issue 1314, 26 July 1926.

Rowing. Issue 1315, 29 July 1926.

Dun Laoghaire Regatta. Issue 1316, 2 August 1926.

In the Wicklow Mountains. Issue 1317, 5 August 1926.

Dublin Horse Show, Issue 1318, 9 August 1926.

International Water Polo; Irish Athletes. Both in Issue 1319, 12 August 1926.

Box On; Heaney–Madden Fight. Issue 1320, 16/8/1926.

Mid–Summer Dance Festival. Issue 1321, 19 August 1926.

Erin Remembers Her Fallen Sons; A Bird's Eye View of the Liffey Swim; Greystones Gala Day; Religious Day in Waterford. All in Issue 1323, 26 August 1926.

Griffith Collins Commemoration. Issue 1324, 30 August 1926.

Bray Regatta; Marshal Joffre Unveils Memorial at Guillemont. Both in Issue 1325, 2 September 1926.

Motor Cycling at 70 Miles an Hour; Ulster Grand Prix. Issue 1327, 9 September 1926.

37,500 at Football Final. Issue 1328, 13 September 1926.

Irish National Army. Issue 1329, 16 September 1926.

Irish Army Reviews; New Irish National Party (Waterford). Issue 1330, 20 September 1926.

The Free State Army; The Fight for Dublin, Irish Free State Army Manoeuvres in the Wicklow Mountains. Issue 1332, 27 September 1926.

St Francis of Assisi; The Coming Elections. Both in Issue 1337, 14 October 1926.

His Grace the Archbishop. Issue 1338, 18 October 1926.

Kerry Defeat Kildare. Issue 1339, 21 October 1926.

First International of the Season; Hunting Season Opens in Ireland. Issue 1340, 25 October 1926.

Cork's Great Victory. Issue 1341, 28 October 1926.

Ireland's National Game; Launch 'Southland'. Issue 1342, 1 November 1926.

The Ward Union Hunt. Issue 1343, 4 November 1926.

Students' Day Out. Issue 1345, 11 November 1926.

Degree Days and 'Joy Day'; Ladies Hockey. Both in Issue 1349, 25 November 1926.

North v. South. Queen's University v. University College. Issue 1350, 29 November 1926.

Trinity College Ceremony; Distinguished Irishmen's Visit. Issue 1352, 6 December 1926.

Conferring Degrees at Dublin University; GAA Football; Rugby Inter–Provincial. All in Issue 1355, 16 December 1926.

Oxford's Irish Team. Issue 1358, 27 December 1926.

6 Degrees Above Freezing Point. Issue 1359, 30 December 1926.

Lacrosse Match in Dublin. Issue 1362. 10 January 1927.

Hammer and Tongs Hockey; Mr Cosgrave. Both in Issue 1366, 24 January 1927.

Interprovincial Hockey; Passing of Royal Hospital. Both in Issue 1367, 27 January 1927.

Army Review and Presentation. Issue 1371, 10 February 1927.

Twickenham Tradition Prevails; Ploughing Competition & Jumping Competition in Delgany. Issue 1372, 14 February 1927.

Are Alsatians Dangerous? Issue 1373, 17 February 1927.

President Cosgrave. Issue 1374, 21 February 1927.

Powers Court Jumping Competitions. Issue 1375, 23 February 1927.
A Matter of Seconds. Issue 1376, 28 February 1927.
Ireland (6) Defeat Scotland (0). Issue 1377, 3 March 1927.
Ireland v. Wales. Issue 1381, 17 March 1927.
St Patrick's Day Celebrations; Erin for Ever!; Irish Kennel Club Dog Show, Ballsbridge. All in Issue 1382, 21 March 1927.
1,835 Dogs of High Degree; Archbishop of Dublin; International Hockey. All in Issue 1383, 24 March 1927.
Lady Wheeler. Issue 1388, 11 April 1927.
Instonians – The Champion! Issue 1389, 14 April 1927.
Irish Grand National. Issue 1391, 21 April 1927.
Late Bishop of Ardagh. Issue 1392, 25 April 1927.
Irish Thousand Guineas at the Curragh. Issue 1393, 28 April 1927.
Peerless Punchestown; Old Bohs' V. Old Shels'; May Procession. All in Issue 1395, 5 May 1927.
Commemoration Ceremony; Punchestown Races. Issue 1396, 9 May 1927.
Famous Garda Boxers. Issue 1397, 12 May 1927.
Dublin Spring Show. Issue 1398, 16 May 1927.
The New Sport; Jumping Competitions at Dublin Spring Show. Issue 1399, 19 May 1927.
Women's Open Golf Championship; Greyhound Racing. Both in Issue 1400, 23 May 1927.
University College Sports. Issue 1402, 30 May
8th Bridge Sports at Portobella. Issue 1403, 2 June 1927.
A Little Bit of Ireland in England; Religious Festival. Issue 1405, 9 June 1927.
Great Tennis Display, Fitzwilliam Club; Garda Athletes in Training. Issue 1406, 13 June 1927.
Dáil Éireann Assembles; Knight of the Grail Wins Irish Derby. Both in Issue 1410, 27 June 1927.
Athletics. Issue 1412, 4 July 1927.
Mr Kevin O'Higgins; Irish Athletic Championships. Both in Issue 1415, 14 July 1927.
Swimming. Issue 1417, 21 July 1927.
First US Minister. Issue 1420, 1 August 1927.
Dublin Horse Show. Issue 1421, 4 August 1927.
Royal Dublin Horse Show. Issue 1422, 8 August 1927.
Swimming. Issue 1423, 11 August 1927.
Horse Jumping. Issue 1424, 15 August 1927.
Dáil Crisis. Personalities and Scenes Around Parliament Houses. Issue 1425, 18 August 1927.
Leinster 100. Issue 1426, 22 August 1927.
Ireland Welcomes New York's Mayor. Issue 1427, 25 August 1927.
5th Anniversary of Collins and Griffith. Issue 1428, 29 August 1927.
Ulster Grand Prix; Dublin Defeat Cork; Ireland – America Flight. All in Issue 1431, 8 September 1927.
Ireland's National Game. Issue 1432, 12 September 1927.
Atlantic Flight Fails. Issue 1434, 19 September 1927.
McIntosh – Fitzmaurice Atlantic Flight from Ireland. Issue 1435, 22 September 1927.
Ireland Through the Ages; All Ireland Football Championships at Croke Park. Both in Issue 1437, 29 September 1927.
Launched in Dublin. Issue 1439, 6 October 1927.

Rugby Season Opens. Issue 1441, 13 October 1927.

The Irish Cesarewitch. Issue 1444, 24 October 1927.

Requiescat in Pace! Issue 1445, 27 October 1927.

Hunting. Issue 1446, 31 October 1927.

Erin Mourns. Issue 1447, 3 November 1927.

Remembrance Day. Issue 1450, 14 November 1927.

Waratahs (5 points) Defeat Ireland (3 points). Issue 1451, 17 November 1927.

Isseu d'Or Wins Irish Cambridgeshire. Issue 1452, 21 November 1927.

Blackpool Defeat Redmonds. Issue 1456, 5 December 1927.

The New Cork. Issue 1457, 8 December 1927.

Leinster Trial Match. Issue 1458, 12 December 1927.

Tennis Tournament; Famous Irish Tenor Honoured; Gallant Swimmers. All in Issue 1464, 2 January 1928.

Lieutenant Coughlan. Issue 1467, 12 January 1928.

Irish Rugby Problem. Issue 1469, 19 January 1928.

Ladies Hockey Trials. Issue 1471, 26 January 1928.

Launch of the SS Isola; The Shamrock's Triumph. Both in Issue 1472, 30 January 1928.

President Cosgrave in America. Issue 1473, 2 February 1928.

Mr James McNeill Installed New Governor–General. Issue 1474, 6 February 1928.

Hockey Inter–Provincial. Issue 1475, 9 February 1928.

England's Dramatic Last Minute Win. Issue 1477, 16 February 1928.

France Beats Ireland. Issue 1480, 27 February 1928.

Cross–Country Running Junior Championship; Ireland Wins Soccer International with Scotland. Both in Issue 1481, 1 March 1928.

Channel Swim. Issue 1482, 5 March 1928.

Wales Conquers Ireland; Scout Ceremony. Both in Issue 1483, 8 March 1928.

Aonach Tailteann. Issue 1485, 15 March 1928.

Inspection and Presentation of Shamrock to Catholic Boy Scouts (Fairview); St Patrick's Day in Dublin; Irish Dog Show at Ballsbridge. All in Issue 1487, 22 March 1928.

Don Sancho Winss [sic] *Irish Guard National.* Issue 1493, 12 April 1928.

Atlantic Flown Westward for First Time!; Lacrosse. Both in Issue 1494, 16 April 1928.

Dublin Chamber of Commerce; World Honours Atlantic Flight Hero. Both in Issue 1495, 16 April 1928.

Peerless Punchestown. Issue 1496, 23 April 1928.

Archbishop of Dublin Blesses New Church at Crooksling Sanatorium. Issue 1498, 30 April 1928.

May Procession. Issue 1501, 10 May 1928.

First of the Spring 'Shows'; Men of 1916. Both in Issue 1502, 14 May 1928.

Lawn Tennis. Issue 1503, 17 May 1928.

Dancers Rehearse; Ulster Houses of Parliament. Both in Issue 1505, 25 May 1928.

Walter Hagen. Issue 1507, 31 May 1928.

The Battle of Castleknock. Issue 1511, 14 June 1928.

Wolfe Tone Anniversary; Bowling; International Boxing. All in Issue 1513, 21 June 1928.

Baytown Wins Irish Derby. Issue 1516, 2 July 1927.

Back to the Start; Fancy Dress Parade. Issue 1517, 5 July 1928.

A State Welcome. Issue 1518, 9 July 1928.

Wnha Fete. Issue 1519, 12 July 1928.

German Students; For Tailteann Games. Both in Issue 1521, 19 July 1928.

Greystone Gala. Issue 1523, 26 July 1928.

The Dublin Horse Show. Issue 1528, 13 August 1928.
The Tailteann Games. Issue 1529, 16 August 1928.
Leinster 100. Issue 1530, 20 August 1928.
Britain Wins International Tourist Trophy; *Erin Remembers Her Fallen Sons*; *Aonach Tailteann*. All in Issue 1531, 23 August 1928.
Titles Missing: Cosgrave welcomes Gene Tunney; Tailteann Games. Both in Issue 1532, 27 August 1928.
Gene Tunney Goes Racing; *Girl Guides Give Display of Irish Dancing*. Both in Issue 1534, 30 August 1928.
Ireland Welcomes Mr Kellogg; *Tailteann Pageant*. Both in Issue 1534, 3 September 1928.
World's Fastest Road Race. Issue 1535, 6 September 1928.
General Mulcahy Opens New Tennis Courts. Issue 1536, 10 September 1928.
Artane Boys Give a Clever Gymnastic Display. Issue 1537, 13 September 1928.
Rugby Season Opens. Issue 1541, 27 September 1928.
Thrilling Riding. Issue 1543, 4 October 1928.
A Great Adventure. Issue 1544, 8 October 1928.
Cead Mille Faite; *His Grace the Archbishop of Dublin Blesses and Opens the New Church at Marino*. Both in Issue 1545, 11 October 1928.
Ulster's Loyal Welcome. Issue 1546, 15 October 1928.
Catholic Truth Week. Issue 1548, 22 October 1928.
Students University Rag in Dublin. Issue 1551, 1 November 1928.
Degree Day is Joy Day. Issue 1552, 5 November 1928.
Trinity's Dead Honoured. Issue 1555, 15 November 1928.
The Shannon Scheme. Issue 1557, 22 November 1928.
A Titan Task; *The Shannon Scheme*. Both in Issue 1558, 26 November 1928.
Six Points Each. Issue 1559, 29 November 1928.
Trinity Boxers; *North and South, Soccer*. Both in Issue 1560, 3 December 1928.
Fast on the Rocks; *Irish Ladies' Hockey*. Issue 1563, 13 December 1928.
No Mercy Given or Required. Issue 1565, 20 December 1928.
Look Back on 1928. Issue 1567, 27 December 1928.
Swimming at Clontarf. Issue 1569, 3 January 1929.
Irish Aero Club. Issue 1573, 17 January 1929.
Ladies' International Trial at Clonskeagh. Issue 1575, 24 January 1929.
Holy Relic of St Brigid; *Probabilities and Possibilities for International Rugby*. Both in Issue 1577, 31 January 1929.
Honours Even. Issue 1579, 7 February 1929.
By the Narrowest of Margins; *College of Surgeons*. Both in Issue 1580, 11 February 1929.
A 'Brooklands' in Dublin City. Issue 1583, 21 February 1929.
Season's Most Thrilling Rugby International. Issue 1585, 28 February 1929.
Honours Even! Issue 1589, 14 March 1929.
Cinema Ball of Masque. Issue 1593, 28 March 1929.
2143 Canine Aristocrats; *Preparing for Electricity Era*. Both in Issue 1594, 1 April 1929.
Irish Grand National. Issue 1595, 4 April 1929.
Notable Dublin Wedding. Issue 1596, 8 August 1929.
Soloptic Wins the 1,000 Irish Guineas at the Curragh. Issue 1602, 29 April 1929.
Horse Jumping Competitions. Issue 1603, 2 May 1929.
May Day; *Ireland's Davis Cup*. Issue 1605, 9 May 1929.
Conclusion of Dublin Spring Show. Issue 1607, 16 May 1929.
President Cosgrave; *Davis Cup – Ireland v. Italy*. Both in Issue 1608, 20 May 1929.

The Davis Cup – Italy v. Ireland Display by Maguire. Issue 1609, 23 May 1929.
American Golfers in Dublin. Issue 1613, 6 June 1929.
Emancipation! Issue 1614, 10 June 1929.
Kopi Wins Irish Derby. Issue 1620, 1 July 1929.
Around the Maypole. Issue 1621, 4 July 1929.
After Thirteen Years. Issue 1624, 14 July 1929.
International Motor Racing. Issue 1625, 17 July 1929.
King of Spain in a Coal Mine!; *South African Ladies.* Both in Issue 1626, 22 July 1929.
Royal Dublin Horse Show. Issue 1632, 12 August 1929.
The Greatest Road Race 'Ever'; *Irish Dancing Competitions.* Both in Issue 1634, 19
　　August 1929.
President Cosgrave. Issue 1637, 29 August 1929.
Irish Military Tattoo. Issue 1640, 9 September 1929.
The Ulster Grand Prix. Issue 1641, 12 September 1929.
Dublin Manufacturers Represented in the Civic Week Pageant of Industry. Issue 1642,
　　16 September 1929.
Hockey; *President Cosgrave.* Both in Issue 1651, 17 October 1929.
Duke of Abercorn. Issue 1652, 21 October 1929.
Clongowes College Ceremony. Issue 1658, 11 November 1929.
Heriotonians. Issue 1659, 14 November 1929.
Ireland's Great New Harbour. Issue 1669, 19 December 1929.
Pretty Dublin Wedding. Issue 1670, 23 December 1929.
Irish 2,000 Guineas. Issue 1673, 2 January 1930.
Shelbourne v. Shamrock. Issue 1676, 13 January 1930.
Rugby Trial Match. Issue 1677, 16 January 1930.
With State Honours. Issue 1678, 20 January 1930.
The Papal Nuncio; *Thrilling Rugby International.* Both in Issue 1680, 27 January 1930.
Relic of St Brigid. Issue 1683, 6 February 1930.
By Narrowest of Margins. Issue 1685, 13 February 1930.
The Famous Kilkenny Hunt. Issue 1687, 20 February 1930.
Our Northern Visitors. Issue 1691, 6 March 1930.
Well Played Wales! Cross Country. Both in Issue 1693, 13 March 1930.
Ward Union Hunt. Issue 1694, 17 March 1930.
St Patrick's Day Celebrations; *Emblem of St Patrick*; *Irish Kennel Club Show.* All in
　　Issue 1695, 20 March 1930.
General Brennen. Issue 1696, 24 March 1930.
2,209 Dogs! Issue 1697, 27 March 1930.
Irish Championships. Issue 1701, 10 April 1930.
Schools Cup Final. 14 April 1930.
Zoological Students Congress. Issue 104, 21 April 1930.
Irish Grand National Won by Fannond. Issue 1705, 24 April 1930.
Ireland v. Monaco. Issue 1708, 5 May 1930.
Dublin Spring Show. Issue 1710, 12 May 1930.
An Irish Lourdes. Issue 1711, 15 May 1930.
Ireland v. Australia. Issue 1712, 19 May 1930.
Baby 'Jehus'. Issue 1713, 22 May 1930.
A Worthy Cause. Issue 1714, 26 May 1930.
University College. Issue 1715, 29 May 1930.
The Irish Victory. Issue 30/1, 2 June 1930.
Dublin Scouts Ceremony; *Fire Drill Display.* 9 June 1930. No issue number given on

NoS or www.britishpathe.com.

The Great Adventure. 12 June 1930. No issue number given on NoS or www.britishpathe.com.

The Globe Circled by Air!; *Corpus Christi.* Both in Issue 30/8, 26 June 1930.

The Irish Derby; *Irish Police Ceremony.* Both in Issue 30/9, 30 June 1930.

Irish Dances/Model Engineers Regatta. Issue 30/10. 3 July 1930.

The Atlantic Flown Again; *Revival of Irish Dances.* Both in Issue 30/28, 7 July 1930.

In Good Old Irish Style; The Metropolitan Regatta. 10 July 1930. No issue number given on NoS or www.britishpathe.com.

Irish Lawn Tennis Championships. Issue 30/14, 17 July 1930

World's Speed Kings. Issue 30/15, 21 July 1930.

International Motor Racing in Ireland. Issue 30/16, 24 July 1930.

Cricket. Issue 30/17, 28 July 1930.

Tramway Sports. 31 July 1930. No issue number given on NoS or www. britishpathe.com.

With Full State Honours. Issue 30/19, 4 August 1930.

Revolutionary Electrical Invention. Issue 30/20, 7 August 1930.

Royal Dublin Horse Show. Issue 30/21, 11 August 1930.

Jumping 'Blue Riband'. Issue 30/22, 14 August 1930.

Erin Remembers!; *Dublin Motor Cycle Races.* Both in Issue 30/24, 21 August 1930.

The Greatest Road Race Ever! Issue 30/25, 24 August 1930.

New Cadets for Free State. Issue 30/27, 1 September 1930.

Juvenile Championships – Tennis. Issue 30/28, 4 September 1930.

Ulster Grand Prix. Issue 30/29, 8 September 1930.

National Army Championships. Issue 30/30, 11 September 1930.

Dublin Military Wedding. Issue 30/38, 9 October 1930.

Duchess of Aberdeen. Issue 30/39, 13 October 1930.

International Hockey. Issue 30/40, 16 October 1930.

Earl Jellicoe's Visit to Dublin; *Gaelic Football.* Both in Issue 30/41, 20 October 1930.

Australian Ladies. Issue 30/44, 30 October 1930.

150 Miles an Hour on a Motorcycle; *Irish Army Ceremony.* No issue number given on NoS or www.britishpathe.com.

Cyclists v. Harriers. 13 November 1930. No issue number given on NoS or www.britishpathe.com.

The Drama of a Million Hopes. Issue 30/50, 20 November 1930.

Irish Free State Army; *President Cosgrave.* Both in Issue 30/51, 24 November 1930.

Cheers – All the Way! Issue 32/93, 21 November 1932.

Meet the Lucky Three!; *Future Leader of Ireland's Army.* Both in Issue 30/52, 27 November 1930.

Soldier Boxers; *No. 1 Army Band.* Both in Issue 30/53, 1 December 1932.

Irish Army; *Dublin Winter Sc Gala Day.* Both in Issue 30/54, 4 December 1930.

Leinster Hockey Test. Issue 30/57, 15 December 1930.

Ulster and Leinster in Inter–Provincial. Issue 30/58, 18 December 1930.

Their Great Day. 29 December 1930. No issue number given on NoS or www.britishpathe.com.

Football. 5 January 1931. No issue number given on NoS or www.britishpathe.com.

By Narrowest of Margins. Issue 31/3, 8 January 1931.

A Bygone Craft. Issue 31/4, 12 January 1931.

Warming Her Up! Issue 31/7, 22 January 1931.

Rugby Trial Match. Issue G1677, 29 January 1931.

Over Miles of Ireland's Moor and Bog. Issue 31/7, 26 February 1931

Hard Going – Even for Horses. Issue 31/21, 12 March 1931.

Ireland v. Wales. Issue 31/22, 16 March 1931.

On St Patrick's Day. 19 March 1931. No issue number given on NoS or www.britishpathe.com.

Pretty Dublin Wedding; *St Patrick's Day*; *Irish Kennel Club Show.* All in Issue 31/24, 23 March 1931.

Lacrosse; *Motor Cycling.* Both in Issue 31/31, 16 April 1931.

Punchestown. Issue 31/33, 23 April 1931.

Hockey. Issue 31/35, 30 April 1931.

Captain Hawkes – London to Baldoyle. Issue 36, 4 May 1931.

A Sporting Victory. Issue 37, 7 May 1931.

Spring Show Opens. Issue 38, 11 May 1931.

Davis Cup Tennis; *Shamrock Rovers Win Free State Cup.* Issue 31/39, 14 May 1931.

College Boy Actors. Issue 31/45, 4 June 1931.

The Battle of the Baby Cars. Issue 31/46, 8 June 1931.

Ladies Open Golf Championship. Issue 31/47, 11 June 1931.

Damaged Polar Submarine. Issue 31/51, 25 June 1931.

Sea Serpent Wins Irish Derby. Issue 31/52, 29 June 1931.

Irish Motor Traders Outing. Issue 31/57, 16 July 1931.

Irish Tennis Championships. Issue 31/60, 27 July 1931.

Leinster Motor Club; *Pembroke Club Gala.* Both in Issue 31/61, 30 July 1931.

Irish Aero Club. Issue 31/62, 2 August 1931.

Erin Remembers. Issue 31/67, 20 August 1931.

The Greatest Road Race Ever! Issue 31/68, 24 August 1931.

All Motor–Cycle Records Broken. Issue 31/73, 10 September 1931.

Irish Lady Athletes. Issue 31/75, 17 September 1931.

Kerry v. Kildare. 1 October 1931. No issue number given on NoS or www.britishpathe. com.

For Ireland's Great Eucharistic Congress; *Clonmel Dog Show.* Both in Issue 31/85, 22 October 1931.

A Dour Struggle. Issue 31/86, 28 October 1931.

Dublin University College 'Rag'. Issue 31/87, 29 October 1931.

Degree Day is Joy Day. Issue 31/88, 2 November 1931.

Great Hurling Final. Issue 31/89, 5 November 1931.

1931's Largest New Ship Takes the Water. Issue 31/92, 16 November 1931.

Luxury Liner Gutted. Issue 31/94, 23 November 1931.

A Revolution of Transport. Issue 31/98, 17 December 1931.

Spain Defeat Irish Free State. Issue 31/98, 17 December 1931.

Springboks Defeat Ireland. Issue 31/102, 21 December 1931.

Springboks Unbeatable. Issue 31/103, 24 December 1931.

Temperature – No Object! Issue 31/105, 31 December 1931.

Ladies Hockey Test. Issue 1885, 14 January 1932.

Horse Jumping Competitions at Dundrum. Issue 1886, 18 January 1932.

Blues v. Whites. Issue 1887, 21 January 1932.

Irish Boxers. Issue 1888, 25 January 1932.

Pike Fishing Contest at the Dublin Zoo; *Hockey – Eek!*; *A Drawn Game – Munster v. Ulster.* All in Issue 1889, 28 January 1932.

By Narrowest of Margins. Issue 1895, 18 February 1932.

Patland Cup Motor Cycle Reliability Trial. Issue 1897, 25 February 1932.

Ward Union Hunt. Issue 1899, 3 March 1932.

Dublin Bullshow. Issue 32/19, 7 March 1932.
Fiánna Fail Personalities in the New Dáil; *Cross Country Race for the National Senior Championship*. Both in Issue 32/20, 10 March 1932.
Big Dublin Fire. Issue 32/21, 14 March 1932.
The Wheel of Fortune. Issue 32/22, 17 March 1932.
Hockey. Issue 32/23, 23 March 1932.
Easter Week in Dublin; *Fairyhouse Races*. Both in Issue 32/26, 31 March 1932.
Binnie Pulls Through. Issue 32/30, 14 April 1932.
Irish Cup Final; *Dublin Car Rally*. Issue 32/30, 21 April 1932.
Punchestown Races. Issue 32/33, 25 April 1932.
Wedding of Earl of Dumfries and Lady Eileen Forbes. 28 April 1932. No issue number given on NoS or www.britishpathe.com.
President De Valera. Issue 32/36, 6 May 1932.
Dublin Spring Show. Issue 32/37, 9 May 1932.
Leinster '200'. Issue 32/38, 12 May 1932.
Irish and Agricultural Fair at Cork. Issue 32/39, 16 May 1932.
All–Ireland Schools Championships; *Irish Native Dogs Annual Show*; *Youthful Dancers at Dun Laughaire* [sic]. All in Issue 32/40, 19 May 1932.
Davis Cup Tennis. Issue 32/41, 23 May 1932.
Irish Sweepstake. Issue 32/43, 30 May 1932.
Dublin Sweepstake Section. Issue 32/44. 2 June 1932.
Mr De Valera. Issue 32/47, 13 June 1932.
Tailteann Preparations. Issue 32/48, 14 June 1932.
The Papal Legate's Great Welcome! Issue 32/50, 23 June 1932.
Congress Mass Meeting. Issue 32/51, 27 June 1932.
A Million People Kneel in Worship. Issue 32/52, 30 June 1932.
Erin Bids Goodbye to Cardinal Legate; *Ireland Defeats America in International Hurling Match*. Both in Issue 32/57, 7 July 1932.
International Diving Championships. Issue 32/58, 11 July 1932.
Irish Tennis Finals at Fitzwilliam. Issue 32/59, 14 July 1932.
Tailteann Football Championships. 18 July 1932. No issue number given on NoS or www.britishpathe.com.
Metropolitan Regatta. Issue 32/60, 29 July 1932.
Dublin Horse Show. Issue 32/62, 4 August 1932.
Royal Dublin Society's Show at Ballsbridge. Issue 32/63, 8 August 1932.
Fiercest Road Race in History! Issue 32/68, 25 August 1932.
New Cadets for Free State. Issue 32/72, 8 September 1932.
Cheers – All the Way! Issue 32/93, 21 November 1932.
M Doral Buckley. Issue 32/96, 1 December 1932.
Boys Rugby Test. Issue 32/97, 5 December 1932.
Ladies Hockey Trial at Kimmage. 15 December 1932. No issue number given on NoS or www.britishpathe.com.
Ulster v. Leinster Rugby Clash. Issue 32/102, 22 December 1932.
Xmas Day Swim. Issue 33/1, 2 January 1933.
Two Leinster Trial Matches. Issue 33/3, 9 January 1933.
Election – It Is at Fever Heat in Ireland. Issue 33/6, 19 January 1933.
Cosgrave or De Valera? Issue 32/8, 25 January 1933.
Irish Election Result. Issue 33/9, 30 January 1933.
Irish Rugby. Issue 33/10, 2 February 1933.
The Scene of the Derailed Passenger Train Near Dundalk. Issue 33/11, 6 February 1933.

This is incorrectly titled *The Scene of the Derailed Passenger Train near Dunkirk* on NoS.

Opening of the Dáil; *The Triumph of the 'Rose'*. Both in Issue 33/13, 13 February 1933.

National Ploughing Championships. Issue 33/15, 20 February 1933.

Baldoyle Races. Issue 33/16, 23 February 1933.

Blizzard Aftermath. Issue 33/18, 2 March 1933.

Irish Pedigree Show. Issue 33/21, 13 March 1933.

Bravo Ireland! Issue 33/22, 16 March 1933.

St Patrick's Day Celebrations. Issue 33/23, 20 March 1933.

Champions All! Issue 33/24, 23 March 1933.

The International; *Mannequins Wear Irish*. Both in Issue 33/26, 30 March 1933.

The Last Rugger International. 6 April 1933. No issue number given on NoS or www.britishpathe.com.

Fairyhouse Races. Issue 33/32, 20 April 1933.

Shure – It Was a Lovely Wedding. Issue 33/33, 24 April 1933.

Peerless Punchestown. Issue 33/34, 27 April 1933.

Dublin Spring Show. Issue 33/37, 8 May 1933.

Leinster '200'. Issue 33/38, 11 May 1933.

Davis Cup Tie. Issue 33/41, 22 May 1933.

Davis Cup Tennis. Issue 33/42, 25 May 1933.

The Drum of Fortune. Issue 33/44, 1 June 1933.

Ladies Golf. Issue 33/45, 5 June 1933.

World Economic Conference. Issue 33/50, 22 June 1933.

Irish Championships. Issue 33/52, 29 June 1933.

In Full Civic State. Issue 33/58, 20 July 1933.

Mr De Valera and the Minister of Defence. Issue 33/65, 14 August 1933.

Fiercest Road Race in History. Issue 33/67, 21 August 1933.

Roosevelt. Issue 33/68, 24 August 1933.

Speed 'Gladiators' Most Thrilling Duel. Issue 33/71, 4 September 1933.

Irish Army in the Field. Issue 33/75, 18 September 1933.

All Ireland Football Final; *President De Valera*. Both in Issue 33/78, 28 September 1933.

One Goal Each. Issue 33/80, 5 October 1933.

Soliman's Feast. 9 October 1933. No issue number given on NoS or www.british pathe.com.

A Steed of Fortune. Issue 33/85, 23 October 1933.

Cycle Road Race. Issue 33/94, 23 November 1933.

Hunting in Wicklow. Issue 33/95, 27 November 1933.

13 Points All. Issue 33/98, 7 December 1933.

Irish Army Jumpers. 28 December 1933. No issue number given on NoS or www.britishpathe.com.

Xmas Day Swim; *Faultless*. Both in Issue 34/1, 1 January 1934.

Lord Mayor. Issue 34/2, 4 January 1934.

13 Points to 3. Issue 34/13, 12 February 1934.

Thrills Galore. Issue 34/16, 22 February 1934.

Honours Even! Issue 34/18, 1 March 1934.

The Wheel of Fortune; *St Patrick's Day Parade*. Both in Issue 34/24, 22 March 1934.

Back to Tennessee. Issue 34/31, 16 April 1934.

Punchestown Races. Issue 34/32, 19 April 1934.

Novel and Useful Contest. Issue 34/34, 26 April 1934.

Dublin Spring Agricultural Show. Issue 34/37, 7 May 1934.

The Leinster 200. Issue 34/38, 10 May 1934.

Rugby Match. Issue 34/40, 17 May 1934.

Round the Houses. Issue 34/42, 24 May 1934.

Draw for the Irish Sweep. Issue 34/46, 7 June 1934.

Dublin Horse Show; Camogie International. Issue 34/64, 9 August 1934.

Parade of Hunters. Issue 34/65, 13 August 1934.

Dublin Horse Show. Issue 34/66, 16 August 1934.

A Test of Stamina. Issue 34/71, 2 September 1934.

To Fight Again. Issue 34/72, 5 September 1934.

Baby Byrne. Issue 34/75, 17 September 1934.

Speed in Phoenix Park. Issue 34/76, 20 September 1934.

Football Final in Dublin. Issue 34/78, 27 September 1934.

The Flying Fortune. Issue 34/86, 25 October 1934.

Fortune's Fairies. Issue 34/87, 29 October 1934.

Rugby International. Issue 35/12, 12 February 1934.

International Rugby. Issue 35/16, 25 February 1934.

Rugby International in Belfast. Issue 35/20, 11 March 1935.

St Patrick's Day in Dublin; Presentation of Shamrock to the Irish Guards at Wellington Barracks. Issue 35/23, 21 March 1935.

The Fortune Procession. Issue 35/24, 25 March 1935.

Irish Sweep Draw. Issue 35/25, 28 March 1935.

Easter Week Demonstrations. Issue 35/33, 25 April 1935.

Sweep Palace Gutted. Issue 35/34, 29 April 1935.

Punchestown Races. Issue 35/35, 2 May 1935.

Punchestown Races. Issue 35/36, 6 May 1935.

The Leinster '200'. Issue 35/37, 9 May 1935.

Sweepstake Mixing and Drawing. 3 June 1935. No issue number given on NoS or www.britishpathe.com.

Pilgrimage to Dundalk. 11 July 1935. No issue number given on NoS or www.britishpathe.com.

Picking the Winners. Issue PT286, 8 August 1935.

Dublin Horse Show. Issue 35/64, 12 August 1935.

Liners After Collision in Irish Sea; All Ireland Football Semi–Final. Both in Issue 35/67, 21 August 1935.

Ulster Grand Prix. Issue 35/69, 28 August 1935.

Kilkenny v. Limerick. 5 September 1935. No issue number given on NoS or www.britishpathe.com.

RAC International Race. Issue 35/72, 9 September 1935.

St Patrick's Country; Cavan Defeat Kildare. Both in Issue 912, 26 September 1935.

Irish Military Tattoo. Issue 35/78, 30 September 1935.

Ulster in Mourning; Dublin Goes Oriental. Both in Issue 35/86, 28 October 1935.

Cambridgeshire Sweep Draw. Issue 35/87, 31 October 1935.

Ireland v. All Blacks at Dublin. Issue 35/98, 9 December 1935.

New Australian Liner Launched at Belfast. 16 December 1935. No issue number given on NoS or www.britishpathe.com.

Bohemians Defeat Waterford. 16 January 1935. No issue number given on NoS or www.britishpathe.com.

Ireland v. England. Issue 36/12, 10 February 1936.

Wales v. Ireland Rugby. Issue 36/22, 16 March 1923.

All Irish Edition. Issue 36/23, 19 March 1936.

Mr Alfred Byrne – Lord Mayor of Dublin; Irish Kennel Club Show. Both in Issue 36/24,

23 March 1936.

Mixing Counterfoils and Bran. Issue 36/26, 26 March 1936.

Irish Aviation Day in Dublin. Issue 36/38, 14 May 1936.

Cork Motor Race over Carrigrohena Circuit; Ireland Beat Sweden. Issue 36/41, 21 May 1936.

Derby Sweepstake – Mixing the Counterfoils. Issue 36/42, 25 May 1936.

Ireland v. Switzerland – Davis Cup Tie. Issue 36/46, 8 June 1936.

Galway Dog Show. Issue 36/54, 15 July 1936.

Irishman Plans Atlantic Hop. Issue 36/55, 16 July 1936.

O'Mahoney's Homecoming at Cove and Ballydehob. Issue 36/61, 30 July 1936.

Galway Races. 3 August 1936. No issue number given on NoS or www.britishpathe.com.

Dublin Horse Show; Limerick Grand Prix. Both in Issue 36/63, 6 August 1936.

Police Sports in Dublin. Issue 36/69, 27 August 1936.

Tourist Trophy Race. Issue 36/72, 7 September 1936.

Hurling Final in Dublin. 10 September 1936. No issue number given on NoS or www.britishpathe.com.

Pretty Dublin Wedding. Issue 36/74, 14 September 1936.

Lord Mayor of Dublin Inaugurates New Air Service. Issue 36/75, 17 September 1936.

All Ireland Football Final. Issue 36.79, 1 October 1936.

Dublin's Firemen's Funeral; Dublin – Drogheda Cycling Race. Both in Issue 36/83, 15 October 1936.

Pretty Wedding at Glasthule. Issue 26/84, 18 October 1936.

Ireland Defeat Germany at Dalymour Park. Issue 36/85, 22 October 1936.

Sweepstake Draw at Mansion House. Issue 36/86, 26 October 1936.

Irish Hockey Girls Lose to US. 19 November 1936. No issue number given on NoS or www.britishpathe.com.

Ireland v. Hungary Football International. Issue 36/99, 10 December 1936.

St. James's Gate v. Sligo Rovers. Issue 37/12, 11 February 1937.

International Rugby, 37/13, 15 February 1937.

South County Dublin Harriers. 22 February 1937. No issue number given on NoS or www.britishpathe.com.

International Rugby – Ireland v. Scotland. 1 March 1937. No issue number given on NoS or www.britishpathe.com.

Galway Market; Bob and Alf Pearson. Both in Issue NSP 50, 11 March 1937.

Ireland v. Germany Ladies Hockey. 15 March 1937. No issue number given on NoS or www.britishpathe.com.

Mixing Counterfoils. Issue 37/42, 15 March 1937.

Sweepstake Draw. Issue 37/43, 18 March 1937.

St Patrick's Day Parade in Dublin; Irish Kennel Club Dog Show. Both in Issue 37/44, 22 March 1937.

Punchestown Races. 3 May 1937. No issue number given on NoS or www.britishpathe.com.

Irish Spring Show at Ballsbridge. 10 May 1937. No issue number given on NoS or www. britishpathe.com.

Physical Training Display in Ireland. Issue 37/38, 13 May 1937.

Irish Sweepstake Pageantry; Cork Motor Race. Both in Issue 37/44.

Irish Press Outing at Bundoran. Issue 37/37. Dated 18 June 1937 on NoS and 10 May 1937 on www.britishpathe.com.

Irish Troops Return from Spain; School Sports at Croke Park. 24 June 1937. No issue number given on NoS or www.britishpathe.com.

President Valera's Final Election Meeting in Dublin. 5 July 1937. No issue number given on NoS or www.britishpathe.com.

Service on Patrol. 22 July 1937. No issue number given on NoS or www.britishpathe.com.

Their Majesties in Ireland. Issue 37/60, 29 July 1937.

Galway Races; Royal Dublin Horse Show. Both in Issue 37/63, 9 August 1937.

Guard Sports in Dublin. Issue 37/64, 12 August 1937.

Pretty Dublin Wedding. 16 August 1937. No issue number given on NoS or www.britishpathe.com.

Irish Hurling Final at Killarney. Issue 37/72, 9 September 1937.

All Ireland Football Final. Issue 37/78, 30 September 1937.

New Bishop of Kilmore Consecrated. Issue 37/80, 7 October 1937.

All Ireland Football Final Replay; Cesarewitch Sweepstake – Mixing Counterfoils. Both in Issue 37/84, 21 October 1937.

Sweepstake Draw. Issue 37/85, 25 October 1937.

Irish Fusiliers' New Colours. Issue 37/88, 4 November 1937.

Irish Sweepstake Winners in US. Issue 37/89, 8 August 1937.

Ireland v. Norway. Issue 37/90, 11 November 1937.

Robert Ashley. Issue NSP 94, 13 January 1938.

President De Valera Arrives at Holyhead. 17 January 1938. No issue number given on NoS or www.britishpathe.com.

The Irish Question – Mr De Valera Visits Downing Street. Issue 38/6, 20 January 1938.

Ireland v. England Rugby International. Issue 38/14, 14 February 1938.

De Valera Revisits London; Irish Hockey Match. Both in Issue 38/15.

Ireland v. Scotland Rugby. Issue 38/18, 3 March 1938.

St Patrick's Day in London; Mrs Chamberlain Opens New Airport at Belfast and Launches HMS 'Belfast'; St Patrick's Day Parade. All in Issue 38/23, 21 March 1938.

Dublin's New President; Motor Racing Thrills at Cork. Both in Issue 38/34, 28 April 1938.

Punchestown Races. Issue 38/35, 2 May 1938.

New President of Éire; Royal Dublin Spring Show. Both in Issue 38/38, 9 May 1938.

Ireland v. Italy Davis Cup Tie. Issue 39/38, 12 May 1938.

The Derby – Sweep Procession in Ireland. Issue 38/52, 25 May 1938.

De Valera Received Seal of Office. Issue 38/53, 4 July 1938.

Solo Atlantic Flight. Issue 38/58, 21 July 1938.

Dublin Horse Show. Issue 38/64, 11 August 1938.

Blessing Missionaries. Issue 38/76, 22 September 1938.

Jacky Saunders Training. Issue 38/76, 22 September 1938.

All Ireland Football. Issue 38/78, 29 September 1938.

All Ireland Gaelic Football Final. Issue 38/86, 27 October 1938.

Survivors of the 1916 Rising. Issue 38/86, 27 October 1938.

Bicycle Polo at Dublin. Issue 38/98, 8 December 1938.

Irish Society Wedding. Issue 38/100, 15 December 1938.

Post Early. Issue 38/101, 19 December 1938.

Turkeys, Trees, Toys. Issue 38/102, 22 December 1938.

St Patrick's Day; Grand National Sweep; President Installed; Dublin Show; Éire Takes Over. All in Issue 38/104, 29 December 1938.

Bomb Outrages. Issue 39/6, 19 January 1939.

Actors Play at Donnybrooke. Issue 39/9, 30 January 1939.

More Bomb Outrages. Issue 39/11, 6 February 1939.
Rugby International at Twickenham – Ireland 5 v. England 0. Issue 39/13, 6 February 1939.
Service to the Pope. Issue 39/15, 20 February 1939.
Rugby International. Issue 39/17, 27 February 1939.
Ladies Hockey in Dublin. Issue 39/20, 9 March 1939.
Ireland v. Wales – Rugby International. Issue 39/20, 16 March 1939.
St Patrick's Day Parade in Dublin. Issue 39/23, 20 March 1939.
Irish Kennel Club Show. Issue 39/24, 23 March 1939.
Dr Hyde Plants Tree of Commemoration; Dublin v. Belfast Ladies Lacrosse; St Patrick's Day in New York. All in Issue 39/26. 30 March 1939.
Irish Sweep Winners Toast 'Lady Luck'. Issue 39/28, 6 April 1939.
President Hyde Gives Children's Display. Issue 39/29, 11 April 1939.
All–Ireland Ballroom Dancing Championships. Issue 39/32, 20 April 1939.
Punchestown Races at Dublin. Issue 39/35, 1 May 1939.
Model Plane Enthusiasts Meet in Dublin. Issue 39/43, 28 May 1939.
Irish Bomb Outrage. Issue 39/52, 26 June 1939.
Old Crocks Run. Issue 39/52, 29 June 1939.
Dublin's New Lord Mayor. Issue 39/53, 3 July 1939.
Universities' Sports in Dublin. Issue 39/54, 6 July 1939.
Dublin's New Airport Under Construction. Issue 39/55, 10 July 1939.
Irish Volunteers Commissioned. Issue 39/57, 17 July 1939.
Glorious Goodwood. Issue 39/60, 27 July 1939.
Air Display at Belfast. Issue 39/62, 3 August 1939.
Ulster Motorcycle Grand Prix. Issue 39/68, 24 August 1939.
War! Issue 39/71, 11 September 1939.
Farr v. Abrew Fight in Dublin. Issue 39/90, 16 November 1939.
International Rugby at Richmond. Issue 39/100
Gaelic Football Championship. 18 September 1939. No issue number available on NoS.
Ireland's Largest Bullock on Show. Issue 40/1, 1 January 1940.
Irish Cabbies Meet in Phoenix Park, Dublin. Issue 40/4, 11 January 1940.
Dig For Victory. Issue 40/7, 22 January 1940.
Fancy Dress Hockey at Kimmage, Dublin. Issue 40/7, 22 January 1940.
Red Cross Steeplechase at Leopardstown. Issue 40/10, 1 February 1940.
Over There News Flashes From France. Issue 40/14, 15 February 1940.
Boxing in Dublin. Issue 40/22, 13 March 1940.
St Patrick's Day. Issue 40/24, 21 March 1940.
Irish Kennel Club Show. Issue 40/25, 25 March 1940.
Irish Trade Mission for London; International Football in Dublin. Both in Issue 40/37, 6 May 1940.
Timber Fire in Dublin. Issue 40/38, 9 May 1940.
SS President Roosevelt Sails for USA; Putting Green Opened. Both in Issue 40/46, 6 June 1940.
All for Defence. Issue 40/50, 20 June 1940.
Outposts of Peace – Irish Army Manoeuvres. Issue 40/54, 4 July 1940.
Éire Menaced by Germany. Issue 40/55, 8 July 1940.
Mining the Coasts of Éire. Issue 40/58, 18 July 1940.
Testing Defences Mines. Issue 40/61, 29 July 1940.
Galway Races. Issue 40/64, 8 August 1940.
Limerick Horse Show. Issue 40/73, 9 September 1940.

Irish Cesarewitch. Issue 40/91, 11 November 1940.
Ulster's New Prime Minister. Issue 40/100, 12 December 1940.
Éire Bombed. Issue 41/4, 13 January 1941.
Dublin Parade. Issue 41/34, 28 April 1941.
Germans Bomb Dublin. Issue 41/46, 9 June 1941.
Corpus Christi Parade in Bandon, Éire. Issue 41/52, 30 June 1941.
Irish Red Cross. Issue 41/55, 10 July 1941.
Fencing in Ireland; Hurling Final. Issue 41/82, 13 October 1941.
Realism in Training. Issue 41/86, 27 October 1941.
On Their Toes in Northern Ireland. Issue 41/88, 3 November 1941.
Good News for Farmers. Issue 41/91, 13 November 1941.
Rugby in Ireland. Issue 41/97, 4 December 1941.
Mr De Valera in Limerick. Issue 41/100, 15 December 1941.
American Troops in Northern Ireland. Issue 42/9, 29 January 1942.
Atlantic Crossings Make History. Issue 42/10, 2 January 1942.
Americans in Northern Ireland. Issue 42/14, 16 January 1942.
Mr Winant at US Camps in Ireland. Issue 42/18, 2 March 1942.
Film Conference. Issue 42/20, 9 March 1942.
The Passing of Barney Mellows. Issue 42/23, 19 March 1942.
Coming Over – American Expeditionary Force; International Cross Country. Both in
   Issue 42/24, 23 March 1942.
Invasion Tactics by US Troops. Issue 42/28, 6 April 1942.
Letters from Home. Issue 42/30, 13 April 1942.
Springtime at the Zoo; LDF (Local Defence Force) Parades. Both in Issue 42/32, 20
   April 1942.
General Marshall Reviews US Troops. Issue 42/34, 27 April 1942.
Dundalk's First Cup; Baby Boxers. Both in Issue 42/38, 11 May 1942.
Dough for Doughboys. Issue 42/41, 21 May 1942.
Newsbriefs. Issue 42/44, 1 June 1942.
Their Majesties in Northern Ireland. Issue 42/53, 2 July 1942.
Episcopal Jubilee Mass. Issue 42/56, 13 July 1942.
Newsbriefs. Issue 42/59, 23 July 1942.
Transporting Wounded. Issue 43/63, 6 August 1942.
Swimming at Blackrock. Issue 42/65, 13 August 1942.
Cork Memorial. NSP Issue 333, 17 August 1942.
Tennis Champions Love Match. Issue 42/77, 24 September 1942.
Defence Minister at LDF Parade. Issue 42/89, 5 November 1942.
Entertainment Workers Entertained. Issue 42/98, 7 December 1942.
News from the Éire Border. Issue 44/25, 27 March 1944.
Newsbriefs. Issue 45/43, 28 May 1945.
Royal Visit to Ulster. Issue 45/60, 26 July 1945.
Spotlight on Sport. Issue 45/101, 17 December 1945.
Princess Elizabeth Launches Mightiest Carrier. Issue 46/24.
Food: Éire May Help. Issue 46/61, 1 August 1946.
Bira Wins Ulster TT. Issue 46/65
Scotland Nil – Ireland Nil. Issue 46/96, 2 December 1946.
No Title. Princess Margaret in Belfast. Issue 47/84, 20 October 1947.
No Title. Ulster celebrities attend Belfast matinee. Issue 48/26. 23 March 1948.
Scotland's Keen Tussle with Ireland. Issue 48/94, 22 November 1948.
Blarney Stone. Issue 230, 7 February 1949.

Irish Story. NSP Issue 233, 28 February 1949.
A New Export – Houses! Issue 49/31, 18 April 1949.
Éire Leaves the Empire. Issue 49/33, 25 April 1949.
Belfast Golfer Wins Amateur Crown. Issue 49/44.
Pilgrims Flock to Ireland's Holy Mountain. Issue 49/63, 8 August 1949.
Ireland Wins Horse Show. Issue 49/64, 11 August 1949.
Irish Pilgrims Fly to Lourdes. Issue 49/67, 22 August 1949.
Gaelic Football. Issue 49/69, 29 August 1949.
England – Lacking Lawton and Matthews – Upset by Éire. Issue 49/77, 26 September
    1949.
Goals Rain at Manchester. Issue 49/93, 21 November 1949.
Belfast Cheers Princess and Duke. Issue 49/44, 2 June 1949.

Topical Budget

Derry Election Day. Issue 75–2, 1 February 1913.
St Patrick's Day Celebration, Issue 82–1, 19 March 1913.
National Cross Country. Issue 83–2, 29 March 1913.
Orange Day. Issue 151–1, 15 July 1914.
Sir Edward Carson in Belfast. Issue 151–2, 18 July 1914.
Dublin Civic Exhibition. Issue 151–2, 18 July 1914.
Ireland's New Viceroy. Issue 190–2, 17 April 1915.
Ireland Welcomes O'Leary VC. Issue 202–2, 10 July 1915.
Viceroy at Limerick. Issue 208–2, 21 August 1915.
Vice–Regal Procession. Issue 208–2, 21 August 1915.
Nationalists in Khaki. Issue 215–1, 6 October 1915.
St Patrick's Day. Issue 238–2, 18 March 1916.
St Patrick's Day. Issue 239–1, 21 March 1916.
Irish Soldiers at Mass. Issue 239–1, 22 March 1916.
The Dublin Rebellion. Issue 245–2, 6 May 1916.
Irish Viceroy Resigns. Issue 246–2, 13 May 1916.
German Rifles; *Trial of Casement*; *Mr Asquith in Dublin, Irish Volunteers*. All in Issue
    247–1, 17 May 1916.
Sinn Féin Rebels. Issue 247–2, 20 May 1916.
The Battle of the Somme, 11 August 1916.
Hospital Ship 'Britannic', the Largest British Liner, Sunk by the Germans. Issue 274–2,
    15 November 1916.
St Patrick's Day. Issue 291–1, 21 March 1917.
With the North and South Irish at the Front, 1915–1917.
Shamrock Day. Issue 343–1, 20 March 1918.
Ireland and the War. Issue 350–1, 8 May 1918.
Lord French in Ireland. Issue 351–2, 20 May 1918.
Firm Hand in Ireland. Issue 352–1, 23 May 1918.
Recruiting in Ireland. Issue 358—2, 8 July 1918.
Sinn Féin to Be Suppressed. Issue 359–1, 11 July 1918.
War Time Orange Festival. Issue 360–1, 18 July 1918.
Lord French and Irish Boys. Issue 361–2, 29 July 1918.
Ruthless Sea Hun Victims. Issue 362–1, 1 August 1918.
Irish Mail Boat Leinster Torpedoed by the Huns; *Royal Irish Mail Steamer Leinster
    Torpedoed by German Submarine*. Both in Issue 373–1, 17 October 1918.
Loyal Irish Celebrate Great Victory. Issue 377–2, 18 November 1918.

Sinn Féin Parliament. Issue 387–2, 27 January 1919
The Mystery of de Valera. Issue 389–2, 10 February 1919.
Sport in Ireland. Issue 391–1, 20 February 1919.
New Chief Secretary for Ireland. Issue 393–2, 10 March 1919.
In Memory of John Redmond. Issue 395–2, 24 March 1919.
Canadians in Ireland. Issue 396–1, 27 March 1919.
Re–Enter de Valera. Issue 397–1, 3 April 1919.
Irish Point–To–Point Races. Issue 399–2, 21 April 1919.
Triumphant Atlantic Airmen. Issue 408–1, 19 June 1919.
Ulster Celebrates Peace. Issue 416–1, 14 August 1919
Wonderful Irish Hunters. Issue 418–1, 28 August 1919.
Ladies Water Polo. Issue 419–1, 4 September 1919.
The Sweet Little Shamrock. Issue 447–1, 18 March 1920.
Irish but not Sinn Féin. Issue 447–2, 22 March 1920.
Dublin's Barbed–Wire Easter. Issue 450–1, 8 April 1920.
First Canadian to Become Secretary for Ireland; *Scenes at an Irish Murder Trial.* Both in
  Issue 453–1, 29 April 1920.
Dublin's Society Show. Issue 455–2, 17 May 1920.
Sir E. Carson. Issue 464–1, 15 July 1920.
Sinn Féin Trafalgar Square. Issue 469–1, 19 August 1920.
Faith Healing in Ireland. Issue 470–2, 30 August 1920.
Belfast Riots. Issue 471–2, 6 September 1920.
Ireland Bradbriggan [sic]. Issue 474–2, 27 September 1920.
Macsweeney. Issue 479–1, 28 October 1920.
Funeral Procession L. Mayor of Cork. Issue 479–2, 1 November 1920.
Lord Mayor's Funeral Cork. Issue 480–1, 4 November 1920.
Ireland. Issue 482–1, 18 November 1920.
Dublin Murders. Issue 483–1, 25 November 1920.
Sinn Féin Gunmen's Victims' Funeral. Issue 483–2, 29 November 1920.
Ditto. Issue 483–2, 29 November 1920.
Liverpool Sinn Féin Outrages/London Guarding Parliament. Issue 484–1, 2 December 1920.
Ireland's Agony. Issue 486–1, 16 December 1920.
Rounding Up the Rebels. Issue 486–2, 20 December 1920.
Mrs Macswiney. Issue 488–1, 30 December 1920.
Cup Final 1921. Issue 504–2, 25 April 1921.
Ulster's Parliament Assembles. Issue 511–1, 9 June 1921.
King at Belfast. Issue 513–1, 23 June 1921.
Is it the Dawn? Issue 515–2, 11 July 1921.
I Want Peace; *Ulster Will Not Yield.* Both in Issue 516–1, 14 July 1921.
Getting Acquainted. Issue 516–2, 18 July 1921.
Dublin Horse Show. Issue 520–1, 11 August 1921.
Ireland's Fate decided in the Highlands. Issue 524–1, 8 September 1921.
Is it Peace? Issue 529–1, 13 October 1921.
Government's Answer to de Valera. Issue 529–2, 17 October 1921.
Rebel Flags on Nelson's Column. Issue 819, 27 October 1921
Will there be peace in Ireland? Issue 533, 10 November 1921.
Historic Unionist Conference in Liverpool. Issue 534–1, 17 November 1921.
Forgive and Forget; *Irish Free State*; *Peace Council at the Palace.* All in Issue 537–1, 8
  December 1921.
Irish Peace Imperilled by Extremists. Issue 537–2, 12 December 1921.

Further Pictures of Irish Peace. Issue 538, 15 December 1921.
Irish Bishops Meet. Issue 538, 15 December 1921.
Sinn Féin Members meet at Dublin Parliament House. Issue 538–2, 19 December 1921.
Ulster Day the Twelfth. Topical Budget, 1921. This appears on the Digital Film Archive.
    There is an item of the same name in Issue 568–2, dated 17 July 1922.
Ireland. Issue 541–2, 19 December 1921.
The 'Surrender' of Dublin Castle. Issue 543–1, 19 January 1922.
British Evacuate Ireland after Hundreds of Years of Occupation. Issue 543–2, 23 January
    1922.
The Great Trek. Issue 544–1, 26 January 1922.
Hunting in Full Swing in Irish Free State. Issue 544–2, 30 January 1922.
Peace in Ireland Means 'Business as Usual' at Aldershot. Issue 545–1, 2 February 1922.
Loyal Southern Irish Regiments. 12 June 1922. No corresponding entry on NoS.
The Shamrock of Ireland. Issue 551–2, 20 March 1922.
New York Americans. Issue 554–1, 6 April, 1922.
Ulster's Gallant Woman Admiral. Issue 563–2, 12 June 1922.
The Battle of Belleek; Ireland Refugees. Issue 564–1, 15 June 1922.
Irish Free State to Maintain the Constitution; De Valera. Both in Issue 564–2, 19 June 1922.
Civil War in Ireland. Issue 566–2, 3 July 1922.
Hemming in the Rebels. Issue 567–1, 6 July 1922.
Dublin's Civil War; Ireland. Both in Issue 567–2, 10 July 1922.
Fall of Limerick. Issue 570–1, 29 July 1922.
Irish National Army Sweeping On. Issue 571–1, 3 August 1922.
Passing of Mr Arthur Griffith; Fall of Cork. Both in Issue, 573–1, 17 August 1922.
Irish Linen in the Making; Griffith Funeral. Both in Issue 573–2, 21 August 1922.
Michael Collins. Issue 574–1, 24 August 1922.
Michael Collins. Issue 574–2, 28 August 1922.
Let the Dublin Guards Bury Me! Issue 575–1, 31 August 1922.
The New Government. Issue 584–1, 2 November 1922.
Rebirth of a Nation. Issue 589–2, 11 December 1922.
British Evacuate Ireland. Issue 543–2, 23 January 1923.
State Entry into Belfast. Issue 601–1, 1 March 1923.
Fleet Visits Belfast. Issue 613–2, 28 May 1923.
Free State or Republic? Issue 627–1, 30 August 1923.
Wales V. Ireland International. Issue 655–1, 13 March 1924.
St Patrick's Day. Issue 656–1, 20 March 1924.
Duke & Duchess of York in Ulster. Issue 674–1, 24 July 1924.
Duke and Duchess of York. Issue 674–2, 28 July 1924.
Irish Boundary Problem. Issue 674–2, 28 July 1924.
Scotland v. Ireland. Issue 688–1, 30 October 1924.
Tournadic Titans. Issue 704–1, 19 February 1925.
Ladies Hockey International Match. Issue 705–2, 2 March 1925.
Shamrock Day. Issue 708–1, 19 March 1925.
Scotland V. Ireland. Issue 757–2, 1 March 1926.
Brown and Ireland. Issue 785–1, 9 September 1926.
International Rugby. Issue 802–1, 6 January 1927.
The Rose & the Shamrock. Issue 807–2, 14 February 1927.
Ladies Hockey International: Scotland v. Ireland. Issue 808–2, 21 February 1927.
The Wearing O' the Green. Issue 812–2, 21 March 1927.
In Training. Issue 838–1, 15 September 1927.

England Swamped. Issue 844–1, 27 October 1927.
Shamrock for the Irish Guards. Issue 864–2, 19 March 1928.
Belfast. British Wine in Race of Thrills! Issue 887–1, 23 August 1928.
Everton. Victory Against Odds. Issue 896–1, 25 October 1928.
A Twickenham Bogey Laid. Issue 911–2, 11 February 1929.
A Double International. Issue 95–2, 7 October 1929.
United Kingdom at Play. Issue 972–2, 14 April 1930.
A Complete Italian Triumph. Issue 991–2, 25 August 1930.

Universal

England, Scotland, Ireland Athletic Contest. Issue 2, 17 July 1930.
Holland Acclaims Evert Van Dyl who Accompanied Wing–Commander Kingsford Smith on Ireland to America Flight in Southern Cross. Issue 9, 11 August 1930.
International TT Belfast. Issue 14, 28 August 1930.
Miss England Does it. Issue 57, 26 January 1931.
International Grand Prix. Issue 96, 11 June 1931.
Ulster TT Race. Issue 118, 27 August 1931.
The Big Sweep. Issue 176, 17 March 1932.
The Mixture (as Before); Angling International. Both in Issue 197, 30 May 1932.
The Big Sweep. Issue 198, 2 June 1932.
Army Athletics. Issue 199, 6 June 1932.
Eucharistic Congress. Issue 206, 30 June 1932.
1,200 Scotsmen Home from America. Issue 212, 21 July 1932.
Tourist Trophy Race. Issue 222, 25 August 1932.
Prince of Wales in Ulster. Issue 247, 21 November 1932.
Italian Air Armada. Issue 312, 6 July 1933.
The Big Mix–Up. Issue 343, 23 October 1933.
International Rugby. Issue 384, 15 March 1934.
Irish Sweepstakes Draw. Issue 386, 21 March 1934.
Duke of Gloucester in Belfast; Sweepstake Counterfoils. Both in Issue 407, 4 June 1934.
Ulster TT Race. Issue 433, 3 September 1934.
The Irish 'Sweep'. Issue 448 and Issue 554, 25 October 1934.
Trooping of the French Drums. Issue 450, 1 November 1934.
Rugby at Twickenham. Issue 479, 11 February 1925.
International Water Polo. Issue 534, 18 July 1935.
No Title. Belfast. Issue 525, 22 July 1935.
Girl Guides of All Nations at Camp in Ireland. Issue 526, 25 July 1935.
Tourist Trophy. Issue 539, 9 September 1935.
Lord Carson. Issue 553, 28 October 1935.
Arroyo Dos Molinos. Issue 554, 31 October 1935.
Rugby Championship. Issue 593, 16 March 1936.
Motor Racing in Ireland. Issue 612, 21 May 1936.
Ulster Grand Prix. Issue 639, 24 August 1936.
Ulster TT Race. Issue 643, 7 September 1936.
England v. Ireland. Issue 689, 15 February 1937.
No Title. Crowning of Irish Linen Queen. Issue 723, 14 June 1937.
Their Majesties in Ireland. Issue 736, 29 July 1937.
No Title. Ulster Grand Prix. Issue 743, 28 August 1937.
Belfast Launches Biggest Liner Since Queen Mary. Issue 753, 27 September 1937.
New French Government and Arrival of Mr De Valera. Issue 785, 17 January 1938.

Rugby! Issue 801, 14 March 1938.
Royal Constabulary Sports at Belfast. Issue 825, 6 June 1938.
Belfast Launch 'Durban Castle'. Issue 828, 16 June 1938.
American Flyer Crosses Atlantic. Issue 838, 21 July 1938.
Ulster TT Race. Issue 847, 22 August 1938.
Rugby. Issue 897, 13 February 1939.
No Title. Launch of SS *Andes.* Issue 904, 9 March 1939.
RAF Display at Belfast. Issue 946, 3 March 1939.
Ulster Grand Prix. Issue 952, 24 August 1939.
With Our Troops in Northern Ireland. Issue 1177, 27 October 1941.
With Our Army in Ulster. Issue 1179, 3 November 1941.
American Expeditionary Force Lands in Northern Ireland. Issue 1204, 29 January 1942.
Americans Settling Down in Ireland. Issue 1209, 29 January 1942.
Mr Winant Inspects American Troops in Ireland. Issue 1213, 2 March 1942.
More American Troops Arrive in Ireland. Issue 1215, 9 March 1942.
No Title. Americans in Northern Ireland. Issue 1237, 18 May 1942.
More Americans in Northern Ireland. Issue 1237, 25 May 1942.
American Troops in Ireland. Issue 1239, 1 June 1942.
AEF in Ireland Toughening Courses. Issue 1245, 22 June 1942.
American Troops in Britain. Issue 1248, 2 July 1942.
Royal Visit to Ulster. Issue 1568, 26 July 1945.
GBS Gets Freedom of Dublin (exclusive). Issue 1683, 2 September 1946.
No Title. Liners *Accra* and *Parthia* launched. Issue 1736, 6 March 1947.
Milk Supplies Threatened. Issue 1793, 22 September 1947.
England v. Ireland. Issue 1836, 19 February 1948.
International Soccer. Issue 1915, 22 November 1948.
Ireland Win Rugby International. Issue 1944, 3 March 1949.
Ireland Beat Wales in Rugby International. Issue 1948, 17 March 1949.
Visit to Northern Ireland. Issue 1970, 2 June 1949.
Dublin Horse Show. Issue 1990, 11 August 1949.
Skymaster Air Disaster. Issue 1992, 18 August 1949.
England v. Ireland. Issue 2019, 21 November 1949.
No Title. Snow in Ireland. Issue 2026, 15 December 1949.

Warwick Bioscope Chronicle
Ulster Day. Issue 58, 28 September 1912.

Indigenous Irish Material
All of the following indigenous material was viewed in the Irish Film Archive.

Late Queen's Visit to Dublin. 1900, filmed by Cecil Hepworth.
Republican Loan Film/Dáil Bonds Film. Ireland, April 1920, directed by John MacDonagh.

Irish Events
Funeral of Terence MacSwiney. Although an intertitle for this film states 'October 1921'
    it is actually footage from the previous year.
The Agony of Belfast. Dated circa 1920 on Digital Film Archive and 1922 at the Irish
    Film Archive.

The following appear as compilation shots in the Irish Film Archives 'Four Provinces' collection. They are undated in the accompanying notes.

Funeral of Thomas Ashe.
A Funeral in Cork. The Imposing Cortege at Internment of Seamus Quirke.
Funeral of the Late Clancy and R. McKee.
Funeral of Lieut Col Beattie Gallant Officer Who Attempted to Rescue Civilian From Burning Building In Templemore.
Obsequies of Capt. White and Major Smith. Military Police. Forces Pay Impressive Tribute To Fallen Comrades.

The Youghal Gazette
Sinn Féin. 1916.
A Day by the Sea. 1917.
Leaving Sunday Mass. 1917.
Peace Celebrations. 1918.

Bibliography

Records consulted in the Public Record Office of Northern Ireland, Belfast (PRONI), the National Archives of Ireland, Dublin (NAI) and the Irish Military Archives, Dublin, have been fully referenced in the endnotes to the relevant chapters.

Publications

'142 Managers Pool Results from Odeon Child Matinees', *Today's Cinema*, 2 November 1938, pp.1, 48.

Advertisement, *Bioscope*, 35, 554 (24 May 1917), pp.788–9.

Aldgate, Anthony, 'Newsreel Scripts: A Case Study', *History*, 61 (1976), pp.390.

Aldgate, Anthony, *Cinema and History: British Newsreels and the Spanish Civil War* (London: Scolar Press, 1979).

Andrews, J.M., 'Northern Ireland Today', *Glasgow Herald*, 17 August 1939.

Aubert, Michelle, 'La Naissance de la Presse Filmée en France 1895–1914' (1996), in Jeavons et al. (1996), pp.11–13.

Baechlin, Peter and Muller–Strauss, Maurice, 'How the Newsreels Grew', in *The Press Annual* (New York, 1954–55).

Ballantyne, James (ed.), *Researcher's Guide to British Newsreels, Vol. 1* (London: BUFVC, 1983).

Ballantyne, James (ed.), *Researcher's Guide to British Newsreels, Vol. 2* (London: BUFVC, 1988).

Ballantyne, James (ed.), *Researcher's Guide to British Newsreels, Vol. 3* (London: BUFVC, 1993).

Bardon, Jonathan, *A History of Ulster* (Belfast: Blackstaff Press, 1992).

Bartlett, Thomas and Jeffrey, Keith (eds), *A Military History of Ireland* (Cambridge: Cambridge University Press, 1997).

Barton, Brian, *Northern Ireland in the Second World War* (Belfast: Ulster Historical Foundation, 1995).

Barton, Brian, *Brookborough: The Making of a Prime Minister* (Belfast: Institute of Irish Studies, Queen's University 1988).

Barton, Ruth, *Irish National Cinema* (Routledge: New York, 2004).

Beckett, J.C., *The Making of Modern Ireland 1603–1923* (London: Faber & Faber, 1966).

Beere, Thekla, 'Cinema Statistics, Saorstát Éireann', *Journal of the Statistical and Social Inquiry of Ireland*, 15, 6 (1936), pp.83–110.

Bishop, H.W., 'Newsreel in the Making', *Sight and Sound*, 3, 12 (1934), pp.150–2.

Blake, John W., *Northern Ireland in the Second World War* (Belfast: Her Majesty's Stationery Office, 1956).

British Universities Film and Video Council, *The BUFVC Handbook* (London: BUFVC, 2001).

British Universities Film Council, *Film and the Historian* (London: BUFC, 1969).

Buchanan, Andrew, 'News Reels or Real News', *Film Art*, 3, 4 (1935), pp.22–4.

Cohen, Stanley and Young, Jock (eds), *The Manufacture of News: Deviance, Social Problems and the Mass Media* (London: Constable, 1973).

Cole, Robert, *Propaganda, Censorship and Irish Neutrality in the Second World War* (Edinburgh: Edinburgh University Press, 2006).

Coogan, Tim Pat, *Ireland in the Twentieth Century* (London: Hutchinson, 2003).

'Craig Replies to Newsreel "Bias" Charge', *Cinema*, 10 August 1949.

Cummings, Adelaide, *History of American Newsreels, 1927–1950* (New York: New York University, 1967).

De Valera, Eamon, *Ireland's Stand: being a Selection of the Speeches of Eamon de Valera During the War: 1939–1945* (Dublin: Gill, 1946).

'De Valera's Land of Silence', *Daily Mail*, 15 January 1942.

Doherty, James, *Standing Room Only: Memories of Belfast Cinemas* (Belfast: Lagan Historical Society, 1997).

Donnings, Hastings and Wilson, Thomas M. (eds), *Border Approaches: Anthropological Perspectives on Frontiers* (London: University Press of America, 1994).

Dyer, Richard, 'Introduction to Film Studies', in Hill and Church Gibson (eds), *Oxford Guide to Film Studies* (1998), pp.3–10.

'Editing and Presenting Film "Copy": The Great Improvements, Editorial Technique and Other Factors, the Production of Brighter News Films'. *Kinematograph Weekly*, 25 October 1934, News Reel and Shorts Supplement, p 20.

'Éire Objects to Film', *Daily Telegraph*, 7 February 1942, p.3.

Elvin, George H., 'This Freedom – An Enquiry into Film Censorship', *Cine–Technician*, January–February 1939, pp.141–6.

Erhardt, Erwin, *War Aims for the Workforce: British Workers Newsreels During the Second World War* (Cincinnati, OH: University of Cincinnati. 1996).

Fennell, Corry W., 'Television Will be no Rival – What we Want is Longer Newsreels!', *Kinematograph Weekly*, 9 August 1945, p.5.

Fielding, Raymond, 'Mirror of Discontent: The March of Time and its Politically Controversial Film Issues', *Western Political Quarterly*, 12, 1 (1959) pp.145–52.

Fielding, Raymond, *The American Newsreel 1911–67* (Norman, OH: University of Oklahoma Press, 1972).

Fielding, Raymond, *The March of Time 1935–1951* (New York: Oxford University Press, 1978).

Fisk, Robert, *In Time of War: Ireland, Ulster and the Price of Neutrality 1939–45* (London: André Deutsch, 1983).

Foster, John Wilson, 'Imagining the Titanic', in Patten (ed.), *Returning to Ourselves* (1995), pp.325–43.

Foster, R.F., *Modern Ireland 1600–1972* (London: Penguin, 1988).

Frazer, David, 'Orange Drummers Have Not Learned Lesson of Somme', *Belfast Telegraph*, 8 July 2006.

Galtung, Johan and Ruge, Mari, 'Structuring and Selecting News', in Cohen and Young (eds), *Manufacture of News* (1973), pp.62–72.

Gibney, Jim, 'Fresh Eyes Revisit Battle of the Somme', *Irish News*, 6 July 2006.

Gill, Alan, 'The Story of the Newsreels', *Amateur Cine World*, 11 July 1963 pp.70–1.

Girvin, Brian, *The Emergency: Neutral Ireland 1939–45* (London: Macmillan, 2006).

Grierson, John, *Grierson on Documentary* (London: Collins, 1946).

Grinley, Charles, 'The News–Reel', *Life and Letters Today*, 17, 10 (1937), pp.122–8.

Gripsrud, Jostein, 'Film Audiences', in Hill and Church Gibson (eds), *Oxford Guide to Film Studies* (1998), pp.02–11.

Hammerton, Jenny, *For Ladies Only? Eve's Film Review: Pathé Cinemagazine* (Hastings: Projection Box, 2001).

Hannigan, Dave, *De Valera in America* (Dublin: O'Brien Press, 2008).

Hart, Peter, *Mick: The Real Michael Collins* (London: Macmillan, 2005).

Hill, John, *Cinema and Northern Ireland* (London: BFI, 2006).

Hill, John and Church Gibson, Pamela (eds), *The Oxford Guide to Film Studies* (Oxford: Oxford University Press, 1998).

Hill, John, McLoone, Martin and Hainsworth, Paul (eds), *Border Crossing: Film in Ireland, Britain and Europe* (Belfast: Institute of Irish Studies in association with the University of Ulster and the BFI, 1994).

Hogenkamp, Bert, 'Workers' Newsreels, the 1920s and 1930s', *Our History*, 68, 36pp.

House of Commons Debates, cols. 1261–1319, Vol. 342, 7 December 1938, in McKernan, *Yesterday's News* (2002), pp.121–33.

'House of Lords Debate on Newsreel Censorship', *Daily Film Renter*, 25 January 1940, pp.1, 7.

Houston, Penelope, 'The Nature of the Evidence', *Sight and Sound*, Spring 1967, p.290. Cited in McKernan (2002), pp290–99.

'How Your News is Rushed to You', *Picturegoer*, 29 April 1933, p.22.

Hugon, P.D., *Hints to a Newsreel Cameraman* (Jersey City, NJ: Pathé News, 1916).

Hulbert, Jeff, 'The Newsreel Association of Great Britain and Ireland' in McKernan (ed.), *Yesterday's News* (2002), pp.257–66.

Hulbert, Norman, 'What I Demand of the Newsreel Editor', *Kinematograph Weekly*, 25 October 1934, Supplement, p.5.

Izod, John and Kilborn, Richard, 'The Documentary', in Hill and Church Gibson (eds), *Oxford Guide to Film Studies* (1998), pp.426–33.

Jackson, Alvin, 'Unionist Myths, 1912–85', *Past & Present*, 136 (1992), pp.164–85.

Jackson, Alvin, 'Irish Unionist Imagery, 1850–1920', in Patten (ed.), *Returning to Ourselves* (1995), pp.344–57.

Jeavons, Clyde, Mercer, Jane and Kirchner, Daniela (eds), *The Story of the Century: An International Newsfilm Conference* (London: BUFVC, 1998).

Kee, Robert, *Ireland A History* (Norwich: Jarrold, 1981).

Kennedy, Dennis, *The Widening Gulf: Northern Attitudes to the Independent Irish State 1919–1949* (Belfast: Blackstaff Press, 1988).

Kissane, Bill, *The Politics of the Irish Civil War* (Oxford: Oxford University Press, 2005).

Lee, J.J., *Ireland 1912–1985: Politics and Society* (Trowbridge: Redwood Books, 1989).

'London Letter', *The Irish Times*, 24 December 1945.

Lopez, Ana M., '(Not) Looking for Origins: Postmodernism, Documentary, and America', in Renov (ed.), *Theorizing Documentary* (1993), pp.151–63.

Loughlin, James, *Ulster Unionism and British National Identity Since 1885* (London: Cassell, 1995).

Low, Rachel, *The History of the British Film 1896–1906* (London: George Allen & Unwin, 1948).

Low, Rachel, *The History of the British Film 1906–1914* (London: George Allen & Unwin, 1949).

Low, Rachel, *The History of the British Film 1914–1918* (London: George Allen & Unwin, 1950).

Low, Rachel, *The History of the British Film 1918–1929* (London: George Allen & Unwin, 1971).

Low, Rachel, *Documentary and Educational Films of the 1930s* (London: George Allen & Unwin, 1979).

Low, Rachel, *Films of Comment and Persuasion of the 1930s* (London: George Allen & Unwin, 1979).

Malins, Geoffrey, *How I Filmed the War* (London: Imperial War Museum, 1993).

Manvell, Roger, *The Living Screen* (London: G. Harrap, 1961).

Martin, Peter, *Censorship in the Two Irelands 1922–1939* (Dublin: Irish Academic Press, 2006).

McBain, Janet and Gomes, Maryann, 'As Others Saw Us – Local Cinema Newsreels' (1996), in Jeavons, Mercer and Kirchner (eds), *Story of the Century* (1998), pp.75–8.

McDonald, Henry, 'De Valera Denounced Reports of Holocaust as "Propaganda" ', *Observer*, 8 May 2005.

McDowell, Michael, 'Reconciliation – the Unfinished Business of the Easter Rising' *The Irish Times*, 11 April 2006.

McGarry, Fearghal, *The Rising Ireland:1916* (Oxford: Oxford University Press, 2010).

McKernan, Luke, *Topical Budget: The Great British News Film* (London: British Film Institute, 1992).

McKernan, Luke, 'Witnessing the Past', in Ballantyne (ed.), *Researcher's Guide to British Newsreels Vol. 3* (1993), pp.35–8.

McKernan, Luke, 'Newsreels, the Silent Era' (1996), in Jeavons, Mercer and Kirchner (eds), *Story of the Century* (1998), pp.17–27.

McKernan, Luke, 'Useless if Delayed? Newsreel Research at the BUFVC', in British Universities Film and Video Council, *BUFVC Handbook* (2001), pp.86–92.

McKernan, Luke (ed.), *Yesterday's News: The British Cinema Newsreel Reader* (London: BUFVC, 2002).

McLaine, Ian, *Ministry of Morale* (London: Allen & Unwin, 1979).

McLoone, Martin, 'The Construction of a Partitionist Mentality: Early Broadcasting, Ireland', in Martin McLoone (ed.), *Public Service Broadcasting in a Divided Community: Seventy Years of the BBC in Northern Ireland* (Institute of Irish Studies, Queen's University Belfast, 1996), pp.20–34.

McMurtry, Des, 'British Army is a Force for Good', *Belfast Telegraph*, 15 July 2006.

Moynihan, Maurice (ed.), *Speeches and Statements by Eamon de Valera 1917–1973* (Dublin: Gill & Macmillan, 1980).

Myers, Kevin, 'Dublin Remembers Too', *Spectator*, 18 November 1995, pp.13–14.

Neill–Brown, J., 'The Industry's Front Page News', *Cine–Technician: The Journal of Association of Cine–Technicians*, 4, 20 (1939), pp.199–200.

'The Newspaper "Boss" – and the Kinema', *Kinematograph Weekly*, 4 March 1920, p.79.

'Newsreels, Demand Again by Éire', *Cinema*, 16 October 1946, pp.3, 40.

'Newsreel Rushes', *World Film News*, 2, 4 (July 1937).

Newton, Robin, 'Somme Sacrifice Will Not be Forgotten', *Belfast Telegraph*, 12 July 2006.

Nichols, Bill, *Representing Reality: Issues and Concepts in Documentary* (Bloomington: Indiana University Press, 1991).

Noble, Ronnie, *Shoot First! Assignments of a Newsreel Cameraman* (London: G. Harrap, 1955).

Norman, Philip, 'The Newsreel Boys', *Sunday Times Magazine*, 10 January 1971.

O'Brien, Harvey, *The Real Ireland: The Evolution of Ireland in Documentary Film* (Manchester: Manchester University Press, 2004).

O'Broin, León, *In Great Haste* (Dublin: Gill & Macmillan, 1983).

Ó'Drisceoil, Donal, *Censorship in Ireland 1939–45* (Cork: Cork University Press, 1996).

O'Flynn, Sunniva, 'Irish Newsreels: an Expression of National Identity?', in Smither and Klaue (eds), *Newsreels in Film Archives* (1996), pp.57–62.

O'Halpin, Eunan, *MI5 and Ireland, 1939–45* (Dublin: Irish Academic Press, 2003).

Open, Michael, *Fading Lights Silver Screens* (Antrim: Greystone Books, 1985).

Partridge, Eric, *A Dictionary of Slang* (London: Routledge, 1984).

'Party Unity in Éire', *The Times*, 29 May 1940.

Patten, Eve (ed.), *Returning to Ourselves* (Belfast: Lagan Press, 1995).

'Politics on the Screen', *Kinematograph Weekly*, 26 October 1933, p.4.

Pratschke, Mairéad, 'A Look at Irish Ireland: Gael Linn's *Amharc Éireann* Films, 1956–64', *New Hibernia Review*, 9, 3 (2005), pp.17–38.

Priestley, J.B., 'If I Owned Newsreels ... What A Row There Would Be!', *Daily Herald*, 11 June 1948.

Pronay, Nicholas, 'British Newsreels, the 1930s – Audience and Producers', *History*, 56 (1971), pp 411–18.

Pronay, Nicholas, 'British Newsreels, the 1930s – their Policies and Impact', *History*, 57 (1972), pp.63–72.

Pronay, Nicholas, 'The Newsreels: The Illusion of Actuality', in Smith (ed.), *Historian and Film* (1976), pp.95–120.

Pronay, Nicholas and Spring, D.W. (eds), *Propaganda, Politics and Film* (London: Macmillan Press, 1982).

Pronay, Nicholas, 'Defeated Germany, British Newsreels', in Short and Dolezel (eds), *Hitler's Fall* (1988), pp.28–49.

'Public and the War Newsreels', *Cinema*, 12 June 1940, p.25.

'The Real Trouble', *Daily Film Renter*, 12 October 1937, p.2 (leading article).

Reeves, Nicholas, *Official British Film Propaganda During the First World War* (London: Croom Helm, 1986).

Regan, John M., *The Irish Counter-Revolution 1921–1936* (Dublin: Gill & Macmillan, 2001).

Renov, Michael (ed.), *Theorizing Documentary* (Routledge: New York, 1993).

Rockett, Kevin, *Irish Film Censorship* (Dublin: Four Courts Press, 2004).

Rockett, Kevin, Gibbons, Luke and Hill, John, *Cinema and Ireland* (London: Routledge, 1987).

Rockett, Kevin, with Emer Rockett, *Film Exhibition and Distribution in Ireland: 1909–2010* (Dublin: Four Courts Press, 2011).

Rowson, Simon, 'A Statistical Survey of the Cinema Industry, Great Britain, 1934', *Journal of the Royal Statistical Society*, 99 (1936), pp.67–129.

Ruah, Lester, 'A Criticism of the News-Film', *Kinematograph Weekly*, 26 March 1914, cited in McKernan (ed.), *Yesterday's News* (2002), pp.21–3.

Ruddock, Alan, 'It Didn't Have to be Like This', *The Sunday Times*, 16 April 2006, News Review.

Russell, Elizabeth, 'Holy Crosses, Guns and Roses: Themes, Popular Reading Material', in Joost Augusteijn (ed.), *Ireland in the 1930s* (Dublin: Four Courts Press, 1999), pp.11–28.

Ryan, Meda, *The Day Michael Collins Was Shot* (Dublin: Poolbeg Press, 1989).

Sanger, Gerald F., 'The Programme of a News Theatre: How it Should be Treated and Presented', *Kinematograph Weekly*, 25 October 1934, Supplement, p.15.

Sanger, Gerald F., 'Developments, News Presentation', *Kinematograph Weekly*, 28 March 1935, Supplement, p.17.

Sanger, Gerald F., 'Star Values, News', *Kinematograph Weekly*, 14 November 1935, Supplement, p.17.

Short, K.R.M. and Stephan Dolezel (eds), *Hitler's Fall: The Newsreel Witness* (London: Croom Helm, 1988).

Sillars, Stuart, 'Things to Come and "Newsreel: Versions of Cinematic Influence" ', *Notes and Queries*, March 2002, pp.91–2.

Simmonds, Roy, 'Newsreels of the Future', *Kinematograph Weekly*, 25 October 1934, Supplement, p.4.

Sinkins, M.A.A., 'A Salute to the Newsreel Cameramen', *Kinematograph Weekly*, 14 January 1943, p.41.

Smith, Paul (ed.), *The Historian and Film* (Cambridge: Cambridge University Press, 1976).

Smither, Roger and Klaue, Wolfgang (eds), *Newsreels in Film Archives* (Trowbridge: Flicks Books, 1996).

Sorenssen, Bjorn, 'The Voice of Reconstruction: the Norwegian Postwar Newsreel', in Smither and Klaue (eds), *Newsreels in Film Archives* (1996), pp.44–56.

Talbot, Frederick A., *Moving Pictures: How They Are Made and Worked* (London: Heinemann, 1912).

Taylor, A.J.P., *Beaverbrook* (London: Hamish Hamilton, 1972).

Taylor, Fred (ed.), *Goebbels' Diaries* (London: Hamish Hamilton, 1982).

Taylor, Philip M., *British Propaganda in the Twentieth Century* (Edinburgh: Edinburgh University Press, 1999).

Taylor, Richard, *Film Propaganda* (London: Croom Helm, 1979).

'The Technique of the Commentator', *Kinematograph Weekly*, 28 March 1935, Supplement, p.15.

Thorpe, Frances and Pronay, Nicholas, *British Official Films in the Second World War* (Oxford: Clio Press, 1980).

Turner, Graeme, *Film as Social Practice* (London: Routledge, 1993).

Turner, John, *Filming History: The Memoirs of John Turner, Newsreel Cameraman* (London: BUFVC, 2001).

Ward, Ken, *Mass Communications and the Modern World* (London: Macmillan, 1989).

Watts, Editor (1928), 'Just "PIC and EVE"', *Pathé Pictorial Press Review*, cited in Hammerton (2001) *For Ladies Only?*, pp.117–18.

Williams, Martin, 'Ancient Mythology and Revolutionary Ideology, Ireland', *Historical Journal*, 26, 2 (1983), pp.307–28.

Wills, Clair, *That Neutral Island* (London: Faber, 2007)

Wood, Ian S., *Ireland During the Second World War* (London: Caxton, 2002).

Unpublished Sources

Brown, Richard, *The History of the British Mutoscope and Biograph Company & an Account of the Biograph Film Studios* (unpublished thesis, 1992, held in the library of the British Film Institute, London).

O'Donovan, Dermot, *Sacred Egoism: Neutral Éire on the Screen 1939–45* (unpublished thesis, University College Dublin, 1996).

Reid, M.J., *British State Propaganda on Irish Neutrality in the Second World War* (unpublished thesis, Thames Valley University, 1996).

Mass Observation Reports

Faking of Newsreels, File Report 16, 7 January 1940.
Newsreel Report (2), File Report 141, 27 January 1940.

Content of Newsreels, File Report 22, 28 January 1940.
Newsreels, File Report 215, 10 June 1940.
Memo on Newsreels, File Report 314, 2 August 1940.
Mass Observation Film Work, File Report 394, 10 September 1940.
Newsreel Report (3), File Report 444, 7 October 1940.
Memo on Newsreels, File Report 524, 11 December 1940.

Index

Entries in italics are newsreel titles.